Oakland Community College
Highland Lakes Library
7350 Cooley Lake Road
Union Lake, Michigan

THE EMANCIPATION OF MASSACHUSETTS
THE DREAM AND THE REALITY

BY

BROOKS ADAMS

REVISED AND ENLARGED EDITION

BOSTON AND NEW YORK
HOUGHTON MIFFLIN COMPANY
The Riverside Press Cambridge

CONTENTS

I AM indebted to Mrs. Robert Homans for permission to quote from the letters of Brooks Adams to Henry Adams, deposited in the Adams Collection at the Houghton Library, Harvard University. I thank the Honorable Henry Cabot Lodge for permission to use the letter of Brooks Adams to his grandfather in 1887. I was promptly and effectively guided through the relevant Adams material by Dr. Lyman H. Butterfield, Editor-in-Chief of the immense operation which will eventually publish the Adams Papers. I thank the Massachusetts Historical Society for providing me with the text of the letter to Lodge, and for materials from the Adams Papers, the Deane Collection, and Brooks Adams's manuscript "Life of John Quincy Adams." I am obliged to the Houghton Library for permission to use papers from the William James Collection.

PERRY MILLER

CAMBRIDGE, *July*, 1961

INTRODUCTION
BY PERRY MILLER

THE VOLUME here reproduced is in fact two virtually separate books. Yet they are related, if only by such a fantastic link as the capricious genius of Brooks Adams (1848–1927) could devise and such an one, perhaps, as only he could suppose logical.

The first of these two (in point of time) is *The Emancipation of Massachusetts*, which Houghton Mifflin published in January, 1887. This is reproduced from the text of the second edition, 1919, in which Adams made a few minor changes of style or phrase. For that edition he wrote what is really a second treatise in the form of a 168-page "Preface," which remains both to intrigue and to baffle us.

The Emancipation of 1887 was Brooks Adams's first book. He had been publishing articles since 1874 and by this time was perfecting a facility for the printed word which ultimately would make him a voluminous author, even though the act of composition would always be for him an ordeal by torture.

The "Preface" is his next-to-last major effort. In 1920 he made his final stand with another preface, entitled "The Heritage of Henry Adams," which he placed before a gathering of the late essays of his brother Henry (1838–1918). Brooks gave this volume a title of his own devising, *The Degradation of the Democratic Dogma*, which is much more the theme of his introduction than of the essays by Henry. This piece, published the year after the "Preface" and probably written in close conjunction with it, has to be consulted if some of the otherwise impenetrable enigmas of the "Preface" are to be expounded — though even so, several remain happily unsolved. Thus between the original book and the "Preface" come all of Adams's prodigious productions — all his restless search of the universe and of world history for the purport of human existence and social order, his flow of sweeping predictions, his fabulous adventures in politics and the amazing tergiversations of his political loyalties.

In retrospect, from the elevation of 1919, *The Emancipation* was the work of a mind as yet relatively uncomplicated, though to many of its contemporaries it was sufficiently opaque. By the time of the "Preface" he had passed through the "phases" memorialized by (to name only his books, apart from the myriad articles and legal briefs), *The Gold Standard* (1894), *The Law of Civilization and Decay* (1895), *America's Economic Supremacy* (1900), *The New Empire* (1902), and *The Theory of Social Revolutions* (1913). To this list we must add the uncompleted, only recently available, manuscript "Life of John Quincy Adams" (1767–1848), upon which Brooks was working in 1908 and 1909. He abandoned this because (it seems) of criticisms by Henry. But he drew upon it both for this "Preface" and for "The Heritage of Henry Adams."

None of Brooks Adams's published books was a financial success, but they all stirred up discussion, most of it hostile. By 1919, the author of the "Preface" had become a man of wide erudition (although never achieving the patience to be a true "scholar" in any of the innumerable areas about which he pontificated), tortuous, contemptuous of the masses of mankind. He had deliberately cultivated a brutality of statement such as, in this same year of 1919: "To carry on anything great, war for instance, we need to establish something close to a dictatorship." [1] By most of his associates — the number dwindled — he was held to be unbalanced and dogmatic to the point of madness. His lifelong complaint was that only a handful of men in the country were capable of comprehending him. By the end, his egomania was a tedious tirade. He was generally dismissed as "the learned eccentric" who dealt in horrendous and manifestly absurd prophecies of impending doom. For twenty years or so after his death, whatever image of him survived was not only that of an "unusable man," his own phrase, but of one headed for total oblivion, except in that he might be remembered as a brother of Henry.

However, with the horrors of a second world war rained upon humanity, many persons suddenly recollected the works of Brooks Adams, and commenced to search them out as precious items in secondhand bookstores. They were republished, with appreciative prefaces; critical essays and biographies appeared. Young students, for whom at first he was not even a name, discovered in him one who spoke directly to their anxieties, even more than did Henry's *Education.* What his contemporaries had dismissed as wild extravagance no longer seemed exaggeration to the epoch in-

---

[1] *Debates in the Massachusetts Constitutional Convention* (Boston, 1919–1920), I, 737.

augurated at Hiroshima. In 1901 Henry Adams had
reported, with that tone of condescension which was a
lifelong trial for the younger man, that Brooks wrote
him "a sort of howl because his prophecies become true
so fast that he can't keep ahead on new ones." [1] Yet,
closely pursued though he might be, Brooks kept ahead.
He uttered many foolish statements, and he generalized
irresponsibly without ever doing the requisite grubbing
among factual records. Even so, there are so many
respects in which the world has only recently caught up
with him, has been forced to look down vistas he alone
opened to the mind, that he now looms as an intellect
which, with all its perversity, read the lesson of modern
civilization as profoundly as any in his time, or, for
that matter, in our own.

II

Brooks Adams commenced his theme song of lacking
an audience able to follow him with the critical reception of *The Emancipation*. In the main, that was
spluttering indignation. The organs of the Protestant
denominations were solidly indignant, even where their
church had no historical ties to New England or had
rejected the Calvinism of the Puritans. They saw it as
an attack upon all sorts and conditions of clergymen,
upon Protestantism, upon religion itself. The review
in *Bibliotheca Sacra* for April, 1877, published at Oberlin
College, is typical of the lot. It is the more interesting
because at Oberlin, under the powerful sway of Charles
Grandison Finney, a theology of "perfectionism" was

[1] Worthington Chauncey Ford, *Letters of Henry Adams*, II (Boston,
1938), 328.

propounded which the Puritans would have condemned in precisely the same terms they used for their eradication of Antinomians. But Brooks Adams, said the review, is disqualified for the task he has brazenly assumed by his manifest lack of sympathy with the clergy, by his constant use of such pejorative terms as "venemous priests." Furthermore, he is utterly ignorant of Christian doctrine. He presents as an astonishing discovery the fact "that the Puritans believed in the authority of the Bible!" His account of the Antinomians is invalidated by "his utter ignorance of the meaning of their doctrine to the Puritans." Yet the supremely pernicious defect of the book is that it is "history written to prove a theory," that it perverts a religious story into "brief essays in the philosophy of history on the Spencerian theory." The only use for the thing at all is that it exhibits to all devout regions outside Boston "how entirely the circle in which the author moves is ignorant of those sublime ideas, convictions, and experiences which the Christian church cherishes as the great gift of God to men." [1]

Brooks Adams could shrug off such notices from the religious press. In fact, he might derive some satisfaction because this sort of periodical got at least a hint that the book did contain a "philosophical" thesis, and properly associated it with the "optimistic" deductions of Darwinism that the universe was an expression of universal law. What galled him, however, was that readers for the more liberal journals missed the point entirely — to him the obvious point — and that also several of his most devoted friends failed to perceive it,

[1] *Bibliotheca Sacra*, New Series, 44 (April, 1887), 384–387.

and that, most humiliating of all, his adored brother
Henry seemed not to be much impressed.

William Dean Howells undoubtedly assumed he was
highly praising the work when he wrote in *Harper's*
(May, 1887) that, while Adams may have overdone a
bit the denunciation, still it was a welcome relief from
the hitherto bland genuflections of New England writers
to their ancestors.

> In fact, the theocracy of New England seems to have
> been a pretty ugly mixture of the dregs of Mosaism and
> feudalism, all the bitterer because they were the dregs.
> The Puritan rulers, cleric and laic, were undoubtedly
> sincere, conscientious, and courageous; all this has been
> recognized in full measure, pressed down and running
> over, by their posterity; and it is well at last to have one
> of their descendants uncover their faults, show their
> limitations, and rebuke their errors, their wilful cruelties,
> their crimes against humanity.[1]

A benign Howells could have no notion that he was
rubbing salt in Adams's already bleeding wounds by
his innocent supposition that this is what *The Emancipation* is "about."

For Adams had been irreparably hurt by a notice in
the *Atlantic Monthly*, dated February, 1887, which he
read in January. This too proved its liberality by not
flinching from the accusation against the Puritan
founders. Had a foreigner written this, we would all
be up in arms, but when an Adams does it, all right-
thinking Americans can breathe a sigh of relief:

> Without fear and without favor he reports what assidu-
> ous study has enabled him to see. It illustrates this

[1] *Harper's New Monthly Magazine*, 74 (May, 1887), 985.

uncompromising sincerity that a more severely just estimate of Samuel Adams has not been published in this
country than that which has here been set down by the
pen of an Adams.

He has been a bit one-sided, but he speaks through the
sources; we had better admit that fundamentally he is
correct, even though we then have to join him in
indicting our revered ancestors:

> As a consequence, the book, though dealing with matter
> of which so much has been written and spoken, and with
> which we had all supposed ourselves quite familiar, is
> fresh, salient, striking, almost startling; and this from
> the nature of the facts revealed, not from any mere effect
> of style. It is as if a fog of ancient continuance should
> suddenly rise from a landscape which had hitherto been
> seen only under that veil, and show it at once the same
> and not the same, the same and yet surprising.

Not to be outdone by Adams in declaring itself "emancipated," the *Atlantic* acknowledged that the clergy, in
their contest with those whom they esteemed servants
of the Devil, "used weapons and methods that must
seem to us little better than devilish, and there ensued
a sad, a dreadful chapter of our history."

Brooks Adams might writhe under the suffocation of
this empty-minded agreement, but he would be plunged
into furious grief when the *Atlantic* thereupon assumed
to admonish him for his two — according to its reviewer — basic errors. First, he is so fanatical a
"liberal" that he can see no good at all in conservatism.
"But," objected the *Atlantic*, "conservatism is a force
without which no human society could exist." (For the
full irony of *this* comment to be comprehended, there

would be needed the next three decades of Adams's
truculent career, culminating in the "Preface" of 1919!)
Secondly, and on this Adams would almost lose the
power of speech, he is a "zealous professor of the mechanical philosophy cherished and promulgated in our
day by a particular set of doctrinaires, and in various
passages . . . he has indulged himself in confident expression of it." Not only did this philosophy, when
thus characterized or thus fabricated out of miscompre-
hension, seem as reprehensible to sophisticated Boston
as it did to provincial Oberlin or to Andover Theological
Seminary, but this stately vehicle of Boston respecta-
bility had the temerity to add that "the introduction of
this speculative doctrine is gratuitous" because the facts
would remain the same under any point of view, pietistic
or agnostic!

> One may assert, if he will, that when Calef, as Mr. Adams
> relates, exposed the witchcraft delusion a mechanical
> force passed from him to the readers he instructed, to
> operate upon their minds in the same way with that which
> drives an engine or turns a mill-wheel; but he will merely
> assert an opinion as little verified by the scientific method,
> and as little capable of verification by it, as the opinion
> of John Stuart Mill that in some other world parallel
> lines may meet.

Wherefore, concluded the *Atlantic*, as though giving
sage advice to a novice, the issue is not whether Adams's
doctrine be true or false (though patently it was false),
but of a needless intrusion of it as if it were ascertained
fact. This, assuredly, is "at least a literary infelicity." [1]
Remembering these words, with his rancorous tenacity,
Brooks Adams would henceforth take care to repeat

[1] *Atlantic Monthly*, 59 (February, 1887), 251–257.

this infelicity (even though the "doctrine" might be radically altered) amid the lengthening inventory of the abuse he would heap upon his contemporaries.

Evidently Henry Cabot Lodge (1850–1924), Henry's former colleague in History at Harvard College, wrote Brooks about the *Atlantic* piece. Lodge, it may be noted, in 1887 was seeking election to the House of Representatives. From the tone of Brooks's response we gather that Lodge was endeavoring, as were always the friends of Brooks, to soften the blow. Yes, Brooks replied, he had read it. Of course, every theocracy is a "strong" government. Massachusetts had the customary vices of all despotisms. So is Russia today, so was France under Louis XIV, so was Spain in 1600. All unions of church and state, wrote Brooks in a tone bewilderingly at variance with some of the impassioned orations in the text, are necessarily strong.

Then, January 22, 1887, he tried to explain to "Cabot," who was already and for the duration of his life would remain a faithful ally, what the book really was "about." (Adams was to repeat this explanation again and again in the next few months, and always in vain.)

> What I feel the lack of, is appreciation of the unity of cause and effect in the notices I see of my book. It is really not a history of Massachusetts but a metaphysical and philosophical inquiry as to the action of the human mind in the progress of civilization; illustrated by the history of a small community, isolated and allowed to work itself free. I could have done as much for any other people in the same phase.

With the introduction of this — to the Adams family —

cabalistic word "phase," Brooks exhibits the compulsive habit of repetition which was to persist as a blemish in all his writing. No, no, he protests: *The Emancipation* "is not an attempt to break down the Puritans or to abuse the clergy, but to follow out the action of the human mind as we do that of the human body." The hidden theme is that which all reviewers have missed: "I believe that they [i.e., laws of mind and of body] are one and subject to the same laws."

Horace Scudder, the Houghton Mifflin editor who invited Adams to do the volume and who faithfully printed it although profoundly shocked by it, and all his ilk were "church-men," insisted Adams. They simply put out of sight whatever value his view contained. They evaded the "scope and force." Or rather, they just would not see it. As for the "story" — that is, the historical narrative which reviewers were monotonously summarizing — "I look on [it] as only an illustration of a law." He protested, with uncharacteristic modesty, that he did not flatter himself as having sounded the depths of knowledge. Still, he did think that he had "hit on a plausible explanation of the necessary working out of certain eras of mental growth," and that in these terms he deserved serious consideration.[1]

[1] B. Adams to H. C. Lodge, Lodge Collection, January 22, 1887. Compare the comment of *New Englander and Yale Review*, in the issue for July, 1887 (47, 1–11), which, after inviting readers to "the spectacle of a bird fouling its own nest," observes:

> Mr. Adams has gotten together some isolated notions of current science and philosophy and has worked them for all they are worth; and is evidently of the opinion that he has a theory of things, but few will be persuaded to share his opinion on the point, and certainly the cultivation of his philosophy is only a secondary aim of this work.

We know not what Lodge thought of this epic presumption, other than that he preserved the letter. Perhaps Lodge, through his fairly extensive association with Adamses, had imbibed an appreciation for their penchant of prescribing, on the slightest hints, how the laws of mental growth would function in the future — at least, once any Adams took them under surveillance. But Brooks Adams came up against a much more hardheaded, and, although friendly, a highly sceptical scholar when he addressed himself, as usual, for "help," to the foremost and most rigorous of New England antiquarians, Charles Deane (1813–1889).

Deane made a fortune in Boston out of a dry-goods concern; all the time he was accumulating money his real interest was not his business but his avocation, American colonial history. By the time he could afford to retire, in 1864, he had become a professional scholar. He supervised eleven volumes of the *Proceedings* of the Massachusetts Historical Society (in which he allowed no comma to escape). By the time Adams addressed him, Deane had set a high standard for accuracy in minute research. He was the admiration and the ideal for all hesitant students in the field supposedly covered by *The Emancipation.* In every respect, Deane's methods and processes of thought were utterly foreign to those of Brooks Adams.

We can imagine, therefore, how profoundly Charles Deane was dismayed when Brooks, in July, 1885, brashly entreated his "help," confessing himself utterly ignorant of "church history," a topic that was bound to be central for the undertaking he was blithely assuming. Possibly Deane was amused — though this is an improbable speculation. At any rate, he seems to have given his time freely, as is the manner of such majestic scholars, especially when confronted by a Brooks Adams. In asking for his first appointment, Adams says he needs clarification on points where "I can't find much light on in the books," though it is evident from his treatment of ecclesiastical polity in *The Emancipation* that he gave a minimum of attention to the information readily available in "books." But, since he despised pedants and professors, it hardly behooved him to waste time on them!

As with whatever letter or letters Lodge must have addressed to the author of *The Emancipation*, those of Deane to him have also disappeared — probably consumed in the holocaust of his papers which Adams is reputed to have made near the end of his life, he being the only member of his family ever to commit such an atrocity. But Deane preserved Adams's letters, and from these it is evident that Deane strove to teach him the rudiments of the Puritan order. Also, these reveal that Adams was running all over town and even going to Cambridge in search of "help" — he uses the word insistently. He wanted to know, for instance, how many of the undertakers of the Brattle Street Church were church members before their secession.

Hence we surmise that Charles Deane would sigh (whether or not he had a sense of humor) upon receiving in September of 1886 another note of fulsome thanks which said that Adams would like publicly to express his debt, "but as my opinions will be, I have no doubt, most offensive to most people, I should not think of doing so without your permission." The "Prefatory

Note" of 1887 acknowledges the obligation, and so
Deane must have consented. But when he read the
book he was certainly very disturbed, as we can make
out from a letter Adams wrote in reply to another one
from him. It is dated January 26, four days after the
letter to Lodge.

In the domain of scholarship Adams could not take
the high-and-mighty with Charles Deane, and he meekly
confessed, feeling the "leniency" of Deane's criticism,
that he had made many errors of fact. But thereupon
Adams swung into what already had become his arma-
dillo defense, the stance he was to maintain about the
book for the rest of his pugnacious existence:

> But I want to put myself right in your eyes. My book
> is not a "history," it is not intended for one. It is an
> attempt to set forth a scientific theory of the action of
> the mind illustrated by a section of history which happens
> to be taken from Massachusetts, but which might as
> well be taken from India.

He might be right and he might be wrong — out of
courtesy he would acknowledge the possibility of the
latter, though he clearly felt it remote — but he had
attempted to explain "certain results by material causes
of a mechanical kind." It was *this* import of the volume
he wanted discussed, not the anti-clerical part, which to
most reviewers seemed the burden, and this import, he
was obliged to conclude, the average American mind
was unable even to recognize, much less to cope with.

The remainder of the letter, as do others which survive from this unhappy spring, deteriorates into something near to incoherence; yet it and the others maintain
the patrician arrogance. He had been, Brooks confided

to Deane, so crowded in space that he could not pretend
to have read all the materials. Even so, he had read
more "divinity" than history, and somehow had read
considerably in what he felt particularly pertinent,
"physiology." Thus, he concluded, in one of those
obfuscations which are the despair of his biographers,
"My references I admit I am ashamed of. I got them
in a bad mess and was unable to get them straight
again." [1] In terms of the standard academic evaluation,
nothing more devastating about *The Emancipation*
needs to be said. Yet the very nonchalance of Adams's
admission of scholarly carelessness is his way of asserting that *The Emancipation* was never conceived as
a contribution to local historiography. It was an effort
to inform American Protestants, especially those who
in the nineteenth century had settled into a complacent
"liberalism," of the line through which they had
descended.

As the spring wore on, reviews piled up, most of them
falling into an instinctively standardized pattern and
each goading Adams to a frenzy. While they acknowledge that it was a good thing to have the persecutions
of the seventeenth-century Puritans frankly confessed,
they increasingly snarled at Brooks Adams himself.
For example, *The Literary World* (published in Boston)
for February decried "*odium theologicum*" but condemned as being even more odious "*odium anti-
theologicum.*" This disease, it said, masquerades "as
scientific impartiality," of which Adams's volume would
be an exasperating example were it not utterly ridicu-

[1] B. Adams to C. Deane, Deane Collection, July 8, 1885; January
13, 1886; September 12, 1886; January 26, 1887.

lous. It is a travesty of ecclesiastical history, and Adams "has utterly failed to do justice to the nobler traits of the Puritan character, which, enlightened by culture, have brought to life the best elements of American civilization." [1]

A still more virulent expression of the anger Adams aroused among his readers was a review by William F. Poole (1821–1894) in *The Dial* (published in Chicago) for March. This mighty pundit had been librarian at the Boston Athenaeum for thirteen years, of the Chicago Public Library for another thirteen, and in 1887 was translating himself to the Newberry Library. He was almost as immensely learned about New England as Charles Deane; in 1869 he had published a sturdy tract, *Cotton Mather and Salem Witchcraft*, which vigorously exonerated the New England clergy from the charge of complicity in the persecutions of 1692. In 1888 Poole was to become President of the American Historical Association. He made it abundantly clear that he intensely disliked Brooks Adams.

The heroes of Brooks Adams, sneered Poole, are invariably "interlopers, anarchists . . . the malcontents, the disturbers of the peace, the heady, exorbitant ranters . . . lunatics and cranks." His opinions of men are based on false standards, in which the past and present jostle each other, to create sheer confusion. "His book has no perspective, and no proper adjustment of lights and shades." Assuredly there has been an "emancipation" of human thought within Western society in the last two centuries. It is all the more unfortunate, then, that Adams did not appreciate his

[1] *The Literary World*, 18 (February 19, 1887).

opportunity to lay aside prejudice and passion. "For an historian has no right to misrepresent facts and absolve himself from an honest code of criticism; and this error is here charged upon Mr. Brooks Adams." [1]

As we work through these reviews — there were some fifty or more of them — and in them chart the crescendo of range, we realize that Adams's book, with all its faults of scholarly method heaped upon its head, precipitated a minor but severe crisis in America's estimation of itself. In this weird way it becomes even more valuable to us the more such demonstrations of its wrongheadedness accumulate.

But worse was yet in store for Adams. Probably he ought to have anticipated it; because he did not, it was the unkindest cut of all. He assumed that if any one journal in the country would do him justice it would be the foremost "liberal" and intellectual magazine of its day, *The Nation*, edited by his and Henry's good friend, E. L. Godkin (1831–1902). Its review in March broke his heart. If *The Nation* could not even perceive the cryptic thesis, who in America, or who in the wide, wide world, would ever properly grasp it?

The Nation started with the conventional concession: the book does perform a service in so far as it challenges the excessive filial reverence of the orthodox New England historians, but that is all that can be said in favor of the author. "Filled with rage against the Puritan clergy as a class, he reiterates certain charges against them with tiresome monotony, and finally leaves the reader in utter darkness as to the object of the entire volume." He fails to show from what

[1] *The Dial*, 7 (March, 1887), 263–268.

Massachusetts was emancipated, or by whom.   The
eleven chapters are distinct essays without any organic
connection; they do not begin to cover the history of
the colony.   Adams sheds no new light — or any light —
on any topic, "and the highest praise we can give him
is that he has used the standard printed authorities."
His excesses will provoke rebuttals, and that may prove
a benefit, but to the serious student this volume "will
be an amusing curiosity, a proof both of the vigor of the
Adams stock and its inherited tendency to forcible
utterances."   But Adams must be aware that every
censure he utters will be quoted by enemies of New
England, more for the parentage than for the truth.
He ought to give up history and turn to writing fiction
in the manner of — here was insult of the most calculated sort — Rider Haggard!   The long review then
concluded, "It may be that Massachusetts needed to
be scourged, but it does not follow that an Adams
should wield the rod." [1]

III

In this extremity, Brooks Adams turned to the one
being who, since the dawn of his consciousness, had been
its tutelary deity, his brother Henry.   Herein, though
this part of the drama was enacted after the publication
and after most of the reviews were in, consists the
poignance of the book, reaching back to Brooks's original conception of it.   In 1908 Henry Adams would
write to Charles Gaskell that Brooks and he "are too
much alike, and agree too well in all our ideas.   We have

[1] *The Nation,* 109 (March, 1887), 189–190.

nothing to give each other." [1]   Any reader at all ac-
climated to the bizarre climate of Henry Adams's
letters recognizes this incongruity as another touch to
the mythological portrait he painted, over the years, of
his hapless junior. Some strokes were laid on fairly
crudely, as when (1894) he spoke slightingly of "my
idiot-brother Brooks." [2] Four years later he lamented
that Brooks "is a singularly impatient and unsteady
workman." [3]   In the usual tone of humorous patron-
izing he speaks of Brooks as "the ferocious anarchist," [4]
and, when Brooks was being most Republican, as "a
Jeffersonian Jacksonian Byronian democrat" (1900). [5]
By 1910, Henry could say to him, with what persons
outside the Adams pale may rashly conclude was
cruelty, "I have known you for sixty-odd years, and
since you were a baby I've never known you when you
weren't making yourself miserable over the failings of
the universe." [6]   Toward the end, in 1917, Henry
Adams, according to the latest and most meticulous of
the biographers of Brooks, retained only the dregs of
friendship for him and scornfully characterized him to
Mrs. Cameron as "my solemn brother Brooks." [7]

It is difficult, and also hazardous, for outsiders to try
to say how much Brooks understood or failed to understand about the relationship. In the astoundingly frank,
"Heritage" preface of 1921 he states, in seeming naïveté,
that in the last years a change had come over Henry
which troubled him. Henry complained that he could
not be agitated — Brooks relays this information to the

---

[1] Ford, *Letters*, II, 504.   [2] *Ibid.*, p. 57.   [3] *Ibid.*, p. 144.
[4] *Ibid.*, p. 270.   [5] *Ibid.*, p. 284.   [6] *Ibid.*, p. 532.
[7] Arthur F. Beringause, *Brooks Adams: A Biography* (New York,
1955), p. 370.

public without apparently realizing that he was about the most agitating personality of his generation. Wherefore, Henry "came rather to shun me, seeming to prefer women's society, in which he could be amused and tranquillized." Brooks calls this a "slight estrangement," [1] yet could still write a hymn of praise to his brother, recounting the many services Henry had rendered him over the years — hammering out his ideas, reading his proofs, improving his style, arranging for publication, and for hailing the *Law* as "the Bible of Anarchy." [2] But for us, with the hindsight provided by the extensive documentation of this intense, ferocious and ambivalent fraternal partnership, we can see that the interchange in 1887 over *The Emancipation* is highly prophetic, full of premonitions for both comedy and anguish.

On March 7 Brooks wrote Henry to request "a considerable favor." Would he take half an hour to write a note (Brooks thought it could be done in ten lines!) to *The Nation* pointing out wherein the reviewer had utterly missed the point of the whole argument? It is not an onslaught on the Puritans "but an attempt to apply certain general laws to a particular phase of developement." It is not a partisan attack "but an attempt to prove the identity of the laws which control mind and matter, and to illustrate my theory from Mass[achusetts] history, as I might have done from that of India." He had assumed that the "theory" was obvious, "but I thought people would be brighter than they are." And so, "You my dear fellow are, permit

[1] B. Adams, "The Heritage of Henry Adams," *The Degradation of the Democratic Dogma* (New York, 1920), p. 102.
[2] Ford, *Letters*, II, 83.

me to say, almost the only man who has understood the point." Whereupon Henry flatly refused and evidently advised Brooks to defend himself in the newspapers!

Brooks did not allow Henry's reply to survive, any more than he permitted those of Lodge and Deane to enter an archive. We can, however, once more guess at the tone, because Brooks's next letter commences straight off, "My dear fellow — don't get mad." He explains, plaintively, that he had written after dining with a friend, a clever man, who told him the book could not be understood; Brooks was "cross" at hearing this criticism, "but I humbled myself and wrote you — thinking pride sinful."

After still another rejoinder from Henry (also destroyed), Brooks wrote once more, exposing painfully his state of mind: "If you think you can do me no good why let matters alone. I am myself absolutely sick. I can't make up my mind." Here we get the full-throated cry of Brooks Adams: "I wrote trusting in God to the chance of finding one man bright enough to review me and to point out my meaning. I put my gauge of intelligence too high." His "dilemma" was: "I don't . . . want to be a fool," but personally "I feel like saying 'to hell with it all.'" What in the name of God is a man to do? If you have a "theory," you have to put it in, but in such a manner as not to break the dramatic movement: "If you put it in as I do in such quantities and such places as I think the modern taste will stand, then you are read indeed for the story — but you are not understood by your audience." [1]

[1] B. Adams to H. Adams, Adams Collection, March 7, 1887; March 8, 1887; March 11, 1887.

Another friend, Professor Henry C. Chapman, to whom also in the "Prefatory Note" he expressed indebtedness, told him that there were not more than thirty men in America who could be made to comprehend *The Emancipation*. If there was anybody who assuredly belonged in such a listing of the thirty top intellects, Professor William James (1842–1910) was the man. He was another to whom Brooks had gone for "help," and he too was listed in the "Prefatory Note." By April, James indicated, though he was gracious and had enjoyed reading *The Emancipation*, that not even he could come within Chapman's elite band. Furthermore, he had to confess himself in the dark as to what "help" he had ever given Brooks Adams!

So, for the last time this spring, Brooks struggled to say what in his own mind he thought he had been about, and what he had failed to communicate. He had, he told James, felt himself fitted to deal with politics, law and theology, but he knew nothing about science. He got what little information he had acquired from his conversations with James! And then, he went on, probably to James's increasing bewilderment, what he had received from James primarily, and what nobody had detected as being in the book at all, was this: "For example: my theory of ritual. It may be all stated somewhere, I only know I could find nothing to help me; but I believe it to lie at the root of all human development; and I believe it the more I study; I believe it more firmly far now than six months ago." To this basic insight James had "helped" him! "I could have done nothing without you."

Thanks to what Adams had thus learned from James,

he could in turn instruct the philosopher: "My dear sir, the deepest passion of the human mind is fear. Fear of the unseen, the spiritual world, represented by the priest; fear of the tangible world, represented by the soldier." The conflict of these two has engendered all civilization! Now this "theory," though it owed so much to James, was, Brooks hospitably allowed, "perfectly antagonistic" to him, yet still this "is all I care for." In the light of this vision, *The Emancipation* must be interpreted.

> If you mean that I have given a side, it is very true; I can't conceive what is meant by impartial history, any more than impartial science. There are a set of facts; your business is to state them accurately and then criticise the evidence, and draw a conclusion; and at the same time, if you can, throw in enough interest to sugar-coat the pill. I have tried to show what I believe to be the crucial point of a certain phase of development, and then to show that what is true of this is universally true. It is a point of view so contrary to that which has been received that it strikes you as one-sided; I think it only seems one-sided because all the evidence is in, and it has not been before.

Perhaps, he granted, he had made the "story" too personal, but he had wanted to make his characters as real to his readers (if any) as they were to him, and above all he had endeavored not to be dull.[1]

Whether *The Emancipation* is dull or not every reader must determine for himself. For Brooks Adams further explanation of the inner "theory" of it had become a bore. As he remarks in the first sentence of the 1919 "Preface," with an indifference which only an Adams

[1] B. Adams to W. James, William James Collection, April 16, 1887.

could manifest so casually, in the three decades since
the thing was published "I have hardly opened it."[1]
Confronted by misapprehension, abuse and denunciation, he did what he and Henry were always to do
when faced with the unpleasant: he traveled.

IV

The next June, Brooks Adams was in England, where
Henry's good friend, Sir Cecil Arthur Spring-Rice
(1859–1918), arranged for him to be put up at an Oxford
College. Brooks was charmed by Spring-Rice: "It is
so seldom that I meet a man who cares for the sort of
thing I care for, or sees in it what absorbs me." He
was cast down when Rice could not join him in Oxford,
but concluded that perhaps all was for the best: "My
dear fellow, I'm a crank; very few human beings can
endure to have me near them, but I like to be with you,
and I suppose I like to be with those who are sympathetic[,] the more since they are so few." [2]
The polished courtesy of Spring-Rice was as far removed from crankiness as a gentleman's breeding could
be, but Brooks Adams was also a gentleman and
Spring-Rice could very well be sympathetic. With his
note Brooks in effect summed up the experience of
writing and publishing *The Emancipation*, and so provided this editor, fortunate enough to have access to
these documents, with an introduction more revealing,
more explanatory, than any he himself might compose
today. Yet also, with this note, Brooks Adams was

[1] Below, p. 3.
[2] B. Adams to Spring-Rice, Adams Papers, June 23, 1888; June?,
1888.

fully embarked on the headlong course that would lead
to the "Preface" of the second edition.

In "The Heritage of Henry Adams," Brooks looks
back to 1887 and betrays how deeply the hostile reaction
accorded *The Emancipation* still rankled in his memory.
He says he had warned Mr. Scudder that he would
produce thoughts over which he had no control, which
often astonished, even alarmed himself. Scudder refused to take him seriously, but realized the horrid
truth when he was obliged by contract to gulp hard and
swallow the volume. "Thus I became the author of
the 'Emancipation of Massachusetts,' which greatly
scandalized all the reputable historians of Massachusetts
and elsewhere, but none, I fear, more than my own
brother Charles." [1]

It appears that almost from the day of his birth,
Brooks's relations with the two eldest of his brothers,
John Quincy (1833–1894) and Charles Francis (1835–
1915), were strained. In his tenth year they made life
so miserable for him that his mother appealed to Henry,
who then wrote Charles Francis Junior that they all
ought to try "to tolerate the child, who is really a
first-rate little fellow, apart from his questions, and we
ought not to snub him so much." It really wasn't
right "to make home disagreeable to him." [2] I find it
somewhat puzzling to make out why *The Emancipation*
should have scandalized Charles Francis, but we have
to note that Brooks took public glee in remembering
that it did. In 1893 Charles Francis delivered four
lectures at Harvard and made them into a book,

[1] B. Adams, "The Heritage," *op. cit.*, p. 88.
[2] Ford, *Letters of Henry Adams*, I (Boston, 1930), 10.

Massachusetts: Its Historians and Its History. This
went over the same ground covered by *The Emancipation*, from which two brief quotations were pushed
into footnotes but which was otherwise ignored. By
implication Charles Francis seemed to sneer at it when
he announced *his* thesis to be "the Emancipation of Man
from Superstition and Caste." He directed a much
more concentrated attack than had Brooks upon "the
filio-pietistic" school of New England historians, naming
them specifically and holding up passages of their
apologetics to scorn. Obviously, he worked from a
sounder basis of knowledge among the sources than
Brooks ever mastered, and he did not get them into
"a bad mess." Perhaps this rude treatment of *The
Emancipation* is one more of those "snubs" to which
Brooks had early been subjected; it is certain that
Charles Francis, though equally iconoclastic, does not
ask the "questions" which to Brooks were the whole
reason for studying Massachusetts at all.

The manuscript "Life of John Quincy Adams,"
most of which Henry read and on which Brooks ultimately gave up (though he drew whole pages out of it
for "The Heritage"), declares that the two Presidential
Adamses, John (1735–1826) and John Quincy "offered
indeed the precise antithesis to Jefferson for they represented physical force," that John Adams "stood ready
to grapple with Napoleon, and held light appeals to the
reason of an adversary such as England when unsupported by broadsides." [1] Without capitalizing on any
psychologizing hunches, one can hardly help suspecting
that in the unsparing give-and-take of the family tussle

[1] B. Adams, manuscript "Life of John Quincy Adams," p. 138.

the boy Brooks learned the lesson of physical force, which for the man became a cult of what seemed to his critics sheer brutality.

In his astonishing paragraphs about *The Emancipation* in "The Heritage," Brooks Adams — still speaking to the public — moves rapidly from the book of 1887 to the summer of 1889 when he asked Evelyn Davis, sister to the wife of Henry Cabot Lodge, to marry him, explaining to her as he had to Scudder, "that I was eccentric almost to madness, and that, if she married me, she must do so on her own responsibility and at her own risk." He says that she, like Scudder, "seemed to regard this as a kind of poor joke, but, in the end she found it serious enough." The 1919 "Preface" must be read as the work of a man who by that late date could speak of himself and of his marital tragedy in these bruising terms.[1]

There can be little comprehension of both the "Preface" and "The Heritage," of the eccentric course of Brooks Adams's development, unless we consider the abortive "Life of John Quincy Adams," which, as I have remarked, Brooks left in manuscript, with instructions that it be shown to no one. Since he reproduced the "theory" of it in "The Heritage," there seems no longer any reason for conspiratorial restraint. The "theory" is alarmingly simple. His grandfather, "like Moses, and a host of other idealists and reformers," dreamed that by his interpretation of the divine mind, "as manifested in nature, he could covenant with God, and thus regenerate mankind." President Adams labored "to bring the democratic principle of equality into such a

[1] B. Adams, "The Heritage," *op. cit.*, pp. 88–89.

relation with science and education that it would yield itself into becoming, or being formed into, an efficient instrument for collective administration." But God Almighty abandoned John Quincy Adams, just as He had abandoned Moses. In the language of the Puritans, He "deserted" them. With the triumph of Jackson, the instinct of greed assumed domination over the Republic; the Adamses, being innocent of greed, were pushed aside.[1] The character of "Moses" in the "Preface" becomes meaningful only when seen as an allegory of the fall of the House of Adams from control over the destiny of America — and so of Brooks Adams's desolation upon the demise of Theodore Roosevelt.

The anagram collapses with the average reader, or becomes positively absurd, when the "Preface" contends that not only the Mosaic civilization but Moses himself "broke down" at the point where mind and matter clashed. John Quincy Adams, in his own Mosaical incarnation, suffered not at all from any such internal conflict. However, let us consider the total situation of American civilization in 1828: then we perceive the point of Brooks Adams's lifelong researches. Just as matter (i.e., greed) overcame mental optimism (the Ten Commandments), so did General Jackson triumph over the optimistic ideals of education, of science, and over a coherent program for internal improvements. Moses was restrained from venturing into the promised land, but his henchmen fulfilled his forecast; so John Quincy Adams will never be understood unless it be appreciated that he "represented the incarnation of that modern civilization, the product of applied sciences, which was destined during the civil war to annihilate the old." [1] President Adams had the ill-fortune to become chief magistrate at a moment when the courtly qualities of a Washington or of a Monroe had suddenly become a liability. As Brooks put it — and here as elsewhere in the manuscript he was thinking not only of his grandfather but of himself:

> The basis of Adams's character was a stern enthusiasm transmitted through his mother from a long line of clerical ancestors. He was morever a puritan trained in politics by Washington. He might die and rot but he could not betray his ideal, and this idealist, so fettered by nature, was selected by fate to confront a combination as adroit, as unscrupulous and as bold as any which ever flourished upon earth. He languished under the ordeal. [2]

At this point we get our first glimmering of the elaborate process Brooks Adams had imposed upon himself to rectify the condemnation of 1887. If Moses is a thinly disguised surrogate for President Adams, then the latter is constructed in the image of Brooks Adams (whence the special bravado of his saying in "The Heritage" that Henry was, among the family, the only inheritor of John Quincy Adams's skill in science!). Viewed in this perspective, the otherwise inexplicable passion of the "Preface" becomes plausible as Brooks's unrepentant *apologia* for his intransigent self.

This construction may seem too labored to be even momentarily respected; those who would impulsively reject it have yet to make an acquaintance (not, I assure them, easy to obtain) with the disturbing functions of his mind. We can hardly pretend otherwise than that,

---

[1] B. Adams, manuscript "Life of John Quincy Adams," p. 429.
[2] *Ibid.*, p. 406.

when Brooks says John Quincy Adams was not a politician in the conventional sense and therefore approached politics from a "scientific" standpoint, Brooks
Adams speaks either of himself in American history or
of the self he still imagined he might be. John Quincy
Adams, being deeply read in history, "reasoned from
the past to the future with an astounding grasp of the
relation of cause and effect, and in drawing deductions
from his premises seldom fell wide of the mark." Whenever he did err, it was usually — this remark is certainly
significant — from "self-distrust, and, possibly, from a
tendency toward depression." On the whole John
Quincy was accurate, and though he might "estimate
that a catastrophe was nearer than the event proved
to be," his forecast generally "prepared him for all
emergencies." [1] The "Preface" of 1919, along with
"The Heritage," was Brooks Adams's desperate effort
to play the part of John Quincy Adams, to prepare the
democracy for what — if it continued to pursue the
ignis fatuus of Jackson and of greed — would become
catastrophe.

It is worth further noting that the manuscript "Life"
reveals more cogently than does "The Heritage" that
this position of the prophet was assumed upon the
premise of a total disillusionment with, or rather an
abject despair of, the intelligence of the American popu-
lace. Brooks Adams wrote the concluding paragraphs
of the "Preface" after he had stated to himself the
predicament in which John Quincy Adams felt himself
mired in 1837, a passage which again he surely composed with his own self in mind:

[1] *Ibid.*, p. 128.

A few weeks earlier, at the opening of the session, he had
sadly admitted to himself [that] on those issues which
were fundamental he could not reach the understanding
of his countrymen by calm and moderate argument, and
he could not do so because of the deterioration of the
American mind. By 1837 intelligence had sunk so low
that no considerable part of the community could discard
local and sordid interests, and give to a public man the
confidence and support which made Washington's career
possible.[1]

Whereupon Brooks Adams took large satisfaction in
noting that John Quincy Adams was excoriated not only
by Southern slaveholders but by wealthy manufacturers
and bankers of the North — by "State Street." The
latter "thought him a semi-demented incendiary."[2]
This judgment those of their type who bothered to pay
attention to Brooks Adams also pronounced upon him.

The result was that in Brooks Adams's view not only
America but the entire universe, to the utmost reaches
of infinite space, "is a chaos which admits of reaching
no equilibrium, and with which man is doomed eternally
and hopelessly to contend."[3] Moses, "the first great
optimist,"[4] is the archetypal figure of all such, down
through John Quincy Adams and (presumably) Brooks
Adams. Moses dramatized the way in which civilizations are repeatedly and inexorably destroyed by the
warfare of matter against mind. The lesson was therefore plain for a competitive American democracy entering into an era in which, if Asia is to be kept subordinate,
force will need to be used. "But it is not imaginable
that Asiatics will submit to this discrimination in
silence."[5]

[1] *Ibid.*, p. 559.   [2] *Ibid.*, p. 565.   [3] Below, p. 5.   [4] Below, p. 8.
[5] Below, p. 167.

Brooks and Henry greatly enjoyed — to the point of nausea — the game of fixing the date when Western civilization would go to smash. By 1918 it had survived several of their appointed terminations; but during 1914–1918 it had barely got through. We can make fun of the predilection of the Adamses for counting on catastrophe. Yet they have a way of thrusting their detractors into the awkward position of becoming, not too comfortably, what Brooks smeared as "optimists." Whereupon these lay themselves open to the dissection which Brooks administered upon his grandfather. If mankind cannot attain a balance between mind and matter, "the future promises to be stormy."[1] With this observation no thinking or responsive mind, unless blinded by an optimism more hollow than the emptiest of nineteenth-century slogans, can hardly, four decades after Brooks Adams made it, dare to disagree.

V

The habit in the Adams family, or at least, as we have noted, among the four sons of the elder Charles Francis Adams (1807–1886), was never, under any sentimental notions of sensitivity, to spare each others' feelings. So, while Henry toiled over Brooks's manuscripts he was free in his criticism, and Brooks treasured every word of it, especially what stung. In "The Heritage" he represents Henry as saying (repeatedly), "Don't you see, Brooks . . . that you, with your lawyer's method, only state sequences of fact, and explain no causes? Granting that your sequences are correct, and I believe they are, and that your law is sound, which I

[1] Below, p. 166.

am willing to suppose, you do not tell us why man has
been a failure, and could be nothing but a failure. You
only show that he has failed." But the task of writing
a "scientific summary" was by that time, Brooks insists,
beyond him.[1] A great part of the charm and equally
of the pathos of the "Preface" — along with his futile
endeavors to link it with the early "scientific" principles
which in 1887 he had passionately entertained — is that,
with Henry gone, Brooks tried, all alone, to do what
Henry had told him to do, to explain everything.

In this light, to repeat, the scholarly deficiencies of
the original book are no longer matters of controversy,
but neither are the wild projections of the "Preface."
What stands out is the intellectual biography of one of
the most interesting minds ever produced in New
England, and a vindication of its often shaky reputation for cantankerousness. The two segments con-
stitute a mental record of what happened between the
optimistic "Darwinian" phase of the 1880's and the
post-world-war year of 1919. Indeed, fully to follow
the bedeviled course of this development, and to
appreciate the impact of ideas and events upon Brooks
Adams, one must go through the books and articles
produced in the long interval. But the beginning and
the end of the pilgrimage are here.

It is not entirely a pleasant tale. There are unlovely
aspects to the mind of Brooks Adams as there were to
his personality. He was by no means the stylist that
his brother Henry became, and by contrast seems
deficient in taste. Yet there is a vigor in everything
he writes, regardless of whether as in 1887 he considers

[1] B. Adams, "The Heritage," *op. cit.*, pp. 100–101.

himself a "Liberal" or as in 1919 a violent conservative. His onslaught — for such it was — upon the sanctified monuments of Puritan piety was valuable if only for the hostility it aroused, and so played a vital part in what I am fain to hope has become a more objective and rounded scholarship of recent years within this treacherous field.

Many of the critics of 1887, especially William F. Poole, were entirely correct in pointing out the shocking limitations of his first-hand knowledge of the sources or of the period. He simply had no comprehension of the contours of the seventeenth-century Puritan intellect, of its metaphysics or of its political doctrine, and his ignorance of the vast structure of the theology is nothing short of profound. But I must insist that Brooks Adams was not writing a history of Puritan New England. Hence his book is not to be read as though it were such. We may not be able today to take seriously the "theory" which he imagined he had exemplified by the narrative, but we have to take the book seriously as a "tract for the times" in 1887, as we must also take the "Preface" for a document of 1919.

However, most important to remark, the gloom of the "Preface" does not, somehow, have anything like the enervating effect of the delicious hopelessness of Henry's last years. To read Henry's letters of his final decade, or of his several decades, in a steady perusal, is to invite exasperation against his cultivated pose and his tedious repetitions of a thin wail of pessimism. But Brooks Adams's "Preface," though madder than any utterance of the Hatter, is paradoxically exhilarating. It is still fighting, just as the *Emancipation* was a combative book. In 1917, Henry, in one of his very last letters, noticed that Brooks "considers the world to be going to the devil with the greatest rapidity quite apart from the war; and I endeavor, as you know, to console him by the assurance it went there at least ten years ago." At the moment Henry wrote this, Brooks was making his last public stand as a delegate to the Massachusetts constitutional convention, where, according to Henry, he was "trying to frame a new fabric for the Society of the next century which will satisfy some one," but for the time being Brooks had "got only to the point of dissatisfying everyone more than ever."[1] So Brooks had begun; so he ended.

It would have been a terrible task to attempt to live with Brooks Adams, as Evelyn Davis discovered to her sorrow. A reader does not have to dwell with him perpetually. He was the man who, a neighbor reported, sang the tune of an Irish ballad while shaving with simple words of his own composition: "God damn it! God damn it! God damn it!"[2] He had so many pairs of shoes that they went, when stacked, completely around the walls of his bedroom; when a young doctor, attending him for the illness that shortly would kill him, asked why he had so many, Brooks Adams answered, "To wear 'em, you damned fool."[3]

Such anecdotes about Brooks Adams have long since become part of the legend of Boston eccentricity. But they are not funny in any comforting sense; they bespeak a man living in deep distress, to which all his

[1] Ford, *Letters*, II, 645.

[2] Thornton Anderson, *Brooks Adams Constructive Conservative* (Ithaca, 1951), p. xiii.

[3] Beringause, *op. cit.*, p. 388.

experience contributed. I would venture to say, using the words with utmost caution, that his whole life was a spiritual crisis. This fact became more clear in his last years when he sought, apparently with his usual ferocity, to find solace in Christianity. In 1921 he made a "retreat" in a Benedictine monastery on the Isle of Wight and later another in the monastery at Portsmouth, New Hampshire. Of the first he is said to have reported, "A moment comes when you must jump the chasm, but unless someone kicks you, unless someone waits on the other side, you don't get across." The monks at Portsmouth remember him standing at the door while they were saying Mass, and report him as telling them: "I have no real belief. I stand at that door — I prefer to stand outside — and I am then one of yourselves. When I talk with you apart from your chapel I am a pagan."[1] The two parts of the 1919 *Emancipation* are a chronicle of this pilgrimage of anguish.

Brooks Adams reports himself as telling Henry, sometime in the 1910's, that it was now four generations since John Adams wrote the constitution of Massachusetts, and that the time had come for all Adamses to perish: "The world is tired of us."[2] It might well have grown tired of Brooks Adams had he been only the profane eccentric of Quincy; but the fact is, he persists as a figure in our national expression. Henry wrote to him in 1900: "Thanks entirely to our family habit of writing, we exist in the public mind only as a typical expression of disagreeable qualities. Our dogmatism

[1] *Ibid.*, pp. 385–386.
[2] B. Adams, "The Heritage," *op. cit.*, p. 93.

is certainly odious, but it was not extravagant till we made it a record."[1]   Brooks Adams gives his readers a highly peculiar sort of pleasure, if only because he made his chapter in the record the most extravagant in the great saga — although, as I have indicated, and as he pleaded, such a work as *The Emancipation* has inherently more substantial claims to our recognition. As Howells concluded in the one fully appreciative review that *The Emancipation* elicited in 1887, it is a story "which Mr. Adams tells absorbingly, clearly, strenuously — not to say athletically."[2]   These adverbs denote rare qualities in American writing, and are to be treasured wherever they appear, whether we be attracted to or positively repelled by the "theory" of the writer.   We can not afford to sacrifice our interest in one who could speak his own epitaph while purporting to compose that of his magnificent grandfather: "In other words he was disappointed because he was not supernatural."[3]

---

[1] Harold Dean Cater, *Henry Adams and His Friends* (Boston, 1947), p. 487.

[2] *Harper's, op. cit.,* p. 985.

[3] B. Adams, "The Heritage," *op. cit.,* p. 35.

PREFACE
TO THE 1919 EDITION

PREFATORY NOTE
TO THE FIRST EDITION

I AM under the deepest obligations to the Hon. Mellen Chamberlain and Mr. Charles Deane.

The generosity of my friend Mr. Frank Hamilton Cushing in putting at my disposal the unpublished results of his researches among the Zuñis is in keeping with the originality and power of his mind. Without his aid my attempt would have been impossible. I have also to thank Prof. Henry C. Chapman, J. A. Gordon, M. D., Prof. William James, and Alpheus Hyatt, Esq., for the kindness with which they assisted me. I feel that any merit this volume may possess is due to these gentlemen; its faults are all my own.

BROOKS ADAMS.

QUINCY, *September* 17, 1886.

PREFACE
TO THE 1919 EDITION
CHAPTER I.

I WROTE this little volume more than thirty years ago, since when I have hardly opened it. Therefore I now read it almost as if it were written by another man, and I find to my relief that, on the whole, I think rather better of it than I did when I published it. Indeed, as a criticism of what were then the accepted views of Massachusetts history, as expounded by her most authoritative historians, I see nothing in it to retract or even to modify. I do, however, somewhat regret the rather acrimonious tone which I occasionally adopted when speaking of the more conservative section of the clergy. Not that I think that the Mathers, for example, and their like, did not deserve all, or, indeed, more than all I ever said or thought of them, but because I conceive that equally effective strictures might have been conveyed in urbaner language; and, as I age, I shrink from anything akin to invective, even in what amounts to controversy.

Therefore I have now nothing to alter in the *Emancipation of Massachusetts*, viewed as history, though I might soften its asperities somewhat, here and there; but when I come to consider it as philosophy, I am startled to observe the gap which separates the present epoch from my early middle life.

The last generation was strongly Darwinian in the sense that it accepted, almost as a tenet of religious faith, the theory that human civilization is a progressive evolution, moving on the whole steadily toward perfection, from a lower to a higher intellectual plane, and, as a necessary part of its progress, developing a higher degree of mental vigor. I need hardly observe that all belief in democracy as a final solution of social ills, all confidence in education as a means to attaining to universal justice, and all hope of approximating to the rule of moral right in the administration of law, was held to hinge on this great fundamental dogma, which, it followed, it was almost impious to deny, or even to doubt. Thus, on the first page of my book, I observe, as if it were axiomatic, that, at a given moment, toward the opening of the sixteenth century, "Europe burst from her mediæval torpor into the splendor of the Renaissance," and further on I assume, as an equally self-evident axiom, that freedom of thought was the one great permanent advance which western civilization made by all the agony and bloodshed of the Reformation. Apart altogether from the fact that I should doubt whether, in the year 1919, any intelligent and educated man would be inclined to maintain that the twelfth and thirteenth centuries were, as contrasted with the nineteenth, ages of intellectual torpor, what startles me in these paragraphs is the self-satisfied assumption of the finality of my conclusions. I posit, as a fact not to be controverted, that our universe is an expression of an universal law, which the nineteenth century had discovered and could formulate.

During the past thirty years I have given this subject my best attention, and now I am so far from assenting to this proposition that my mind tends in the opposite direction. Each day I live I am less able to withstand the suspicion that the universe, far from being an expression of law originating in a single primary cause, is a chaos which admits of reaching no equilibrium, and with which man is doomed eternally and hopelessly to contend. For human society, to deserve the name of civilization, must be an embodiment of order, or must at least tend toward a social equilibrium. I take, as an illustration of my meaning, the development of the domestic relations of our race.

I assume it to be generally admitted, that possibly man's first and probably his greatest advance toward order — and, therefore, toward civilization — was the creation of the family as the social nucleus. As Napoleon said, when the lawyers were drafting his Civil Code, "Make the family responsible to its head, and the head to me, and I will keep order in France." And yet although our dependence on the family system has been recognized in every age and in every land, there has been no restraint on personal liberty which has been more resented, by both men and women alike, than has been this bond which, when perfect, constrains one man and one woman to live a joint life until death shall them part, for the propagation, care, and defence of their children.

The result is that no civilization has, as yet, ever succeeded, and none promises in the immediate future to succeed, in enforcing this primary obligation, and we are thus led to consider the cause, inherent in our complex nature, which makes it impossible for us to establish an equilibrium between mind and matter. A difficulty which never has been even partially overcome, which wrecked the Roman Empire and the Christian Church, which has wrecked all systems of law, and which has never been more lucidly defined than by Saint Paul, in the Epistle to the Romans, "For we know that the law is spiritual: but I am carnal, sold under sin. For that which I do, I allow not: for what I would, that do I not; but what I hate, that do I. . . . Now then it is no more I that do it, but sin that dwelleth in me. . . . For the good that I would, I do not: but the evil which I would not, that I do. . . . For I delight in the law of God after the inward man: . . . But I see another law in my members, warring against the law of my mind, and bringing me into captivity to the law of sin which is in my members. O wretched man that I am! who shall deliver me from the body of this death?" [1]

And so it has been since a time transcending the limits of imagination. Here in a half-a-dozen sentences Saint Paul exposes the ceaseless conflict between mind and matter, whose union, though seemingly the essence of life, creates a condition which we cannot comprehend and to which we could not hope to con-

[1] Romans VII, 14-24.

form, even if we could comprehend it. In short, which indicates chaos as being the probable core of an universe from which we must evolve order, if ever we are to cope with violence, fraud, crime, war, and general brutality. Wheresoever we turn the prospect is the same. If we gaze upon the heavens we discern immeasurable spaces sprinkled with globules of matter, to which our earth seems to be more or less akin, but all plunging, apparently, both furiously and aimlessly, from out of an infinite past to an equally immeasurable future.

Whence this material mass comes, or what its wild flight portends, we neither know nor could we, probably, comprehend even were its secret divulged to us by a superior intelligence, always conceding that there be such an intelligence, or any secret to disclose. These latter speculations lie, however, beyond the scope of my present purpose. It suffices if science permits me to postulate (a concession by science which I much doubt if it could make) that matter, as we know it, has the semblance of being what we call a substance, charged with a something which we define as energy, but which at all events simulates a vital principle resembling heat, seeking to escape into space, where it cools. Thus the stars, having blazed until their vital principle is absorbed in space, sink into relative torpor, or, as the astronomers say, die. The trees and plants diffuse their energy in the infinite, and, at length, when nothing but a shell remains, rot. Lastly, our fleshly bodies, when the union between mind and matter is dissolved, crumble into dust. When the involuntary partnership between mind and matter ceases through death, it is possible, or at least conceivable, that the impalpable soul, admitting that such a thing exists, may survive in some medium where it may be free from material shackles, but, while life endures, the flesh has wants which must be gratified, and which, therefore, take precedence of the yearnings of the soul, just as Saint Paul points out was the case with himself; and herein lies the inexorable conflict between the moral law and the law of competition which favors the strong, and from whence comes all the abominations of selfishness, of violence, of cruelty and crime.

Approached thus, perhaps no historical fragment is more suggestive than the exodus of the Jews from Egypt under Moses, who was the first great optimist, nor one which is seldomer read with an eye to the contrast which it discloses between Moses the law-giver, the idealist, the religious prophet, and the visionary; and Moses the political adventurer and the keen and unscrupulous man of the world. And yet it is here at the point at which mind and matter clashed, that Moses merits most attention. For Moses and the Mosaic civilization broke down at this point, which is, indeed, the chasm which has engulfed every progressive civilization since the dawn of time. And the value of the story as an illustration of scientific history is its familiarity, for no Christian child lives who has not been brought up on it.

We have all forgotten when we first learned how the Jews came to migrate to Egypt during the years of the famine, when Joseph had become the minister of Pharaoh through his acuteness in reading dreams. Also how, after their settlement in the land of Goshen, — which is the Egyptian province lying at the end of the ancient caravan road, which Abraham travelled, leading from Palestine to the banks of the Nile, and which had been the trade route, or path of least resistance, between Asia and Africa, probably for ages before the earliest of human traditions, — they prospered exceedingly. But at length they fell into a species of bondage which lasted several centuries, during which they multiplied so rapidly that they finally raised in the Egyptian government a fear of their domination. Nor, considering subsequent events, was this apprehension unreasonable. At all events the Egyptian government is represented, as a measure of self-protection, as proposing to kill male Jewish babies in order to reduce the Jewish military strength; and it was precisely at this juncture that Moses was born. Moses, indeed, escaped the fate which menaced him, but only by a narrow chance, and he was nourished by his mother in an atmosphere of hate which tinged his whole life, causing him always to feel to the Egyptians as the slave feels to his master. After birth the mother hid the child as long as possible, but when she could conceal the infant no longer she platted a basket of reeds, smeared it with pitch, and set it adrift in the Nile, where it was likely to be found, leaving her eldest daughter, named Miriam, to watch over it. Presently Pharaoh's daughter came, as was her habit, to the river to bathe, as Moses's mother expected that she would, and there she noticed the "ark" floating among the bulrushes. She had it brought her, and, noticing Miriam, she caused the girl to engage her mother, whom Miriam pointed out to her, as a nurse. Taking pity on the baby the kind-hearted princess adopted it and brought it up as she would had it been her own, and, as the child grew, she came to love the boy, and had him educated with care, and this education must be kept in mind since the future of Moses as a man turned upon it. For Moses was most peculiarly a creation of his age and of his environment; if, indeed, he may not be considered as an incarnation of Jewish thought gradually shaped during many centuries of priestly development.

According to tradition, Moses from childhood was of great personal beauty, so much so that passers by would turn to look at him, and this early promise was fulfilled as he grew to be a man. Tall and dignified, with long, shaggy hair and beard, of a reddish hue tinged with gray, he is described as "wise as beautiful." Educated by his foster-mother as a priest at Heliopolis, he was taught the whole range of Chaldean and Assyrian literature, as well as the Egyptian, and thus became acquainted with all the traditions of oriental magic: which, just at that period, was in its fullest development. Consequently, Moses must have been familiar with the ancient doctrines of Zoroaster.

Men who stood thus, and had such an education, were called Wise Men, Magi, or Magicians, and had great influence, not so much as priests of a God, as enchanters who dealt with the supernatural as a profession. Daniel, for example, belonged to this class. He was one of three captive Jews whom Nebuchadnezzar, King of Babylon, gave in charge to the master of his eunuchs, to whom he should teach the learning and the tongue of the Chaldeans. Daniel, very shortly, by his natural ability, brought himself and his comrades into favor with the chief eunuch, who finally presented them to Nebuchadnezzar, who conversed with them and found them "ten times better than all the magicians and astrologers that were in all his realm."

The end of it was, of course, that Nebuchadnezzar dreamed a dream which he forgot when he awoke and he summoned "the magicians, and the astrologers, and the sorcerers, and the Chaldeans, for to shew the king his dreams," but they could not unless he told it them. This vexed the king, who declared that unless they should tell him his dream with the interpretation thereof, they should be cut in pieces. So the decree went forth that all "the wise men" of Babylon should be slain, and they sought Daniel and his fellows to slay them. Therefore, it appears that together with its privileges and advantages the profession of magic was dangerous in those ages. Daniel, on this occasion, according to the tradition, succeeded in revealing and interpreting the dream; and, in return,

Nebuchadnezzar made Daniel a great man, chief governor of the province of Babylon.

Precisely a similar tale is told of Joseph, who, having been sold by his brethren to Midianitish merchantmen with camels, bearing spices and balm, journeying along the ancient caravan road toward Egypt, was in turn sold by them to Potiphar, the captain of Pharaoh's guard.

And Joseph rose in Potiphar's service, and after many alternations of fortune was brought before Pharaoh, as Daniel had been before Nebuchadnezzar, and because he interpreted Pharaoh's dream acceptably, he was made "ruler over all the land of Egypt" and so ultimately became the ancestor whom Moses most venerated and whose bones he took with him when he set out upon the exodus.

It is true also that Josephus has preserved an idle tale that Moses was given command of an Egyptian army with which he made a successful campaign against the Ethiopians, but it is unworthy of credit and may be neglected. His bringing up was indeed the reverse of military. So much so that probably far the most important part of his education lay in acquiring those arts which conduce to the deception of others, such deceptions as jugglers have always practised in snake-charming and the like, or in gaining control of another's senses by processes akin to hypnotism; — processes which have been used by the priestly class and their familiars from the dawn of time. In especial there was one miracle performed

by the Magi, on which not only they, but Moses himself, appear to have set great store, and on which
Moses seemed always inclined to fall back, when
hard pressed to assert his authority. They pretended
to make fire descend onto their altars by means of
magical ceremonies.[1] Nevertheless, amidst all these
ancient eastern civilizations, the strongest hold which
the priests or sorcerers held over, and the greatest
influence which they exercised upon, others, lay in
their relations to disease, for there they were supposed to be potent. For example, in Chaldea, diseases
were held to be the work of demons, to be feared in
proportion as they were powerful and malignant,
and to be restrained by incantations and exorcisms.
Among these demons the one, perhaps most dreaded,
was called Namtar, the genius of the plague. Moses
was, of course, thoroughly familiar with all these
branches of learning, for the relations of Egypt were
then and for many centuries had been, intimate with
Mesopotamia. Whatever aspect the philosophy may
have, which Moses taught after middle life touching
the theory of the religion in which he believed, Moses
had from early childhood been nurtured in these
Mesopotamian beliefs and traditions, and to them —
or, at least, toward them — he always tended to re
vert in moments of stress. Without bearing this
fundamental premise in mind, Moses in active life
can hardly be understood, for it was on this foundation that his theories of cause and effect were based.

[1] Lenormant, *Chaldean Magic*, 226.

As M. Lenormant has justly and truly observed,
go back as far as we will in Egyptian religion, we find
there, as a foundation, or first cause, the idea of a
divine unity, — a single God, who had no beginning
and was to have no end of days, — the primary cause
of all.[1]   It is true that this idea of unity was early
obscured by confounding the energy with its manifestations. Consequently a polytheism was engendered which embraced all nature.   Gods and demons
struggled for control and in turn were struggled
with. In Egypt, in Media, in Chaldea, in Persia,
there were wise men, sorcerers, and magicians who
sought to put this science into practice, and among
this fellowship Moses must always rank foremost.
Before, however, entering upon the consideration of
Moses, as a necromancer, as a scientist, as a statesman, as a priest, or as a commander, we should first
glance at the authorities which tell his history.

Scholars are now pretty well agreed that Moses and
Aaron were men who actually lived and worked probably about the time attributed to them by tradition.
That is to say, under the reign of Ramses II, of the
Nineteenth Egyptian dynasty who reigned, as it is
computed, from 1348 to 1281 B.C., and under whom
the exodus occurred. Nevertheless, no very direct or
conclusive evidence having as yet been discovered
touching these events among Egyptian documents,
we are obliged, in the main, to draw our information
from the Hebrew record, which, for the most part,

[1] *Chaldean Magic,* 79.

is contained in the Pentateuch, or the first five books of the Bible.

Possibly no historical documents have ever been subjected to a severer or more minute criticism than have these books during the last two centuries. It is safe to say that no important passage and perhaps no paragraph has escaped the most searching and patient analysis by the acutest and most highly trained of minds; but as yet, so far as the science of history is concerned, the results have been disappointing. The order in which events occurred may have been successfully questioned and the sequence of the story rearranged hypothetically; but, in general, it has to be admitted that the weight of all the evidence obtained from the monuments of contemporary peoples has been to confirm the reliability of the Biblical narrative. For example, no one longer doubts that Joseph was actually a Hebrew, who rose, through merit, to the highest offices of state under an Egyptian monarch, and who conceived and successfully carried into execution a comprehensive agrarian policy which had the effect of transferring the landed estates of the great feudal aristocracy to the crown, and of completely changing Egyptian tenures. Nor does any one question, at this day, the reality of the power which the Biblical writers ascribed to the Empire of the Hittites. Under such conditions the course of the commentator is clear. He should treat the Jewish record as reliable, except where it frankly accepts the miracle as a demonstrated fact, and even then regard the miracle as an important and most suggestive part of the great Jewish epic, which always has had, and always must have, a capital influence on human thought.

The Pentateuch has, indeed, been demonstrated to be a compilation of several chronicles arranged by different writers at different times, and blended into a unity under different degrees of pressure, but now, as the book stands, it is as authentic a record as could be wished of the workings of the Mosaic mind and of the minds of those of his followers who supported him in his pilgrimage, and who made so much of his task possible, as he in fact accomplished.

Moses, himself, but for the irascibility of his temper, might have lived and died, contented and unknown, within the shadow of the Egyptian court. The princess who befriended him as a baby would probably have been true to him to the end, in which case he would have lived wealthy, contented, and happy and would have died overfed and unknown. Destiny, however, had planned it otherwise.

The Hebrews were harshly treated after the death of Joseph, and fell into a quasi-bondage in which they were forced to labor, and this species of tyranny irritated Moses, who seems to have been brought up under his mother's influence. At all events, one day Moses chanced to see an Egyptian beating a Jew, which must have been a common enough sight, but a sight which revolted him. Whereupon Moses, thinking himself alone, slew the Egyptian and hid his body in the sand. Moses, however, was not alone. A day or so later he again happened to see two men fighting, whereupon he again interfered, enjoining the one who was in the wrong to desist. Whereupon the man whom he checked turned fiercely on him and said, "Who made thee a prince and a judge over us? Intendest thou to kill me, as thou killedst the Egyptian?"

When Moses perceived by this act of treachery on the part of a countryman, whom he had befriended, that nothing remained to him but flight, he started in the direction of southern Arabia, toward what was called the Land of Midian, and which, at the moment, seems to have lain beyond the limits of the Egyptian administrative system, although it had once been one of its most prized metallurgical regions. Just at that time it was occupied by a race called the Kenites, who were more or less closely related to the Amalekites, who were Bedouins and who relied for their living upon their flocks, as the Israelites had done in the time of Abraham. Although Arabia Patrea was then, in the main, a stony waste, as it is now, it was not quite a desert. It was crossed by trade routes in many directions along which merchants travelled to Egypt, as is described in the story of Joseph, whose brethren seized him in Dothan, and as they sat by the side of the pit in which they had thrown him, they saw a company of Ishmaelites who came from Gilead and who journeyed straight down from Damascus to Gilead and from thence to Hebron, along the old caravan road, toward Egypt, with camels bearing spices and myrrh, as had been their custom since long beyond human tradition, and which had been the road along which Abraham had travelled before them, and which was still watered by his wells. This was the famous track from Beersheba to Hebron, where Hagar was abandoned with her baby Ishmael, and if the experiences of Hagar do not prove that the wilderness of Shur was altogether impracticable for women and children it does at least show that for a mixed multitude without trustworthy guides or reliable sources of supply, the country was not one to be lightly attempted.

It was into a region similar to this, only somewhat further to the south, that Moses penetrated after his homicide, travelling alone and as an unknown adventurer, dressed like an Egyptian, and having nothing of the nomad about him in his looks. As Moses approached Sinai, the country grew wilder and more lonely, and Moses one day sat himself down, by the side of a well whither shepherds were wont to drive their flocks to water. For shepherds came there, and also shepherdesses; among others were the seven daughters of Jethro, the priest of Midian, who came to water their father's flocks. But the shepherds drove them away and took the water for themselves. Whereupon Moses defended the girls and drew water for them and watered their flocks. This naturally pleased the young women, and they took Moses home with them to their father's tent, as Bedouins still would do. And when they came to their father, he asked how it chanced that they came home so early that day. "And they said, an Egyptian delivered us out of the hand of the shepherds, and also drew water enough for us, and watered the flock." And Jethro said, "Where is he? Why is it that ye have left the man? Call him that he may eat bread."

"And Moses was content to dwell with" Jethro, who made him his chief shepherd and gave him Zipporah, his daughter. And she bore him a son. Seemingly, time passed rapidly and happily in this peaceful, pastoral life, which, according to the tradition preserved by Saint Stephen, lasted forty years, but be the time long or short, it is clear that Moses loved and respected Jethro and was in return valued by him. Nor could anything have been more natural, for Moses was a man who made a deep impression at first sight — an impression which time strengthened. Intellectually he must have been at least as notable as in personal appearance, for his education at Heliopolis set him apart from men whom Jethro would have been apt to meet in his nomad life. But if Moses had strong attractions for Jethro, Jethro drew Moses toward himself at least as strongly in the position in which Moses then stood. Jethro, though a child of the desert, was the chief of a tribe or at least of a family, a man used to command, and to administer the nomad law; for Jethro was the head of the Kenites, who were akin to the Amalekites, with whom the Israelites were destined to wage mortal war. And for Moses this was a most important connection, for Moses after his exile never permitted his relations with his own people in Egypt to lapse. The possibility of a Jewish revolt, of which his own banishment was a precursor, was constantly in his mind. To Moses a Jewish exodus from Egypt was always imminent. For centuries it had been a dream of the Jews. Indeed it was an article of faith with them. Joseph, as he sank in death, had called his descendants about him and made them solemnly swear to "carry his bones hence." And to that end Joseph had caused his body to be embalmed and put in a coffin that all might be ready when the day came. Moses knew the tradition and felt himself bound by the oath and waited in Midian with confidence until the moment of performance should come. Presently it did come. Very probably before he either expected or could have wished it, and actually, as almost his first act of leadership, Moses did carry the bones of Joseph with him when he crossed the Red Sea. Moses held the tradition to be a certainty. He never conceived it to be a matter of possible doubt, nor probably was it so. There was in no one's mind a question touching Joseph's promise nor about his expectation of its fulfilment. What Moses did is related in Exodus XIII, 19: "And Moses took the bones of Joseph with him; for he had straitly sworn the children of Israel, saying, God will surely visit you; and ye shall carry up my bones away hence with you."

In fine, Moses, in the solitude of the Arabian wilderness, in his wanderings as the shepherd of Jethro, came to believe that his destiny was linked with that of his countrymen in a revolution which was certain to occur before they could accomplish the promise of Joseph and escape from Egypt under the guidance of the god who had befriended and protected him. Moreover, Moses was by no means exclusively a religious enthusiast. He was also a scientific man, after the ideas of that age. Moses had a high degree of education and he was familiar with the Egyptian and Chaldean theory of a great and omnipotent prime motor, who had had no beginning and should have no end. He was also aware that this theory was obscured by the intrusion into men's minds of a multitude of lesser causes, in the shape of gods and demons, who mixed themselves in earthly affairs and on whose sympathy or malevolence the weal or woe of human life hinged. Pondering deeply on these things as he roamed, he persuaded himself that he had solved the riddle of the universe, by identifying the great first cause of all with the deity who had been known to his ancestors, whose normal home was in the promised land of Canaan, and who, beside being all-powerful, was also a moral being whose service must tend toward the welfare of mankind. For Moses was by temperament a moralist in whom such abominations as those practised in the worship of Moloch created horror. He knew that the god of Abraham would tolerate no such wickedness as this, because of the fate of Sodom on much less provocation, and he believed that were he to lead the Israelites, as he might lead them, he could propitiate such a deity, could he but by an initial success induce his congregation to obey the commands of a god strong enough to reward them for leading a life which should be acceptable to him. All depended, therefore, should the opportunity of leadership come to him, on his being able, in the first place, to satisfy himself that the god who presented himself to him was verily the god of Abraham, who burned Sodom, and not some demon, whose object was to vex mankind: and, in the second place, assuming that he himself were convinced of the identity of the god, that he could convince his countrymen of the fact, and also of the absolute necessity of obedience to the moral law which he should declare, since without absolute obedience, they would certainly merit, and probably suffer, such a fate as befell the inhabitants of Sodom, under the very eyes of Abraham, and in spite of his prayers for mercy.

There was one other apprehension which may have troubled, and probably did trouble, Moses. The god of the primitive man, and certainly of the Bedouin, is usually a local deity whose power and whose activity is limited to some particular region, as, for instance, a mountain or a plain. Thus the god of Abraham might have inhabited and absolutely ruled the plain of Mamre and been impotent elsewhere. But this, had Moses for a moment harbored such a notion, would have been dispelled when he thought of Joseph. Joseph, when his brethren threw him into the pit, must have been under the guardianship of the god of his fathers, and when he was drawn out, and sold in the ordinary course of the slave-trade, he was bought by Potiphar, the captain of the guard. "And the Lord was with Joseph and he was a prosperous man." Thenceforward, Joseph had a wonderful career. He received in a dream a revelation of what the weather was to be for seven years to come. And by this dream he was able to formulate a policy for establishing public graineries like those which were maintained in Babylon, and by means of these graineries, ably administered, the crown was enabled to acquire the estates of the great feudatories, and thus the whole social system of Egypt was changed. And Joseph, from being a poor waif, cast away by his brethren in the wilderness, became the foremost man in Egypt and the means of settling his compatriots in the province of Gotham, where they still lived when Moses fled from Egypt. Such facts had made a profound impression upon the mind of Moses, who very reasonably looked upon Joseph as one of the most wonderful men who had ever lived, and one who could not have succeeded as he succeeded, without the divine interposition. But if the god who did these things could work such miracles in Egypt, his power was not confined by local boundaries, and his power could be trusted in the desert as safely as it could be on the plain of Mamre or elsewhere. The burning of Sodom was a miracle equally in point to prove the stern morality of the god. And that also, was a fact, as incontestable, to the mind of Moses, as was the

rising of the sun upon the morning of each day. He
knew, as we know of the battle of Great Meadows,
that one day his ancestor Abraham, when sitting in
the door of his tent toward noon, "in the plain of
Mamre," at a spot not far from Hebron and perfectly
familiar to every traveller along the old caravan road
hither, on looking up observed three men standing
before him, one of whom he recognized as the "Lord."
Then it dawned on Abraham that the "Lord" had
not come without a purpose, but had dropped in for
dinner, and Abraham ran to meet them, "and bowed
himself toward the ground." And he said, "Let a
little water be fetched, and wash your feet, and rest
yourselves under the tree: And I will fetch a morsel
of bread, and comfort ye your hearts; after that you
shall pass on." "And Abraham ran unto the herd,
and fetcht a calf tender and good, and gave it unto a
young man; and he hasted to dress it. And he took
butter, and milk, and the calf which he had dressed,
and set it before them; and he stood by them under
the tree, and they did eat." Meanwhile, Abraham
asked no questions, but waited until the object of the
visit should be disclosed. In due time he succeeded in
his purpose. "And they said unto him, Where is
Sarah thy wife? And he said, Behold, in the tent.
And he [the Lord] said, . . . Sarah thy wife shall have
a son. . . . Now Abraham and Sarah were old, and
well stricken in age." At this time Abraham was
about one hundred years old, according to the tradition, and Sarah was proportionately amused, and

"laughed within herself." This mirth vexed "the
Lord," who did not treat his words as a joke, but
asked, "Is anything too hard for the Lord?" Then
Sarah took refuge in a lie, and denied that she had
laughed. But the lie helped her not at all, for the
Lord insisted, "Nay, but thou didst laugh." And this
incident broke up the party. The men rose and
"looked toward Sodom": and Abraham strolled with
them, to show them the way. And then the "Lord"
debated with himself whether to make a confidant of
Abraham touching his resolution to destroy Sodom
utterly. And finally he decided that he would, "because the cry of Sodom and Gomorrah is great and
because their sin is very grievous." Whereupon
Abraham intervened, and an argument ensued, and
at length God admitted that he had been too hasty
and promised to think the matter over. And finally,
when "the Lord" had reduced the number of righteous for whom the city should be saved to ten, Abraham allowed him to go "his way . . . and Abraham
returned to his place."

In the evening of the same day two angels came to
Sodom, who met Lot at the gate, and Lot took them
to his house and made them a feast and they did eat.
Then it happened that the mob surrounded Lot's
house and demanded that the strangers should be
delivered up to them. But Lot successfully defended
them. And in the morning the angels warned Lot to
escape, but Lot hesitated, though finally he did escape to Zoar.

"Then the Lord rained upon Sodom and upon Gomorrah brimstone and fire from the Lord out of heaven."

"And Abraham gat up early in the morning to the place where he stood before the Lord:

"And he looked toward Sodom and Gomorrah, and toward all the land of the plain, and beheld, and, lo, the smoke of the country went up as the smoke of a furnace."

We must always remember, in trying to reconstruct the past, that these traditions were not matters of possible doubt to Moses, or indeed to any Israelite. They were as well established facts to them as would be the record of volcanic eruptions now. Therefore it would not have astonished Moses more that the Lord should meet him on the slope of Horeb, than that the Lord should have met his ancestor Abraham on the plain of Mamre. Moses' doubts and perplexities lay in another direction. Moses did not question, as did his great ancestress, that his god could do all he promised, if he had the will. His anxiety lay in his doubt as to God's steadiness of purpose supposing he promised; and this doubt was increased by his lack of confidence in his own countrymen. The god of Abraham was a requiring deity with a high moral standard, and the Hebrews were at least in part somewhat akin to a horde of semi-barbarous nomads, much more likely to fall into offences resembling those of Sodom than to render obedience to a code which would strictly conform to the requirements which

alone would ensure Moses support, supposing he
accepted a task which, after all, without divine aid,
might prove to be impossible to perform.

When the proposition which Moses seems, more or
less confidently, to have expected to be made to him
by the Lord, came, it came very suddenly and very
emphatically.

"Now Moses kept the flock of Jethro his father-in-
law, the priest of Midian: and he led the flock to the
backside of the desert, and came to the mountain of
God, even to Horeb.

"And the angel of the Lord appeared unto him in
a flame of fire out of the midst of a bush: and he looked,
and, behold, the bush burned with fire, and the bush
was not consumed."

And Moses, not, apparently, very much excited,
said, "I will now turn aside, and see this great sight."
But "God called unto him out of the midst of the
bush, and said, Moses, Moses. And he said, Here am
I." Then the voice commanded him to put off his
shoes from off his feet, for the place he stood on was
holy ground.

"Moreover," said the voice, "I am the God of thy
father, the God of Abraham, the God of Isaac, and
the God of Jacob. And Moses hid his face; for he was
afraid to look upon God.

"And the Lord said, I have surely seen the affliction
of my people . . . and have heard their cry by reason
of their taskmasters; for I know their sorrows.

"And I am come down to deliver them out of the

hand of the Egyptians, and to bring them up out of that land unto a good land and a large, unto a land flowing with milk and honey; unto the place of the Canaanites, and the Hittites, and the Amorites, and the Perizzites. . . .

"Come now, therefore, and I will send thee unto Pharaoh, that thou mayest bring forth my people, the children of Israel, out of Egypt.

"And Moses said unto God, Who am I, that I should go unto Pharaoh, and that I should bring forth the children of Israel out of Egypt? . . . And Moses said unto God, Behold, when I am come unto the children of Israel, and shall say unto them, The God of your fathers hath sent me unto you; and they shall say to me, What is his name? what shall I say unto them?

"And God said unto Moses, *I am That I Am;* and he said, Thus shalt thou say unto the children of Israel, *I Am* hath sent me unto you.

"And God said, moreover, unto Moses, Thus shalt thou say unto the children of Israel, The Lord God of your fathers, the God of Abraham, the God of Isaac, and the God of Jacob, hath sent me unto you: this is my name forever, and this is my memorial unto all generations."

Then the denizen of the bush renewed his instructions and his promises, assuring Moses that he would bring him and his following out of the land of affliction of Egypt and into the land of the Canaanites, and the Hittites, and the Amorites, and others, unto a land flowing with milk and honey. In a word to Palestine. And he insisted to Moses that he should gain an entrance to Pharaoh, and that he should tell him that "the Lord God of the Hebrews hath met with us: and now let us go, we beseech thee, three days' journey into the wilderness, that we may sacrifice to the Lord our God."

Also God did not pretend to Moses that the King of Egypt would forthwith let them go; whereupon he would work his wonders in Egypt and after that Pharaoh would let them go.

Moreover, he promised, as an inducement to their avarice, that they should not go empty away, for that the Lord God would give the Hebrews favor in the sight of the Egyptians, "so that every woman should borrow of her neighbor, and of her that sojourneth in her house, jewels of silver, jewels of gold, and raiment," and that they should spoil the Egyptians. But all this time God did not disclose his name; so Moses tried another way about. If he would not tell his name he might at least enable Moses to work some wonder which should bring conviction to those who saw it, even if the god remained nameless. For Moses appreciated the difficulty of the mission suggested to him. How was he, a stranger in Egypt, to gain the confidence of that mixed and helpless multitude, whom he was trying to persuade to trust to his guidance in so apparently desperate an enterprise as crossing a broad and waterless waste, in the face of a well-armed and vigorous foe. Moses apprehended that there was but one way in which he could by possibility succeed. He might prevail by convincing the Israelites that he was commissioned by the one deity whom they knew, who was likely to have both the will and the power to aid them, and that was the god who had visited Abraham on the plain of Mamre, who had destroyed Sodom for its iniquity, and who had helped Joseph to become the ruler of Egypt. Joseph above all was the man who had made to his descendants that solemn promise on whose faith Moses was, at that very moment, basing his hopes of deliverance; for Joseph had assured the Israelites in the most solemn manner that the god who had aided him would surely visit them, and that they should carry his bones away with them to the land he promised. That land was the land to which Moses wished to guide them. Now Moses was fully determined to attempt no such project as this unless the being who spoke from the bush would first prove to him, Moses, that he was the god he purported to be, and should beside give Moses credentials which should be convincing, by which Moses could prove to the Jews in Egypt that he was no impostor himself, nor had he been deceived by a demon. Therefore Moses went on objecting as strongly as at first:

"And Moses answered and said, But behold they will not believe me, nor hearken to my voice; for they will say, the Lord hath not appeared unto thee."

Then the being in the bush proceeded to submit his method of proof, which was of a truth feeble, and which Moses rejected as feeble. A form of proof which never fully convinced him, and which, in his judgment could not be expected to convince others, especially men so educated and intelligent as the Egyptians. For the Lord had nothing better to suggest than the ancient trick of the snake-charmer, and even the possessor of the voice seems implicitly to have admitted that this could hardly be advanced as a convincing miracle. So the Lord proposed two other tests: the first was that Moses should have his hand smitten with leprous sores and restored immediately by hiding it from sight in "his bosom." And in the event that this test left his audience still sceptical, he was to dip Nile water out of the river, and turn it into blood on land.

Moses at all these three proposals remained cold as before. And with good reason, for Moses had been educated as a priest in Egypt, and he knew that Egyptian "wise men" could do as well, and even better, if it came to a magical competition before Pharaoh. And Moses had evidently no relish for a contest in the presence of his countrymen as to the relative quality of his magic. Therefore, he objected once more on another ground: "I am not eloquent, neither heretofore nor since thou hast spoken unto thy servant: but I am slow of speech, and of a slow tongue." This continued hesitancy put the Lord out of patience; who retorted sharply, "Who hath made man's mouth? or who maketh the dumb, or deaf, or the seeing, or the blind? Have not I the Lord?

"Now therefore go, and I will be with thy mouth, and teach thee what thou shalt say."

Then Moses made his last effort. "O my Lord, send, I pray thee, by the hand of him whom thou wilt send." Which was another way of saying, Send whom you please, but leave me to tend Jethro's flock in Midian.

"And the anger of the Lord was kindled against Moses; and he said, Is not Aaron the Levite thy brother? I know that he can speak well. And also, behold, he cometh forth to meet thee; and when he seeth thee, he will be glad in his heart.

"And he shall be, . . . to thee instead of a mouth, and thou shalt be to him instead of God."

Then Moses, not seeming to care very much what Aaron might think about the matter, went to Jethro, and related what had happened to him on the mountain, and asked for leave to go home to Egypt, and see how matters stood there. And Jethro listened, and seems to have thought the experiment worth trying, for he answered, "Go in peace."

"And the Lord said unto Moses," — but where is not stated, probably in Midian, — "Go, return into Egypt," which you may do safely, for all the men are dead which sought thy life.

"And Moses took his wife and his sons, and set them upon an ass, and he returned to the land of Egypt. And Moses took the rod of God in his hand."

It was after this, apparently, that Aaron travelled to meet Moses in Midian, and Moses told Aaron what had occurred, and performed his tests, and, seemingly, convinced him; for then Moses and Aaron went together into Egypt and called the elders of the children of Israel together, "and did the signs in the sight of the people. And the people believed: and . . . bowed their heads and worshipped." Meanwhile God had not, as yet, revealed his name. But as presently matters came to a crisis between Moses and Pharaoh, he did so. He said to Moses, "I am the Lord:

"I appeared unto Abraham, unto Isaac, and unto Jacob, by the name of God Almighty; but by my name Jehovah was I not known to them. . . .

"Wherefore say unto the children of Israel, I am the Lord. . . . And I will bring you in unto the land, concerning the which I did swear to give it to Abraham, to Isaac, and to Jacob; and I will give it you for an heritage: I am the Lord.

"And Moses spake so unto the children of Israel: but they hearkened not unto Moses, for anguish of spirit, and for cruel bondage. . . .

"And Moses spake before the Lord, saying, Behold the children of Israel have not hearkened unto me; how then shall Pharaoh hear me?" And from this form of complaint against his countrymen until his death Moses never ceased.

Certain modern critics have persuaded themselves to reject this whole Biblical narrative as the product of a later age and of a maturer civilization, contending that it would be childish to attribute the reasoning of the Pentateuch to primitive Bedouins like the patriarchs or like the Jews who followed Moses into the desert. Setting aside at once the philological discussion as to whether the language of the Pentateuch could have been used by Moses, and admitting for the sake of argument that Moses did not either himself write, or dictate to another, any part of the documents in question, it would seem that the application of a little common sense would show pretty conclusively that Moses throughout his whole administrative life acted upon a single scientific theory of the application of a supreme energy to the affairs of life, and upon the belief that he had discovered what that energy was and understood how to control it.

His syllogism amounted to this:

Facts, which are admitted by all Hebrews, prove that the single dominant power in the world is the being who revealed himself to our ancestors, and who, in particular, guided Joseph into Egypt, protected him there, and raised him to an eminence never before or since reached by a Jew. It can also be proved, by incontrovertible facts, that this being is a moral being, who can be placated by obedience and by attaining to a certain moral standard in life, and by no other means. That this standard has been disclosed to me, I can prove to you by sundry miraculous signs. Therefore, be obedient and obey the law which I shall promulgate "that ye may prosper in all that ye do."

Indeed, the philosophy of Moses was of the sternly practical kind, resembling that of Benjamin Franklin. He did not promise his people, as did the Egyptians, felicity in a future life. He confined himself to prosperity in this world. And to succeed in his end he set an attainable standard. A standard no higher certainly than that accepted by the Egyptians, as it is set forth in the 125th chapter of the Book of the Dead, a standard to which the soul of any dead man had to attain before he could be admitted into Paradise. Nor did Moses, as Dr. Budde among others assumes, have to deal with a tribe of fierce and barbarous Bedouins, like the Amalekites, to whom indeed the Hebrews were antagonistic and with whom they waged incessant war.

The Jews, for the most part, differed widely from such barbarians. They had become sedentary at the time of the exodus, whatever they may have been when Abraham migrated from Babylon. They were accustomed in Egypt to living in houses, they cultivated and cooked the cereals, and they fed on vegetables and bread. They did not live on flesh and milk as do the Bedouins; and, indeed, the chief difficulty Moses encountered in the exodus was the ignorance of his followers of the habits of desert life, and their dislike of desert fare. They were forever pining for the delights of civilization. "Would to God we had died by the hand of the Lord in the land of Egypt, when we sat by the flesh-pots, and when we did eat bread to the full! for ye have brought us forth into this wilderness, to kill this whole assembly with hunger."[1]

---

[1] Ex. XVI, 3.

"We remember the fish, which we did eat in Egypt freely; the cucumbers, and the melons, and the leeks, and the onions, and the garlick." These were the wants of sedentary and of civilized folk, not of barbarous nomads who are content with goat's flesh and milk. And so it was with their morality and their conceptions of law. Moses was, indeed, a highly civilized and highly educated man. No one would probably pretend that Moses represented the average Jew of the exodus, but Moses understood his audience reasonably well, and would not have risked the success of his whole experiment by preaching to them a doctrine which was altogether beyond their understanding. If he told them that the favor of God could only be gained by obeying the laws he taught, it was because he thought such an appeal would be effective with a majority of them.

Dr. Budde, who is a good example of the modern hypercritical school, takes very nearly the opposite ground. His theory is that Moses was in search of a war god, and that he discovered such a god, in the god of the Bedouin tribe of the Kenites whose acquaintance he first made when dwelling with his father-in-law Jethro at Sinai. The morality of such a god he insists coincided with the morality which Moses may have at times countenanced, but which was quite foreign to the spirit of the decalogue.

Doubtless this is, in a degree, true. The religion of the pure Bedouin was very often crude and shocking, not to say disgusting. But to argue thus is to ignore the fact that all Bedouins did not, in the age of Moses, stand on the same intellectual or moral level, and it is also to ignore the gap that separated Moses and his congregation intellectually and morally from such Bedouins as the Amalekites.

Dr. Budde, in his *Religion of Israel to the Exile,* insists that the Kenite god, Jehovah, demanded "The sacred ban by which conquered cities with all their living beings were devoted to destruction, the slaughter of human beings at sacred spots, animal sacrifices at which the entire animal, wholly or half raw, was devoured, without leaving a remnant, between sunset and sunrise, — these phenomena and many others of the same kind harmonise but ill with an aspiring ethical religion."

He also goes on to say: "We are further referred to the legislation of Moses, . . . comprising civil and criminal, ceremonial and ecclesiastical, moral and social law in varying compass. This legislation, however, cannot have come from Moses. . . . Such legislation can only have arisen after Israel had lived a long time in the new home."

To take these arguments in order, — for they must be so dealt with to develop any reasonable theory of the Mosaic philosophy, — Moses, doubtless, was a ruthless conqueror, as his dealings with Sihon and Og sufficiently prove. "So the Lord our God delivered into our hands Og also, the king of Bashan, and all his people: and we smote him until none was left to him remaining. . . .

"And we utterly destroyed them, as we did unto Sihon, king of Heshbon, utterly destroying the men, women, and children of every city." [1]

There is nothing extraordinary, or essentially barbarous, in this attitude of Moses. The same theory of duty or convenience has been held in every age and in every land, by men of the ecclesiastical temperament, at the very moment at which the extremest doctrines of charity, mercy, and love were practised by their contemporaries, or even preached by themselves. For example:

At the beginning of the thirteenth century the two great convents of Cluny and Citeau, together, formed the heart of monasticism, and Cluny and Citeau were two of the richest and most powerful corporations in the world, while the south of France had become, by reason of the eastern trade, the wealthiest and most intelligent district in Europe. It suffices to say here that, just about this time, the people of Languedoc had made up their minds, because of the failure of the Crusades, the cost of such magnificent establishments was not justified by their results, and accordingly Count Raymond of Toulouse, in sympathy with his subjects, did seriously contemplate secularization. To the abbots of these great convents, it was clear that if this movement spread across the Rhone into Burgundy, the Church would face losses which they could not contemplate with equanimity. At this period one Arnold was Abbot of Citeau, universally

[1] Deut. III, 3-6.

recognized as perhaps the ablest and certainly one of the most unscrupulous men in Europe. Hence the crusade against the Albigenses which Simon de Montfort commanded and Arnold conducted. Arnold's first exploit was the sack of the undefended town of Béziers, where he slaughtered twenty thousand men, women, and children, without distinction of religious belief. When asked whether the orthodox might not at least be spared, he replied, "Kill them all; God knows his own."

This sack of Béziers occurred in 1209. Exactly contemporaneously Saint Francis of Assisi was organizing his order whose purpose was to realize Christ's kingdom upon earth, by the renunciation of worldly wealth and by the practice of poverty, humility, and obedience. Soon after, Arnold was created Archbishop of Narbonne and became probably the greatest and richest prelate in France, or in the world. This was in 1225. In 1226 the first friars settled in England. They multiplied rapidly because of their rigorous discipline. Soon there were to be found among them some of the most eminent men in England. Their chief house stood in London in a spot called Stinking Lane, near the Shambles in Newgate, and there, amidst poverty, hunger, cold, and filth, these men passed their lives in nursing horrible lepers, so loathsome that they were rejected by all but themselves, while Arnold lived in magnificence in his palace, upon the spoil of those whom he had immolated to his greed.

In the case of Moses the contrast between precept

and practice in the race for wealth and fortune was
not nearly so violent. Moses, it is true, according to
Leviticus, declared it to be the will of the Lord that
the Israelites should love their neighbors as themselves,[1] while on the other hand in Deuteronomy he
insisted that obedience was the chief end of life, and
that if the Israelites were to thoroughly obey the
Lord's behests, they were to "consume all the people
which the Lord thy God shall deliver thee; thine eye
shall have no pity upon them: neither" should thou
serve their gods, "for the Lord thy God is a jealous
God."[2]   And the penalty for slackness was "lest
the anger of the Lord thy God be kindled against
thee, and destroy thee from off the face of the earth."[3]
There is, nevertheless, this much to be said in favor
of the morality of Moses as contrasted with that of
thirteenth-century orthodox Christians like Arnold;
Moses led a crusade against a foreign and hostile
people, while Arnold slaughtered the Albigenses, who
were his own flock, sheep to whom he was the shepherd, communicants in his own church, and wor-
shippers of the God whom he served. What concerns
us, however, is that the same stimulant animated
Moses and Arnold alike. The stimulant, pure and
simple, of greed. On these points Moses was as out-
spokenly, one may say as brutally, frank as was
Arnold. In the desert Moses commanded his followers
to exterminate the inhabitants of the kingdom of
Bashan in order that they might appropriate their

[1] Lev. xix, 18.   [2] Deut. vii, 16.   [3] Deut. vi, 15.

possessions, which he enumerated, and Moses had no other argument to urge but the profitableness of it by which to secure obedience to his moral law.

Arnold stood on precisely the same platform. He did not accuse Count Raymond of heresy or any other crime, nor did Pope Innocent III consider Raymond as morally guilty of a criminal offence, or worthy of punishment. Indeed, the pope would have protected the Count had it been possible, and summoned him before the Fourth Lateran Council for that purpose. But Arnold told his audience that were Raymond allowed to escape there would be an end of the Catholic faith in France. Or, in other words, monastic property would be secularized. Perhaps he was right. At all events, this argument prevailed, and Raymond and his family and people were sacrificed.

Moses promised his congregation that, if they would spare nothing they should enjoy abundance of good things, without working for them. He was much more pitiless than such a man as King David thought it necessary to be, but Moses was not a soldier like David. He could not promise to win victories himself, he could but promise what he had in hand, and that was the spoil of those they massacred. Moses never had but one appeal to make for obedience, one incentive to offer to obey. In this he was perfectly honest and perfectly logical. His congregation and he, finding Egypt untenable, were engaged in a common land speculation to improve their condition; a speculation in which Moses believed, but which could only

be brought to a successful end by obtaining control of
the dominant energy of the world. This energy, he
held, could be handled by no one but himself, and
then only in case those who acted with him were absolutely obedient to his commands, which, taken together, were equivalent to a magical exorcism or spell.
Then only could they hope that the Lord of Abraham
and Isaac would give them "great and goodly cities,
which thou buildedst not, And houses full of all good
things, which thou filledst not, and wells digged,
which thou diggedst not, vineyards and olive trees,
which thou plantedst not." [1]

Very obviously, if the theory which Moses propounded were sound the assets which he offered as
an inducement for docility could be obtained, at so
cheap a rate, in no other way. All Moses' moral teaching amounted, therefore, to this — "It pays to be
obedient and good." No argument could have been
better adapted to Babylonish society, and it seems to
have answered nearly as well with the Israelites, which
proves that they stood on nearly the same intellectual
plane. The chief difficulty with which Moses had to
contend was that his countrymen did not thoroughly
believe in him, nor in the efficacy of his motor. They
always were tempted to try experiments with other
motors which were operated by other prophets and
by other peoples who were, apparently, as prosperous
as they, or even more so. His trouble was not that his
followers were nomads unprepared for a sedentary life

[1] Deut. vi, 10, 11.

or a moral law like his, or unable to appreciate the value of the property of a people further advanced in civilization than they were. The Amalekites would have responded to no such system of bribery as Moses offered the Israelites, who did respond with intelligence, if not always with enthusiasm.

The same is true of the Mosaic legislation which Dr. Budde curtly dismisses as impossible to have come from Moses,[1] as presupposing a knowledge of a settled agricultural life, which "Israel did not reach until after Moses' death."

All this is an assumption of fact unsupported by evidence; but quite the contrary, as we can see by an examination of the law in question. Whatever may have been the date of the establishment of the cities of refuge, I suppose that it will not be seriously denied that the law of the covenant as laid down in Exodus xx, 1, Numbers xxxv, 6, is at least as old as the age of Moses, in principle, if not in words; and this legal principle is quite inconsistent with, if not directly antagonistic to, all the prejudices and regulations, moral, religious, or civil, of a pure nomadic society, since it presupposes a social condition which, if adopted, would be fatal to a nomad society.

The true nomad knows no criminal law save the law of the blood feud, which is the law of revenge, and which prevailed among the Hebrews much earlier. In the early Saxon law it was expressed by the apothegm "*Factum reputabitur pro volunte.*" The act implies

---

[1] *Religion of Israel to the Exile,* 31.

the intent. That is to say, the tribe is an enlarged family who, since they have no collective system of sovereignty which gives them common protection by an organized police, and courts with power to enforce process, have no option but to protect each other. Therefore, it is incumbent on each member of the tribe or family to avenge an injury to any other member, whether the injury be accidental or otherwise; and to be himself the judge of what amounts to an injury. Such a condition prevailed among the Hebrews at a very early period; "And God blessed Noah and his sons, and said unto them: . . . at the hand of every man's brother will I require the life of man. Whoso sheddeth man's blood, by man shall his blood be shed." [1] These customs and the type of thought which sustain them are very tenacious and change slowly. Moses could not have altered the nomadic customs of thought and of blood revenge, had he tried, more than could Canute. It would have been impossible. The advent of a civilized conception of the law is the work of centuries as the history of England proves.

We know not how long ago it was that the law of the blood feud was fully recognized in England, but it had already been shaken at the conquest, and its death-blow was given it by the Church, which had begun to tire of the responsibility entailed by the trial by ordeal or miracle, and the obloquy which it involved, at a relatively early date. For the purposes

[1] Gen. IX, 1, 5, 6.

of the Church and the uses of confession it was more convenient to regard crime or tort, as did the Romans; as a mental condition, dependent altogether upon the state of the mind or "animus." Malice in the eye of the Church was the virus which poisoned the otherwise innocent act, and made the thought alone punishable. Indeed, this conception is one which has not yet been completely established even in the modern law. The first signs of such a revolution in jurisprudence only began to appear in England some seven centuries ago. As Mr. Maitland has observed in his *History of English Law*,[1] "We receive a shock of surprise when we meet with a maxim which has troubled our modern lawyers, namely, *Reum non facit nisi mens rea*, in the middle of the *Leges Henrici.*" That is to say somewhere about the year 1118 A.D. This maxim was taken bodily out of a sermon of Saint Augustine, which accounts for it, but at that time the Church had another process to suggest by which she asserted her authority. She threw the responsibility for detecting guilt, in cases of doubt, upon God. By the ordeal, if a homicide, for example, were committed, and the accused denied his guilt, he was summoned to appear, and then, after a solemn reference to God by the ecclesiastics in charge, he was caused either to carry a red-hot iron bar a certain distance or to plunge his arms in boiling water. If he were found, after a certain length of time, during which his arms were bandaged, to have been injured, he was held to have been guilty.

[1] Vol. II, 476.

If he had escaped unhurt he was innocent. Gradually, however, the ordeal began to fall into ridicule. William Rufus gibed at it, for of fifty men sent to the ordeal of iron, under the sacred charge of the clerks, all escaped, which certainly, as Mr. Maitland intimates, looks as if the officiating ecclesiastics had an interest in the result.[1] At length, by the Lateran Council of 1215, the Church put an end to the institution, but long afterward it found its upholders. For example, the *Mirror*, written in the reign of Edward I (circa 1285) complained, "It is an abuse that proofs and compurgations be not by the miracle of God where other proof faileth." Nor was the principle that "attempts" to commit indictable offences are crimes, established as law, until at least the time of the Star Chamber, before its abolition in the seventeenth century. Though doubtless it is the law to-day.[2] And this, although the means used may have been impossible. Moreover, the doctrine is still in process of enlargement.

Very convincing conclusions may be drawn from these facts. The subject is obscure and difficult, but if the inception of the process of breaking down the right of enforcing the blood feud be fixed provisionally toward the middle of the tenth century, — and this date is early enough, — the movement of thought cannot be said to have attained anything like ultimate results before at least the year 1321 when a case is

[1] *History of English Law*, II, 599, note 2.
[2] Stephen, *Digest of the Criminal Law*, 192.

cited wherein a man was held guilty because he had attempted to kill his master, and the "*voluntas in isto casu reputabitur pro facto.*"

Measuring by this standard five hundred years is a short enough period to estimate the time necessary for a community to pass from the stage when the blood feud is recognized as unquestioned law, to the status involved in the administration of the cities of refuge, for in these cities not only the mental condition is provided for as a legitimate defence, but the defence of negligence is made admissible in a secular court.

"These six cities shall be a refuge, both for the children of Israel, and for the stranger, and for the sojourner among them; that every one that killeth any person unawares may flee thither. . . .

"If he thrust him of hatred, or hurl at him by laying of wait that he die;

"Or in enmity smite him with his hand, that he die: he that smote him shall surely be put to death; for he is a murderer: the revenger of blood shall slay the murderer, when he meeteth him.

"But if he thrust him suddenly without enmity, or have cast upon him anything without laying of wait,

"Or with any stone, wherewith a man may die, seeing him not, and cast it upon him, that he die, and was not his enemy, neither sought his harm:

"Then the congregation shall judge between the slayer and the revenger of blood according to these judgments:

"And the congregation shall deliver the slayer out

of the hand of the revenger of blood, and the congregation shall restore him to the city of his refuge, whither he was fled.". . . [1]

Here we have a defendant in a case of homicide setting up the defence that the killing happened through an accident, but an accident not caused by criminal negligence, and this defence is to be tried by the congregation, which is tantamount to trial by jury. It is not left to God, under the oversight of the Church; and this is precisely our own system at the present day. We now come to the inferences to be drawn from these facts. Supposing that the Israelites when they migrated to Egypt, in the time of Joseph, were in the condition of pure nomads among whom the blood feud was fully recognized as law, an interval of four or five hundred years, such as they are supposed to have passed in Goshen would bring them to the exodus. Now, assuming that the Israelites during those four centuries, when they lived among civilized neighbors and under civilized law, made an intellectual movement corresponding in velocity to the movement the English made after the conquest, they would have been, about the time when the cities of refuge were created, in the position described in Numbers, which is what we should expect assuming the Biblical tradition to be true.

To us the important question is not whether a certain piece of the supposed Mosaic legislation actually went into effect during the life of Moses, for that is

[1] Numbers xxxv, 15, 20–25.

relatively immaterial, but whether the Biblical narrative is, on the whole, worthy of credence, and this correlation of dates gives the strongest possible evidence in its favor. Very possibly, perhaps it may even be said certainly, the order in which events occurred may have been transposed, but, taken as a whole, it is impossible to resist the inference that the Bible story is excellent history and that, due allowance being made for the prejudice of the various scribes who wrote the Pentateuch in favor of the miraculous, where Moses was concerned, the Biblical record is good and trustworthy history, and frank at that; — much superior to quantities of modern documents which we accept without question.

Of all the achievements of Moses' life none equals the exodus itself, either in brilliancy or success. How it was possible for Moses, with the assistance he had at command, to marshal and move a column of a million or a million and a half of men, women, and children, without discipline or cohesion, and encumbered with their baggage, beside their cattle, is an insoluble mystery. "And the children of Israel did according to the word of Moses; and they borrowed of the Egyptians jewels of silver, and jewels of gold, and raiment: . . . And they spoiled the Egyptians. And the children of Israel journeyed from Ramses to Succoth, about six hundred thousand on foot that were men, beside children. And a mixed multitude went up also with them; and flocks and herds, even very much cattle." They started from Ramses and Succoth.

The position of Ramses has been identified; that of Succoth is more questionable. Ramses and Pithom were fortified places, built by the Israelites for Ramses II, of the Nineteenth Dynasty, but apparently Succoth was the last halting-place before coming to the difficult ground which was overflowed by the sea.

The crossing was made at night, but it is hard to understand how, even under the most favorable conditions of weather, such a vast and confused multitude of women and children could have made the march in darkness with an active enemy pursuing, without loss of life or material. Indeed, even at that day the movement seemed to the actors so unparalleled that it always passed for a miracle, and its perfect success gave Moses more reputation with the Israelites and more practical influence over them than anything else he ever did, or indeed than all his other works together. "And Israel saw that great work which the Lord did upon the Egyptians: and the people feared the Lord and believed the Lord and his servant Moses."

"And Miriam, the prophetess, the sister of Aaron; and all the women went after her with timbrels and with dances." Now Miriam was in general none too loyal a follower of her younger brother, but that day, or rather night, she did proclaim Moses as a conqueror; which was a great concession from her, and meant much. And Moses exulted openly, as he had good cause to do, and gave vent to his exultation in

a song which tradition has ever since attributed to
him, and has asserted to have been sung by him and
his congregation as they stood by the shore of the sea
and watched the corpses of the Egyptians lying in the
sand. And, if ever man had, Moses then had, cause
for exultation, for he had seemingly proved by the
test of war, which is the ultimate test to which a man
can subject such a theory as his, that he had indeed
discovered the motor which he sought, and, more important still, that he knew how to handle it. Therefore, he was master of supreme energy and held his
right to command by the title of conquest. This was
the culminating moment of his life; he never again
reached such exaltation. From this moment his slow
and gradual decline began.

And, indeed, great as had been the momentary success of Moses, his position was one of extreme difficulty, and probably he so understood it, otherwise
there would be no way to account for his choosing the
long, difficult, and perilous journey by Sinai, instead
of approaching the "Promised Land" directly by
way of Kadesh-Barnea, which was, in any event, to
be his ultimate objective. It may well have been
because Moses felt himself unable alone to cope with
the difficulties confronting him that he decided at
any cost to seek Jethro in Midian, who seems to have
been the only able, honest, and experienced man within
reach. Joshua, indeed, might be held to be an exception to this generalization, but Joshua, though a good
soldier, was a man of somewhat narrow understanding,

and quite unfit to grapple with questions involving jurisprudence and financial topography.

And at this juncture Moses must have felt his own deficiencies keenly. As a captain he made no pretence to efficiency. The Amalekites were, as he well knew, at this moment lying in wait for him, and forthwith he recognized that he had no alternative but to retire into the background himself and surrender the active command of the army to Joshua, a fatal concession had Joshua been ambitious or unscrupulous. And this was but the beginning. Before he could occupy Palestine he had to encounter and overcome numbers of equally formidable foes, a defeat by any one of whom might well be fatal. A man like Jethro, therefore, would be invaluable in guiding the caravan to spots favorable for action, from whence retreat to a place of safety would be open in case of a check. A reverse which happened on a later occasion gave Moses a shock he never forgot.

Furthermore, though Moses lived many years with Jethro, as his chief servant, he never seems to have travelled extensively in Arabia, and to have been ignorant of the chief trade routes along which wells were dug, and of the oases where pasture was to be found; so that Moses was nearly worthless as a guide, and this was a species of knowledge in which Jethro, according to Moses' own statement, excelled. Meanwhile, the lives of all his followers depended on such knowledge. And Moses, when he reached Sinai, left no stone unturned to overcome Jethro's reluctance to join him and to instruct him on the march north.

More important and pressing than all, Moses was ignorant of how, practically, to administer the law which he taught. His only idea was to do all in person, but this, with so large a following, was impossible. And here also his hope lay in Jethro. For when he got to Sinai, and Jethro remonstrated with him upon his methods, pointing out that they were impracticable, all Moses had to say in reply was that he sat all day to hear disputes and "I judge between one and another; and I do make them know the statutes of God, and his laws." Further than this he had nothing to propose. It was Jethro who explained to him a constructive policy.

On the whole, upon this analysis, it appears that in all those executive departments in which Moses, by stress of the responsibilities which he had assumed, was called upon, imperatively, to act, there was but one, that of the magician or wise man, in which, by temperament and training, he was fitted to excel, and the functions of this profession drove him into an intolerably irksome and distressing position, yet a position from which throughout his life he found it impossible to escape. No one who attentively weighs the evidence can, I apprehend, escape the conviction that Moses was at bottom an honest man who would have conformed to the moral law he laid down in the name of the Lord had it been possible for him to do so. Among these precepts none ranked higher than a regard for truth and honesty. "Ye shall not steal, neither deal falsely, neither lie one to another." [1] And this text is but one example of a general drift of thought.

Whether these particular words of Leviticus, or any similar phrases, were ever used by Moses is immaterial. No one can doubt that, in substance, they contained the gist of his moral doctrine and that he enforced the moral duty which they convey to the best of his power. And here the burden lay, which crushed this man, from which he never thenceforward could, even for an instant, free himself, and which Saint Paul avers to be the heaviest burden man can bear. Moses, to fulfil what he conceived to be his destiny and which at least certainly was his ambition, was condemned to lead a life of deceit and to utter no word during his long subsequent march which was not positively or inferentially a lie. And the bitterest of his trials must have been the agony of anxiety in which he must have lived lest some error in judgment on his part, some slackness in measuring the exact credulity of his audience, should cause his exposure and lead to his being cast out of the camp as an impostor and hunted to death as a false prophet: a fate which more than once nearly overtook him. Indeed, as he aged and his nerves lost their elasticity under the tension, he became obsessed with the fixed idea that God had renounced him and that some horror would overtake him should he attempt to cross the Jordan

[1] Leviticus XIX, 11.

and enter the "Promised Land." Defeated at Hormah, he dared not face another such check and, therefore, dawdled away his time in the wilderness until further dawdling became impossible. Then followed his mental collapse which is told in Deuteronomy, together with his suicide on Mount Nebo. And thus he died because he could not gratify at once his lust for power and his instinct to live an honest man.

CHAPTER II.

THE interval during which Moses led the exodus falls, naturally, into three parts of unequal length. The first consists of the months which elapsed between the departure from Ramses and the arrival at Sinai. The second comprises the halt at Sinai, while the third contains the story of the rest of his life, ending with Mount Nebo.

His trials began forthwith. The march was hardly a week old before the column was in quasi-revolt because he had known so little of the country, that he had led the caravan three days through a waterless wilderness where they feared to perish from thirst. And matters grew steadily worse. At Rephidim, "And the people murmured against Moses, and said, Wherefore is this that thou hast brought us up out of Egypt, to kill us and our children and our cattle with thirst?" Not impossibly Moses may still, at this stage of his experiences, have believed in himself, in the God he pretended to serve, and in his mission. At least he made a feint of so doing. Indeed, he had to. Not to have done so would have caused his instant downfall. He always had to do so, in every emergency of his life. A few days later he was at his wits' end. He cried unto the Lord, "What shall I do unto this people? They be almost ready to stone me." In short, long before the congregation reached Sinai, and indeed before Moses had fought his first battle with Amalek, the people had come to disbelieve in Moses and also to question whether there was such a god as he pretended.

"And he called the name of the place Massah, and Meribah, because of the chiding of the children of Israel, and because they tempted the Lord, saying, Is the Lord among us, or not?"

"Then came Amalek, and fought with Israel in Rephidim." [1]

Under such conditions it was vital to Moses to show resolution and courage; but it was here that Moses, on the contrary, flinched; as he usually did flinch when it came to war, for Moses was no soldier.

"And Moses said unto Joshua, Choose us out men and go out, fight with Amalek: to-morrow I will stand on the top of the hill with the rod of God in mine hand."

And Moses actually had the assurance to do as he proposed, nor did he even have the endurance to stand. He made Aaron and Hur fetch a stone on which he should sit and then hold up his hands for him, pretending the while that when Moses held up his hands the Hebrews prevailed and when he lowered them Amalek prevailed. Notwithstanding, Joshua won a victory. But it may readily be believed that this performance of his functions as a captain, did little to strengthen the credit of Moses among the fighting men. Nor evidently was Moses satisfied with the

[1] Exodus XVII, 7, 8.

figure that he cut, nor was he confident that Joshua approved of him, for the Lord directed Moses to make excuses, promising to do better the next time, by assuring Joshua that "I will utterly put out the remembrance of Amalek from under heaven." This was the best apology Moses could make for his weakness. However, the time had now come when Moses was to realize his plan of meeting Jethro.

"And Jethro . . . came with his sons and his wife unto Moses into the wilderness, where he encamped at the mount of God: . . . And Moses went out to meet his father-in-law, and did obeisance, and kissed him; and they asked each other of their welfare; and they came into the tent.

"And Moses told his father-in-law all that the Lord had done unto Pharaoh and to the Egyptians for Israel's sake, and all the travail that had come upon them by the way, and how the Lord had delivered them. . . .

"And Jethro said, Blessed be the Lord, who hath delivered you out of the hand of the Egyptians. . . . Now I know that the Lord is greater than all gods. . . . And Aaron came, and all the elders of Israel, to eat bread with Moses' father-in-law before God."

It is from all this very plain that Jethro had a controlling influence over Moses, and was the proximate cause of much that followed. For the next morning Moses, as was his custom, "sat to judge the people: and the people stood by Moses from the morning unto the evening." And when Jethro saw how

Moses proceeded he remonstrated, "Why sittest thou thyself alone, and all the people stand by thee from morning unto even?"

And Moses replied: "Because the people come unto me to enquire of God."

And Jethro protested, saying "The thing thou doest is not good. Thou wilt surely wear away, both thou and this people that is with thee: for this thing is too heavy for thee; thou art not able to perform it thyself alone.

"Hearken, . . . I will give thee counsel, and God shall be with thee; Be thou for the people to God-ward, that thou mayest bring the causes unto God."

Then it was that Moses perceived that he must have a divinely promulgated code. Accordingly, Moses made his preparations for a great dramatic effect, and it is hard to see how he could have made them better. For, whatever failings he may have had in his other capacities as a leader, he understood his part as a magician.

He told the people to be ready on the third day, for on the third day the Lord would come down in the sight of all upon Mount Sinai. But, "Take heed to yourselves that ye go not up into the mount, or touch the border of it: whosoever toucheth the mount shall be surely put to death:

"There shall not an hand touch it, but he shall surely be stoned or shot through; whether it be beast or man, it shall not live: when the trumpet soundeth long, they shall come up to the mount."

It must be admitted that Moses either had wonderful luck, or that he had wonderful judgment in weather, for, as it happened in the passage of the Red Sea, so it happened here. At the Red Sea he was aided by a gale of wind which coincided with a low tide and made the passage practicable, and at Sinai he had a thunder-storm.

"And it came to pass on the third day, in the morning, that there were thunders and lightnings, and a thick cloud upon the mount, and the voice of the trumpet exceeding loud; so that all the people that was in the camp trembled." Moses had undoubtedly sent some thoroughly trustworthy person, probably Joshua, up the mountain to blow a ram's horn and to light a bonfire, and the effect seems to have been excellent.

"And Mount Sinai was altogether on a smoke, because the Lord descended upon it in fire: and the smoke thereof ascended as the smoke of a furnace, and the whole mount quaked greatly.

"And when the voice of the trumpet sounded long, and waxed louder and louder, Moses spake, and God answered him by a voice.

"And the Lord came down upon Mount Sinai, on the top of the mount; and the Lord called Moses up to the top of the mount; and Moses went up." And the first thing that Moses did on behalf of the Lord was to "charge the people, lest they break through unto the Lord to gaze, and many of them perish."

And Moses replied to God's enquiry, "The people

cannot come up to Mount Sinai: for thou chargedst us, saying, Set bounds about the mount.

"And the Lord said unto him, Away, get thee down, and thou shalt come up, thou, and Aaron with thee: but let not the priests and the people break through to come up unto the Lord, lest he break forth upon them.

"So Moses went down unto the people, and spake unto them."

Whether the decalogue, as we know it, was a code of law actually delivered upon Sinai, which German critics very much dispute as being inconsistent with the stage of civilization at which the Israelites had arrived, but which is altogether kindred to the Babylonish law with which Moses was familiar, is immaterial for the present purpose. What is essential is that beside the decalogue itself there is a considerable body of law chiefly concerned with the position of servants or slaves, the difference between assaults or torts committed with or without malice, theft, trespass, and the regulation of the *lex talionis*. There are beside a variety of other matters touched upon all of which may be found in the 21st, 22d, and 23d chapters of Exodus.

Up to this point in his show Moses had behaved with discretion and had obtained a complete success. The next day he went on to demand an acceptance of his code, which he prepared to submit in form. But as a preliminary he made ready to take Aaron and his two sons, together with seventy elders of the congregation up the mountain, to be especially impressed with a sacrifice and a feast which he had it in his mind to organize. In the first place, "Moses . . . rose up early in the morning, and builded an altar, . . . and sacrificed peace offerings of oxen unto the Lord. . . .

"And he took the book of the covenant, and read in the audience of the people: and they said, All that the Lord hath said will we do, and be obedient."

Had Moses been content to end his ceremony here and to return to the camp with his book of the covenant duly accepted as law, all might have been well. But success seems to have intoxicated him, and he conceived an undue contempt for the intelligence of his audience, being, apparently, convinced that there were no limits to their credulity, and that he could do with them as he pleased.

It was not enough for him that he should have them accept an ordinary book admittedly written by himself. There was nothing overpoweringly impressive in that. What he wanted was a stone tablet on which his code should be engraved, as was the famous code of Hammurabi, which he probably knew well, and this engraving must putatively be done by God himself, to give it the proper solemnity.

To have such a code as this engraved either by himself or by any workman he could take into the mountain with him, would be a work of time and would entail his absence from the camp, and this was a very serious risk. But he was over-confident and determined to run it, rather than be baulked of his purpose.

"And Moses rose up, and his minister Joshua; and Moses went up into the mount of God.

"And he said unto the elders, Tarry you here for us, until we come again unto you: and, behold, Aaron and Hur are with you: and if any man have matters to do, let him come unto them. And Moses went into the midst of the cloud, and gat him up into the mount: and Moses was in the mount forty days and forty nights."

But Moses had made the capital mistake of under-valuing the intelligence of his audience. They had, doubtless, been impressed when Moses, as a showman, had presented his spectacle, for Moses had a commanding presence and he had chosen a wonderful locality for his performance. But once he was gone the effect of what he had done evaporated and they began to value the exhibition for what it really was. As men of common sense, said they to one another, why should we linger here, if Moses has played this trick upon us? Why not go back to Egypt, where at least we can get something to eat? So they decided to bribe Aaron, who was venal and would do anything for money.

"And when the people saw that Moses delayed to come down out of the mount, the people gathered themselves together unto Aaron, and said unto him, Up, make us gods, which shall go before us; for as for this Moses, the man that brought us up out of the land of Egypt, we wot not what is become of him."

When Aaron heard this proposition he showed no

objection to accept, provided the people made it worth his while to risk the wrath of Moses; so he answered forthwith, "Break off the golden earrings, which are in the ears of your wives, of your sons, and of your daughters, and bring them unto me."

These were the ornaments of which the departing Israelites had spoiled the Egyptians and they must have been of very considerable value. At all events, Aaron took them and melted them and made them into the image of a calf, such as he had been used to see in Egypt. The calf was probably made of wood and laminated with gold. Sir G. Wilkinson thinks that the calf was made to represent Mnevis, with whose worship the Israelites had been familiar in Egypt. Then Aaron proclaimed a feast for the next day in honor of this calf and said, "To-morrow is a feast to the Lord," and they said, "These be thy gods, O Israel, which brought thee up out of the land of Egypt."

"And they rose up early on the morrow, and offered burnt offerings, and brought peace offerings: and the people sat down to eat and to drink, and rose up to play."

It was not very long before Moses became suspicious that all was not right in the camp, and he prepared to go down, taking the two tables of testimony in his hands. These stone tablets were covered with writing on both sides, which must have taken a long time to engrave considering that Moses was on a bare mountain-side with probably nobody to help but Joshua. Of course all that made this weary expedition worth the doing was that, as the Bible says, "the tables were" to pass for "the work of God, and the writing was the writing of God." Accordingly, it is not surprising that as Moses "came nigh unto the camp," and he "saw the calf, and the dancing": that his "anger waxed hot, and he cast the tables out of his hands, and brake them beneath the mount.

"And he took the calf which they had made, and burnt it in the fire, and ground it to powder, and strewed it upon the water, and made the children of Israel drink of it.

"And Moses said unto Aaron, What did this people unto thee, that thou hast brought so great a sin upon them?

"And Aaron said, Let not the anger of my lord wax hot: thou knowest the people, that they are set on mischief.

"For they said unto me, Make us gods, which shall go before us: for as for this Moses, the man that brought us up out of the land of Egypt, we wot not what is become of him.

"And I said unto them, Whosoever hath any gold, let them break it off. So they gave it me: then I cast it into the fire, and there came out this calf.

"And when Moses saw that the people were naked; (for Aaron had made them naked unto their shame among their enemies:)" that is to say, the people had come to the feast unarmed, and without the slightest fear or suspicion of a possible attack; then Moses saw his opportunity and placed himself in a gate of the camp, and said: "Who is on the Lord's side? Let him come unto me. And all the sons of Levi gathered themselves together unto him.

"And he said unto them, Thus saith the Lord God of Israel, Put every man his sword by his side, and go in and out from gate to gate throughout the camp, and slay every man his brother, and every man his companion, and every man his neighbour.

"And the children of Levi did according to the word of Moses: and there fell of the people that day about three thousand men."

There are few acts in all recorded history, including the awful massacres of the Albigenses by Simon de Montfort and the Abbot Arnold, more indefensible than this wholesale murder by Moses of several thousand people who had trusted him, and whom he had entrusted to the care of his own brother, who participated in their crime, supposing that they had committed any crime saving the crime of tiring of his dictatorship.

The effect of this massacre was to put Moses, for the rest of his life, in the hands of the Levites with Aaron at their head, for only by having a body of men stained with his own crimes and devoted to his fortunes could Moses thenceforward hope to carry his adventure to a good end. Otherwise he faced certain and ignominious failure. His preliminary task, therefore, was to devise for the Levites a reward which would content them. His first step in this direction was to go back to the mountain and seek a new inspiration and a revelation more suited to the existing conditions than the revelation conveyed before the golden calf incident.

Up to this time there is nothing in Jewish history to show that the priesthood was developing into a privileged and hereditary caste. With the consecration of Aaron as high priest the process began. Moses spent another six weeks in seclusion on the mount. And as soon as he returned to the camp he proclaimed how the people should build and furnish a sanctuary in which the priesthood should perform its functions. These directions were very elaborate and detailed, and part of the furnishings of the sanctuary consisted in the splendid and costly garments for Aaron and his sons "for glory and for beauty."

"And thou shalt put upon Aaron the holy garments, and anoint him, and sanctify him; that he may minister unto me in the priest's office. And thou shalt bring his sons, and clothe them with coats: And thou shalt anoint them, as thou didst anoint their father, that they may minister unto me in the priest's office: for their anointing shall surely be an everlasting priesthood, throughout their generations.

"Thus did Moses: according to all that the Lord commanded him, so did he."

It followed automatically that, with the creation of a great vested interest centred in an hereditary caste of priests, the pecuniary burden on the people was correspondingly increased and that thenceforward Moses became nothing but the representative of that vested

interest: as reactionary and selfish as all such representatives must be. How selfish and how reactionary
may readily be estimated by glancing at Numbers
XVIII, where God's directions are given to Aaron touching what he was to claim for himself, and what the
Levites were to take as their wages for service. It was
indeed liberal compensation. A good deal more than
much of the congregation thought such services worth.

In the first place, Aaron and the Levites with him
for their service "of the tabernacle" were to have "all
the tenth in Israel for an inheritance." But this was
a small part of their compensation. There were beside perquisites, especially those connected with the
sacrifices which the people were constrained to make
on the most trifling occasions; as, for example, whenever they became *unclean*, through some accident, as
by touching a dead body:

"This shall be thine of the most holy things, reserved
from the fire: every oblation of their's, every meat
offering of their's, and every sin offering of their's, and
every trespass offering of their's, which they shall render unto me, shall be most holy for thee and thy sons.

"In the most holy place shalt thou eat it; every male
shall eat it; it shall be holy unto thee.

"And this is thine. . . . All the best of the oil, and all
the best of the wine, and of the wheat, the firstfruits of
them which they shall offer unto the Lord, them have
I given thee; . . . every one that is clean in thine house
shall eat of it.

"Everything devoted in Israel shall be thine. . . .

"All the heave offerings of the holy things, which the children of Israel offer unto the Lord, have I given thee, and thy sons and thy daughters with thee, by a statute forever: it is a covenant of salt forever before the Lord unto thee and to thy seed with thee."

Also, on the taking of a census, such as occurred at Sinai, Aaron received a most formidable perquisite.

The Levites were not to be numbered; but there was to be a complicated system of redemption at the rate of "five shekels by the poll, after the shekel of the sanctuary."

"And Moses took the redemption money of them that were over and above them that were redeemed by the Levites: Of the first-born of the children of Israel took he the money; a thousand three hundred and three score and five shekels, after the shekel of the sanctuary; And Moses gave the money of them that were redeemed unto Aaron and to his sons."

Assuming the shekel of those days to have weighed two hundred and twenty-four grains of silver, its value in our currency would have been about fifty-five cents, but its purchasing power, twelve hundred years before Christ, would have been, at the very most moderate estimate, at least ten for one, which would have amounted to between six and seven thousand dollars in hard cash for no service whatever, which, considering that the Israelites were a wandering nomadic horde in the wilderness, was, it must be admitted, a pretty heavy charge for the pleasure of observing the performances of Aaron and his sons, in their gorgeous garments.

Also, under any sedentary administration it followed that the high priest must become the most considerable personage in the community, as well as one of the richest. And thus as payment for the loyalty to himself of the Levites during the massacre of the golden calf, Moses created a theocratic aristocracy headed by Aaron and his sons, and comprising the whole tribe of Levi, whose advancement in fortune could not fail to create discontent. It did so: a discontent which culminated very shortly after in the rebellion of Korah, which brought on a condition of things at Kadesh which contributed to make the position of Moses intolerable.

Moses was one of those administrators who were particularly reprobated by Saint Paul; Men who "do evil," as in the slaughter of the feasters who set up the golden calf, "that good may come," and "whose damnation," therefore, "is just." [1]

And Moses wrought thus through ambition, because, though personally disinterested, he could not endure having his will thwarted. Aaron had nearly the converse of such a temperament. Aaron appears to have had few or no convictions; it mattered little to him whether he worshipped Jehovah on Sinai or the golden calf at the foot of Sinai, provided he were paid at his own price. And he took care to exact a liberal price. Also the inference to be drawn from the way in which Moses behaved to him is that Moses understood what manner of man he was.

Jethro stood higher in the estimation of Moses, and

[1] Romans III, 8.

Moses did his best to keep Jethro with him, but, apparently, Jethro had watched Moses closely and was not satisfied with his conduct of the exodus. On the eve of departure from Sinai, just as the Israelites were breaking camp, Moses sought out Jethro and said to him; "We are journeying unto the place of which the Lord said, I will give it you; come thou with us, and we will do thee good; for the Lord has spoken good concerning Israel.

"And he said unto him, I will not go; but I will depart to mine own land, and to my kindred."

Not discouraged, Moses kept on urging: "Leave us not, I pray thee; forasmuch as thou knowest how we are to encamp in the wilderness, and thou mayest be to us instead of eyes.

"And it shall be, if thou go with us, yea, it shall be, that what goodness the Lord shall do unto us, the same will we do unto thee." It has been inferred from a passage in Judges,[1] that Moses induced Jethro to reconsider his refusal and that he did accompany the congregation in its march to Kadesh, but, on the whole, the text of the Bible fails to bear out such inference, for there is no subsequent mention of Jethro in the books which treat directly of the trials of the journey, although there would seem to have been abundant occasion for Moses to have called upon Jethro for aid had Jethro been present. In his apparent absence the march began, under the leadership of the Lord and Moses, very much missing Jethro.

[1] Judges I, 16.

They departed from the mount: "And the cloud of the Lord was upon them by day," when they left the camp "to search out a resting-place." Certainly, on this occasion, the Lord selected a poor spot for the purpose, quite different from such an one as Jethro would have been expected to have pointed out; for the children of Israel began complaining mightily, so much so that it displeased the Lord who sent fire into the uttermost parts of the camp, where it consumed them.

"And the people cried unto Moses, and when Moses prayed unto the Lord, the fire was quenched."

This suggestion of a divine fire under the control of Moses opens an interesting speculation.

The Magi, who were the priests of the Median religion, greatly developed the practices of incantation and sorcery. Among these rites they "pretended to have the power of making fire descend on to their altars by means of magical ceremonies." [1] Moses appears to have been very fond of this particular miracle. It is mentioned as having been effective here at Taberah, and it was the supposed weapon employed to suppress Korah's rebellion. Moses was indeed a powerful enchanter. His relations with all the priestcraft of central Asia were intimate, and if the Magi had secrets which were likely to be of use to him in maintaining his position among the Jews, the inference is that he would certainly have used them to the utmost; as he did the brazen serpent, the ram's horns at Sinai, and the like. But in spite of all his miracles Moses

[1] Lenormant, *Chaldean Magic*, 226, 238.

found his task too heavy, and he frankly confessed that he wished himself dead.

"Then Moses heard the people weep throughout their families . . . and the anger of the Lord was kindled greatly; Moses also was displeased.

"And Moses said unto the Lord, Wherefore hast thou afflicted thy servant? . . . that thou layest the burden of all this people upon me?

"Have I conceived all this people? have I begotten them, that thou shouldest say unto me, Carry them in thy bosom, as a nursing father beareth the sucking child, unto the land which thou swarest unto their fathers?

"Whence should I have flesh to give unto all this people? for they weep unto me saying, Give us flesh that we may eat.

"I am not able to bear all this people alone, because it is too heavy for me.

"And if thou deal thus with me, kill me, I pray thee, out of hand, if I have found favour in thy sight; and let me not see my wretchedness."

Leaving aside for the moment all our childish preventions, and considering this evidence in the cold light of history, it becomes tolerably evident that Moses had now reached the turning-point in his career, the point whither he had inexorably tended since the day on which he bid good-bye to Jethro to visit Egypt and attempt to gain control of the exodus, and the point to which all optimists must come who resolve to base a religious or a political movement on the manip-

ulation of the supernatural. However pure and disinterested the motives of such persons may be at the
outset, and however thoroughly they may believe in
themselves and in their mission, sooner or later, to
compass their purpose, they must resort to deception
and thus become impostors who flourish on the credulity of their dupes.

Moses, from the nature of the case, had to make such
demands on the credulity of his followers that even
those who were bound to him by the strongest ties of
affection and self-interest were alienated, and those
without such commanding motives to submit to his
claim to exact from them absolute obedience, revolted,
and demanded that he should be deposed. The first
serious trouble with which Moses had to contend
came to a head at Hazeroth, the second station after
leaving Sinai. The supposed spot is still used as a
watering-place. There Miriam and Aaron attacked
Moses because they were jealous of his wife, whom
they decried as an "Ethiopian." And they said,
"Hath the Lord indeed spoken only by Moses? hath
he not spoken also by us?" Instantly, it became evident to Moses that if this denial of his superior inti-
macy with God were to be permitted, his supremacy
must end. Accordingly the Lord came down "in the
pillar of the cloud, and stood in the door of the tabernacle, and called Aaron and Miriam: and they both
came forth." And the Lord explained that he had no
objection to a prophet; if any one among the congregation had an ambition to be a prophet he would com-

municate with him in a dream; but there must always be a wide difference between such a man or woman and Moses with whom he would "speak mouth to mouth, even apparently, and not in dark speeches." And then God demanded irritably, "Wherefore, then, were ye not afraid to speak against my servant Moses?" "Afterward the cloud," according to the Bible, departed and God with it.

Ever since the dawn of time the infliction of or the cure of disease has been the stronghold of the necromancer, the wise man, the magician, the saint, the prophet and the priest, and Moses was no exception to the rule, only hitherto he had had no occasion to display his powers of this kind. Nevertheless, among the Hebrews of the exodus, the field for this form of miracle was large. Leprosy was very prevalent, so much so that in Egypt the Jews were called a nation of lepers. And in the camp the regulations touching them were strict and numerous. But the Jews were always a dirty race.

In chapter XIII of Leviticus, elaborate directions are given as to how the patient shall be brought before Aaron himself, or at least some other of the priests, who was to examine the sore and, if it proved to be a probable case of leprosy, the patient was to be excluded from the camp for a week. At the end of that time the disease, if malignant, was supposed to show signs of spreading, in which case there was no cure and the patient was condemned to civil death. On the contrary, if no virulent symptoms developed during the week, the patient was pronounced clean and returned to ordinary life.

The miracle in the case of Miriam was this: When the cloud departed from off the tabernacle, Miriam was found to be "leprous, white as snow," just as Moses' hand was found to be white with leprosy after his conversation with the Lord at the burning bush. Upon this Aaron, who had been as guilty as Miriam, and was proportionately nervous, made a prayer to Moses: "Alas, my lord, I beseech thee, lay not the sin upon us, wherein we have done foolishly. . . . Let her not be as one dead.

"And Moses cried unto the Lord, saying, Heal her now, O God, I beseech thee."

But the Lord replied: "If her father had but spit in her face, should she not be ashamed seven days? Let her be shut out from the camp seven days, and after that let her be received in again."

This was the Mosaic system of discipline. And it was serious for all parties concerned. Evidently it was very serious for Miriam, who had to leave her tent and be exiled to some spot in the desert, where she had to shift for herself. We all know the almost intolerable situation of those unfortunates who, in the East, are excluded from social intercourse, and sit without the gate, and are permitted to approach no one. But it was also a serious infliction for the congregation, since Miriam was a personage of consequence, and had to be waited for. That is to say, a million or two of people had to delay their pilgrimage until Moses had determined how much punishment Miriam deserved for her insubordination, and this was a question which lay altogether within the discretion of Moses. In that age there were at least seven varieties of eruptions which could hardly, if at all, be distinguished, in their early stages, from leprosy, and it was left to Moses to say whether or not Miriam had been attacked by true leprosy or not. There was no one, apparently, to question his judgment, for, since Jethro had left the camp, there was no one to controvert the Mosaic opinion on matters such as these. Doubtless Moses was content to give Aaron and Miriam a fright; but also Moses intended to make them understand that they lay absolutely at his mercy.

After this outbreak of discontent had been thus summarily suppressed and Miriam had been again received as "clean," the caravan resumed its march and entered into the wilderness of Paran, which adjoined Palestine, and from whence an invasion of Canaan, if one were to be attempted, would be organized. Accordingly Moses appointed a reconnaissance, who in the language of the Bible are called "spies," to examine the country, report its condition, and decide whether an attack were feasible.

On this occasion Moses seems to have remembered the lesson he learned at Sinai. He did not undertake to leave the camp himself for a long interval. He sent the men whom he supposed he could best trust, among whom were Joshua and Caleb. These men, who corresponded to what, in a modern army, would be called the general-staff, were not sent to manufacture a report which they might have reason to suppose would be pleasing to Moses, but to state precisely what they saw and heard together with their conclusions thereon, that they might aid their commander in an arduous campaign; and this duty they seem, honestly enough, to have performed. But this was very far from satisfying Moses, who wanted to make a strenuous offensive, and yet sought some one else to take the responsibility therefor.

The spies were absent six weeks and when they returned were divided in opinion. They all agreed that Canaan was a good land, and, in verity, flowing with milk and honey. But the people, most of them thought, were too strong to be successfully attacked. "The cities were walled and very great," and moreover "we saw the children of Anak there."

"The Amalekites dwell in the land of the south; and the Hittites, and the Jebusites, and the Amorites, dwell in the mountains; and the Canaanites dwell by the sea, and by the coast of Jordan.

"And Caleb stilled the people before Moses, and said, Let us go up at once, . . . for we are well able to overcome it.

"But the men that went up with him said, We be not able to go up against the people; for they are stronger than we.

"And they brought up an evil report of the land which they had searched, . . . saying, . . . all the people that we saw in it are men of great stature.

"And there we saw the giants, the sons of Anak, . . . and we were in our own sight as grasshoppers, and so were we in their sight."

Had Moses been gifted with military talent, or with any of the higher instincts of the soldier, he would have arranged to have received this report in private and would then have acted as he thought best. Above all he would have avoided anything like a council of war by the whole congregation, for a vast popular meeting of that kind was certain to become unmanageable the moment a division appeared in their command, upon a difficult question of policy.

Moses did just the opposite. He convened the people to hear the report of the "spies." And immediately the majority became dangerously depressed, not to say mutinous.

"And all the congregation lifted up their voice, and cried; and the people wept that night.

"And all the children of Israel murmured against Moses and against Aaron: and the whole congregation said unto them, Would God that we had died in the land of Egypt! Or would God we had died in this wilderness! . . .

"And they said one to another, Let us make a captain, and let us return into Egypt.

"Then Moses and Aaron fell on their faces before all the assembly of the congregation of the children of Israel."

But Joshua, who was a soldier, when Moses thus somewhat ignominiously collapsed, retained his pres-

ence of mind and his energy. He and Caleb "rent
their clothes," and reiterated their advice.

"And they spake unto all the company of the children of Israel, saying, The land which we passed
through to search it, is an exceeding good land.

"If the Lord delight in us, then he will bring us into
this land, and give it us; a land which floweth with
milk and honey.

"Only rebel not ye against the Lord, neither fear
ye the people of the land; for they are bread for us:
their defence is departed from them . . . fear them not.

"But all the congregation bade stone them with
stones."

By this time Moses seems to have recovered some
composure. Enough, at least, to repeat certain violent
threats of the "Lord."

Nothing is so impressive in all this history as the difference between Moses when called upon to take
responsibility as a military commander, and Moses
when, not to mince matters, he acted as a quack. On
the one hand, he was all vacillation, timidity, and ir-
ritability. On the other, all temerity and effrontery.

In this particular emergency, which touched his
very life, Moses vented his disappointment and vexation in a number of interviews which he pretended to
have had with the "Lord," and which he retailed to the
congregation, just at the moment when they needed,
as Joshua perceived, to be steadied and encouraged.

"How long," vociferated the Lord, when Moses had
got back his power of speech, "will this people provoke

me? and how long will it be ere they believe me, for all the signs which I have shewed among them?

"I will smite them with the pestilence, and disinherit them, and will make of thee a greater nation and mightier than they."

But when Moses had cooled a little and came to reflect upon what he had made the "Lord" say, he fell into his ordinary condition of hesitancy. Supposing some great disaster should happen to the Jews at Kadesh, which lay not so very far from the Egyptian border, the Egyptians would certainly hear of it, and in that case the Egyptian army might pursue and capture Moses. Such a contingency was not to be contemplated, and accordingly Moses began to make reservations. It must be remembered that all these ostensible conversations with the "Lord" went on in public; that is to say, Moses proffered his advice to the Lord aloud, and then retailed his version of the answer he received.

"Now if thou shalt kill all this people as one man, then the nations which have heard the fame of thee will speak, saying,

"Because the Lord was not able to bring this people into the land which he sware unto them, therefore he hath slain them in the wilderness. . . .

" Pardon, I beseech thee, the iniquity of this people according unto the greatness of thy mercy, and as thou hast forgiven this people from Egypt even until now.

"And the Lord said, I have pardoned according to thy word."

Had Moses left the matter there it would not have been so bad, but he could not contain his vexation, because his staff had not divined his wishes. Those men, though they had done their strict duty only, must be punished, so he thought, to maintain his ascendancy.

Of the twelve "spies" whom Moses had sent into Canaan to report to him, ten had incurred his bitter animosity because they failed to render him such a report as would sustain him before the people in making the campaign of invasion to which he felt himself pledged, and on the success of which his reputation depended. Of these ten men, Moses, to judge by the character of his demands upon the Lord, thought it incumbent on him to make an example, in order to sustain his own credit.

To simply exclude these ten spies from Palestine, as he proposed to do with the rest of the congregation, would hardly be enough, for the rest of the Hebrews were, at most, passive, but these ten had wilfully ignored the will of Moses, or, as he expressed it, of the Lord. Therefore it was the Lord's duty, as Moses saw it, to punish them. And this Moses proposed that the Lord should do in a prompt and awful manner: the lesson being pointed by the immunity of Joshua and Caleb, the two spies who had had the wit to divine the will of Moses. Therefore, all ten of these men died of the plague while the congregation lay encamped at Kadesh, though Joshua and Caleb remained immune.

Moses, as the commanding general of an attacking army, took a course diametrically opposed to that of Joshua, and calculated to be fatal to victory. He vented his irritation in a series of diatribes which he attributed to the "Lord," and which discouraged and confused his men at the moment when their morale was essential to success.

Therefore, the Lord, according to Moses, went on: "But as truly as I live, all the earth shall be filled with the glory of the Lord.

"Because all those men which have seen my glory, and my miracles, which I did in Egypt and in the wilderness, have tempted me now these ten times, and have not hearkened to my voice;

"Surely they shall not see the land which I swear unto their fathers, neither shall any of them that provoked me see it:

"But my servant Caleb, because he had another spirit with him, and hath followed me fully, him will I bring into the land whereinto he went; . . ."

Having said all this, and, as far as might be, disorganized the army, Moses surrendered suddenly his point. He made the "Lord" go on to command: "To-morrow turn you, and get you into the wilderness by the way of the Red Sea." But, not even yet content, Moses assured them that this retreat should profit them nothing.

"And the Lord spake unto Moses and unto Aaron, saying, How long shall I bear with this evil congregation, which murmur against me? I have heard the murmurings of the children of Israel, which they murmur against me." And the Lord continued:

"Say unto them, As truly as I live, . . . as ye have spoken in mine ears, so will I do to you.

"Your carcases shall fall in this wilderness; and all that were numbered of you, . . . from twenty years old and upward, which have murmured against me,

"Doubtless ye shall not come into the land. . . .

"But as for you, your carcases, they shall fall in this wilderness. . . .

"And the men which Moses sent to search the land, who returned, and made all the congregation to murmur against him, by bringing up a slander upon the land, —

"Even those men that did bring up the evil report upon the land, died by the plague before the Lord.

"But Joshua . . . and Caleb, . . . which were of the men that went to search the land, lived still.

"And Moses told these sayings unto all the children of Israel and the people mourned greatly."

The congregation were now completely out of hand. They knew not what Moses wanted to do, nor did they comprehend what Moses was attempting to make the Lord threaten: except that he had in mind some dire mischief. Accordingly, the people decided that the best thing for them was to go forward as Joshua and Caleb proposed. So, early in the morning, they went up into the top of the mountain, saying, "We be here, and will go up unto the place which the Lord hath promised: for we have sinned."

But Moses was more dissatisfied than ever. "Wherefore now do you transgress the commandment of the Lord? But it shall not prosper." Notwithstanding, "they presumed to go up unto the hilltop: nevertheless the ark of the covenant of the Lord, and Moses, departed not out of the camp.

"Then the Amalekites came down, and the Canaanites, which dwelt in that hill, and smote them, and discomfited them, even unto Hormah"; which was at a very considerable distance, — perhaps not less than thirty miles, though the positions are not very well established.

This is the story as told by the priestly chronicler, who, of course, said the best that could be said for Moses. But he makes a sorry tale of it. According to him, Moses, having been disappointed with the report made by his officers on the advisability of an immediate offensive, committed the blunder of summoning the whole assembly of the people to listen to it, and then, in the midst of the panic he had created, he lost his self-possession and finally his temper. Whereupon his soldiers, not knowing what to do or what he wanted, resolved to follow the advice of Joshua and advance.

But this angered Moses more than ever, who committed the unpardonable crime in the eyes of the soldier; he abandoned his men in the presence of the enemy and by this desertion so weakened them that they sustained the worst defeat the Israelites suffered during the whole of their wanderings in the wilderness. Such a disaster brought on a crisis. The only wonder is that it had been so long delayed. Moses had had since the exodus a wonderful opportunity to test the truth of his theories. He had asserted that the universe was the expression of a single and supreme mind, which operated according to a fixed moral law. That he alone, of all men, understood this mind, and could explain and administer its law, and that this he could and would do were he to obtain absolute obedience to the commands which he uttered. Were he only obeyed, he would win for his followers victory in battle, and a wonderful land to which they should march under his guidance, which was the Promised Land, and thereafter all was to be well with them.

The disaster at Hormah had demonstrated that he was no general, and even on that very day the people had proof before their eyes that he knew nothing of the desert, and that the Lord knew no more than he, since there was no water at Kadesh, and to ask the congregation to encamp in such a spot was preposterous. Meanwhile Moses absorbed all the offices of honor and profit for his family. Aaron and his descendants monopolized the priesthood, and this was a bitter grievance to other equally ambitious Levites. In short, the Mosaic leadership was vulnerable on every hand. Attack on Moses was, therefore, inevitable, and it came from Korah, who was leader of the opposition.

Korah was a cousin of Moses, and one of the ablest and most influential men in the camp, to whom Dathan and Abiram and "two hundred and fifty" princes of the assembly, famous in the congregation, men of renown, joined themselves. "And they gathered them-

selves together against Moses and against Aaron, and
said unto them, Ye take too much upon you, seeing
all the congregation are holy, every one of them, and
the Lord is among them: wherefore then lift you up
yourselves above the congregation of the Lord?"

Korah's grievance was that he had been, although
a Levite, excluded from the priesthood in favor of the
demands of Aaron and his sons.

"And when Moses heard it, he fell upon his face."

And yet something had to be done. Moses faced
an extreme danger. His life hung upon the issue.
As between him and Korah he had to demonstrate
which was the better sorcerer or magician, and he could
only do this by challenging Korah to the test of the ordeal: the familiar test of the second clause of the code
of Hammurabi; "If the holy river makes that man to
be innocent, and has saved him, he who laid the spell
upon him shall be put to death. He who plunged into
the holy river shall take to himself the house of him
who wove the spell upon him." [1] And so with Elijah,
to whom Ahaziah sent a captain of fifty to arrest him.
And Elijah said to the captain of fifty, "If I be a man
of God, then let fire come down from heaven, and consume thee and thy fifty. And there came down fire
from heaven, and consumed him and his fifty." [2]

In a word, the ordeal was the common form of test
by which the enchanter, the sorcerer, or the magician
always was expected to prove himself. Moses already

[1] Code of Laws promulgated by Hammurabi, King of Babylon.
Translated by C. H. W. Johns, M.A., § 2.
[2] 2 Kings i, 10.

had tried the test by fire at least once, and probably oftener. So now Moses reproached Korah because he was jealous of Aaron; "and what is Aaron, that ye murmur against him? . . . This do; Take you censers, Korah, and all his company; and put fire therein, and put incense in them before the Lord to-morrow; and . . . whom the Lord doth choose, he shall be holy: ye take too much upon you, ye sons of Levi."

But it was not only about the priesthood that Moses had trouble on his hands. He had undertaken, with the help of the Lord, to lead the Israelites through the wilderness. But at every step of the way his incompetence became more manifest. Even there, at that very camp of Kadesh, there was no water, and all the people clamored. And, therefore, Dathan and Abiram taunted him with failure, and with his injustice to those who served him. And Moses had no reply, except that he denied having abused his power.

"And Moses sent to call Dathan and Abiram, the sons of Eliab: which said, We will not come up:

"Is it a small thing that thou hast brought us up out of a land that floweth with milk and honey, to kill us in the wilderness, except thou make thyself altogether a prince over us?

"Moreover, thou hast not brought us into a land that floweth with milk and honey, or given us inheritance of fields and vineyards: wilt thou put out the eyes of these men [probably alluding to the "spies"]? We will not come up."

This was evidently an exceedingly sore spot. Moses

had boasted that, because the "spies" had rendered to the congregation what they believed to be a true report instead of such a report as he had expected, the "Lord" had destroyed them by the plague. And it is pretty evident that the congregation believed him. It could hardly have been by pure accident that out of twelve men, the ten who had offended Moses should have died by the plague, and the other two alone should have escaped. Moses assumed to have the power of destroying whom he pleased by the pestilence through prayer to the "Lord," and he, indeed, probably had the power, in such a spot as an ancient Jewish Nomad camp, not indeed by prayer, but by the very human means of communicating so virulent a poison as the plague: means which he very well understood.

Therefore it is not astonishing that this insinuation should have stung Moses to the quick.

"And Moses was very wroth, and said unto the Lord, Respect not thou their offering: I have not taken one ass from them, neither have I hurt one of them."

Then Moses turned to Korah, "Be thou and all thy company before the Lord, thou, and they, and Aaron, to-morrow:

"And take every man his censer, and put incense in them, and bring ye before the Lord every man his censer, two hundred and fifty censers."

And Korah, on the morrow, gathered all the congregation against them unto the door of the tabernacle. And the "Lord" then as usual intervened and advised Moses to "separate yourselves from among this

congregation, that I may consume them in a moment."
And Moses did so. That is to say, he made an effort
to divide the opposition, who, when united, he seems
to have appreciated, were too strong for him.

What happened next is not known. That Moses
partially succeeded in his attempt at division is admitted, for he persuaded Dathan and Abiram and their
following to "depart . . . from the tents of these wicked
men, and touch nothing of theirs, lest ye be consumed
in all their sins."

Exactly what occurred after this is unknown. The
chronicle, of course, avers that "the earth opened her
mouth, and swallowed them up, and their houses, and
all the men that appertained unto Korah, and all their
goods." But it could not have been this or anything
like it, for the descendants of Korah, many generations
after, were still doing service in the Temple, and at
the time of the miracle the spectators were not intimidated by the sight, although all "Israel that were
round about them fled at the cry of them: for they
said, Lest the earth swallow us up also.

"And there came out a fire from the Lord, and consumed the two hundred and fifty men that offered
incense."

Notwithstanding all which, the congregation next
day were as hostile and as threatening as ever.

"On the morrow all the congregation of the children
of Israel murmured against Moses and against Aaron,
saying, Ye have killed the people of the Lord. . . .

"And they fell upon their faces."

In this crisis of his fate, when it seemed that nothing could save Moses from a conflict with the mass of his followers, who had renounced him, Moses showed that audacity and fertility of resource, which had hitherto enabled him, and was destined until his death to enable him, to maintain his position, at least as a prophet, among the Jewish people.

The plague was always the most dreaded of visitations among the ancient Jews: far more terrible than war. It was already working havoc in the camp, as the death of the "spies" shows us. Moses always asserted his ability to control it, and at this instant, when, apparently, he and Aaron were lying on their faces before the angry people, he conceived the idea that he would put his theurgetic powers to the proof. Suddenly he called to Aaron to "take a censer and put fire therein from off the altar, and put on incense, and go quickly unto the congregation, and make an atonement for them: for there is wrath gone out from the Lord; the plague is begun."

"And Aaron took as Moses commanded, and ran into the midst of the congregation; and, behold, the plague was begun among the people: . . . and made an atonement for the people.

"And he stood between the dead and the living; and the plague was stayed.

"Now they that died in the plague were fourteen thousand and seven hundred, beside them that died about the matter of Korah."

Even this was not enough. The discontent continued, and Moses went on to meet it by the miracle of Aaron's rod.

Moses took a rod from each tribe, twelve rods in all and on Aaron's rod he wrote the name of Levi, and Moses laid them out in the tabernacle. And the next day Moses examined the rods and showed the congregation how Aaron's rod had budded. And Moses declared that Aaron's rod should be kept for a token against the rebels: and that they must stop their murmurings "that they die not."

This manipulation of the plague by Moses, upon what seems to have been a sudden inspiration, was a stroke of genius in the way of quackery. He was, indeed, in this way almost portentous. It had a great and terrifying effect upon the people, who were completely subdued by it. Against corporeal enemies they might hope to prevail, but they were helpless against the plague. And they all cried out with one accord, "Behold we die, we perish, we all perish. Whosoever cometh anything near unto the tabernacle of the Lord shall die: shall we be consumed with dying?"

As I have already pointed out, Moses was a very great theurgist, as many saints and prophets have been. When in the actual presence of others he evidently had the power of creating a belief in himself which approached the miraculous, so far as disease was concerned. And he presumed on this power and took correspondingly great risks. The case of the brazen serpent is an example. The story is — and there is no reason to doubt its substantial truth — that the Hebrews were attacked by venomous serpents probably in the neighborhood of Mount Hor, where Aaron died, and thereupon Moses set up a large brazen serpent on a pole, and declared that whoever would look upon the serpent should live. Also, apparently, it did produce an effect upon those who believed: which, of course, is not an unprecedented phenomenon among faith healers. But what is interesting in this historical anecdote is not that Moses performed certain faith cures by the suggestion of a serpent, but that the Israelites themselves, when out of the presence of Moses, recognized that he had perpetrated on them a vulgar fraud. For example, King Hezekiah destroyed this relic, which had been preserved in the Temple, calling it "Nehushtan," "a brazen thing," as an expression of his contempt. And what is more remarkable still is that although Hezekiah reigned four or five centuries after the exodus, yet science had made no such advance in the interval as to justify this contempt. Hezekiah seems to have been every whit as credulous as were the pilgrims who looked on the brazen serpent and were healed. Hezekiah "was sick unto death, and Isaiah came to see him, and told him to set his house in order; for thou shalt die, and not live. . . . And Hezekiah wept sore."

Then, like Moses, Isaiah had another revelation in which he was directed to return to Hezekiah, and tell him that he was to live fifteen years longer. And Isaiah told the attendants to take "a lump of figs." "And they took it and laid it on the boil, and he recovered."

Afterward Hezekiah asked of Isaiah how he was to know that the Lord would keep his word and give him fifteen additional years of life. Isaiah told him that the shadow should go back ten degrees on the dial. And Isaiah "cried unto the Lord," and he brought the shadow ten degrees backward "by which it had gone down in the dial of Ahaz." [1] And yet this man Hezekiah, who could believe in this marvellous cure of Isaiah, repudiated with scorn the brazen serpent as an insult to credulity. The contrast between Moses, who hesitated not to take all risks in matters of disease with which he felt himself competent to cope, and his timidity and hesitation in matters of war, is astounding. But it is a common phenomenon with the worker of miracles and indicates the limit of faith at which the saint or prophet has always betrayed the impostor. For example: Saint Bernard, when he preached in 1146 the Second Crusade, made miraculous cures by the thousand, so much so that there was danger of being killed in the crowds which pressed upon him. And yet this same saint, when chosen by the crusaders four years later, in 1150, to lead them because of his power to constrain victory by the intervention of God, wrote, after the crusaders' defeat, in terror to the pope to protect him, because he was unfit to take such responsibility.

But even with this reservation Moses could not gain the complete confidence of the congregation and the insecurity of his position finally broke him down.

[1] 2 Kings xx, 11.

At this same place of Kadesh, Miriam died, "and the people chode with Moses because there was no water for the congregation." [1] Moses thereupon withdrew and, as usual, received a revelation. And the Lord directed him to take his rod, "and speak ye unto the rock before their eyes; and it shall give forth his water."

And Moses gathered the congregation and said unto them, "Hear now, ye rebels; must we fetch you water out of this rock?"

"And he smote the rock twice: and the water came out abundantly."

But Moses felt that he had offended God, "Because ye believed me not, to sanctify me in the eyes of the children of Israel, therefore ye shall not bring this congregation into the land which I have given them."

Moses had become an old man, and he felt himself unequal to the burden he had assumed. He recognized that his theory of cause and effect had broken down, and that the "Lord" whom at the outset he had firmly believed to be an actual and efficient power to be dominated by him, either could not or would not support him in emergency. In short, he had learned that he was an adventurer who must trust to himself. Hence, after Hormah he was a changed man. Nothing could induce him to lead the Jews across the Jordan to attack the peoples on the west bank, and though the congregation made a couple of campaigns against Sihon and Og, whose ruthlessness has always been a

[1] Numbers xx, 3.

stain on Moses, the probability is that Moses did not meddle much with the active command. Had he done so, the author of Deuteronomy would have given the story in more detail and Moses more credit. All that is attributed to Moses is a division of the conquests made together with Joshua, and a fruitless prayer to the Lord that he might be permitted to cross the Jordan.

Meanwhile life was ending for him. His elder sister Miriam died at Kadesh, and Aaron died somewhat later at Mount Hor, which is supposed to lie about as far to the east of Kadesh as Hormah is to the west, but there are circumstances about the death of Aaron which point to Moses as having had more to do with it than of having been a mere passive spectator thereof.

The whole congregation is represented as having "journeyed from Kadesh and come unto Mount Hor . . . by the coast of the land of Edom," and there the "Lord" spoke unto Moses and Aaron, and explained that Aaron was to be "gathered unto his people, . . . because ye rebelled . . . at the water of Meribah." Therefore Moses was to "take Aaron and Eleazar his son, and bring them up unto Mount Hor: and strip Aaron of his garments, and put them upon Eleazar," . . . and that Aaron . . . shall die there.

"And they went up into Mount Hor in the sight of all the congregation. And Moses stripped Aaron of his garments, and put them upon Eleazar his son; and Aaron died there in the top of the mount: and Moses and Eleazar came down from the mount." [1]

[1] Numbers xx, 22–28.

Now it is incredible that all this happened as straightforwardly as the chronicle would have us believe. Aaron was an old man and probably failing, but his death was not imminent. On the contrary, he had strength to climb Mount Hor with Moses, without aid, and there is no hint that he suffered from any ailment likely to end his life suddenly. Moses took care that he and Eleazar should be alone with Aaron so that there should be no witness as to what occurred, and Moses alone knew what was expected.

Moses had time to take off the priestly garments, which were the insignia of office and to put them on Eleazar, and then, when all was ready, Aaron simply ceased to breathe at the precise moment when it was convenient for Moses to have him die, for the policy of Moses evidently demanded that Aaron should live no longer. Under the conditions of the march Moses was evidently preparing for his own death, and for a complete change in the administration of affairs. Appreciating that his leadership had broken down and that the system he had created was collapsing, he had dawdled as long on the east side of the Jordan as the patience of the congregation would permit. An advance had become inevitable, but Moses recognized his own inability to lead it. The command had to be delegated to a younger man and that man was Joshua. Eleazar, on the other hand, was the only available candidate for the high priesthood, and Moses took the opportunity of making the investiture on Mount Hor. So Aaron passed away, a sacrifice to the optimism of

Moses. Next came the turn of Moses himself. The whole story is told in Deuteronomy. Within, probably, something less than a year after Aaron's death the "Lord" made a like communication to Moses.

"Get thee up . . . unto Mount Nebo, which is in the land of Moab, that is over against Jericho;

"And die in the Mount whither thou goest up, and be gathered unto thy people; as Aaron, thy brother died in Mount Hor;

"Because ye trespassed against me among the children of Israel at the waters of Meribah-Kadesh, in the wilderness of Zin, because ye sanctified me not in the midst of the children of Israel.

"And Moses went up from the plains of Moab unto the mountain of Nebo, . . . And the Lord showed him all the land of Gilead, unto Dan.

"And Moses the servant of the Lord died there in the land of Moab, according to the word of the Lord. . . . But no man knoweth of his sepulchre unto this day.

"And Moses was an hundred and twenty years old when he died: his eye was not dim, nor his natural force abated."

The facts, as preserved by Josephus, appear to have been these: Moses ascended the mountain with only the elders, the high priest Eleazar, and Joshua. At the top of the mountain he dismissed the elders, and then, as he was embracing Joshua and Eleazar and still speaking, a cloud covered him, and he disappeared in a ravine. In other words, he killed himself.

Such is the story of Moses, a fragment of history interesting enough in itself, but especially material to us not only because of the development of the thought dealt with in the following volumes, but of the inferences which, at the present time, it permits us to draw touching our own immediate future.

Moses was the first great optimist of whom any record remains, and one of the greatest. He was the prototype of all those who have followed. He was a visionary. All optimists must be visionaries. Moses based the social system which he tried to organize, not on observed facts, but on *a priori* theories evolved out of his own mind, and he met with the failure that all men of that cast of mind must meet with when he sought to realize his visions. His theory was that the universe about him was the expression of an infinite mind which operated according to law. That this mind, or consciousness, was intelligent and capable of communicating with man. That it did, in fact, so communicate through him, as a medium, and that other men had only to receive humbly and obey implicitly his revelations to arrive at a condition nearly approaching, if not absolutely reaching, perfection, while they should enjoy happiness and prosperity in the land in which they should be permitted, by an infinite and supernatural power and wisdom, to dwell. All this is not alien to the attitude of scientific optimists at the present day, who anticipate progressive perfection.

Let us consider, for a moment, whither these *a priori*

theories led, when put in practice upon human beings, including himself. And, in the first place, it will probably be conceded that no optimist could have, or ever hope to have, a fairer opportunity to try his experiment than had Moses on that plastic Hebrew community which he undertook to lead through Arabia. Also it must be admitted that Moses, as an expounder of a moral code, achieved success. The moral principles which he laid down have been accepted as sound from that day to this, and are still written up in our churches, as a standard for men and women, however slackly they may be observed. But when we come to mark the methods by which Moses obtained acceptance of his code by his contemporaries, and, above all, sought to constrain obedience to himself and to it, we find the prospect unalluring. To begin with, Moses had only begun the exodus when he learned from his practical father-in-law that the system he employed was fantastic and certain to fail: his notion being that he should sit and judge causes himself, as the mouthpiece of the infinite, and that therefore each judgment he gave would demand a separate miracle or imposture. This could not be contemplated. Therefore Moses was constrained to impose his code in writing, once for all, by one gigantic fraud which he must perpetrate himself. This he tried at Sinai, unblushingly declaring that the stone tablets which he produced were "written with the finger of God"; wherefore, as they must have been written by himself, or under his personal supervision, he brazenly and deliberately lied. His good faith was obviously suspected, and this suspicion caused disastrous results. To support his lie Moses caused three thousand unsuspecting and trusting men to be murdered in cold blood, whose only crime was that they would have preferred another leadership to his, and because, had they been able to effect their purpose, they would have disappointed his ambition.

To follow Moses further in the course which optimism enforced upon him would be tedious, as it would be to recapitulate the story which has already been told. It suffices to say shortly that, at every camp, he had to sink to deeper depths of fraud, deception, lying, and crime in order to maintain his credit. It might be that, as at Meribah, it was only claiming for himself a miracle which he knew he could not work, and for claiming which, instead of giving the credit to God, he openly declared he deserved and must receive punishment; or it might be some impudent quackery, like the brazen serpent, which at least was harmless; or it might have been complicated combinations which suggest a deeper shade; as, for example, the outbreak of the plague, after Korah's rebellion, which bears the aspect of a successful effort at intimidation to support his own wavering credit. But the result was always the same. Moses had promised that the supernatural power he pretended to control should sustain him and give victory. Possibly, when he started on the exodus he verily believed that such a power existed, was amenable and could be constrained to intervene. He found that he had been mistaken on all these heads, and when he accepted these facts as final, nothing remained for him but suicide, as has been related. It only remains to glance, for a single moment, at what befell, when he had gone, the society he had organized on the optimistic principle of the approach of human beings toward perfection. During the period of the Judges, when "there was no king in Israel, but every man did that which was right in his own eyes," [1] anarchy supervened, indeed, but also the whole Mosaic system broke down because of the imbecility of the men on whom Moses relied to lift the people toward perfection.

Eli, a descendant of Aaron, was high priest, and a judge, being the predecessor of Samuel, the last of the judges. Now Eli had two sons who "were sons of Belial; they knew not the Lord."

Eli, being very old, "heard all that his sons did unto all Israel; and how they lay with the women that assembled at the door of the tabernacle. . . ." And Eli argued with them; "notwithstanding they harkened not unto the voice of their father."

Samuel succeeded Eli. He was not a descendant of Aaron, but became a judge, apparently, upon his own merits. But as a judge he did not constrain his sons any better than Eli had his, for "they took bribes, and perverted judgment." So the elders of Israel came to Samuel and said, "Give us a king to judge us." "And Samuel prayed unto the Lord," though he disliked the idea. Yet the result was inevitable. The king-

[1] Judges xvii, 6.

dom was set up, and the Mosaic society perished. Nothing was left of Mosaic optimism but the tradition. Also there was the Mosaic morality, and what that amounted to may best, perhaps, be judged by David, who was the most perfect flower of the perfection to which humanity was to attain under the Mosaic law, and has always stood for what was best in Mosaic optimism. David's morality is perhaps best illustrated by the story of Uriah the Hittite.

One day David saw Uriah's wife taking a bath on her housetop and took a fancy to her. The story is all told in the Second of Samuel. How David sent for her, took her into the palace, and murdered Uriah by sending him to Joab who commanded the army, and instructing Joab to set Uriah in the forefront of the hottest battle, and "retire ye from him that he may be smitten and die." And Uriah was killed.

Then came the famous parable by Nathan of the ewe lamb. "And David's anger was greatly kindled against the man; and he said to Nathan, As the Lord liveth, the man who hath done this thing shall surely die.

"And Nathan said to David, Thou art the man."

And Nathan threatened David with all kinds of disaster and even with death, and David was very repentant and "he fasted and lay all night upon the earth." But for all that, when assured that nothing worse was to happen to him than the loss of the son Bathsheba had borne him, David comforted Bathsheba. He by no means gave her up. On the contrary, "he went in unto her . . . and she bare him a son, and he called his name Solomon: and the Lord loved him."

Again the flesh had prevailed. And so it has always been with each new movement which has been stimulated by an idealism inspired by a belief that the spirit was capable of generating an impulse which would overcome the flesh and which could cause men to move toward perfection along any other path than the least resistant. And this because man is an automaton, and can move no otherwise. In this point of view nothing can be more instructive than to compare the Roman with the Mosaic civilization, for the Romans were a sternly practical people and worshipped force as Moses worshipped an ideal.

As Moses dreamed of realizing the divine consciousness on earth by introspection and by prayer, so the Romans supposed that they could attain to prosperity and happiness on earth by the development of superior physical force and the destruction of all rivals. Cato the Censor was the typical Roman landowner, the type of the class which built up the great vested interest in land which always moved and dominated Rome. He expressed the Roman ideal in his famous declaration in the Senate, when he gave his vote for the Third Punic War; *"Delenda est Carthago,"* Carthage must be destroyed. And Carthage was destroyed because to a Roman to destroy Carthage was a logical competitive necessity. Subsequently, the Romans took the next step in their social adjustment at home. They deified the energy which had destroyed Carthage. The incarnation of physical force became the head of the State; — the Emperor when living, the Divus, when dead. And this conception gained expression in the law. This godlike energy found vent in the Imperial will; "*Quod principi placuit, legis habet vigorem.*" [1]

Nothing could be more antagonistic to the Mosaic philosophy, which invoked the supernatural unity as authority for every police regulation. Moreover, the Romans carried out their principle relentlessly, to their own destruction. That great vested interest which had absorbed the land of Italy, and had erected the administrative entity which policed it, could not hold and cultivate its land profitably, in competition with other lands such as Egypt, North Africa, or Assyria, which were worked by a cheaper and more resistant people. Therefore the Roman landowners imported this competitive population from their homes, having first seized them as slaves, and cultivated their own Italian fields with them after the eviction of the original native peasants, who could not survive on the scanty nutriment on which the eastern races throve. [2]

---

[1] Inst. 1, 2, 6.

[2] I have dealt with this subject at length in my *Law of Civilization and Decay*, chapter II, to which I must refer the reader. More fully still in the French translation. "This unceasing emigration gradually changed the character of the rural population, and a similar alteration took place in the army. As early as the time of Cæsar, Italy was exhausted; his legions were mainly raised in Gaul, and as the native farmers sank into serfdom or slavery, and then at last vanished, recruits were drawn more and more from beyond the limits of the empire." I cannot repeat my arguments here, but I am not aware that they have been seriously controverted.

The Roman law, the *Romana lex*, was as gigantic, as original, and as comprehensive a structure as was the empire which gave to it expression. Modern European law is but a dilution thereof. The Roman law attained perfection, as I conceive, about the time of the Antonines, through the great jurists who then flourished. If one might name a particular moment at which so vast and complex a movement culminated, one would be tempted to suggest the reign of Hadrian, who appointed Salvius Julianus to draw up the *edictum perpetuum*, or permanent edict, in the year 132 A.D. Thenceforward the magistrate had to use his discretion only when the edict of Julianus did not apply.

I am not aware that any capital principle of municipal law has been evolved since that time, and the astonishing power of the Roman mind can only be appreciated when it is remembered that the whole of this colossal fabric was original. Modern European law has been only a servile copy. But, regard being had to the position of the emperor in relation to the people, and more especially in relation to the vast bureaucracy of Rome, which was the embodiment of the vested interest which was Rome itself, the adherence of Roman thought to the path of least resistance was absolute. "So far as the cravings of Stoicism found historical and political fulfilment, they did so in the sixty years of Hadrian and the Antonines, and so far again as an individual can embody the spirit of an age, its highest and most representative impersonation is unquestionably to be found in the person of Marcus

Antoninus. . . . Stoicism faced the whole problem of existence, and devoted as searching an investigation to processes of being and of thought, to physics and to dialectic, as to the moral problems presented by the emotions and the will." [1]

Such was stoicism, of which Marcus Aurelius was and still remains the foremost expression. He admitted that as emperor his first duty was to sacrifice himself for the public and he did his duty with a constancy which ultimately cost him his life. Among these duties was the great duty of naming his successor. The Roman Empire never became strictly hereditary. It hinged, as perhaps no other equally developed system ever hinged, upon the personality of the emperor, who incarnated the administrative bureaucracy which gave effect to the *Pax Romana* and the *Romana lex* from the Euphrates to the Atlantic and from Scotland to the Tropic of Cancer. Of all men Marcus Aurelius was the most conscientious and the most sincere, and he understood, as perhaps no other man in like position ever understood, the responsibility which impinged on him, to allow no private prevention to impose an unfit emperor upon the empire But Marcus had a son Commodus, who was nineteen when his father died, and who had already developed traits which caused foreboding. Nevertheless, Marcus associated Commodus with himself in the empire when Commodus was fourteen and Commodus at-

[1] *Marcus Aurelius Antoninus*, in English, by Gerald H. Rendall, Introduction, XXVII.

tained to absolute power when Marcus died. Subsequently, Commodus became the epitome of all that was basest and worst in a ruler. He was murdered by the treachery of Marcia, his favorite concubine, and the Senate decreed that "his body should be dragged with a hook into the stripping room of the gladiators, to satiate the public fury." [1]

From that day Rome entered upon the acute stage of her decline, and she did so very largely because Marcus Aurelius, the ideal stoic, was incapable of violating the great law of nature which impelled him to follow not reason, but the path of least resistance in choosing a successor; or, in other words, the instinct of heredity. Moreover, this instinct and not reason is or has been, among the strongest which operate upon men, and makes them automata. It is the basis upon which the family rests, and the family is the essence of social cohesion. Also the hereditary instinct has been the prime motor which has created constructive municipal jurisprudence and which has evolved religion.

With the death of Marcus Aurelius individual competition may be judged to have done its work, and presently, as the population changed its character under the stress thereof, a new phase opened: a phase which is marked, as such phases usually are, by victory in war. Marcus Aurelius died in 180 A.D. Substantially a century later, in 312, Constantine won the battle of the Milvian Bridge with his troops fighting under

[1] *Decline and Fall*, chap. IV.

the Labarum, a standard bearing a cross with the device "*In hoc signo vinces*"; By this sign conquer. Probably Constantine had himself scanty faith in the Labarum, but he speculated upon it as a means to arouse enthusiasm in his men. It served his purpose, and finding the step he had taken on the whole satisfactory, he followed it up by accepting baptism in 337 A.D.

From this time forward the theory of the possibility of securing divine or supernatural aid by various forms of incantation or prayer gained steadily in power for about eight centuries, until at length it became a passion and gave birth to a school of optimism, the most overwhelming and the most brilliant which the world has ever known and which evolved an age whose end we still await.

The Germans of the fourth century were a very simple race, who comprehended little of natural laws, and who therefore referred phenomena they did not understand to supernatural intervention. This intervention could only be controlled by priests, and thus the invasions caused a rapid rise in the influence of the sacred class. The power of every ecclesiastical organization has always rested on the miracle, and the clergy have always proved their divine commission as did Moses. This was eminently the case with the mediæval Church. At the outset Christianity was socialistic, and its spread among the poor was apparently caused by the pressure of servile competition; for the sect only became of enough importance to be persecuted under Nero, contemporaneously with the first signs of distress which appeared through the debasement of the denarius. But socialism was only a passing phase, and disappeared as the money value of the miracle rose, and brought wealth to the Church. Under the Emperor Decius, about 250, the magistrates thought the Christians opulent enough to use gold and silver vessels in their service, and by the fourth century the supernatural so possessed the popular mind that Constantine, as we have seen, not only allowed himself to be converted by a miracle, but used enchantment as an engine of war.

The action of the Milvian Bridge, fought in 312, by which Constantine established himself at Rome, was probably the point whence nature began to discriminate decisively against the vested interest of Western Europe. Capital had already abandoned Italy; Christianity was soon after officially recognized, and during the next century the priest began to rank with the soldier as a force in war.

Meanwhile, as the population sank into exhaustion, it yielded less and less revenue, the police deteriorated, and the guards became unable to protect the frontier. In 376, the Goths, hard pressed by the Huns, came to the Danube and implored to be taken as subjects by the emperor. After mature deliberation the Council of Valens granted the prayer, and some five hundred thousand Germans were cantoned in Mœsia. The intention of the government was to scatter this multitude through the provinces as *coloni*, or to draft them into the legions; but the detachment detailed to handle them was too feeble, the Goths mutinied, cut the guard to pieces, and having ravaged Thrace for two years, defeated and killed Valens at Hadrianople. In another generation the disorganization of the Roman army had become complete, and Alaric gave it its death-blow in his campaign of 410.

Alaric was not a Gothic king, but a barbarian deserter, who, in 392, was in the service of Theodosius. Subsequently he sometimes held imperial commands, and sometimes led bands of marauders on his own account, but was always in difficulty about his pay. Finally, in the revolution in which Stilicho was murdered, a corps of auxiliaries mutinied and chose him their general. Alleging that his arrears were unpaid, Alaric accepted the command, and with this army sacked Rome.

During the campaign the attitude of the Christians was more interesting than the strategy of the soldiers. Alaric was a robber, leading mutineers, and yet the orthodox historians did not condemn him. They did not condemn him because the sacred class instinctively loved the barbarians whom they could overawe, whereas they could make little impression on the materialistic intellect of the old centralized society. Under the empire the priests, like all other individuals, had to obey the power which paid the police; and as long as a revenue could be drawn from the provinces, the Christian hierarchy were subordinate to the monied bureaucracy who had the means to coerce them.

Yet only very slowly, as the empire disintegrated, did the theocratic idea take shape. As late as the ninth century the pope prostrated himself before Charlemagne, and did homage as to a Roman emperor.[1]

Saint Benedict founded Monte Cassino in 529, but centuries elapsed before the Benedictine order rose to power. The early convents were isolated and feeble, and much at the mercy of the laity, who invaded and debauched them. Abbots, like bishops, were often soldiers, who lived within the walls with their wives and children, their hawks, their hounds, and their men-at-arms; and it has been said that, in all France, Corbie and Fleury alone kept always something of their early discipline.

Only in the early years of the most lurid century of the Middle Ages, when decentralization culminated, and the imagination began to gain its fullest intensity, did the period of monastic consolidation open with the foundation of Cluny. In 910 William of Aquitaine draw a charter [2] which, so far as possible, provided for the complete independence of his new corporation. There was no episcopal visitation, and no interference with the election of the abbot. The monks were put directly under the protection of the pope, who was made their sole superior. John XI confirmed this charter by his bull of 932, and authorized the affiliation of all converts who wished to share in the reform.[3]

[1] Perz, *Annales Lauressenses*, I, 188.

[2] Bruel, *Recueil des Chartes de l'Abbaye de Cluny*, I, 124.

[3] *Bull. Clun.* p. 2, col. 1. Also Luchaire, *Manuel des Institutions Françaises*, 93, 95, where the authorities are collected.

The growth of Cluny was marvellous; by the twelfth century two thousand houses obeyed its rule, and its wealth was so great, and its buildings so vast, that in 1245 Innocent IV, the Emperor Baldwin, and Saint Louis were all lodged together within its walls, and with them all the attendant trains of prelates and nobles with their servants.

In the eleventh century no other force of equal energy existed. The monks were the most opulent, the ablest, and the best organized society in Europe, and their effect upon mankind was proportioned to their strength. They intuitively sought autocratic power, and during the centuries when nature favored them, they passed from triumph to triumph. They first seized upon the papacy and made it self-perpetuating; they then gave battle to the laity for the possession of the secular hierarchy, which had been under temporal control since the very foundation of the Church.

According to the picturesque legend, Bruno, Bishop of Toul, seduced by the flattery of courtiers and the allurements of ambition, accepted the tiara from the emperor, and set out upon his journey to Italy with a splendid retinue, and with his robe and crown. On his way he turned aside at Cluny, where Hildebrand was prior. Hildebrand, filled with the spirit of God, reproached him with having seized upon the seat of the vicar of Christ by force, and accepted the holy office from the sacrilegious hand of a layman. He exhorted Bruno to cast away his pomp, and to cross the Alps humbly as a pilgrim, assuring him that the priests and people of Rome would recognize him as their bishop, and elect him according to canonical forms. Then he would taste the joys of a pure conscience, having entered the fold of Christ as a shepherd and not as a robber. Inspired by these words, Bruno dismissed his train, and left the convent gate as a pilgrim. He walked barefoot, and when after two months of pious meditations he stood before Saint Peter's, he spoke to the people and told them it was their privilege to elect the pope, and since he had come unwillingly he would return again, were he not their choice.

He was answered with acclamations, and on February 2, 1049, he was enthroned as Leo IX. His first act was to make Hildebrand his minister.

The legend tells of the triumph of Cluny as no historical facts could do. Ten years later, in the reign of Nicholas II, the theocracy made itself self-perpetuating through the assumption of the election of the pope by the college of cardinals, and in 1073 Hildebrand, the incarnation of monasticism, was crowned under the name of Gregory VII.

With Hildebrand's election, war began. The Council of Rome, held in 1075, decreed that holy orders should not be recognized where investiture had been granted by a layman, and that princes guilty of conferring investiture should be excommunicated. The Council of the next year, which excommunicated the emperor, also enunciated the famous propositions of Baronius — the full expression of the theocratic idea. The priest had grown to be a god on earth.

"So strong in this confidence, for the honour and defence of your Church, on behalf of the omnipotent God, the Father, the Son, and the Holy Ghost, by your power and authority, I forbid the government of the German and Italian kingdoms, to King Henry, the son of the Emperor Henry, who, with unheard-of arrogance, has rebelled against your Church. I absolve all Christians from the oaths they have made or may make to him, and I forbid that any one should obey him as king." [1]

Henry marched on Italy, but in all European history there has been no drama more tremendous than the expiation of his sacrilege. To his soldiers the world was a vast space, peopled by those fantastic beings which are still seen on Gothic towers. These demons obeyed the monk of Rome, and his army, melting from about the emperor under a nameless horror, left him helpless.

Gregory lay like a magician in the fortress of Canossa: but he had no need of carnal weapons, for when the emperor reached the Alps he was almost alone. Then his imagination also took fire, the panic seized him, and he sued for mercy.

On August 7, 1106, Henry died at Liège, an outcast and a mendicant, and for five long years his body lay at the church door, an accursed thing which no man dared to bury.

Gregory prevailed because, to the understanding of the eleventh century, the evidence at hand indicated that he embodied in a high degree the infinite energy.

[1] Migne, CXLVIII, 790.

The eleventh century was intensely imaginative and the evidence which appealed to it was those phenomena of trance, hypnotism, and catalepsy which are as mysterious now as they were then, but whose effect was then to create an overpowering demand for miracle-working substances.   The sale of these substances gradually drew the larger portion of the wealth of the community into the hands of the clergy, and with wealth went temporal power.   No vested interest in any progressive community has probably ever been relatively stronger, for the Church found no difficulty, when embarrassed, in establishing and operating a thorough system for exterminating her critics.

Under such a pressure modern civilization must have sunk into some form of caste had the mediæval mind resembled any antecedent mind, but the middle age, though superficially imaginative, was fundamentally materialistic, as the history of the crusades showed.

At Canossa the laity conceded as a probable hypothesis that the Church could miraculously control nature; but they insisted that if the Church possessed such power, she must use that power for the common good.   Upon this point they would not compromise, nor would they permit delay.   During the chaos of the ninth century turmoil and violence reached a stage at which the aspirations of most Christians ended with self-preservation; but when the discovery and working of the Harz silver had brought with it some semblance of order, an intense yearning possessed both men and women to ameliorate their lot.   If relics could give protection against oppression, disease, famine, and death, then relics must be obtained, and, if the cross and the tomb were the most effective relics, then the cross and the tomb must be conquered at any cost. In the north of Europe especially, misery was so acute that the people gladly left their homes upon the slenderest promise of betterment, even following a vagrant like Peter the Hermit, who was neither soldier nor priest. There is a passage in William of Tyre which has been often quoted to explain a frenzy which is otherwise inexplicable, and in the old English of Caxton the words still glow with the same agony which makes lurid the supplication of the litany, — "From battle and murder, and from sudden death, Good Lord deliver us":

"Of charyte men spack not, debates, discordes, and warres were nyhe oueral, in suche wyse, that it seemed, that thende of the world was nyghe, by the signes that our lord sayth in the gospell, ffor pestylences and famynes were grete on therthe, ferdfulness of heuen, tremblyng of therthe in many places, and many other thinges there were that ought to fere the hertes of men. . . .

"The prynces and the barons brente and destroyed the contrees of theyr neyghbours, yf ony man had saved ony thynge in theyr kepyng, theyr owne lordes toke them and put them in prison and in greuous tormentis, for to take fro them suche as they had, in suche qyse that the chyldren of them that had ben riche men, men myght see them goo fro dore to dore, for to begge and gete theyr brede, and some deye for hungre and mesease." [1]

Throughout the eleventh century the excitement touching the virtues of the holy places in Judea grew, until Gregory VII, about the time of Canossa, perceived that a paroxysm was at hand, and considered leading it, but on the whole nothing is so suggestive of the latent scepticism of the age as the irresolution of the popes at this supreme moment. The laity were the pilgrims and the agitators. The kings sought the relics and took the cross; the clergy hung back. Robert, Duke of Normandy, for example, the father of William the Conqueror, died in 1035 from hardship at Nicæa when returning from Palestine, absorbed to the last in the relics which he had collected, but the popes stayed at home. Whatever they may have said in private, neither Hildebrand nor Victor nor Urban moved officially until they were swept forward by the torrent. They shunned responsibility for a war which they would have passionately promoted had they been sure of victory. The man who finally kindled the conflagration was a half-mad fanatic, a stranger to the hierarchy. No one knew the family of Peter the Hermit, or whence he came, but he certainly was not an ecclesiastic in good standing. Inflamed by fasting and penance, Peter followed the throng of pilgrims to Jerusalem, and there, wrought upon by what he saw, he sought the patriarch. Peter asked the patriarch if

[1] *Godeffroy of Bologne*, by William, Archbishop of Tyre, translated from the French by William Caxton, London, 1893, 21, 22.

nothing could be done to protect the pilgrims, and to retrieve the Holy Places. The patriarch replied, "Nothing, unless God will touch the heart of the western princes, and will send them to succor the Holy City." The patriarch did not propose meddling himself, nor did it occur to him that the pope should intervene. He took a rationalistic view of the Moslem military power. Peter, on the contrary, was logical, arguing from eleventh-century premises. If he could but receive a divine mandate, he would raise an invincible army. He prayed. His prayer was answered. One day while prostrated before the sepulchre he heard Christ charge him to announce in Europe that the appointed hour had come. Furnished with letters from the patriarch, Peter straightway embarked for Rome to obtain Urban's sanction for his design. Urban listened and gave a consent which he could not prudently have withheld, but he abstained from participating in the propaganda. In March, 1095, Urban called a Council at Piacenza, nominally to consider the deliverance of Jerusalem, and this Council was attended by thirty thousand impatient laymen, only waiting for the word to take the vow, but the pope did nothing. Even at Clermont eight months later, he showed a disposition to deal with private war, or church discipline, or with anything in fact rather than with the one engrossing question of the day, but this time there was no escape. A vast multitude of determined men filled not only Clermont but the adjacent towns and villages, even sleeping in the fields, al-

though the weather was bitterly cold, who demanded
to know the policy of the Church. Urban seems to
have procrastinated as long as he safely could, but, at
length, at the tenth session, he produced Peter on the
platform, clad as a pilgrim, and, after Peter had spoken,
he proclaimed the war. Urban declined, however, to
command the army. The only effective force which
marched was a body of laymen, organized and led by
laymen, who in 1099 carried Jerusalem by an ordinary
assault. In Jerusalem they found the cross and the
sepulchre, and with these relics as the foundation of
their power, the laity began an experiment which lasted
eighty-eight years, ending in 1187 with the battle of
Tiberias. At Tiberias the infidels defeated the Christians, captured their king and their cross, and shortly
afterward seized the tomb.

If the eleventh-century mind had been as rigid as
the Roman mind of the first century, mediæval civilization could hardly, after the collapse of the crusades,
have failed to degenerate as Roman civilization de-
generated after the defeat of Varus. Being more elas-
tic, it began, under an increased tension, to develop
new phases of thought. The effort was indeed prodigious and the absolute movement possibly slow, but a
change of intellectual attitude may be detected almost
contemporaneously with the fall of the Latin kingdom
in Palestine. It is doubtless true that the thirteenth
century was the century in which imaginative thought
reached its highest brilliancy, when Albertus Magnus
and Saint Thomas Aquinas taught, when Saint Fran-

cis and Saint Clara lived, and when Thomas of Celano wrote the *Dies Iræ*. It was then that Gothic architecture touched its climax in the cathedrals of Chartres and Amiens, of Bourges and of Paris; it was then also that Blanche of Castile ruled in France and that Saint Louis bought the crown of thorns, but it is equally true that the death of Saint Louis occurred in 1270, shortly after the thorough organization of the Inquisition by Innocent IV in 1252, and within two years or so of the production by Roger Bacon of his *Opus Majus*.

The establishment of the Inquisition is decisive, because it proves that sceptical thought had been spread far enough to goad the Church to general and systematic repression, while the *Opus Majus* is a scientific exposition of the method by which the sceptical mind is trained.

Roger Bacon was born about 1214, and going early to Oxford fell under the influence of the most liberal teachers in Europe, at whose head stood Robert Grosseteste, afterward Bishop of Lincoln. Bacon conceived a veneration for Grosseteste, and even for Adam de Marisco his disciple, and turning toward mathematics rather than toward metaphysics he eagerly applied himself, when he went to Paris, to astrology and alchemy, which were the progenitors of the modern exact sciences. In the thirteenth century a young man like Bacon could hardly stand alone, and Bacon joined the Franciscans, but before many years elapsed he embroiled himself with his superiors. His

friend, Grosseteste, died in 1253, the year after Innocent IV issued the bull *Ad extirpanda* establishing
the Inquisition, and Bacon felt the consequences.
The general of his order, Saint Bonaventura, withdrew him from Oxford where he was prominent, and
immured him in a Parisian convent, treating him rigorously, as Bacon intimated to Pope Clement IV.
There he remained, silenced, for some ten years, until
the election of Clement IV, in 1265. Bacon at once
wrote to Clement complaining of his imprisonment,
and deploring to the pope the plight into which scientific education had fallen. The pope replied directing Bacon to explain his views in a treatise, but did
not order his release. In response Bacon composed
the *Opus Majus.*

The *Opus Majus* deals among other things with ex-
perimental science, and in the introductory chapter to
the sixth part Bacon stated the theory of inductive
thought quite as lucidly as did Francis Bacon three
and a half centuries later in the *Novum Organum.*[1]

Clement died in 1268. The papacy remained vacant
for a couple of years, but in 1271 Gregory X came in

[1] Positis radicibus sapientiae Latinorum penes Linguas et Math-
ematicam et Perspectivam, nunc volo revolvere radices a parte Sci-
entiae Experimentalis, quia sine experientia nihil sufficienter
scire protest. Duo enim sunt modi cognoscendi, scilicet per argumentum et experimentum. Argumentum concludit et facit nos
concedere conclusionem, sed non certificat neque removet dubita-
tionem ut quiescat animus in intuitu veritatis, nisi eam inveniat via
experientiae; quia multi habent argumenta ad scibilia, sed quia non
habent experientiam, negligunt ea, nec vitant nociva nex perse-
quuntue bona. J. H. Bridges, *The Opus Majus of Roger Bacon* (Oxford, 1897), ii, 167.

on a conservative reaction. Bacon passed most of the rest of his life in prison, perhaps through his own ungovernable temper, and ostensibly his writings seem to have had little or no effect on his contemporaries, yet it is certain that he was not an isolated specimen of a type of intelligence which suddenly bloomed during the Reformation. Bacon constantly spoke of his friends, but his friends evidently did not share his temperament. The scientific man has seldom relished martyrdom, and Galileo's experience as late as 1633 shows what risks men of science ran who even indirectly attacked the vested interests of the Church. After the middle of the thirteenth century the danger was real enough to account for any degree of secretiveness, and a striking case of this timidity is related by Bacon himself. No one knows even the name of the man to whom Bacon referred as "Master Peter," but according to Bacon, "Master Peter" was the greatest and most original genius of the age, only he shunned publicity. The "Dominus experimentorum," as Bacon called him, lived in a safe retreat and devoted himself to mathematics, chemistry, and the mechanical arts with such success that, Bacon insisted, he could by his inventions have aided Saint Louis in his crusade more than his whole army.[1] Nor is this assertion altogether fantastic. Bacon understood the formula for gunpowder, and if Saint Louis had been provided with even a poor explosive he might have taken Cairo; not to speak of the terror which Greek fire always inspired.

[1] Émile Charles, *Roger Bacon. Sa vie et ses ouvrages,* 17.

Saint Louis met his decisive defeat in a naval battle fought in 1250, for the command of the Nile, by which he drew supplies from Damietta, and he met it, according to Matthew Paris, because his ships could not withstand Greek fire. Gunpowder, even in a very simple form, might have changed the fate of the war.

Scepticism touching the value of relics as a means for controlling nature was an effect of experiment, and, logically enough, scepticism advanced fastest among certain ecclesiastics who dealt in relics. For example, in 1248 Saint Louis undertook to invade Egypt in defence of the cross. Possibly Saint Louis may have been affected by economic considerations also touching the eastern trade, but his ostensible object was a crusade. The risk was very great, the cost enormous, and the responsibility the king assumed of the most serious kind. Nothing that he could do was left undone to ensure success. In 1249 he captured Damietta, and then stood in need of every pound of money and of every man that Christendom could raise; yet at this crisis the Church thought chiefly of making what it could in cash out of the war, the inference being that the hierarchy suspected that even if Saint Louis prevailed and occupied Jerusalem, little would be gained from an ecclesiastical standpoint. At all events, Matthew Paris has left an account, in his chronicle of the year 1249, of how the pope and the Franciscans preached this crusade, which is one of the most suggestive passages in thirteenth-century literature:

"About the same time, by command of the pope,

whom they obeyed implicitly, the Preacher and Minorite brethren diligently employed themselves in preaching; and to increase the devotion of the Christians, they went with great solemnity to the places where their preaching was previously indicated, and granted many days of indulgence to those who came to hear them. . . . Preaching on behalf of the cross, they bestowed that symbol on people of every age, sex and rank, whatever their property or worth, and even on sick men and women, and those who were deprived of strength by sickness or old age; and on the next day, or even directly afterwards, receiving it back from them, they absolved them from their vow of pilgrimage, for whatever sum they could obtain for the favour. What seemed unsuitable and absurd was, that not many days afterwards, Earl Richard collected all this money in his treasury, by the agency of Master Bernard, an Italian clerk, who gathered in the fruit; whereby no slight scandal arose in the Church of God, and amongst the people in general, and the devotion of the faithful evidently cooled." [1]

When the unfortunate Baldwin II became Emperor of the East in 1237, the relics of the passion were his best asset. In 1238, while Baldwin was in France trying to obtain aid, the French barons who carried on the government at Constantinople in his absence were obliged to pledge the crown of thorns to an Italian syndicate for 13,134 perpera, which Gibbon conjectures

[1] Matthew Paris, *English History*, translated by the Rev. J. A. Giles, II, 309.

to have been besants. Baldwin was notified of the pledge and urged to arrange for its redemption. He met with no difficulty. He confidently addressed himself to Saint Louis and Queen Blanche, and "Although the king felt keen displeasure at the deplorable condition of Constantinople, he was well pleased, nevertheless, with the opportunity of adorning France with the richest and most precious treasure in all Christendom." More especially with "a relic, and a sacred object which was not on the commercial market." [1]

Louis, beside paying the loan and the cost of transportation which came to two thousand French pounds (the mark being then coined into £2, 15 sous and 6 pence), made Baldwin a present of ten thousand pounds for acting as broker. Baldwin was so well contented with this sale which he closed in 1239, that a couple of years later he sent to Paris all the contents of his private chapel which had any value. Part of the treasure was a fragment of what purported to be the cross, but the authenticity of this relic was doubtful; there was beside, however, the baby linen, the spear-head, the sponge, and the chain, beside several miscellaneous articles like the rod of Moses.

Louis built the Sainte Chapelle at a cost of twenty thousand marks as a shrine in which to deposit them. The Sainte Chapelle has usually ranked as the most absolutely perfect specimen of mediæval religious architecture. [2]

[1] Du Cange, *Histoire de l'empire de Constantinople sous les empereurs Français*, edition de Buchon, I, 259.

[2] On this whole subject of the inter-relation of mediæval theology

When Saint Louis bought the Crown of Thorns from Baldwin in 1239, the commercial value of relics may, possibly, be said to have touched its highest point, but, in fact, the adoration of them had culminated with the collapse of the Second Crusade, and in another century and a half the market had decisively broken and the Reformation had already begun, with the advent of Wycliffe and the outbreak of Wat Tyler's Rebellion in 1381. For these social movements have always a common cause and reach a predetermined result.

In the eleventh century the convent of Cluny, for example, had an enormous and a perfectly justified hold upon the popular imagination, because of the sanctity and unselfishness of its abbots. Saint Hugh won his sainthood by a self-denial and effort which were impossible to ordinary men, but with Louis IX the penitential life had already lost its attractions and men like Arnold rapidly brought religion and religious thought into contempt. The famous Grosseteste, Bishop of Lincoln, born, probably, in 1175, died in 1253. He presided over the diocese of Lincoln at the precise moment when Saint Louis was building the Sainte Chapelle, but Grosseteste in 1250 denounced in a sermon at Lyons the scandals of the papal court with a ferocity which hardly was surpassed at any later day.

To attempt even an abstract of the thought of the English Reformation would lead too far, however fas-

with architecture and philosophy the reader is referred to *Mont-Saint-Michel et Chartres*, by Henry Adams, which is the most philosophical and thorough exposition of this subject which ever has been attempted.

cinating the subject might be. It must suffice to say
briefly that theology had little or nothing to do with it.
Wycliffe denounced the friars as lazy, profligate impostors, who wrung money from the poor which they
afterwards squandered in ways offensive to God, and
he would have stultified himself had he admitted, in
the same breath, that these reprobates, when united,
formed a divinely illuminated corporation, each member of which could and did work innumerable miracles
through the interposition of Christ. Ordinary miracles, indeed, could be tested by the senses, but the essence of transubstantiation was that it eluded the
senses. Thus nothing could be more convenient to
the government than to make this invisible and in-
tangible necromancy a test in capital cases for heresy.
Hence Wycliffe had no alternative but to deny transubstantiation, for nothing could be more insulting to
the intelligence than to adore a morsel of bread which
a priest held in his hand. The pretension of the priests
to make the flesh of Christ was, according to Wycliffe,
an impudent fraud, and their pretension to possess this
power was only an excuse by which they enforced their
claim to collect fees, and what amounted to extortionate taxes, from the people.[1] But, in the main,
no dogma, however incomprehensible, ever troubled
Protestants, as a class. They easily accepted the Trinity, the double procession, or the Holy Ghost itself,
though no one had the slightest notion what the Holy

[1] Nowhere, perhaps, does Wycliffe express himself more strongly
on this subject than in a little tract called *The Wicket*, written in
English, which he issued for popular consumption about this time.

Ghost might be. Wycliffe roundly declared in the first paragraph of his confession [1] that the body of Christ which was crucified was truly and really in the consecrated host, and Huss, who inherited the Wycliffian tradition, answered before the Council of Constance, "Verily, I do think that the body of Christ is really and totally in the sacrament of the altar, which was born of the Virgin Mary, suffered, died, and rose again, and sitteth on the right hand of God the Father Almighty." [2] That which has rent society in twain and has caused blood to flow like water, has never been abstract opinions, but that economic competition either between states or classes, that lust for power and wealth, which makes a vested interest. Thus by 1382 the eucharist had come to represent to the privileged classes power and wealth, and they would have repudiated Wycliffe even had they felt strong enough to support him. But they were threatened by an adversary equally formidable with heresy in the person of the villeins whom the constantly increasing momentum of the time had raised into a position in which they undertook to compete for the ownership of the land which they still tilled as technical serfs.

[1] Fasciculi Zizaniorum, 115.
[2] Foxe, *Acts and Monuments*, III, 452.

CHAPTER III.

Now the courts may say what they will in support of the vested interests, for to support vested interests is what lawyers are paid for and what courts are made for. Only, unhappily, in the process of argument courts and lawyers have caused blood to flow copiously, for in spite of all that can be said to the contrary, men have practically proved that they do own all the property they can defend, all the courts in Christendom notwithstanding, and this is an issue of physical force and not at all of words or of parchments. And so it proved to be in England in the fourteenth and fifteenth centuries, alike in Church and State. It was a matter of rather slow development. After the conquest villeins could neither in fact nor theory acquire or hold property as against their lord, and the class of landlords stretched upwards from the owner of a knight's fee to the king on his throne, who was the chief landlord of all, but by so narrow a margin that he often had enough to do to maintain some vestige of sovereignty. So, to help himself, it came to pass that the king intrigued with the serfs against their restive masters, and the abler the king, the more he intrigued, like Henry I, until the villeins gained very substantial advantages. Thus it was that toward 1215, or pretty nearly contemporaneously with the epoch when men like Grosseteste began to show restlessness under the extortionate corruption of the Church, the villein was discovered to be able to defend his claim to some portion of the increment in the value of the land which he tilled and which was due to his labor: and this title the manorial courts recognized, because they could not help it, as a sort of tenant right, calling it a customary tenancy by base service. A century later these services in kind had been pretty frequently commuted into a fixed rent paid in money, and the serf had become a freeman, and a rather formidable freeman, too. For it was largely from among these technical serfs that Edward III recruited the infantry who formed his line at Crécy in 1346, and the archers of Crécy were not exactly the sort of men who take kindly to eviction, to say nothing of slavery. As no one meddled much with the villeins before 1349, all went well until after Crécy, but in 1348 the Black Death ravaged England, and so many laborers died that the cost of farming property by hired hands exceeded the value of the rent which the villeins paid. Then the landlords, under the usual reactionary and dangerous legal advice, tried coercion. Their first experiment was the famous Statute of Laborers, which fixed wages at the rates which prevailed in 1347, but as this statute accomplished nothing the landlords repudiated their contracts, and undertook to force their villeins to render their ancient customary services. Though the lay landlords were often hard masters, the ecclesiastics, especially the monks, were harder still, and the ecclesiastics were served by lawyers of their own cloth, whose sharp practice became proverbial. Thus the law declined to recognize rights in property existing in fact, with the inevitable result of the peasant rising in 1381, known as Wat Tyler's Rebellion. Popular rage perfectly logically ran highest against the monks and the lawyers. Both the Archbishop of Canterbury, Simon de Sudbury, the Lord Chancellor, and the Chief Justice were killed, and the insurgents wished to kill, as Capgrave has related, "all the men that had learned ony law." Finally the rebellion was suppressed, chiefly by the duplicity of Richard II. Richard promised the people, by written charters, a permanent tenure as freemen at reasonable rents, and so induced them to go home with his charters in their hands; but they were no sooner gone than vengeance began. Though Richard had been at the peasants' mercy, who might have killed him had they wished, punitive expeditions were sent in various directions. One was led by Richard himself, who travelled with Tresilian, the new Chief Justice, the man who afterward was himself hanged at Tyburn. Tresilian worked so well that he is said to have strung up a dozen villeins to a single beam in Chelmsford because he had no time to have them executed regularly. Stubbs has estimated that seven thousand victims hardly satisfied the landlords' sense of outraged justice. What concerns us, chiefly, is that this repression, however savage, failed altogether to bring tranquillity. After 1381 a full century of social chaos supervened, merging at times into actual civil war, until, in 1485, Henry Tudor came in after his victory at Bosworth, pledged to destroy the whole reactionary class which incarnated feudalism. For the feudal soldier was neither flexible nor astute, and allowed himself to be caught between the upper and the nether millstone. While industrial and commercial capital had been increasing in the towns, capitalistic methods of farming had invaded the country, and, as police improved, private and predatory warfare, as a business, could no longer be made to pay. The importance of a feudal noble lay in the body of retainers who followed his banner, and therefore the feudal tendency always was to overcharge the estate with military expenditure. Hence, to protect themselves from creditors, the landlords passed the Statute *De Donis* [1] which made entails inalienable. Toward the end of the Wars of the Roses, however, the pressure for money, which could only be raised by pledging their land, became too strong for the feudal aristocracy. Edward IV, who was a very able man, perceived, pretty early in his reign, that his class could not maintain themselves unless their land were put upon a commercial basis. Therefore he encouraged the judges, in the collusive litigation known to us as Taltarum's Case, decided in 1472, to set aside the Statute *De Donis*, by the fiction of the Common Recovery. The concession, even so, came too late. The combination against them had grown too strong for the soldiers to resist. Other classes evolved by competition wanted their property, and these made Henry Tudor king of England to seize it for them.

[1] 13 Edw. I, c. 1 (A.D. 1284).

Henry's work was simple enough. After Bosworth, with a competent police force at hand to execute process, he had only to organize a political court, and to ruin by confiscatory fines all the families strong enough, or rash enough, to maintain garrisoned houses. So Henry remodelled the Star Chamber, in 1486,[1] to deal with the martial gentry, and before long a new type of intelligence possessed the kingdom.

The feudal soldiers being disposed of, it remained to evict the monks, who were thus left without their natural defenders. No matter of faith was involved. Henry VIII boasted that in doctrine he was as orthodox as the pope. There was, however, an enormous monastic landed property to be redistributed This was confiscated, and appropriated, not to public purposes, but, as usually happens in revolutions, to the use of the astutest of the revolutionists. Among these, John Russell, afterward Earl of Bedford, stood preeminent. Russell had no particular pedigree or genius, save the acquisitive genius, but he made himself useful to Henry in such judicial murders as that of Richard Whiting, Abbot of Glastonbury. He received in payment, among much else, Woburn Abbey, which has since remained the Bedford country seat, and Covent Garden or Convent Garden, one of the most valuable parcels of real estate in London. Covent Garden the present duke recently sold, anticipating, perhaps, some such legislation as ruined the monks and made his ancestor's fortune. As for the monks whom Henry

[1] 3 Henry 7, C 1.

evicted, they wandered forth from their homes beggars, and Henry hanged all of them whom he could catch as vagrants. How many perished as counterpoise for the peasant massacres and Lollard burnings of the foregoing two centuries can never be known, nor to us is it material. What is essential to mark, from the legal standpoint, is that while this long and bloody revolution, of one hundred and fifty years, displaced a favored class and confiscated its property, it raised up in their stead another class of land monopolists, rather more greedy and certainly quite as cruel as those whom they superseded. Also, in spite of all opposition, labor did make good its claim to participate more or less fully in the ownership of the property it cultivated, for while the holding of the ancient villein grew to be well recognized in the royal courts as a copyhold estate, villeinage itself disappeared.

Yet, unless I profoundly err, in the revolution of the sixteenth century, the law somewhat conspicuously failed in its function of moderating competition, for I am persuaded that competition of another kind sharpened, and shortly caused a second civil war bloodier than the Wars of the Roses.

Fifteen years before the convents were seized, Sir Thomas More wrote *Utopia*, in whose opening chapter More has given an account of a dinner at Cardinal Morton's, who, by the way, presided in the Star Chamber. At this dinner one of the cardinal's guests reflected on the thievish propensities of Englishmen, who were to be found throughout the country hanged as felons, sometimes twenty together on a single gallows. More protested that this was not the fault of the poor who were hanged, but of rich land monopolists, who pastured sheep and left no fields for tillage. According to More, these capitalists plucked down houses and even towns, leaving nothing but the church for a sheep-house, so that "by covin and fraud, or by violent oppression, . . . or by wrongs and injuries," the husbandmen "be thrust out of their own," and, "must needs depart away, poor, wretched souls, men, women, husbands, wives, fatherless children, widows." The dissolution of the convents accelerated the process, and more and more of the weaker yeomanry were ruined and evicted. It is demonstrated that the pauperization of the feebler rural population went on apace by the passage of poor-laws under Elizabeth, which, in the Middle Ages, had not been needed and, therefore, were unknown. This movement, described by More, was the beginning of the system of enclosing common lands which afterward wrought havoc among the English yeomen, and which, I suppose, contributed more than any other single cause to the Great Rebellion of the seventeenth century. In the mediæval village the owners of small farms enjoyed certain rights in the common land of the community, affording them pasturage for their cattle and the like, rights without which small farming could not be made profitable. These commons the land monopolists appropriated, sometimes giving some shadow of compensation, sometimes by undisguised force, but on the whole compensation amounted to so little that the enclosure of the commons must rank as confiscation. Also this seizure of property would doubtless have caused a convulsion as lasting as that which followed the insurrection of 1381, or as did actually occur in Ireland, had it not been for an unparalleled contemporaneous territorial and industrial expansion. Thorold Rogers always insisted that between 1563, the year of the passage of the Statute of Apprentices,[1] and 1824, a regular conspiracy existed between the lawyers "and the parties interested in its success . . . to cheat the English workman of his wages, . . . and to degrade him to irremediable poverty." [2] Certainly the land monopolists resorted to strong measures to accumulate land, for something like six hundred and fifty Enclosure Acts were passed between 1760, the opening of the Industrial Revolution, and 1774, the outbreak of the American War. But without insisting on Rogers's view, it is not denied that the weakest of the small yeomen sank into utter misery, becoming paupers or worse. On the other hand, of those stronger some emigrated to America, others, who were among the ablest and the boldest, sought fortune as adventurers over the whole earth, and, like the grandfather of Chatham, brought home from India as smugglers or even as pirates, diamonds to be sold to kings for their crowns, or, like Clive, became the greatest generals and administrators of the nation. Probably, however, by far the majority of those who were of

[1] 5 Eliz. c. 4.   [2] *Work and Wages*, 398.

average capacity found compensation for the confiscated commons in domestic industry, owning their houses with lots of land and the tools of their trade. Defoe has left a charming description of the region about Halifax in Yorkshire, toward the year 1730, where he found the whole population busy, prosperous, healthy, and, in the main, self-sufficing. He did not see a beggar or an idle person in the whole country. So, favored by circumstances, the landed oligarchy met with no effective resistance after the death of Cromwell, and achieved what amounted to being autocratic power in 1688. Their great triumph was the conversion of the House of Commons into their own personal property, about the beginning of the eighteenth century, with all the guaranties of law. In the Middle Ages the chief towns of England had been summoned by the king to send burgesses to Westminster to grant him money, but as time elapsed the Commons acquired influence and, in 1642, became dominant. Then, after the Restoration, the landlords conceived the idea of appropriating the right of representation, as they had appropriated and were appropriating the common lands. Lord John Russell one day observed in the House of Commons that the burgesses were originally chosen from among the inhabitants of the towns they represented, but that, in the reign of Anne, the landlords, to depress the shipping interest, opened the borough representation to all qualified persons without regard to domicile.[1] Lord John was mistaken

[1] 36 Hansard, Third Series, 548.

in his date, for the change occurred earlier, but he described correctly enough the persistent animus of the landlords. An important part of their policy turned on the so-called Determination Acts of 1696 and 1729, which defined the franchises and which had the effect of confirming the titles of patrons to borough property,[1] thus making a seat in the House of Commons an incorporeal hereditament fully recognized by law. On this point so high an authority as Lord Eldon was emphatic.[2] By the time of the American War the oligarchy had become so narrow that one hundred and fifty-four peers and commoners returned three hundred and seven members, or much more than a majority of the House as then organized.[3] With the privileged class reduced to these contemptible numbers a catastrophe necessarily followed. Almost impregnable as the position of the oligarchy appeared, it yet had its vulnerable point. As Burke told the Duke of Portland, a duke's power did not come from his title, but from his wealth, and the landlords' wealth rested on their ability to draw a double rent from their estates, one rent for themselves, and another to provide for the farmer to whom they let their acres. Evidently British land could not bear this burden if brought in competition with other equally good land that paid only a single rent, and from a pretty early period the landlords appear to have been alive to this fact. Nevertheless, ocean freights afforded a fair protection, and as long as the

[1] Porritt, *Unreformed House of Commons*, i, 9, *et seq.*
[2] 12 Hansard, Third Series, 396.
[3] Grey's motion for Reform, 30 *Parl. Hist.* 795 (A.D. 1793).

industrial population remained tolerably self-support-ing, England rather tended to export than to import grain. But toward 1760 advances in applied science profoundly modified the equilibrium of English so-ciety. The new inventions, stimulated by steam, could only be utilized by costly machinery installed in large factories, which none but considerable capi-talists could build, but once in operation the product of these factories undersold domestic labor, and ruined and evicted the population of whole regions like Hali-fax. These unfortunate laborers were thrust in abject destitution into filthy and dark alleys in cities, where they herded in masses, in misery and crime. In con-sequence grain rose in value, so much so that in 1766 prayers were offered touching its price. Thence-forward England imported largely from America, and in 1773 Parliament was constrained to reduce the duty on wheat to a point lower than the gentry conceded again, until the total repeal of the Corn Laws in 1846.[1] The situation was well understood in London. Burke, Governor Pownall, and others ex-plained it in Parliament, while Chatham implored the landlords not to alienate America, which they could not, he told them, conquer, but which gave them a necessary market, — a market as he aptly said, both of supply and demand. And Chatham was right, for America not only supplied the grain to feed English labor, but bought from England at least one third of all her surplus manufactures.

[1] John Morley, *The Life of Richard Cobden*, 167, note 5.

This brings us to the eighteenth century, which directly concerns us, because the religious superstition, which had previously caused men to seek in a conscious supreme energy the effective motor in human affairs, had waned, and the problem presented was reduced to the operation of that acceleration of movement by the progress of applied science which always has been, and always must be, the prime cause of the quickening of economic competition either as between communities or as between individuals. And this is the capital phenomenon of civilization. For it is now generally admitted that war is nothing but economic competition in its acutest form. When competition reaches a certain intensity it kindles into war or revolution, precisely as when iron is raised to a certain heat it kindles into flame. And, for the purposes of illustration, possibly the best method of showing how competition was quickened, and how it affected adjacent communities during the eighteenth century, is to take navigation, not only because navigation was much improved during the first three quarters of that period, but because both England and France competed for control in America by means of ships. It suffices to mention, very succinctly, a few of the more salient advances which were then made.

Toward 1761 John Harrison produced the chronometer, by which longitude could be determined at sea, making the ship independent in all parts of the world. At the same time more ingenious rigging increased her power of working to windward. With such advantages

Captain Cook became a mighty discoverer both in the southern and western oceans, charted New Zealand and much else, and more important than all, in 1759 he surveyed the Saint Lawrence and piloted ships up the river, of which he had established the channel. Speaking of Cook naturally leads to the solution of the problem of the transportation of men, sailors, soldiers, and emigrants, on long voyages, thereby making population fluid. Cook, in his famous report, read before the Royal Society in March, 1776, after his second voyage, established forever the hygienic principles by observing which a ship's company may safely be kept at sea for any length of time. Previously there had always been a very high mortality from scurvy and kindred diseases, which had, of course, operated as a very serious check to human movement. On land the same class of phenomena were even more marked. In England the Industrial Revolution is usually held to date from 1760, and, by common consent, the Industrial Revolution is attributed altogether to applied science, or, in other words, to mechanical inventions. In 1760 the flying-shuttle appeared, and coal began to replace wood for smelting. In 1764 Hargreaves invented the spinning-jenny; in 1779 Crompton contrived the mule; and in 1768 Watt brought the steam-engine to maturity. In 1761 the first boat-load of coals sailed over the Barton viaduct, which James Brindley built for the Duke of Bridgewater's canal, to connect Worsley with Manchester, thus laying the foundation of British inland navigation, which before the end of the century had covered England; while John Metcalf, the blind roadbuilder, began his lifework in 1765. He was destined to improve English highways, which up to that time had been mostly impossible for wheeled traffic. In France the same advance went on. Arthur Young described the impression made on him in 1789 by the magnificence of the French roads which had been built since the administration of Colbert, as well as by the canal which connected the Mediterranean with the Atlantic.

In the midst of this activity Washington grew up. Washington was a born soldier, engineer, and surveyor with the topographical instinct peculiar to that temperament. As early as 1748 he was chosen by Lord Fairfax, who recognized his ability, though only sixteen years old, to survey his vast estate west of the Blue Ridge, which was then a wilderness. He spent three years in this work and did it well. In 1753 Governor Dinwiddie sent Washington on a mission to the French commander on the Ohio, to warn him to cease trespassing on English territory, a mission which Washington fulfilled, under considerable hardship and some peril, with eminent success. Thus early, for he was then only twenty-two, Washington gained that thorough understanding of the North American river system which enabled him, many years afterward, to construct the Republic of the United States upon the lines of least resistant intercommunication. And Washington's conception of the problem and his solution thereof were, in substance, this:

The American continent, west of the mountains and south of the Great Lakes, is traversed in all directions by the Mississippi and its tributaries, but we may confine our attention to two systems of watercourses, the one to the west, forming by the Wisconsin and the main arm of the Mississippi, a thoroughfare from Lake Michigan to the Gulf; and the other by French Creek and the Allegheny, broken only by one easy portage, affording a perfect means of access to the Ohio, a river which has always operated as the line of cleavage between our northern and southern States. The French starting from Quebec floated from Lake Erie down the Allegheny to Pittsburgh, the English ascended the Potomac to Cumberland, and thence, following the most practicable watercourses, advanced on the French position at the junction of the Allegheny and the Monongahela. There Washington met and fought them in 1754, and ever after Washington maintained that the only method by which a stable union among the colonies could be secured was by a main trunk system of transportation along the line of the Ohio and the Potomac. This was to be his canal which should bind north and south, east and west, together by a common interest, and which should carry the produce of the west, north, and south, to the Atlantic coast, where it should be discharged at the head of deep-water navigation, and which should thus stimulate industry adjacent to the spot he chose for the Federal City, or, in our language, for the City of Washington. Thus the capital of the United States was to become the capital of a true nation, not as a political compromise, but because it lay at the central point of a community made cohesive by a social circulation which should build it up, in his own words, into a capital, or national heart, if not "as large as London, yet of a magnitude inferior to few others in Europe." [1] Maryland and Virginia abounded, as Washington well knew, in coal and iron. His canal passing through this region would stimulate industry, and these States would thus become the focus of exchanges. Manufacturing is incompatible with slavery, hence slavery would gradually and peacefully disappear, and the extremities of the Union would be drawn together at what he described as "the great emporium of the United States." To crown all, a national university was to make this emporium powerful in collective thought.

Doubtless Grenville and Townshend had not considered the American problem as maturely as had Washington, but nevertheless, most well-informed persons now agree that Englishmen in 1763 were quite alive to the advantages which would accrue to Great Britain, by holding in absolute control a rich but incoherent body of colonies whose administrative centre lay in England, and were as anxious that London should serve as the heart of America as Washington was that America should have its heart on the Potomac.

Accordingly, England attempted to isolate Massachusetts and pressed an attack on her with energy, before the whole thirteen colonies should be able to draw

[1] Washington to Mrs. Fairfax, 16 May, 1798; Sparks, xi, 233.

to a unity. On the other hand, Washington, and most sensible Americans, resisted this attack as resolutely as might be under such disadvantages, not wishing for independence, but hoping for some compromise like that which Great Britain has since effected with her remaining colonies. The situation, however, admitted of no peaceful adjustment, chiefly because the imbecility of American administration induced by her incapacity for collective thought, was so manifest, that Englishmen could not believe that such a society could wage a successful war. Nor could America have done so alone. She owed her ultimate victory altogether to Washington and France.

It would occupy too much space for me to undertake to analyze, even superficially, the process by which, after the Seven Years' War, competition between America and England reached an intensity which kindled the American Revolution, but, shortly stated, the economic tension arose thus: As England was then organized, the estates of the English landlords had to pay two rents, one to the landlord himself, the other to the farmer who leased his land, and this it could not do were it brought into direct competition with equally good land which paid but one profit, and which was not burdened by an excessive cost of transportation in reaching its market. As freights between England and America fell because of improved shipping and the greater safety of the seas, England had to have protection for her food and she proposed to get it thus: If competing Continental exports could be excluded from America, and, at the same time, Americans could be prevented from manufacturing for themselves, the colonists might be constrained to take what they needed from England, at prices which would enable labor to buy food at a rate which would yield the double profit, and thus America could be made to pay the cost of supporting the landlords. As Cobden afterward observed, the fortunes of England have turned on American competition. A part of these fortunes were represented by the Parliamentary boroughs which the landlords owned and which were confiscated by the Reform Bill, and these boroughs were held by Lord Eldon to be incorporeal hereditaments: as truly a part of the private property of the gentry who owned them as church advowsons, or the like. And the gentry held to their law-making power which gave them such a privilege with a tenacity which precipitated two wars before they yielded; but this was naught compared to the social convulsion which rent France, when a population which had been for centuries restrained from free domestic movement, burst its bonds and insisted on levelling the barriers which had immobilized it.

The story of the French Revolution is too familiar to need recapitulation here: indeed, I have already dealt with it in my *Social Revolutions;* but the effects of that convulsion are only now beginning to appear, and these effects, without the shadow of a doubt, have been in their ultimate development the occasion of that great war whose conclusion we still await.

France, in 1792, having passed into a revolution
which threatened the vested interests of Prussia, was
attacked by Prussia, who was defeated at Valmy.
Presently, France retaliated, under Napoleon, invaded Prussia, crushed her army at Jena, in 1807, dis-
membered the kingdom and imposed on her many
hardships. To obtain their freedom the Prussians
found it needful to reorganize their social system from
top to bottom, for this social system had descended
from Frederic William, the Great Elector of Brandenburg (1640–1688), and from Frederic the Great (1740–
1786), and was effete and incapable of meeting the
French onset, which amounted, in substance, to a
quickened competition. Accordingly, the new Prussian constitution, conceived by Stein, put the community upon a relatively democratic and highly developed educational basis. By the Emancipating Edict
of 1807, the peasantry came into possession of their
land, while, chiefly through the impulsion of Scharnhorst, who was the first chief of staff of the modern army,
the country adopted universal military service, which
proved to be popular throughout all ranks. Previous
to Scharnhorst, under Frederic the Great, the qualification of an officer had been birth. Scharnhorst defined it as education, gallantry, and intelligence. Simi-
larly, Gneisenau's conception of a possible Prussian
supremacy lay in its army, its science, and its administration. But the civil service was intended to incar-
nate science, and was the product of the modernized
university, exemplified in the University of Berlin or-

ganized by William von Humboldt. Herein lay the initial advantage which Germany gained over England, an advantage which she long maintained. And the advantage lay in this: Germany conceived a system of technical education matured and put in operation by the State. Hence, so far as in human affairs such things are possible, the intelligence of Germans was liberated from the incubus of vested interests, who always seek to use education to advance themselves. It was so in England. The English entrusted education to the Church, and the Church was, by the necessity of its being, reactionary and hostile to science, whereas the army, in the main, was treated in England as a social function, and the officers, speaking generally, were not technically specially educated at all. Hence, in foreign countries, but especially in Germany which was destined to be ultimately England's great competitor, England laid herself open to rather more than a suspicion of weakness, and indeed, when it came to a test, England found herself standing, for several years of war, at a considerable disadvantage because of the lack of education in those departments wherein Germany had, by the attack of France, been forced to make herself proficient. This any one may see for himself by reading the addresses of Fichte to the German nation, delivered in 1807 and 1808, when Berlin was still occupied by the French. In fine, it was with Prussia a question of competition, brought to its ultimate tension by war. Prussia had no alternative as a conquered land but to radically accelerate her momentum, or perish. And so, at the present day, it may not improbably be with us. Competition must grow intenser.

With England the situation in 1800 was very different. It was less strenuous. Nothing is more notable in England than to observe how, after the Industrial Revolution began, there was practically no means by which a poor man could get an education, save by educating himself. For instance, in February 1815, four months before Waterloo, George Stephenson took out a patent for the locomotive engine which was to revolutionize the world. But George Stephenson was a common laborer in the mines, who had no state instruction available, nor had he even any private institution at hand in which the workmen whom he employed in practical construction could be taught. He and his son Robert, had to organize instruction for themselves and their employees independently. So it was even with a man like Faraday, who began life as an errand boy, and later on who actually went abroad as a sort of valet to Sir Humphry Davy. Davy himself was a self-made man. In short, England, as a community, did little or nothing by education for those who had no means, and but little to draw any one toward science. It was at this precise moment that Germany was cast into the furnace of modern competition with England, who had, because of a series of causes, chiefly geographical, topographical, and mineralogical, about a century the start of her. Against this advantage Germany had to rely exclusively upon civil and military education. At first this competition by Germany took a military complexion, and very rapidly wrought the complete consolidation of Germany by the Austrian and the French wars. But this phase presently passed, and after the French campaign of 1870 the purely economic aspect of the situation developed more strenuously still, so much so that intelligent observers, among whom Lord Roberts was conspicuous, perceived quite early in the present century that the heat generated in the conflict must, probably, soon engender war. Nor could it either theoretically or practically have been otherwise, for the relations between the two countries had reached a point where they generated a friction which caused incandescence automatically. And, moreover, the inflammable material fit for combustion was, especially in Germany, present in quantity. From the time of Fichte and Scharnhorst downward to the end of the century, the whole nation had learned, as a sort of gospel, that the German education produced a most superior engine of economic competition, whereas the slack education and frivolous amusements of English civil and military life alike, had gradually created a society apt to crumble. And it is only needful for any person who has the curiosity, to glance at the light literature of the Victorian age, which deals with the army, to see how dominant a part such an amusement as hunting played in the life of the younger officers, especially in the fashionable regiments, to be impressed with the soundness of much of this German criticism.

Assuming, then, for the sake of argument, that these historical premises are sound, I proceed to consider how they bear on our prospective civilization.

This is eminently a scientific age, and yet the scientific mind, as it is now produced among us, is not without tendencies calculated to cause uneasiness to those a little conversant with history or philosophy. For whereas no one in these days would dream of utilizing prayer, as did Moses or Saint Hugh, as a mechanical energy, nevertheless the search for a universal prime motor goes on unabated, and yet it accomplishes nothing to the purpose. On the contrary, the effect is one which could neither be expected nor desired. Instead of being an aid to social coördination, it stimulates disintegration to a high degree as the war has shown. It has stimulated disintegration in two ways. First, it has enormously quickened physical movement, which has already been discussed, and secondly, it has stimulated the rapidity with which thought is diffused. The average human being can only absorb and assimilate safely new forms of thought when given enough time for digestion, as if he were assimilating food. If he be plied with new thought too rapidly he fails to digest. He has a surfeit, serious in proportion to its enormity. That is to say, his power of drawing correct conclusions from the premises submitted to him fails, and we have all sorts of crude experiments in sociology attempted, which end in that form of chaos which we call a violent revolution. The ordinary result is infinite waste fomented by fallacious hopes; in a word, financial disaster, supplemented usually by loss of life. The experience is an old one, and the result is almost invariable.

For example, during the Middle Ages, men like Saint Hugh and Peter the Venerable, and, most of all, Saint Francis, possessed by dreams of attaining to perfection, by leading lives of inimitable purity, self-devotion, and asceticism, inspired the community about them with the conviction that they could work miracles. They thereby, as a reward, drew to the Church they served what amounted to being, considering the age they lived in, boundless wealth. But the effect of this economic phenomenon was far from what they had hoped or expected. Instead of raising the moral standard of men to a point where all the world would be improved, they so debased the hierarchy, by making money the standard of ambition within it, that, as a whole, the priesthood accepted, without any effective protest, the fires of the Council of Constance which consumed Huss, and the abominations of the Borgias at Rome. Perfectly logically, as a corollary to this orgy of crime and bestiality, the wars of the Reformation swept away many, many thousands of human beings, wasted half of Europe, and only served to demonstrate the futility of ideals.

And so it was with the Puritans, who were themselves the children of the revolt against social corruption. They fondly believed that a new era was to be ushered in by the rule of the Cromwellian saints. What the Cromwellian saints did in truth usher in, was the carnival of debauchery of Charles II, in its turn to be succeeded by the capitalistic competitive age which we have known, and which has abutted in the recent war.

Man can never hope to change his physical necessities, and therefore his moral nature must always remain the same in essence, if not in form. As Washington truly said, "The motives which predominate most in human affairs are self-love and self-interest," and "nothing binds one country or one state to another but interest."

If, then, it be true, that man is an automatic animal moving always along the paths of least resistance toward predetermined ends, it cannot fail to be useful to us in the present emergency to mark, as distinctly as we can, the causes which impelled Germany, at a certain point in her career, to choose the paths which led to her destruction rather than those which, at the first blush, promised as well, and which seemed to be equally as easy and alluring. And we may possibly, by this process, expose certain phenomena which may profit us, since such an examination may help us to estimate what avenues are like to prove ultimately the least resistant.

Throughout the Middle Ages North Germany, which is the region whereof Berlin is the capital, enjoyed relatively little prosperity, because Brandenburg, for example, lay beyond the zone of those main trade routes which, before the advent of railways, served as the arteries of the eastern trade.   Not until after the opening of the Industrial Revolution in England, did that condition alter. Nor even then did a change come rapidly because of the inertia of the Russian people. Nevertheless, as the Russian railway system developed, Berlin one day found herself standing, as it were, at the apex of a vast triangle whose boundaries are, roughly, indicated by the position of Berlin itself, Petersburg, Warsaw, Moscow, Kiev, and the Ukraine. Beyond Berlin the stream of traffic flowed to Hamburg and thence found vent in America, as a terminus. Great Britain, more especially, demanded food, and food passed by sea from Odessa. Hence Russia served as a natural base for Germany, taking German manufactures and offering to Germany a reservoir capable of absorbing her redundant population. Thus it had long been obvious that intimate relations with Russia were of prime importance to Germany since all the world could perceive that the monied interests of Russia must more and more fall into German hands, because of the intellectual limitations of the Russians. Also pacification to the eastward always was an integral part of Bismarck's policy. Notwithstanding which other influences conflicted with, and ultimately overbalanced, this eastern trend in Germany.

For many thousand years before written history began, the economic capital of the world, the seat for the time being of opulence and of splendor, and at once the admiration and the envy of less favored rivals, has been a certain ambulatory spot upon the earth's surface, at a point where the lines of trade from east to west have converged. And always the marked idiosyncrasy of this spot has been its unrest. It has constantly oscillated from east to west according as the fortunes of war have prevailed, or as the march of applied science has made one or another route of transportation cheaper or more defensible.

Thus Babylon was conquered and robbed by Rome, and Rome, after a long heyday of prosperity, yielded to Constantinople, while Constantinople lost her supremacy to Venice, Genoa, and North Italy, following the sack of Constantinople by the Venetians in 1202 A.D. The Fairs of Champaign in France, and the cities of the Rhine and Antwerp were the glory of the Middle Ages, but these great markets faded when the discovery of the long sea voyage to India threw the route by the Red Sea and Cairo into eccentricity, and caused Spain and Portugal to bloom. Spain's prosperity did not, however, last long. England used war during the sixteenth century as an economic weapon, pretty easily conquering. And since the opening of the Industrial Revolution, at least, London, with the exception of the few years when England suffered from the American revolt of 1776, has assumed steadily more the aspect of the great international centre of exchanges, until with Waterloo her supremacy remained unchallenged. It was this brilliant achievement of London, won chiefly by arms, which more than any other cause impelled Germany to try her fortunes by war rather than by the methods of peace.

Nor was the German calculation of chances unreasonable or unwarranted. For upwards of two centuries Germany had found war the most profitable of all her economic ventures; especially had she found the French war of 1870 a most lucrative speculation. And she felt unbounded confidence that she could win as easy a triumph with her army, over the French, in the twentieth as in the nineteenth century. But, could she penetrate to Paris and at the same time occupy the littoral of the Channel and Antwerp, she was persuaded that she could do to the commerce of England what England had once done to the commerce of Spain, and that Hamburg and Berlin would supplant London. And this calculation might have proved sound had it not been for her oversight in ignoring one essential factor in the problem. Ever since North America was colonized by the English, that portion of the continent which is now comprised by the Republic of the United States, had formed a part of the British economic system, even when the two fragments of that system were competing in war, as has occurred more than once. And as America has waxed great and rich these relations have grown closer, until of recent years it has become hard to determine whether the centre of gravity of this vast capitalistic mass lay to the east or to the west of the Atlantic. One fact, however, from before the outset of this war had been manifest, and that was that the currents of movement flowed with more power from America to England than from America to Germany. And this had from before the outbreak of hos-

tilities affected the relations of the parties. Should
Germany prevail in her contest with England, the result
would certainly be to draw the centre of exchanges to
the eastward, and thereby to throw the United States,
more or less, into eccentricity; but were England to prevail the United States would tend to become the centre
toward which all else would gravitate. Hence, perfectly automatically, from a time as long ago as the
Spanish War, the balance, as indicated by the weight
of the United States, hung unevenly as between Germany and England, Germany manifesting something
approaching to repulsion toward the attraction of the
United States while Great Britain manifested favor.
And from subsequent evidence, this phenomenon
would seem to have been thus early developed, because
the economic centre of gravity of our modern civilization had already traversed the Atlantic, and by so doing
had decided the fortunes of Germany in advance, in
the greater struggle about to come. Consider attentively what has happened. In April, 1917, when the
United States entered the conflict, Germany, though it
had suffered severely in loss of men, was by no means
exhausted. On the contrary, many months subsequently she began her final offensive, which she pushed
so vigorously that she penetrated to within some sixty
miles of Paris. But there, at Château Thierry, on the
Marne, she first felt the weight of the economic shift.
She suddenly encountered a division of American
troops advancing to oppose her. Otherwise the road
to Paris lay apparently open. The American troops

were raw levies whom the Germans pretended to despise. And yet, almost without making a serious effort at prolonged attack, the Germans began their retreat, which only ended with their collapse and the fall of the empire.

A similar phenomenon occurred once before in German history, and it is not an uncommon incident in human experience when nature has already made, or is on the brink of making, a change in the seat of the economic centre of the world. In the same way, when Constantine won the battle of the Milvian Bridge, with his men fighting under the standard of the Labarum, it was subsequently found that the economic capital of civilization had silently migrated from the Tiber to the Bosphorus, where Constantine seated himself at Constantinople, which was destined to be the new capital of the world for about eight hundred years. So in 1792, when the Prussians and the French refugees together invaded France, they never doubted for an instant that they should easily disperse the mob, as they were pleased to call it, of Kellermann's "vagabonds, cobblers, and tailors." Nevertheless the Germans recoiled on the slope of Valmy from before the republican army, almost without striking a blow, nor could they be brought again to the attack, although the French royalists implored to be allowed to storm the hill alone, provided they could be assured of support. Then the retreat of the Duke of Brunswick began, and this retreat was the prelude to the Napoleonic empire, to Austerlitz, to Jena, to the dismemberment and to the reorganization of Prussia and to the evolution of modern Germany: in short, to the conversion of the remnants of mediæval civilization into the capitalistic, industrial, competitive society which we have known. And all this because of the accelerated movement caused by science.

If it be, indeed, a fact that the victory of Château Thierry and the subsequent retreat of the German army together with the collapse of the German Empire indicate, as there is abundant reason to suppose that they may, a shift in the world's social equilibrium, equivalent to the shift in Europe presaged by Valmy, or to that which substituted Constantinople for Rome and which was marked by the Milvian Bridge, it follows that we must prepare ourselves for changes possibly greater than our world has seen since it marched to Jerusalem under Godfrey de Bouillon. And the tendency of those changes is not so very difficult, perhaps, roughly to estimate, always premising that they are hardly compatible with undue optimism. Supposing, for example, we consider, in certain of their simpler aspects, some of the relations of Great Britain toward ourselves, since Great Britain is not only our most important friend, assuming that she remain a friend, but our most formidable competitor, should competition strain our friendship. Also Great Britain has the social system nearest akin to our own, and most likely to be influenced by the same so-called democratic tendencies. For upwards of a hundred years Great Britain has been, and she still is, absolutely de-

pendent on her maritime supremacy for life. It was on
that issue she fought the Napoleonic wars, and when
she prevailed at Trafalgar and Waterloo she assumed
economic supremacy, but only on the condition that
she should always be ready and willing to defend it,
for it is only on that condition that economic supremacy can be maintained. War is the most potent engine of economic competition. Constantinople and
Antwerp survived and flourished on the same identical
conditions long before the day of London. She must
keep her avenues of communication with all the world
open, and guard them against possible attack. So
long as America competed actively with England on
the sea, even for her own trade, her relations with
Great Britain were troubled. The irritation of the
colonies with the restrictions which England put upon
their commerce materially contributed to foment the
revolution, as abundantly appears in the famous case
of John Hancock's sloop Liberty, which was seized for
smuggling. So in the War of 1812, England could not
endure the United States as a competitor in her contest with France. She must be an ally, or, in other
words, she must function as a component part of the
British economic system, or she must be crushed. The
crisis came with the attack of the Leopard on the
Chesapeake in 1807, after which the possibility of maintaining peace, under such a pressure, appeared, in its
true light, as a phantasm. After the war, with more
or less constant friction, the same conditions continued until the outbreak of the Rebellion, and then

Great Britain manifested her true animus as a competitor. She waged an unacknowledged campaign against the commerce of the United States, building, equipping, arming, manning, and succoring a navy for the South, which operated none the less effectively because its action was officially repudiated. And in this secret warfare England prevailed, since when the legislation of the United States has made American competition with England on the sea impossible. Wherefore we have had peace with England. We have supplied Great Britain with food and raw materials, abandoning to England the carrying trade and an undisputed naval supremacy. Consequently Great Britain feels secure and responds to the full force of that economic attraction which makes America naturally, a component part of the British economic system. But let American pretensions once again revive to the point of causing her to attempt seriously to develop her sea power as of yore, and the same friction would also revive which could hardly, were it pushed to its legitimate end, eventuate otherwise than in the ultimate form of all economic competition.

If such a supposition seems now to be fanciful, it is only necessary to reflect a moment on the rapidity with which national relations vary under competition, to be assured that it is real. As Washington said, the only force which binds one nation to another is interest. The rise of Germany, which first created jealousy in England, began with the attack on Denmark in 1864. Then Russia was the power which the

British most feared and with whom they were on the worst of terms. About that period nothing would have seemed more improbable than that these relations would be reversed, and that Russia and England would jointly, within a generation, wage fierce war on Germany. We are very close to England now, but we may be certain that, were we to press, as Germany pressed, on British maritime and industrial supremacy, we should be hated too. It is vain to disguise the fact that British fortunes in the past have hinged on American competition, and that the wisest and most sagacious Englishmen have been those who have been most alive to the fact. Richard Cobden, for example, was one of the most liberal as he was one of the most eminent of British economists and statesmen of the middle of the nineteenth century. He was a democrat by birth and education, and a Quaker by religion. In 1835, just before he entered public life, Cobden visited the United States and thus recorded his impressions on his return:

"America is once more the theatre upon which nations are contending for mastery; it is not, however, a struggle for conquest, in which the victor will acquire territorial dominion — the fight is for commercial supremacy, and will be won by the cheapest. . . . It is from the silent and peaceful rivalry of American commerce, the growth of its manufactures, its rapid progress in internal improvements, . . . it is from these, and not from the barbarous policy or the impoverishing armaments of Russia, that the grandeur of our commercial and national prosperity is endangered." [1]

It is not, however, any part of my contention that nature should push her love of competition so far as necessarily to involve us in war with Great Britain, at least at present, for nature has various and most unlooked-for ways of arriving at her ends, since men never can determine, certainly in advance, what avenue will, to them, prove the least resistant. They very often make an error, as did the Germans, which they can only correct by enduring disaster, defeat, and infinite suffering. Nature might very well, for example, prefer that consolidation should advance yet another step before a reaction toward chaos should begin.

This last war has, apparently, been won by a fusion of two economic systems which together hold and administer a preponderating mass of fluid capital, and which have partially pooled their resources to prevail. They appear almost as would a gigantic lizard which, having been severed in an ancient conflict, was now making a violent but only half-conscious effort to cause the head and body to unite with the tail, so that the two might function once more as a single organism, governed by a single will. Under our present form of capitalistic life there would seem to be no reason why this fluid capital should not fuse and by its energy furnish the motor which should govern the world. Rome, for centuries, was governed by an emperor, who

[1] John Morley, *The Life of Richard Cobden,* 107, 108.

represented the landed class of Italy, under the forms of a republic. It is not by any means necessary that a plutocratic mass should have a recognized political head. And America and England, like two enormous banking houses, might in effect fuse and yet go on as separate institutions with nominally separate boards of directors.

But it is inconceivable that even such an expedient as this, however successful at the outset, should permanently solve the problem, which resolves itself once more into individual competition. It is not imaginable that such an enormous plutocratic society as I have supposed could conduct its complex affairs upon the basis of the average intelligence. As in Rome, a civil service would inevitably be organized which would contain a carefully selected body of ability. We have seen such a process, in its initial stages, in the recent war. And such a civil service, however selected and however trained, would, to succeed, have to be composed of men who were the ablest in their calling, the best educated, and the fittest: in a word, the representatives of what we call "the big business" of the country. Such as they might handle the railroads, the telegraph lines, the food supply, the question of competitive shipping, and finally prices, as we have seen it done, but only on condition that they belonged to the fortunate class by merit.

But supposing, in the face of such a government, the unfortunate class should protest, as they already do protest in Russia, in Germany, and even in England and here at home, that a legal system which sanctions such a civilization is iniquitous.   Here, the discontented say, you insist on a certain form of competition being carried to its limit.   That is, you demand intellectual and peaceful competition for which I am unfit both by education, training, and mental ability.   I am therefore excluded from those walks in life which make a man a freeman.   I become a slave to capital.   I must work, or fight, or starve according to another man's convenience, caprice, or, in fine, according to his will. I could be no worse off under any despot.   To such a system I will not submit.   But I can at least fight. Put me on a competitive equality or I will blow your civilization to atoms.   To such an argument there is no logical answer possible except the answer which all extreme socialists have always advanced.   The fortunate man should be taxed for all he earns above the average wage, and the State should confiscate his accumulations at death.   Then, with a system of government education, obligatory on all, children would start equal from birth.

Here we come against the hereditary instinct, the creator and the preserver of the family: the instinct which has made law and order possible, so far as our ancestors or we have known order, as far back as the Ice Age.   If the coming world must strive with this question, or abandon the "democratic ideal," the future promises to be stormy.

But even assuming that this problem of individual competition be overcome, we are as far as ever from creating a system of moral law which shall avail us, for we at once come in conflict with the principle of abstract justice which demands that free men shall be permitted to colonize or move where they will. But supposing England and America to amalgamate; they now hold or assume to control all or nearly all the vacant regions of the earth which are suited to the white man's habitation. And the white man cannot live and farm his land in competition with the Asiatic; that was conclusively proved in the days of Rome.

But it is not imaginable that Asiatics will submit to this discrimination in silence. Nothing can probably constrain them to resignation but force, and to apply force is to revert to the old argument of the savage or the despot, who admits that he knows no law save that of the stronger, which is the system, however much we have disguised it and, in short, lied about it, under which we have lived and under which our ancestors have lived ever since the family was organized, and under which it is probable that we shall continue to live as long as any remnant of civilization shall survive.

Nevertheless, it seems to be far from improbable that the system of industrial, capitalistic civilization, which came in, in substance, with the "free thought" of the Reformation, is nearing an end. Very probably it may have attained to its ultimate stages and may dissolve presently in the chaos which, since the Reformation, has been visibly impending. Democracy in America has conspicuously and decisively failed, in the collective administration of the common public property. Granting thus much, it becomes simply a question of relative inefficiency, or degradation of type, culminating in the exhaustion of resources by waste; unless the democratic man can supernaturally raise himself to some level more nearly approaching perfection than that on which he stands. For it has become self-evident that the democrat cannot change himself from a competitive to a non-competitive animal by talking about it, or by pretending to be already or to be about to become other than he is, — the victim of infinite conflicting forces.

BROOKS ADAMS.

QUINCY, *July 20*, 1919.

THE EMANCIPATION
OF MASSACHUSETTS

CHAPTER I.

THE COMMONWEALTH.

THE mysteries of the Holy Catholic Church had been venerated for ages when Europe burst from her mediæval torpor into the splendor of the Renaissance. Political schemes and papal abuses may have precipitated the inevitable outbreak, but in the dawn of modern thought the darkness faded amidst which mankind had so long cowered in the abject terrors of superstition. Already in the beginning of the fifteenth century many of the ancient dogmas had begun to awaken incredulity, and sceptics learned to mock at that claim to infallibility upon which the priesthood based their right to command the blind obedience of the Christian world. Between such adversaries compromise was impossible; and those who afterward revolted against the authority of the traditions of Rome sought refuge under the shelter of the Bible, which they grew to reverence with a passionate devotion, believing it to have been not only directly and verbally inspired by God, but the only channel through which he had made known his will to men.

Thus the movement was not toward new doctrines; on the contrary, it was the rejection of what could no longer be believed. Calvin was no less orthodox than St. Augustine in what he accepted; his heresy lay in the denial of enigmas from which his understanding recoiled. The mighty convulsion of the Reformation, therefore, was but the supreme effort of the race to tear itself from the toils of a hierarchy whose life hung upon its success in forcing the children to worship the myths of their ancestral religion.

Three hundred years after Luther nailed his theses to the church door the logical deduction had been drawn from his great act, and Christendom had been driven to admit that any concession of the right to reason upon matters of faith involved the recognition of the freedom of individual thought. But though this noble principle has been at length established, long years of bloodshed passed before the victory was won; and from the outset the attitude of the clergy formed the chief obstacle to the triumph of a more liberal civilization; for howsoever bitterly Catholic and Protestant divines have hated and persecuted each other, they have united like true brethren in their hatred and their persecution of heretics; for such was their inexorable destiny.

Men who firmly believe that salvation lies within their creed alone, and that doubters suffer endless torments, never can be tolerant. They feel that duty commands them to defend their homes against a deadly peril, and even pity for the sinner urges them to wring from him a recantation before it is too late; and then, moreover, dissent must lessen the power and influence of a hierarchy and may endanger its very existence; therefore the priests of every church have been stimulated to crush out schism by the two strongest passions that can inflame the mind — by bigotry and by ambition.

In England the Reformation was controlled by statesmen, whose object was to invest the crown with ecclesiastical power, and who made no changes except such as they thought necessary for their purpose. They repudiated the papal supremacy, and adopted articles of religion sufficiently evangelical in form, but they retained episcopacy, the liturgy, and the surplice; the cross was still used in baptism, the people bowed at the name of Jesus, and knelt at the communion. Such a compromise with what they deemed idolatry was offensive to the stricter Protestants, and so early as 1550 John Hooper refused the see of Gloucester because he would not wear the robes of office; thus almost from its foundation the church was divided into factions, and those who demanded a more radical reform were nicknamed Puritans. As time elapsed large numbers who could no longer bring themselves to conform withdrew from the orthodox communion, and began to worship by themselves; persecution followed, and many fled to Holland, where they formed congregations in the larger towns, the most celebrated of them being that of John Robinson at Leyden, which afterward founded Plymouth. But

the intellectual ferment was universal, and the same
upheaval that was rending the church was shaking
the foundations of the state : power was passing into
the hands of the people, but a century was to elapse
before the relations of the sovereign to the House of
Commons were fully adjusted. During this interval
the Stuarts reigned and three of the four kings suffered exile or death in the fierce contest for mastery.

The fixed determination of Charles I. was to establish a despotism and enforce conformity with ritualism ; and the result was the Great Rebellion.

Among the statesmen who advised him, none has
met with such scant mercy from posterity as Laud,
who has been gibbeted as the impersonification of
narrowness, of bigotry, and of cruelty. The judgment
is unscientific, for whatever may be thought of the
humanity or wisdom of his policy, he only did what
all have done who have attempted to impose a creed
on men.

The real grievance has never been that an observance has been required, or an indulgence refused, but
that the right to think has been denied. Provided a
boundary be fixed within which the reason must be
chained, the line drawn by Laud is as reasonable as
that of Calvin ; Geneva is no more infallible than
Canterbury or Rome. Comprehension is the dream
of visionaries, for some will always differ from any
confession of faith, however broad ; and where there
are dogmas there will be heretics till all have perished.
But in their fear and hatred of individual free thought

regarding the mysteries of religion, Laud, Calvin, and the Pope agreed.

With the progress of the war, the Puritans, who had at first been united in their opposition to the crown, themselves divided; one party, to which most of the peers and of the non-conforming clergy belonged, being anxious to reëstablish the monarchy, and set up a rigid Presbyterianism; the other, of whose spirit Cromwell was the incarnation, resolving each day more firmly to crush the king and proclaim freedom of conscience; and it was this doctrine of toleration which was the snare and the abomination in the eyes of evangelical divines.

Robert Baillie, the Scotch commissioner, while in London, anxiously watching the rise of the power of the Independents in Parliament, with each victory of their armies in the field wrote, " Liberty of conscience, and toleration of all and any religion, is so prodigious an impiety that this religious parliament cannot but abhor the very meaning of it." Nor did his reverend brethren of the Westminster Assembly fall any whit behind him when they rose to expound the word. In a letter of 17th May, 1644, he thus described their doctrine: "This day was the best that I have seen since I came to England. . . . After D. Twisse had begun with a brief prayer, Mr. Marshall prayed large two hours, most divinely, confessing the sins of the members of the assembly, in a wonderful, pathetick, and prudent way. After, Mr. Arrowsmith preached an hour, then a psalm; thereafter, Mr. Vines prayed near two hours, and Mr. Palmer preached an hour, and Mr. Seaman prayed near two hours, then a psalm; after, Mr. Henderson brought them to a sweet conference of the heat confessed in the assembly, and other seen faults to be remedied, and the conveniency to preach against all sects, especially Anabaptists and Antinomians. Dr. Twisse closed with a short prayer and blessing." [1]

But Cromwell, gifted with noble instincts and transcendent political genius, a layman, a statesman, and a soldier, was a liberal from birth till death.

" Those that were sound in the faith, how proper was it for them to labor for liberty, . . . that men might not be trampled upon for their consciences! Had not they labored but lately under the weight of persecution? And was it fit for them to sit heavy upon others? Is it ingenuous to ask liberty and not to give it? What greater hypocrisy than for those who were oppressed by the bishops to become the greatest oppressors themselves, so soon as their yoke was removed? I could wish that they who call for liberty now also had not too much of that spirit, if the power were in their hands." [2]

" If a man of one form will be trampling upon the heels of another form, if an Independent, for example, will despise him under Baptism, and will revile him and reproach him and provoke him, — I will not suffer it in him. If, on the other side, those of the Anabap-

---

[1] Baillie's *Letters and Journals*, ii. 18.

[2] Speech at dissolution of first Parliament, Jan. 22, 1655. Carlyle's *Cromwell*, iv. 107.

tist shall be censuring the godly ministers of the nation who profess under that of Independency; or if those that profess under Presbytery shall be reproaching or speaking evil of them, traducing and censuring of them, as I would not be willing to see the day when England shall be in the power of the Presbytery to impose upon the consciences of others that profess faith in Christ, — so I will not endure any reproach to them."[1]

The number of clergymen among the emigrants to Massachusetts was very large, and the character of the class who formed the colony was influenced by them to an extraordinary degree. Many able pastors had been deprived in England for non-conformity, and they had to choose between silence or exile. To men of their temperament silence would have been intolerable; and most must have depended upon their profession for support. America, therefore, offered a convenient refuge. The motives are less obvious which induced the leading laymen, some of whom were of fortune and consequence at home, to face the hardships of the wilderness. Persecution cannot be the explanation, for a government under which Hampden and Cromwell could live and be returned to Parliament was not intolerable; nor does it appear that any of them had been severely dealt with. The wish of the Puritan party to have a place of retreat, should the worst befall, may have had its weight with individuals, but probably the influence which swayed the

[1] Speech made September, 1656. Carlyle's *Cromwell*, iv. 234.

larger number was the personal ascendancy of their pastors, for that ascendancy was complete. In a community so selected, men of the type of Baillie must have vastly outnumbered those of the stamp of Cromwell, and in point of fact their minds were generally cast in the ecclesiastical mould and imbued with the ecclesiastical feeling. Governor Dudley represented them well, and at his death some lines were found in his pocket in which their spirit yet glows in all the fierceness of its bigotry.

> " Let men of God in Courts and Churches watch
> O're such as do a Toleration hatch,
> Lest that Ill Egg bring forth a Cockatrice,
> To poison all with heresie and vice." [1]

In former ages churches had been comprehensive to this extent: infants had been baptized, and, when the child had become a man, he had been admitted to the communion as a matter of course, unless his life had given scandal; but to this system the Congregationalist was utterly opposed. He believed that, human nature being totally depraved, some became regenerate through grace; that the signs of grace were as palpable as any other traits of character, and could be discerned by all the world; therefore, none should be admitted to the sacrament who had not the marks of the elect; and as in a well-ordered community the godly ought to rule, it followed that none should be enfranchised but members of the church.

To suppose such a government could be maintained in England was beyond the dreams even of an enthu-

[1] *Magnalia*, bk. 2, ch. v. § 1.

siast, and there can be little doubt that the controlling incentive with many of those who sailed was the hope, with the aid of their divines, of founding a religious commonwealth in the wilderness which should harmonize with their interpretation of the Scriptures.

The execution of such a project was, however, far from easy. It would have been most unsafe for the emigrants to have divulged their true designs, since these were not only unlawful, but would have been highly offensive to the king, and yet they were too feeble to exist without the protection of Great Britain, therefore it was necessary to secure for themselves the rights of English subjects, and to throw some semblance at least of the sanction of law over the organization of their new state. Accordingly, a patent[1] was obtained from the crown, by which twenty-five persons were incorporated under the name of the Governor and Company of Massachusetts Bay in New England; and as the extent of the powers therein granted has given rise to a controversy which is not yet closed, it is necessary to understand the nature of that instrument in order to comprehend the bearings of the bitter strife which darkens the history of the first fifty years of the colony.

The germ of the written charter is so ancient as to be lost in obscurity. During the Middle Ages, oppression was, speaking generally, the accepted condition of society, no man not noble having the right in theory, or the power in practice, to control his own actions without interference from his feudal superior.

[1] March 4, 1629.

Under such circumstances the only hope for the weak was to combine, and most of the early triumphs of freedom were won by combinations of commons against some noble, or of nobles against a king. Organization is difficult for a peasantry, but easy for burghers, and from the outset these seem to have united for their common defense against the neighboring barons; and thus was born the mediæval guild.

The ancient townsmen were not usually strong enough to fight for their liberties, so they generally resorted to purchase; they agreed with their lord upon a price to be paid for a privilege, and were given for their money a grant, which, because it was written, was called a charter.

The following charter of the Merchants' Guild of Leicester is very early and very simple. It presupposes that there could be no doubt about the local customs, which are therefore not enumerated, and it shows that the guild of Leicester existed as a corporation at the Conquest, and must already have held property in succession and been liable to suit through two reigns: —

"Robert, Earl of Mellent, to Ralph, and all his barons, French and English, of all his land in England, greeting: Know ye, that I have granted to my merchants of Leicester their Guild Merchant, with all customs which they held in the time of King William, of King William his son, and now hold in the time of Henry the king.

"Witness: R., the son of Alcitil."

The object of these ancient writings was only to record the fact of corporate existence; the popular custom by which the guilds were regulated was taken for granted; but obviously they must have had succession, been liable to suit, able to contract, and, in a word, to do all those acts which were afterward set forth. And such has uniformly been the process by which English jurisprudence has been shaped; a usage grows up that courts recognize, and, by their decisions, establish as the common law; but judicial decisions are inflexible, and, as they become antiquated, they are themselves modified by legislation. Lawyers observed these customary companies for some centuries before they learned what functions were universal; but, with the lapse of time, the patents became more elaborate, until at length a voluminous grant of each particular power was held necessary to create a new corporation.

A merchants' guild, like the one of Leicester, was an association of the townsmen for their common welfare. Every trader was then called a merchant, and as almost every burgher lived by trade, and was also a landowner, to the extent at least of his dwelling, it followed that the guild practically included all free male inhabitants; the guild hall was used as the town hall, the guild ordinances were the town ordinances, and the corporation became the government of the borough, and as such chose persons to represent it in Parliament, when summoned by the king's writ to send burgesses to Westminster.

London is a corporation by prescription and not by virtue of any particular charter, and to this day its city hall is called by the ancient name, Guild Hall. But with the growth of wealth and population the original fraternity divided into craft organizations (so long ago, indeed, that no record of its existence remains), and each trade organized a guild, with a hall of its own; and thus it came to pass that the twelve livery companies — the Mercers, the Grocers, the Goldsmiths, the Drapers, the Fishmongers, and the rest — became the government of the capital of England.

All mediæval institutions tended to aristocracy and monopoly, and, accordingly, after the merchant guilds had split into these corporate trade unions, boroughs waxed exclusive, and membership, instead of being an incident of citizenship, grew to confer citizenship itself; thus the franchise, being confined to freemen, and freedom or membership having come to depend on birth, marriage, election, or purchase, the constituencies which returned a majority of the House of Commons grew so petty and corrupt as to threaten the existence of parliamentary government itself, and the abuse at last culminated in the agitation which produced the Reform Bill.

When legal forms had taken shape, the land upon which a town stood was not unusually granted to the mayor and commonalty by metes and bounds,[1] to

---

[1] See Charter of Plymouth, granted 1439. *History of Plymouth*, p. 50. The incorporation was by statute.

them and their successors forever, upon payment of
a rent; and the mayor and common council were empowered to make laws and ordinances for the local
government, and to fine, imprison, and sometimes
whip and otherwise punish offenders, so as their statutes, fines, pains, and penalties were reasonable and
not repugnant to law.[1] The foreign trading company
was an offshoot of the guild, and was intended to
protect commerce. Obviously some such organization
must have been necessary, for, if property was inse-
cure within the realm, it was far more exposed without; and, indeed, in the fourteenth century, English
merchants domiciled on the Continent could hardly
have been safer than Europeans are now who garrison
the so-called factories upon the coast of Africa.

At the Conquest, the Hanse merchants had a house
in London, which was afterward famous as the Steel
Yard. They lived a strange life, — a combination of
that of the trader, the soldier, and the monk. Their
fortified warehouse, exposed to the attacks of the ferocious mob, was occasionally taken and sacked ; and the
garrison shut up within was subject to an iron discipline. They were forbidden to marry, no woman
passed the gates, nor did they ever sleep a night without the walls; but, always on the watch, they lay in
their cells ready to repulse a storm. For many years
these Germans seem to have monopolized the carrying
trade, for it was not till the thirteenth century that
Englishmen appear to have made an effort at compe-

[1] *History of Tiverton,* App. 5.

tition. However, about 1296 certain London mercers are said to have obtained a grant of privileges from John, Duke of Brabant, and to have established a wool market at Antwerp.[1] The recognition of the Flemish government was of course necessary; but they could hardly have maintained themselves without some support at home; for, although their warehouse was abroad, they were English merchants, and they must have relied upon English protection. No very early documents remain; but an elaborate charter, granted by Edward IV. in 1463, proves that the corporation had then had a long legal existence.[2] The crown thereby confirmed one Obrey, the governor, in his office during pleasure, with the wages theretofore enjoyed; existing laws were approved; the governor and merchants were empowered to elect twelve Justicers, who were to hold courts for all merchants and mariners in those parts; and the company was authorized to regulate the trade and control the traders, provided no laws were passed contrary to the intent of that charter.

Here, as in the Merchant Guild, the inevitable aristocratic revolution took place, and the old democratic brotherhood became a strict monopoly. The oppression was so flagrant that a petition was presented to Parliament in 1497 against the exactions of the Merchant Adventurers, as the association was then called, by which it appeared that interlopers, trading to Hol

---

[1] Anderson's *History of Commerce.*

[2] Hakluyt's *Voyages,* i. 230.

land and Flanders, were fined £40, whereas any subject might have become a freeman in earlier times for
an old noble, or about 6s. 8d.; [1] and the scandal was
so great that the fine was fixed at 10 marks, or £6
13s. 4d., by statute. During the stagnation of the
Middle Ages few traces of such commercial enter-
prises are to be found, but with the sixteenth century
Europe awoke to a new life and thrilled with a new
energy. Trade shared in the impulse. In 1554 Philip
and Mary incorporated the Russia Company in regular modern form; in 1581 the Turkey Company was
organized; in 1600 the East India Company received
its charter; and, to come directly to what is material, in 1629 Charles I. signed the patent of the Governor and Company of Massachusetts Bay in New
England.

Stripped of its verbiage, the provisions are simple.
The stockholders, or "freemen," as they were then
called, were to meet once a quarter in a "General
Court." This General Court, or stockholders' meeting, chose the officers, of which there were twenty, the
governor, deputy governor, and eighteen assistants
or directors, on the last Wednesday in each Easter
Term. The assistants were intrusted with the business
management, and were to meet once a month or oftener; while the General Court was empowered to admit freemen, and "to make laws and ordinances for
the good and welfare of the said company, and for the
government and ordering of the said lands and planta-

[1] 12 Henry VII. ch. vi.

tion, and the people inhabiting and to inhabit the same, as to them from time to time shall be thought meet, — so as such laws and ordinances be not contrary or repugnant to the laws and statutes of this our realm of England." The criminal jurisdiction was limited to the "imposition of lawful fines, mulcts, imprisonment, or other lawful correction, according to the course of other corporations in this our realm of England."

The "course of corporations" referred to was well established. The Master and Wardens of the Guild of Drapers in London, for example, could make "such . . . pains, punishments, and penalties, by corporal punishment, or fines and amercements," . . . "as shall seem . . . necessary," provided their statutes were reasonable and not contrary to the laws of the kingdom.[1] In like manner, boroughs such as Tiverton might "impose and assess punishments by imprisonments, etc., and reasonable fines upon offenders."[2]

But all lawyers knew that such grants did not convey full civil or criminal jurisdiction, which, when thought needful, was specially conferred, as was done in the case of the East India Company upon their petition in 1624,[3] and in that of Massachusetts by the charter of William and Mary.

Such was the undoubted theory, and evidently there must always have been some practical means of checking the abuse of power by these strong organizations.

---

[1] Herbert's *Livery Companies*, i. 489.

[2] See *History of Tiverton*, App. 5.

[3] Bruce, *Annals*, i. 252.

In semi-barbarous ages the sovereign took matters into his own hands by seizing the franchise, and even the Plantagenets repeatedly suspended or revoked the liberties of London, — often, no doubt, for cause, but sometimes also to make money by a resale ; and a succession of these arbitrary forfeitures demonstrated that charters to be of value must be beyond the grantor's control. Resort was had to the courts, as a matter of course, and finally it was settled that relief should be given by a writ of *quo warranto*, upon which the question of the violation of privileges could be tried ; and curious records still remain of ancient litigations of this nature.

In 1321 complaint was made against the London Weavers for injuring the public by passing regulations tending to raise the price of cloth.[1] It was alleged that the guild, with this intent, had limited the working hours in the day, the working days in the year, and the number of apprentices the freemen might employ ; and the prayer was that for these abuses the charter should be annulled.

The cause was tried before a jury, who found the truth of some of the charges ; but the judgment is lost, as the roll is imperfect.

There was danger, moreover, to the citizen from the oppression of these powerful bodies, as well as to the public from their usurpations ; and were authority wholly wanting, argument would be almost unnecessary to prove that some appellate tribunal must always

[1] *Liber Customarum,* i. 416–424.

have had jurisdiction to pass upon the validity of corporate legislation; for otherwise any summary punishment might have been inflicted upon an individual, though notoriously unlawful, and the only redress possible would have been subsequent proceedings to vacate the charter.

Through appeals, corporations could be controlled; and by none was this control so stubbornly disputed, or its necessity so clearly demonstrated, as by the Governor and Company of Massachusetts Bay in New England. A good illustration is the trial of the Quaker, Wenlock Christison, for his life in 1661.

" William Leddra being thus dispatch'd, it was resolved to make an end also of Wenlock Christison. He therefore was brought from the prison to the court at Boston, where the governor John Indicot, and the deputy governor Richard Billingham, being both present, it was told him, 'Unless you will renounce your religion, you shall surely die.' But instead of shrinking, he said with an undaunted courage, 'Nay, I shall not change my religion, nor seek to save my life; neither do I intend to deny my Master; but if I lose my life for Christ's sake, and the preaching of the gospel, I shall save my life.' . . . John Indicot asked him 'what he had to say for himself, why he should not die?' . . . Then Wenlock asked, 'By what law will you put me to death?' The answer was, 'We have a law, and by our law you are to die.' 'So said the Jews of Christ,' (reply'd Wenlock) 'we have a law, and by our law he ought to die. Who empowered you to make that law?' To which one of the board answered, 'We have a patent, and are the patentees; judge whether we have not power to make laws.' Hereupon Wenlock asked again, 'How, have you power to make laws repugnant to the laws of England?' 'No,' said the governor. 'Then,' (reply'd Wenlock,) 'you are gone beyond your bounds, and have forfeited your patent; and that is more than you can answer.' 'Are you,' ask'd he, 'subjects to the king, yea or nay?' . . . To which one said, 'Yea, we are so.' 'Well,' said Wenlock, 'so am I.' . . . 'Therefore seeing that you and I are subjects to the king, I demand to be tried by the laws of my own nation.' It was answered, You shall be tried by a bench and a jury.' For it seems they began to be afraid to go on in the former course, of trial without a jury. . . . But Wenlock said, 'That is not the law, but the manner of it; for I never heard nor read of any law that was in England to hang Quakers.' To this the governor reply'd 'that there was a law to hang Jesuits.' To which Wenlock return'd, 'If you put me to death, it is not because I go under the name of a Jesuit, but of a Quaker. Therefore, I appeal to the laws of my own nation.' But instead of taking notice of this, one said 'that he was in their hands, and had broken their law, and they would try him.'"[1]

Yet, though the ecclesiastical party in Massachusetts obstinately refused to admit appeals to the British judiciary up to the last moment of their power, for the

[1] Sewel, pp. 278, 279.

obvious reason that the existence of the theocracy depended upon the enforcement of such legislation as that under which the Quakers suffered, there was no principle in the whole range of English jurisprudence more firmly established. By a statute of Henry VI. passed in 1436, corporate enactments were to be submitted to the judges for approval; and the Court of King's Bench always set aside such as were bad, whenever the question of their validity was presented for adjudication.[1]

But discussion is futile; the proposition is self-evident, that an association endowed with the capacity of acting like a single man, for certain defined objects, which shall attempt other objects, or shall seek to compass its ends by unlawful means, violates the condition upon which its life has been granted, transcends the limits of its existence, and forfeits its privileges; and that under such circumstances its ordinances are void, and none are bound to yield them their obedience.

Approached thus from the standpoint of legal history, no doubt can exist concerning the scope of the franchise secured by the Puritans for the Massachusetts colony. The instrument obtained from Charles I. embodied certain of their number in an English corporation, whose only lawful business was the American trade, as the business of the East India Company was

[1] Stat. 15 H. VI. ch. 6.   Stat. 19 H. VII. ch. 7.   Clark's Case, 5 Coke, 633, decided A. D. 1596. See Kyd on Corporations, ii. 107–110, where authorities are collected. Child *v.* Hudson Bay Co., 2 P. W. 207.

trade in Hindostan. To enable them to act effectively, a tract of land in New England, between the
Merrimack and the Charles, was conveyed to them, as
the soil upon which a town stood was conveyed to the
mayor and commonalty. Within this territory they
were authorized to established their plantations and
forts, which they were empowered to defend against
attack, as the Hanse merchants defended the Steel
Yard in London. They were also permitted to govern the country within their grant by reasonable regulations calculated to preserve the peace, and of much
the same character as the municipal ordinances of
towns, subject, of course, to judicial supervision. The
corporation itself was created subject to the municipal
laws of England, and could have no existence without
the realm; and though perhaps even then the American wilderness might have been held to belong to the
British empire, it formed no part of the kingdom,[1]
and was altogether beyond the limits of that jurisdiction from whose customs and statutes the life of
this imaginary being sprang. Therefore, the govern-
ing body could legally exercise its functions only
when domiciled in some English town.[2]

Sir Richard Sheldon, the solicitor-general, advised
the king that he was signing a charter containing "such
. . . clauses for y⁰ electing of Governors and Officers
here in England, . . . and powers to make lawes and

[1] Blackstone's *Commentaries,* i. 109.
[2] On this subject see the able paper of Mr. Deane, in *Massachusetts Historical Society Proceedings,* December, 1869, p. 166.

ordinances for setling ye governement and magistracye for yᵉ plantacõn there, . . . as . . . are usuallie allowed to Corporacõns in England." [1]   And there can be no question that his opinion was sound.

Nothing can be imagined more ill-suited to serve as the organic law of a new commonwealth than this instrument. No provision was made for superior or probate courts, for a representative assembly, for the incorporation of counties and towns, for police or taxation.   In short, hardly a step could be taken toward founding a territorial government based upon popular suffrage without working a forfeiture of the charter by abuse of the franchise.   The colonists, it is true, afterward advanced very different theories of construction; but that they were well aware of their legal position is demonstrated by the fact that after some hesitation from apprehension of consequences, they ventured on the singularly bold and lawless measure of secretly removing their charter to America and establishing their corporation in a land which they thought would be beyond the process of Westminster Hall.[2] The details of the settlement are related in many books, and require only the briefest mention here.   In 1628 an association of gentlemen bought the tract of country lying between the Merrimack and Charles from the Council of Plymouth, and sent Endicott to take charge of their purchase.   A royal patent was, however, thought necessary for the protection of a large colony, and one

[1] *Mass. Hist. Soc. Proc.* 1869–70, p. 173.   [2] 1629, Aug. 29.

having been obtained, the Company of Massachusetts Bay was at once organized in England, Endicott was appointed governor in America, and six vessels sailed during the spring of 1629, taking out several hundred persons and a "plentiful provision of godly ministers." In August the church of Salem was gathered and Mr. Higginson was consecrated as their teacher. In that same month Winthrop, Saltonstall, and others met at Cambridge and signed an agreement binding themselves upon the faith of Christians to embark for the plantation by the following March; "Provided always that before the last of September next, the whole government, together with the patent, . . . be first by an order of court legally transferred and established to remain with us and others which shall inhabite upon the said plantation." [1] The Company accepted the proposition, Winthrop was chosen governor, and he anchored in Salem harbor in June.[2] More than a thousand settlers landed before winter, and the first General Court was held at Boston in October; nor did the emigration thus begun entirely cease until the meeting of the Long Parliament.

From the beginning the colonists took what measures they thought proper, without regarding the limitations of the law. Counties and towns had to be practically incorporated, taxes were levied upon inhabitants, and in 1634 all pretence of a General Court of freemen was dropped, and the towns chose delegates to represent them, though the legislature was

[1] *Hutch. Coll.*, Prince Soc. ed. i. 28.   [2] 1630.

not divided into two branches until ten years later. When the government had become fully organized supreme power was vested in the General Court, a legislature composed of two houses; the assistants, or magistrates, as they were called, and the deputies. The governor, deputy governor, and assistants were elected by a general vote; but each town sent two deputies to Boston.

For some years justice was dispensed by the magistrates according to the Word of God, but gradually a judicial system was established; the magistrate's local court was the lowest, from whence causes went by appeal to the county courts, one of whose judges was always an assistant, and probate jurisdiction was given to the two held at Ipswich and at Salem. From the judgments entered here an appeal lay to the Court of Assistants, and then to the General Court, which was the tribunal of last resort. The clergy and gentry pertinaciously resisted the enactment of a series of general statutes, upon which the people as steadily insisted, until at length, in 1641, "The Body of Liberties" was approved by the legislature. This compilation was the work of the Rev. Mr. Ward, pastor of Ipswich, and contained a criminal code copied almost word for word from the Pentateuch, but apart from matters touching religion, the legislation was such as English colonists have always adopted. A major-general was elected who commanded the militia, and in 1652 money was coined.

The social institutions, however, have a keener interest, for they reflect that strong cast of thought which has stamped its imprint deep into the character of so much of the American people. The seventeenth century was aristocratic, and the inhabitants of the larger part of New England were divided into three classes, the commonalty, the gentry, and the clergy. Little need be said of the first, except that they were a brave and determined race, as ready to fight as Cromwell's saints, who made Rupert's troopers "as stubble to their swords;" that they were intelligent, and would not brook injustice; and that they were resolute, and would not endure oppression. All know that they were energetic and shrewd.

The gentry had the weight in the community that comes with wealth and education, and they received the deference then paid to birth, for they were for the most part the descendants of English country-gentlemen. As a matter of course they monopolized the chief offices; and they were not sentenced by the courts to degrading punishments, like whipping, for their offences, as other criminals were. They even showed some wish at the outset to create legal distinctions, such as a magistracy for life, and a disposition to magnify the jurisdiction of the Court of Assistants, whose seats they filled; but the action of the people was determined though quiet, a chamber of deputies was chosen, and such schemes were heard of no more.

Yet notwithstanding the existence of this aristocratic element, the real substance of influence and power lay with the clergy. It has been taught as an axiom of Massachusetts history, that from the outset the town was the social and political unit; but an analysis of the evidence tends to show that the organization of the Puritan Commonwealth was ecclesiastical, and the congregation, not the town, the basis upon which the fabric rested. By the constitution of the corporation the franchise went with the freedom of the company; but in order to form a constituency which would support a sacerdotal oligarchy, it was enacted in 1631 " that for time to come noe man shalbe admitted to the freedome of this body politicke, but such as are members of some of the churches within . . . the same." [1] Thus though communicants were not necessarily voters, no one could be a voter who was not a communicant; therefore the town-meeting was in fact nothing but the church meeting, possibly somewhat attenuated, and called by a different name. By this insidious statute the clergy seized the temporal power, which they held till the charter fell. The minister stood at the head of the congregation and moulded it to suit his purposes and to do his will; for though he could not when opposed admit an inhabitant to the sacrament, he could peremptorily exclude therefrom all those of whom he disapproved, for "none are propounded to the congregation, except they be first allowed by the elders." [2] In such a community the influence of the priesthood

[1] *Mass. Records,* i. 87.

[2] Winthrop's reply to Vane, *Hutch. Coll.,* Prince Soc. ed. i. 101.

must have been overwhelming. Not only in an age
without newspapers or tolerable roads were their sermons, preached several times each week to every
voter, the most effective of political harangues; but,
unlike other party orators, they were not forced to
stimulate the sluggish, or to convince the hostile, for
from a people glowing with fanaticism, each elder
picked his band of devoted servants of the church,
men passionately longing to do the will of Christ,
whose commands concerning earth and heaven their
pastor had been ordained to declare. Nor was their
power bounded by local limits; though seldom holding
office themselves, they were solemnly consulted by the
government on every important question that arose,
whether of war or peace, and their counsel was rarely
disregarded. They gave their opinion, no matter how
foreign the subject might be to their profession or
their education; and they had no hesitation in passing upon the technical construction of the charter
with the authority of a bench of judges. An amusing example is given by Winthrop: "The General
Court assembled again, and all the elders were sent
for, to reconcile the differences between the magistrates and deputies. When they were come the first
question put to them was, . . . whether the magistrates
are, by patent and election of the people, the standing
council of this commonwealth in the vacancy of the
General Court, and have power accordingly to act in
all cases subject to government, according to the said
patent and the laws of this jurisdiction; and when

any necessary occasions call for action from authority, in cases where there is no particular express law provided, there to be guided by the word of God, till the General Court give particular rules in such cases. The elders, having received the question, withdrew themselves for consultation about it, and the next day sent to know, when we would appoint a time that they might attend the court with their answer. The magistrates and deputies agreed upon an hour " and . . . " their answer was affirmative, on the magistrates behalf, in the very words of the question, with some reasons thereof. It was delivered in writing by Mr. Cotton in the name of them all, they being all present, and not one dissentient." Then the magistrates propounded four more questions, the last of which is as follows : " Whether a judge be bound to pronounce such sentence as a positive law prescribes, in case it be apparently above or beneath the merit of the offence ? " To which the elders replied at great length, saying that the penalty must vary with the gravity of the crime, and added examples: " So any sin committed with an high hand, as the gathering of sticks on the Sabbath day, may be punished with death when a lesser punishment may serve for gathering sticks privily and in some need." [1] Yet though the clerical influence was so unbounded the theocracy itself was exposed to constant peril. In monarchies such as France or Spain the priests who rule the king have the force of the nation at command to dispose of

[1] Winthrop, ii. 204, 205.

at their will; but in Massachusetts a more difficult problem was presented, for the voters had to be controlled. By the law requiring freemen to be church-members the elders meant to grasp the key to the suffrage, but experience soon proved that more stringent regulation was needed.

According to the original Congregational theory each church was complete and independent, and elected its own officers and conducted its own worship, free from interference from without, except that others of the same communion might offer advice or admonition. Under the theocracy no such loose system was possible, for heresy might enter in three different ways; first, under the early law, " blasphemers " might form a congregation and from thence creep into the company; second, an established church might fall into error; third, an unsound minister might be chosen, who would debauch his flock by securing the admission of sectaries to the sacrament. Above all, a creed was necessary by means of which false doctrine might be instantly detected and condemned. Accordingly, one by one, as the need for vigilance increased, laws were passed to guard these points of danger.

First, in 1635 it was enacted,[1] " Forasmuch as it hath bene found by sad experience, that much trouble and disturbance hath happened both to the church & civill state by the officers & members of some churches, wch have bene gathered . . . in an vndue manner . . . it is . . . ordered that . . . this Court

[1] 1635–6, March 3.

doeth not, nor will hereafter, approue of any such com-
panyes of men as shall henceforthe ioyne in any pretended way of church fellowshipp, without they shall
first acquainte the magistrates, & the elders of the
great͛ p̄te of the churches in this jurisdic͂on, with
their intenc͂ons, and have their approbac͂on herein.
And ffurther, it is ordered, that noe pson, being a
member of any churche which shall hereafter be gathered without the approbac͂on of the magistrates, & the
greater p̄te of the said churches, shallbe admitted to
the ffreedome of this com͂onwealthe." [1]

In 1648 all the elders met in a synod at Cambridge;
they adopted the Westminster Confession of Faith
and an elaborate " Platform of Church Discipline,"
the last clause of which is as follows : " If any church
. . . shall grow schismatical, rending itself from the
communion of other churches, or shall walk incor-
rigibly and obstinately in any corrupt way of their
own contrary to the rule of the word ; in such case
the magistrate, . . . is to put forth his coercive power,
as the matter shall require." [2]

In 1658 the General Court declared : " Whereas it
is the duty of the Christian magistrate to take care
the people be fed wth wholesome & sound doctrine, &
in this houre of temptation, . . . it is therefore ordered,
that henceforth no person shall . . . preach to any company of people, whither in church society or not, or be
ordeyned to the office of a teaching elder, where any
two organnick churches, councill of state, or Generall

----

[1] *Mass. Rec.* i. 168.   [2] *Magnalia,* bk. 5, ch. xvii. § 9.

Court shall declare theire dissatisfaction thereat, either in refference to doctrine or practize . . . and in case of ordination . . . timely notice thereof shall be given unto three or fower of the neighbouring organicke churches for theire approbation." [1] And lastly, in 1679, the building of meeting-houses was forbidden, without leave from the freemen of the town or the General Court.[2]

But legislation has never yet controlled the action of human thought. All experience shows that every age, and every western nation, produces men whose nature it is to follow the guidance of their reason in the face of every danger. To exterminate these is the task of religious persecution, for they can be silenced only by death. Thus is a dominant priesthood brought face to face with the alternative of surrendering its power or of killing the heretic, and those bloody deeds that cast their sombre shadow across the history of the Puritan Commonwealth cannot be seen in their true bearing unless the position of the clergy is vividly before the mind.

Cromwell said that ministers were " helpers of, not lords over, God's people," [3] but the orthodox New Englander was the vassal of his priest. Winthrop was the ablest and the most enlightened magistrate the ecclesiastical party ever had, and he tells us that

[1] *Mass. Rec.* iv. pt. 1, p. 328.

[2] *Mass. Rec.* v. 213.

[3] Cromwell to Dundass, letter cxlviii. Carlyle's *Cromwell,* iii. 72.

" I honoured a faithful minister in my heart and could have kissed his feet." [1] If the governor of Massachusetts and the leader of the emigration could thus describe his moral growth, — a man of birth, education, and fortune, who had had wide experience of life, and was a lawyer by profession, — the awe and terror felt by the mass of the communicants can be imagined.

Jonathan Mitchel, one of the most famous of the earlier divines, thus describes his flock : " They were a gracious, savoury-spirited people, principled by Mr. Shepard, liking an humbling, mourning, heart-breaking ministry and spirit; living in religion, praying men and women." And " he would speak with such a transcendent majesty and liveliness, that the people . . . would often shake under his dispensations, as if they had heard the sound of the trumpets from the burning mountain, and yet they would mourn to think, that they were going presently to be dismissed from such an heaven upon earth." . . . " When a publick admonition was to be dispensed unto any one that had offended scandalously . . . the hearers would be all drowned in tears, as if the admonition had been, as indeed he would with much artifice make it be directed unto them all; but such would be the compassion, and yet the gravity, the majesty, the scriptural and awful pungency of these his dispensations, that the conscience of the offender himself, could make no resistance thereunto." [2]

[1] *Life and Letters of Winthrop*, i. 61.
[2] *Magnalia*, bk. 4, ch. iv. §§ 9, 10.

Their arrogance was fed by the submission of the people, and they would not tolerate the slighest opposition even from their most devoted retainers. The Reforming Synod was held in 1679. " When the report of a committee on 'the evils that had provoked the Lord' came up for consideration, 'Mr. Wheelock declared that there was a cry of injustice in that magistrates and ministers were not rated' (taxed), ' which occasioned a very warm discourse. Mr. Stodder' (minister of Northampton) ' charged the deputy with saying what was not true, and the deputy governor' (Danforth) ' told him he deserved to be laid by the heels, etc.'

" ' After we broke up, the deputy and several others went home with Mr. Stodder, and the deputy asked forgiveness of him and told him he freely forgave him, but Mr. Stodder was high.' The next day 'the deputy owned his being in too great a heat, and desired the Lord to forgive it, and Mr. Stodder did something, though very little, by the deputy.' "[1] Wheelock was lucky in not having to smart more severely for his temerity, for the unfortunate Ursula Cole was sentenced to pay £5 [2] or be whipped for the lighter crime of saying " she had as lief hear a cat mew "[3] as Mr.

[1] Palfrey's *History of New England*, iii. 330, note 2. Extract from *Journal* of Rev. Peter Thacher.

[2] Five pounds was equivalent to a sum between one hundred and twenty-five and one hundred and fifty dollars now. Ursula was of course poor, or she would not have been sentenced to be whipped. The fine was therefore extremely heavy.

[3] Frothingham, *History of Charlestown*, p. 208.

Shepard preach. The daily services in the churches consumed so much time that they became a grievance with which the government was unable to cope.

In 1633 the Court of Assistants, thinking " the keepeing of lectures att the ordinary howres nowe obserued in the forenoone, to be dyvers wayes p̄eiudiciall to the comōn good, both in the losse of a whole day, & bringing othʳ charges & troubles to the place where the lecture is kept," ordered that they should not begin before one o'clock.[1] The evil still continued, for only the next year it was found that so many lectures " did spend too much time and proved overburdensome," and they were reduced to two a week.[2] Notwithstanding these measures, relief was not obtained, because, as the legislature complained in 1639, lectures " were held till night, and sometimes within the night, so as such as dwelt far off could not get home in due season, and many weak bodies could not endure so long, in the extremity of the heat or cold, without great trouble and hazard of their health," [3] and a consultation between the elders and magistrates was suggested.

But to have the delights of the pulpit abridged was more than the divines could bear. They declared roundly that their privileges were invaded ; [4] and the General Court had to give way. A few lines in Winthrop's Journal give an idea of the tax this loquacity must have been upon the time of a poor and scattered

[1] *Mass. Rec.* i. 110.
[2] Felt's *Eccl. Hist.* i. 201.
[3] Winthrop, i. 324.
[4] *Idem*, i. 325.

people. " Mr. Hooker being to preach at Cambridge, the governor and many others went to hear him. . . . He preached in the afternoon, and having gone on, with much strength of voice and intention of spirit, about a quarter of an hour, he was at a stand, and told the people that God had deprived him both of his strength and matter, &c. and so went forth, and about half an hour after returned again, and went on to very good purpose about two hours." [1]

Common men could not have kept this hold upon the inhabitants of New England, but the clergy were learned, resolute, and able, and their strong but narrow minds burned with fanaticism and love of power ; with their beliefs and under their temptations persecution seemed to them not only their most potent weapon, but a duty they owed to Christ — and that duty they unflinchingly performed. John Cotton, the most gifted among them, taught it as a holy work: " But the good that is brought to princes and subjects by the due punishment of apostate seducers and idolaters and blasphemers is manifold.

" First, it putteth away evill from the people and cutteth off a gangreene, which would spread to further ungodlinesse. . . .

" Secondly, it driveth away wolves from worrying and scattering the sheep of Christ. For false teachers be wolves, . . . and the very name of wolves holdeth forth what benefit will redound to the sheep, by either killing them or driving them away.

[1] Winthrop, i. 304.

"Thirdly, such executions upon such evill doers causeth all the country to heare and feare, and doe no more such wickednesse. . . . Yea as these punishments are preventions of like wickednesse in some, so are they wholesome medicines, to heale such as are curable of these eviles. . . .

"Fourthly, the punishments executed upon false prophets and seducing teachers, doe bring downe showers of God's blessings upon the civill state. . . .

"Fifthly, it is an honour to God's Justice that such judgments are executed. . . ." [1]

All motives combined to drive them headlong into cruelty ; for in the breasts of the larger number, even the passion of bigotry was cool beside the malignant hate they felt for those whose opinions menaced their earthly power and dominion ; and they never wearied of exhorting the magistrates to destroy the enemies of the church. "Men's lusts are sweet to them, and they would not be disturbed or disquieted in their sin. Hence there be so many such as cry up tolleration boundless and libertinism so as (if it were in their power) to order a total and perpetual confinement of the sword of the civil magistrate unto its scabbard ; (a notion that is evidently distructive to this people, and to the publick liberty, peace, and prosperity of any instituted churches under heaven.)" [2]

"Let the magistrates coercive power in matters of

[1] *Bloody Tenent Washed*, pp. 137, 138.

[2] *Eye Salve*, Election Sermon, by Mr. Shepard of Charlestown, p. 21.

religion (therefore) be still asserted, seing he is one who is bound to God more than any other men to cherish his true religion ; . . . and how wofull would the state of things soon be among us, if men might have liberty without controll to profess, or preach, or print, or publish what they list, tending to the seduction of others." [1] Such feelings found their fit expression in savage laws against dissenting sects ; these, however, will be dealt with hereafter ; only those which illustrate the fundamental principles of the theocracy need be mentioned here. One chief cause of schism was the hearing of false doctrine ; and in order that the people might not be led into temptation, but might on the contrary hear true exposition of the word, every inhabitant was obliged to attend the services of the established church upon the Lord's day under a penalty of fine or imprisonment ; the fine not to exceed 5s. (equal to about $5 now) for every absence.[2]

"If any christian so called . . . shall contemptuously behave himselfe toward y[e] word preached, or y[e] messeng[rs] thereof called to dispence y[e] same in any congregation, . . . or like a sonn of Corah cast upon his true doctrine or himselfe any reproach . . . shall for y[e] first scandole be convented . . . and bound to their good behaviour; and if a second time they breake forth into y[e] like contemptuous carriages, either to pay £5 to y[e] publike treasury or to stand

---

[1] *Eye Salve*, p. 38.

[2] 1634–35, 4 March. *Mass. Rec.* i. 140.

two houres openly upon a block 4 foote high, on a lecture day, wth a pap fixed on his breast wth this, A Wanton Gospeller, written in capitall lett[rs] y[t] oth[rs] may fear & be ashamed of breaking out into the like wickednes." [1]

"Though no humane pow[r] be Lord ov[r] y[e] faith & consciences of men and therefore may not constraine y[m] to beleeve or pfes ag[st] their conscience, yet because such as bring in damnable heresies tending to y[e] subversion of y[e] Christian faith . . . ought duely to be restrained fro[m] such notorious impiety, if any christian . . . shall go about to subvert . . . y[e] Christian faith, by broaching . . . any damnable heresy, as deniing y[e] imortality of y[e] soule, or y[e] resurrection of y[e] body, or any sinn to be repented of in y[e] regen[r]- ate, or any evill done by y[e] outward man to be ac- counted sinn, or deniing y[t] Christ gave himselfe a ran- some for o[r] sinns . . . or any oth[r] heresy of such nature & degree . . . shall pay to y[e] comon treas- ury during y[e] first six months 20*s*. a month and for y[e] next six months 40*s*. p. m., and so to continue dureing his obstinacy ; and if any such pson shall endeav[r] to seduce others . . . he shall forfeit . . . for every sev- erall offence . . . five pounds." [2]

" For y[e] honno[r] of y[e] aetaernall God, whome only wee wor[pp] and serve," (it is ordered that) " no pson w[th]in this jurisdicon, whether X[t]ian or pagan, shall wittingly and willingly psume to blaspheme his

[1] 1646, 4 Nov.   *Mass. Rec.* ii. 179.
[2] 1646, 4 Nov.   *Mass. Rec.* ii. 177.

holy name either by wilfull or obstinate denying y[e] true God, or rep[r]oach y[e] holy religion of God, as if it were but a polliticke devise to keepe ignorant men in awe, . . . or deny his creation or goūm[nt] of y[e] world, or shall curse God, or shall vtter any other eminent kind of blasphemy, of y[e] like nature and degree; if any pson or psons w[t]soeuer w[th]in our jurisdicõn shall breake this lawe they shall be putt to death." [1]

The special punishments for Antinomians, Baptists, Quakers, and other sectaries were fine and imprisonment, branding, whipping, mutilation, banishment, and hanging. Nor were the elders men to shrink from executing these laws with the same ferocious spirit in which they were enacted. Remonstrance and command were alike neglected. The Long Parliament warned them to beware; Charles II. repeatedly ordered them to desist; their trusted and dearest friend, Sir Richard Saltonstall, wrote from London to Cotton: " It doth not a little grieve my spirit to heare what sadd things are reported dayly of your tyranny and persecution in New England, as that you fyne, whip, and imprison men for their consciences," [2] and told them their " rigid wayes have laid you very lowe in the hearts of the saynts." Thirteen of the most learned and eminent nonconforming ministers in England wrote to the governor of Massachusetts imploring him that he and the General Court would not

---

[1] *Mass. Rec.* iii. 98.
[2] *Hutch. Coll.*, Prince Soc. ed. ii. 127.

by their violence " put an advantage into the hands of some who seek pretences and occasions against our liberty." [1] Winthrop, the wisest and ablest champion the clergy ever had, hung back. Like many another political leader, he was forced by his party into measures from which his judgment and his heart recoiled. He tells us how, on a question arising between him and Mr. Haynes, the elders " delivered their several reasons which all sorted to this conclusion, that strict discipline, both in criminal offences and in martial affairs, was more needful in plantations than in a settled state, as tending to the honor and safety of the gospel. Whereupon Mr. Winthrop acknowledged that he was convinced that he had failed in over much lenity and remissness, and would endeavor (by God's assistance) to take a more strict course thereafter." [2] But his better nature revolted from the foul task and once more regained ascendancy just as he sunk in death. For while he was lying very sick, Dudley came to his bedside with an order to banish a heretic : "No," said the dying man, " I have done too much of that work already," and he would not sign the warrant. [3]

Nothing could avail; for the clergy held the state within their grasp, and shrank from no deed of blood to guard the interests of their order.

The case of Gorton may serve as an example of a rigor that shocked even the Presbyterian Baillie ; it

[1] *Magnalia*, bk. 7, ch. iv. § 4.   [2] Winthrop, i. 178.
[3] *Life and Letters of Winthrop*, ii. 393.

must be said in explanation of his story that the magistrates condemned Gorton and his friends to death for the crime of heresy in obedience to the unanimous decision of the elders,[1] but the deputies refusing to concur, the sentence of imprisonment in irons during the pleasure of the General Court was agreed upon as a compromise. "Only they in New England are more strict and rigid than we, or any church, to suppress, by the power of the magistrate, all who are not of their way, to banishment ordinarily and presently even to death lately, or perpetual slavery; for one Jortin, sometime a famous citizen here for piety, having taught a number in New England to cast off the word and sacrament, and deny angels and devils, and teach a gross kind of union with Christ in this life, by force of arms was brought to New Boston, and there with ten of the chief of his followers, by the civil court was discerned perpetual slaves, but the votes of many were for their execution. They lie in irons, though gentlemen; and out of their prison write to the admiral here, to deal with the parliament for their deliverance."[2]

Like all phenomena of nature, the action of the mind is obedient to law; the cause is followed by the consequence with the precision that the earth moves round the sun, and impelled by this resistless power his destiny is wrought out by man. To the ecclesiastic a deep debt of gratitude is due, for it was by his effort that the first step from barbarism was made.

[1] Winthrop, ii. 146.   [2] Baillie's *Letters*, ii. 17, 18.

In the world's childhood, knowledge seems divine, and those who first acquire its rudiments claim, and are believed, to have received it by revelation from the gods. In an archaic age the priest is likewise the lawgiver and the physician, for all erudition is concentrated in one supremely favored class — the sacred caste. Their discoveries are kept profoundly secret, and yet to perpetuate their mysteries among their descendants they found schools which are the only repositories of learning; but the time must inevitably come when this order is transformed into the deadliest enemy of the civilization which it has brought into being. The power of the spiritual oligarchy rests upon superstitious terrors which dwindle before advancing enlightenment; hence the clergy have become reactionary, have sought to stifle the spirit of free inquiry, and have used the schools which they have builded as instruments to keep alive unreasoning prejudice, or to serve their selfish ends. This, then, has been the fiercest battle of mankind; the heroic struggle to break down the sacerdotal barrier, to popularize knowledge, and to liberate the mind, began ages before the crucifixion upon Calvary; it still goes on. In this cause the noblest and the bravest have poured forth their blood like water, and the path to freedom has been heaped with the corpses of her martyrs.

In that tremendous drama Massachusetts has played her part; it may be said to have made her intellectual life; and it is the passion of the combat which gives an interest at once so sombre and so romantic to her story.

In the tempest of the Reformation a handful of the sternest rebels were cast upon the bleak New England coast, and the fervor of that devotion which led them into the wilderness inspired them with the dream of reproducing the institutions of God's chosen people, a picture of which they believed was divinely preserved for their guidance in the Bible. What they did in reality was to surrender their new commonwealth to their priests. Yet they were a race in whose bone and blood the spirit of free thought was bred; the impulse which had goaded them to reject the Roman dogmas was quick within them still, and revolt against the ecclesiastical yoke was certain. The clergy upon their side trod their appointed path with the precision of machines, and, constrained by an inexorable destiny, they took that position of antagonism to liberal thought which has become typical of their order. And the struggles and the agony by which this poor and isolated community freed itself from its gloomy bondage, the means by which it secularized its education and its government, won for itself the blessing of free thought and speech, and matured a system of constitutional liberty which has been the foundation of the American Union, rise in dignity to one of the supreme efforts of mankind.

CHAPTER II.

THE ANTINOMIANS.

HABIT may be defined with enough accuracy for ordinary purposes as the result of reflex action, or the immediate response of the nerves to a stimulus, without the intervention of consciousness. Many bodily functions are naturally reflex, and most movements may be made so by constant repetition; they are then executed independently of the will. It is no exaggeration to say that the social fabric rests on the control this tendency exerts over the actions of men; and its strength is strikingly exemplified in armies, which, when well organized, are machines, wherein subjection to command is instinctive, and insubordination, therefore, practically impossible.

An analogous phenomenon is presented by the church, whose priests have intuitively exhausted their ingenuity in weaving webs of ceremonial, as soldiers have directed their energies to perfecting manuals of arms; and the evidence leads to the conclusion that increasing complexity of ritual indicates a densening ignorance and a deepening despotism. The Hindoos, the Spaniards, and the English are types of the progression.

Within the historic ages unnumbered methods of

sacerdotal discipline have been evolved, but whether the means used to compass the end has been the bewildering maze of a Levitical code, or the rosary and the confessional of Rome, the object has always been to reduce the devotee to the implicit obedience of the trooper. And the stupendous power of these amazingly perfect systems for destroying the capacity for original thought cannot be fully realized until the mind has been brought to dwell upon the fact that the greatest eras of human progress have begun with the advent of those who have led successful insurrection; nor can the dazzling genius of these brilliant exceptions be appreciated, unless it be remembered how infinitely small has been the number of those among mankind who, having been once drilled to rigid conformity, have not lapsed into automatism, but have been endowed with the mental energy to revolt. On the other hand, though ecclesiastics have differed widely in the details of the training they have enforced upon the faithful, they have agreed upon this cardinal principle: they have uniformly seized upon the education of the young, and taught the child to revere the rites in which he was made to partake before he could reason upon their meaning, for they understood well that the habit of abject submission to authority, when firmly rooted in infancy, would ripen into a second nature in after years, and would almost invariably last till death.

But this manual of religion, this deadening of the soul by making mechanical prayers and genu-

flexions the gauge of piety, has always roused the
deepest indignation in the great reformers; and, un-
appalled by the most ghastly perils, they have never
ceased to exhort mankind to cast off the slavery of
custom and emancipate the mind. Christ rebuked
the Pharisees because they rejected the commandment of God to keep their own tradition; Paul proclaimed that men should be justified by faith without
the deeds of the law; and Luther preached that the
Christian was free, that the soul did not live because
the body wore vestments or prayed with the lips, and
he denounced the tyranny of the clergy, who arrogated
to themselves a higher position than others who were
Christian in the spirit. On their side priesthoods
know these leaders of rebellion by an unerring instinct and pursue them to the death.

The ministers of New England were formalists to
the core, and the society over which they dominated
was organized upon the avowed basis of the manifes-
tation of godliness in the outward man. The sad
countenance, the Biblical speech, the sombre garb, the
austere life, the attendance at worship, and, above all,
the unfailing deference paid to themselves, were the
marks of sanctification by which the elders knew the
saints on earth, for whom they were to open the path
to fortune by making them members of the church.

Happily for Massachusetts, there has never been
a time when all her children could be docile under
such a rule; and, among her champions of freedom,
none have been braver than those who have sprung

from the ranks of her ministry, as the fate of Roger Williams had already proved. In such a community, before the ecclesiastical power had been solidified by time, only a spark was needed to kindle a conflagration, and that spark was struck by a woman.

So early as 1634 a restless spirit was abroad, for Winthrop was then set aside, and now, in 1636, young Henry Vane was enthusiastically elected governor, though he was only twenty-four, and had been but a few months in the colony. The future seemed bright and serene, yet he had hardly taken office before the storm burst, which not only overthrew him, but was destined to destroy that unhappy lady whom the Rev. Thomas Welde called the American Jezebel.[1]

John Cotton, the former rector of St. Botolph's, was the teacher of the Boston church. By common consent the leader of the clergy, he was the most brilliant, and, in some respects, the most powerful man in the colony. Two years before, Anne Hutchinson, with all her family, had followed him from her home in Lincolnshire into the wilderness, for, "when our teacher came to New England, it was a great trouble unto me; my brother, Wheelwright, being put by also." [2] A gentlewoman of spotless life, with a kind and charitable heart, a vigorous understanding and dauntless courage, her failings were vanity and a bit-

---

[1] Opinions are divided as to the authorship of the *Short Story*, but I conclude from internal evidence that the ending at least was written by Mr. Welde.

[2] Hutch. *Hist.* ii. 440.

ter tongue toward those whom she disliked.[1] Unfortunately also for herself, she was one of the enthusiasts
who believe themselves subject to divine revelations,
for this pretension would probably in any event have
brought upon her the displeasure of the church.   It
is worth while to attempt some logical explanation of
the dislike felt by the Massachusetts elders to any suggestion of such supernatural interposition.   The half-
unconscious train of reasoning on which they based
their claim to exact implicit obedience from the people seems, when analyzed, to yield this syllogism: All
revelation is contained in the Bible; but to interpret
the ancient sacred writings with authority, a technical training is essential, which is confined to priests;
therefore no one can define God's will who is not of
the ministry.   Had the possibility of direct revelation
been admitted this reasoning must have fallen; for
then, obviously, the word of an inspired peasant would
have outweighed the sermon of an uninspired divine;
it follows, necessarily, that ecclesiastics so situated
would have been jealous of lay preaching, and absolutely intolerant of the inner light.

In May, 1636, the month of Vane's election,
Mrs. Hutchinson had been joined by her brother-in-
law, John Wheelwright, the deprived vicar of Bilsby.
Her social influence was then at its height; her amiable disposition had made her popular, and for some
time past she had held religious meetings for women
at her house.   The ostensible object of these gather-

[1] Cotton, *Way of New England Churches*, p. 52.

ings was to recapitulate the sermons of the week; but the step from discussion to criticism was short, and it soon began to be said that she cast reproach " upon the ministers, . . . saying that none of them did preach the covenant of free grace, but Master Cotton, and that they have not the seale of the Spirit, and so were not able ministers of the New Testament." [1] Or, to use colloquial language, she accused the clergy of being teachers of forms, and said that, of them all, Cotton alone appealed to the animating spirit like Luther or St. Paul.

" A company of legall professors," quoth she, " lie poring on the law which Christ hath abolished." [2]

Such freedom of speech was, of course, intolerable; and so, as Cotton was implicated by her imprudent talk, the elders went to Boston in a body in October to take him to task. In the hope of adjusting the difficulty, he suggested a friendly meeting at his house, and an interview took place. At first Mrs. Hutchinson, with much prudence, declined to commit herself; but the Rev. Hugh Peters besought her so earnestly to deal frankly and openly with them that she, confiding in the sacred character of a confidential conversation with clergymen in the house of her own religious teacher, committed the fatal error of admitting that she saw a wide difference between Mr. Cotton's ministry and theirs, and that they could not preach a covenant of grace so clearly as he, because

[1] *Short Story,* p. 36.

[2] *Wonder-Working Providence,* Poole's ed. p. 102.

they had not the seal of the Spirit.   The progress of
the new opinion was rapid, and it is clear Mrs. Hutchinson had only given expression to a feeling of discontent which was both wide-spread and deep.   Before
winter her adherents, or those who condemned the
covenant of works, — in modern language, the liberals,
— had become an organized political party, of which
Vane was the leader; and here lay their first danger.

Notwithstanding his eminent ability, he was then
but a boy, and the task was beyond his strength.   The
stronghold of his party was Boston, where, except
some half-dozen,[1] the whole congregation followed him
and Cotton : yet even here he met with the powerful
opposition of Winthrop and the pastor, John Wilson.
In the country he was confronted by the solid body
of the clergy, whose influence proved sufficient to hold
together a majority of the voters in substantially all
the towns, so that the conservatives never lost control
of the legislature.

The position was harassing, and his nerves gave
way under the strain.   In December he called a court
and one day suddenly announced that he had received
letters from England requiring his immediate return ;
but when some of his friends remonstrated he " brake
forth into tears and professed that, howsoever the
causes propounded for his departure were such as did
concern the utter ruin of his outward estate, yet he
would rather have hazarded all " . . . " but for the
danger he saw of God's judgment to come upon us

[1] Winthrop, i. 212.

for these differences and dissensions which he saw amongst us, and the scandalous imputations brought upon himself, as if he should be the cause of all." [1]

Such a flight was out of the question. The weight of his name and the protection given his supporters by the power of his family in England could not be dispensed with, and therefore the Boston congregation intervened. After a day's reflection he seems himself to have become convinced that he had gone too far to recede, so he "expressed himself to be an obedient child to the church and therefore . . . durst not go away." [2]

That a young and untried man like Vane should have grown weary of his office and longed to escape will astonish no one who is familiar with the character and the mode of warfare of his adversaries.

In that society a layman could not retort upon a minister who insulted him, nor could Vane employ the arguments with which Cromwell so effectually silenced the Scotch divines. The following is a specimen of the treatment to which he was probably almost daily subjected, and the scene in this instance was the more mortifying because it took place before the assembled legislature.

" The ministers had met a little before and had drawn into heads all the points wherein they suspected Mr. Cotton did differ from them, and had propounded them to him, and pressed him to a direct answer . . . to every one; which he had promised.

[1] Winthrop, i. 207.   [2] *Idem*, i. 208.

. . . This meeting being spoke of in the court the day before, the governour took great offence at it, as being without his privity, &c., which this day Mr. Peter told him as plainly of (with all due reverence), and how it had sadded the ministers' spirits, that he should be jealous of their meetings, or seem to restrain their liberty, &c. The governour excused his speech as sudden and upon a mistake. Mr. Peter told him also, that before he came, within less than two years since, the churches were in peace. . . . Mr. Peter also besought him humbly to consider his youth and short experience in the things of God, and to beware of peremptory conclusions which he perceived him to be very apt unto." [1] This coarse bully was the same Hugh Peters of whom Whitelock afterward complained that he often advised him, though he "understood little of the law, but was very opinionative," [2] and who was so terrified at the approach of death that on his way to the scaffold he had to drink liquor to keep from fainting.[3]

" Mr. Wilson " also " made a very sad speech to the General Court of the condition of our churches, and the inevitable danger of separation, if these differences . . . were not speedily remedied, and laid the blame upon these new opinions . . . which all the magistrates except the governour and two others did confirm and all the ministers but two." [4] Those two were John Cotton and John Wheelwright, the preachers of the covenant of grace.

[1] Winthrop, i. 209.   [2] *Memorials*, p. 521.
[3] Burnet, i. 162.   [4] Winthrop, i. 209.

Their brethren might well make sad speeches, for their cup of bitterness was full ; but they must be left to describe for themselves the tempest of fear and wrath that raged within them. "Yea, some that had beene begotten to Christ by some of their faithfull labours in this land" (England, where the tract was published,) "for whom they could have laid downe their lives, and not being able to beare their absence followed after them thither to New England to enjoy their labours, yet these falling acquainted with those seducers, were suddenly so altered in their affections toward those their spirituall fathers, that they would neither heare them, nor willingly come in their company, professing they had never received any good from them." . . . "Now the faithfull ministers of Christ must have dung cast on their faces . . . must be pointed at as it were with the finger, and reproached by name, such a church officer is an ignorant man, and knows not Christ; such an one is under a covenant of works : such a pastor is a proud man, and would make a good persecutor . . . so that through these reproaches occasion was given to men, to abhorre the offerings of the Lord."[1]

"Now, one of them in a solemne convention of ministers dared to say to their faces, that they did not preach the Covenant of Free Grace, and that they themselves had not the seale of the Spirit. . . . Now, after our sermons were ended at our publike lectures, you might have seene halfe a dozen pistols discharged

[1] Welde's *Short Story*, Pref. §§ 7–11.

at the face of the preacher (I meane) so many objec.
tions made by the opinionists in the open assembly
against our doctrine . . . to the marvellous weaken-
ing of holy truths delivered . . . in the hearts of all
the weaker sort." [1]

John Wheelwright was a man whose character ex-
torts our admiration, if it does not win our love. The
personal friend of Cromwell and of Vane, with a mind
vigorous and masculine, and a courage stern and determined even above the Puritan standard of resolution and of daring, he spoke the truth which was within
him, and could neither be intimidated nor cajoled.
In October an attempt had been made to have him
settled as a teacher of the Boston church in conjunction with Wilson and Cotton, but it had miscarried
through Winthrop's opposition, and he had afterward
taken charge of a congregation that had been gathered
at Mount Wollaston, in what is now Quincy.

On the 19th of January a fast was held on account
of the public dissensions, and on that day Wheelwright preached a great sermon in Boston which brought
on the crisis. He was afterward accused of sedition:
the charge was false, for he did not utter one seditious word; but he did that which was harder to
forgive, he struck at what he deemed the wrong with
his whole might, and those who will patiently pore
over his pages until they see the fire glowing through
his rugged sentences will feel the power of his blow.
And what he told his hearers was in substance this:

[1] Welde's *Short Story*, Pref. §§ 7–11.

It maketh no matter how seemingly holy men be according to the law, if . . . they are such as trust to their own righteousness they shall die, saith the Lord. Do ye not after their works ; for they say and do not. They make broad their phylacteries and enlarge the borders of their garments ; and love the uppermost rooms at feasts, and the chief seats in the synagogues ; and greetings in the market place and to be called of men, Rabbi, Rabbi. But believe on the Lord Jesus Christ, and ye shall be saved, for being justified by faith we have peace with God through our Lord Jesus Christ. And the way we must take if so be we will not have the Lord Jesus Christ taken from us is this, we must all prepare a spiritual combat, we must put on the whole armor of God, and must have our loins girt up and be ready to fight, . . . because of fear in the night if we will not fight the Lord Jesus Christ may come to be surprised.

And when his brethren heard it they sought how they might destroy him ; for they feared him, because all the people were astonished at his doctrine.

In March the legislature met, and Wheelwright was arraigned before a court composed, according to the account of the Quaker Groom, of Henry Vane, " twelve magistrates, twelve priests, & thirty-three deputies." [1] His sermon was produced, and an attempt was made to obtain an admission that by those under a covenant of works he meant his brethren. But the accused was one whom it was hard to entrap and impossible

[1] Groom's *Glass for New England,* p. 6.

to frighten. He defied his judges to controvert his doctrine, offering to prove it by the Scriptures, and as for the application he answered that " if he were shown any that walked in such a way as he had described to be a covenant of works, them did he mean." [1] Then the rest of the elders were asked if they " did walk in such a way, and they all acknowledged they did," [2] excepting John Cotton, who declared that " brother Wheelwright's doctrine was according to God in the parts controverted, and wholly and altogether." [3] He received ecclesiastical justice. There was no jury, and the popular assembly that decided law and fact by a partisan vote was controlled by his adversaries. Yet even so, a verdict of sedition was such a flagrant outrage that the clergy found it impossible to command prompt obedience. For two days the issue was in doubt, but at length " the priests got two of the magistrates on their side, and so got the major part with them." [4] They appear, however, to have felt too weak to proceed to sentence, for the prisoner was remanded until the next session.

No sooner was the judgment made known than more than sixty of the most respected citizens of Boston signed a petition to the court in Wheelwright's behalf. In respectful and even submissive language they pointed out the danger of meddling with the right of

[1] Wheelwright, Prince Soc. ed. p. 17, note 27.
[2] Winthrop, i. 215. Wheelwright, p. 18.
[3] Groom's *Glass for New England*, p. 7.
[4] Felt's *Eccl. Hist.* ii. 611.

free speech. " Paul was counted a pestilent fellow, or
a moover of sedition, and a ringleader of a sect, . . .
and Christ himselfe, as well as Paul, was charged to
bee a teacher of New Doctrine. . . . Now wee beseech
you, consider whether that old serpent work not after
his old method, even in our daies." [1]

The charge of sedition made against them they repudiated in emphatic words, which deserve attention,
as they were afterwards held to be criminal.

" Thirdly, if you look at the effects of his doctrine
upon the hearers, it hath not stirred up sedition in us,
not so much as by accident; wee have not drawn the
sword, as sometimes Peter did, rashly, neither have wee
rescued our innocent brother, as sometimes the Israelites did Jonathan, and yet they did not seditiously.
The covenant of free grace held forth by our brother
hath taught us rather to become humble suppliants
to your worships, and if wee should not prevaile, wee
would rather with patience give our cheekes to the
smiters." [2]

The liberal feeling ran so strongly in Boston that
the conservatives thought it prudent to remove the
government temporarily to Cambridge, that they might
more easily control the election which was to come in
May. Vane, with some petulance, refused to entertain the motion; but Endicott put the question, and it
was carried. As the time drew near the excitement
increased, the clergy straining every nerve to bring up

[1] Wheelwright, Prince Soc. ed. p. 21.
[2] *Idem.*

their voters from the country; and on the morning of the day the feeling was so intense that the Rev. Mr. Wilson, forgetting his dignity and his age, scrambled up a tree and harangued the people from its branches.[1]

Yet, though the freemen were so deeply moved, there was no violence, and Winthrop was peaceably elected governor, with a strong conservative majority in the legislature. It so happened that just at this time a number of the friends of Wheelwright and the Hutchinsons were on their way from England to settle in Massachusetts. The first act of the new government was to exclude these new-comers by passing a law forbidding any town to entertain strangers for more than three weeks without the consent of two of the magistrates.

This oppressive statute caused such discontent that Winthrop thought it necessary to publish a defence, to which Vane replied and Winthrop rejoined. The controversy would long since have lost its interest had it not been for the theory then first advanced by Winthrop, that the corporation of Massachusetts, having bought its land, held it as though it were a private estate, and might exclude whom they pleased therefrom; and ever since this plea has been set up in justification of every excess committed by the theocracy.

Winthrop was a lawyer, and it is but justice to his reputation to presume that he spoke as a partisan, knowing his argument to be fallacious. As a legal proposition he must have been aware that it was unsound.

[1] Hutch. *Hist.* i. 62, note.

Although during the reign of Charles I. monopolies were a standing grievance with the House of Commons, yet they had been granted and enforced for centuries; and had Massachusetts claimed the right to exclude strangers as interlopers in trade, she would have stood upon good precedent. Such, however, was not her contention. The legislation against the friends of Wheelwright was passed avowedly upon grounds of religious difference of opinion, and a monopoly in religion was unknown.

Her commercial privileges alone were exclusive, and, provided he respected them, a British subject had the same right to dwell in Massachusetts as in any of the other dominions of the crown, or, indeed, in any borough which held its land by grant, like Plymouth. To subject Englishmen to restriction or punishment unknown to English law was as outrageous as the same act would have been had it been perpetrated by the city of London, — both corporations having a like power to preserve the peace by local ordinances, and both being controlled by the law of the land as administered by the courts. Such arguments as those advanced by Winthrop were only solemn quibbling to cloak an indefensible policy. To banish freemen for demanding liberty of conscience was a still more flagrant wrong. A precisely parallel case would have been presented had the directors of the East India Company declared the membership of a proprietor to be forfeited, and ordered his stock to be sold, because he disapproved of enforcing conformity in worship among inhabitants of the factories in Hindostan.

Vane sailed early in August, and his departure cleared the last barrier from the way of vengeance. Proceedings were at once begun by a synod of all the ministers, which was held at Cambridge, for the purpose of restoring peace to the churches. " There were about eighty opinions, some blasphemous, others erroneous, and all unsafe, condemned by the whole assembly. . . . Some of the church of Boston . . . were offended at the producing of so many errors, . . . and called to have the persons named which held those errors." To which the elders answered that all those opinions could be proved to be held by some, but it was not thought fit to name the parties. " Yet this would not satisfy some but they oft called for witnesses ; and because some of the magistrates declared to them . . . that if they would not forbear it would prove a civil disturbance . . . they objected. . . . So as he " (probably meaning Winthrop) "was forced to tell one of them that if he would not forbear . . . he might see it executed. Upon this some of Boston departed from the assembly and came no more." [1] Once freed from their repinings all went well, and their pastor, Mr. Wilson, soon had the satisfaction of sending their reputed heresies " to the devil of hell from whence they came." [2] Cotton, seeing that all was lost, hastened to make his peace by a submission which the Rev. Mr. Hubbard of Ipswich describes with unconscious cynicism. " If he were not convinced, yet he

[1] Winthrop, i. 238.
[2] *Magnalia*, bk. 3, ch. iii. § 13.

was persuaded to an amicable compliance with the
other ministers ; . . . for, although it was thought he
did still retain his own sense and enjoy his own apprehension in all or most of the things then controverted
(as is manifest by some expressions of his . . . since
that time published," . . .) yet. " By that means did
that reverend and worthy minister of the gospel re-
cover his former splendour throughout . . . New England." [1]

He was not a sensitive man, and having once determined to do penance, he was far too astute a politician
to do it by halves; he not only gave himself up to the
task of detecting the heterodoxy of his old friends,[2]
but on a day of solemn fasting he publicly professed
repentance with many tears, and told how, " God leaving him for a time, he fell into a spirituall slumber;
and had it not been for the watchfulnesse of his
brethren, the elders, &c., hee might have slept on,
. . . and was very thankfull to his brethren for their
watchfulnesse over him." [3]   Nor to the end of his life
did he feel quite at ease ; " yea, such was his ingenuity
and piety as that his soul was not satisfied without
often breaking forth into affectionate bewailing of his
infirmity herein, in the publick assembly, sometimes
in his prayer, sometimes in his sermon, and that with
tears." [4]

Wheelwright was made of sterner stuff, and was in-

[1] Hubbard, p. 302.   [2] Winthrop, i. 253.
[3] *Hypocrisie Unmasked*, p. 76.
[4] Norton's *Funeral Sermon*, p. 37.

flexible. In fact, however, the difference of dogma, if any existed, was trivial. The clergy used the cry of heresy to excite odium, just as they called their opponents Antinomians, or dangerous fanatics. To support these accusations the synod gravely accepted every unsavory inference which ingenuity could wring from the tenets of their adversaries; and these, together with the fables invented by idle gossip, made up the long list of errors they condemned. Though the scheme was unprincipled, it met with complete success, and the Antinomians have come down to posterity branded as deadly enemies of Christ and the commonwealth; yet nothing is more certain than that they were not only good citizens, but substantially orthodox. On such a point there is no one among the conservatives whose testimony has the weight of Winthrop's, who says: "Mr. Cotton . . . stated the differences in a very narrow scantling; and Mr. Shepherd, preaching at the day of election, brought them yet nearer, so as, except men of good understanding, and such as knew the bottom of the tenents of those of the other party, few could see where the difference was." [1] While Cotton himself complains bitterly of the falsehoods spread about him and his friends: "But when some of . . . the elders of neighbour churches advertised me of the evill report . . . I . . . dealt with Mrs. Hutchinson and others of them, declaring to them the erroneousnesse of those tenents, and the injury done to myself in fathering them upon mee. Both shee and they utterly

[1] Winthrop, i. 221.

denyed that they held such tenents, or that they had
fathered them upon mee. I returned their answer to
the elders. . . . They answered me they had but one
witnesse, . . . and that one loth to be known." . . .[1]
Moreover, it is a remarkable fact that, notwithstanding
the advantage it would have given the reactionists to
have been able to fix subversive opinions upon their
prominent opponents, it was found impossible to prove
heresy in a single case which was brought to trial. The
legislature chosen in May was apparently unfit for the
work now to be done, for the extraordinary step of a
dissolution was decided on, and a new election held, under circumstances in which it was easy to secure the
return of suitable candidates. The session opened on
November 2, and Wheelwright was summoned to appear. He was ordered to submit, or prepare for sentence. He replied that he was guilty of neither sedition
nor contempt; that he had preached only the truth of
Christ, the application of which was for others, not
for him. "To which it was answered by the court
that they had not censured his doctrine, but left it as
it was; but his application, by which hee laid the magistrates and ministers and most of the people of God
in these churches under a covenant of works." [2] The
prisoner was then sentenced to be disfranchised and
banished. He demanded an appeal to the king; it
was refused; and he was given fourteen days to leave
Massachusetts. So he went forth alone in the bit-

[1] Cotton, *Way of New England Churches*, pp. 39, 40.
[2] *Short Story*, p. 24.

ter winter weather and journeyed to the Piscataqua, — yet "it was marvellous he got thither at that time, when they expelled him, by reason of the deep snow in which he might have perished."[1] Nor was banishment by any means the trivial penalty it has been described. On the contrary, it was a punishment of the utmost rigor. The exiles were forced suddenly to dispose of their property, which, in those times, was mostly in houses and land, and go forth among the savages with helpless women and children. Such an ordeal might well appall even a brave man; but Wheelwright was sacrificing his intellectual life. He was leaving books, friends, and the mental activity, which made the world to him, to settle in the forests among backwoodsmen; and yet even in this desolate solitude the theocracy continued to pursue him with persevering hate.

But there were others beside Wheelwright who had sinned, and some pretext had to be devised by which to reach them. The names of most of his friends were upon the petition that had been drawn up after his trial. It is true it was a proceeding with which the existing legislature was not concerned, since it had been presented to one of its predecessors; it is also true that probably never, before or since, have men who have protested they have not drawn the sword rashly, but have come as humble suppliants to offer their cheeks to the smiters, been held to be public enemies. Such scruples, however, never hampered

---

[1] Wheelwright, Prince Soc. ed. *Mercurius Americanus*, p. 24.

the theocracy. Their justice was trammelled neither
by judges, by juries, nor by laws; the petition was
declared to be a seditious libel, and the petitioners
were given their choice of disavowing their act and
making humble submission, or exile.

Aspinwall was at once disfranchised and banished.[1]
Coddington, Coggeshall, and nine more were given
leave to depart within three months, or abide the
action of the court; others were disfranchised; and
fifty-eight of the less prominent of the party were
disarmed in Boston alone.[2]

Thus were the early liberals crushed in Massachusetts; the bold were exiled, the timid were terrified;
as a political organization they moved no more till the
theocracy was tottering to its fall; and for forty years
the power of the clergy was absolute in the land.

The fate of Anne Hutchinson makes a fit ending to
this sad tale of oppression and of wrong. In November, 1637, when her friends were crushed, and the tri-
umphant priests felt that their victim's doom was sure,
she was brought to trial before that ghastliest den of
human iniquity, an ecclesiastical criminal court. The
ministers were her accusers, who came burning with
hate to testify to the words she had spoken to them at
their own request, in the belief that the confidence she
reposed was to be held sacred. She had no jury to
whose manhood she could appeal, and John Winthrop,
to his lasting shame, was to prosecute her from the
judgment seat. She was soon to become a mother,

---

[1] *Mass. Rec.* i. 207.   [2] *Idem,* i. 223.

and her health was feeble, but she was made to stand till she was exhausted; and yet, abandoned and forlorn, before those merciless judges, through two long, weary days of hunger and of cold, the intrepid woman defended her cause with a skill and courage which even now, after two hundred and fifty years, kindles the heart with admiration.   The case for the government was opened by John Winthrop, the presiding justice, the attorney - general, the foreman of the jury, and the chief magistrate of Massachusetts Bay.   He upbraided the prisoner with her many evil courses, with having spoken things prejudicial to the honor of the ministers, with holding an assembly in her house, and with divulging the opinions held by those who had been censured by that court; closing in these words, which sound strangely in the mouth of a New England judge : —

We have thought good to send for you . . . that if you be in an erroneous way we may reduce you that so you may become a profitable member here among us, otherwise if you be obstinate . . . that then the court may take such course that you may trouble us no further, therefore I would entreat you . . . whether you do not justify Mr. Wheelwright's sermon and the petition.

Mrs. H. I am called here to answer before you, but I hear no things laid to my charge.

Gov. I have told you some already, and more I can tell you.

Mrs. H. Name one, sir.

Gov. Have I not named some already?

Mrs. H. What have I said or done? . . .

Gov. You have joined with them in the faction.

Mrs. H. In what faction have I joined with them?

Gov. In presenting the petition. . . .

Mrs. H. But I had not my hand to the petition.

Gov. You have counselled them.

Mrs. H. Wherein?

Gov. Why, in entertaining them.

Mrs. H. What breach of law is that, sir?

Gov. Why, dishonoring of parents. . . .

Mrs. H. I may put honor upon them as the children of God and as they do honor the Lord.

Gov. We do not mean to discourse with those of your sex but only this; you do adhere unto them, and do endeavor to set forward this faction, and so you do dishonor us.

Mrs. H. I do acknowledge no such thing, neither do I think that I ever put any dishonor upon you.

And, on the whole, the chief justice broke down so hopelessly in his examination, that the deputy governor, or his senior associate upon the bench, thought it necessary to interfere.

Dep. Gov. I would go a little higher with Mrs. Hutchinson. Now . . . if she in particular hath disparaged all our ministers in the land that they have preached a covenant of works, and only Mr. Cotton a covenant of grace, why this is not to be suffered. . .

Mrs. H. I pray, sir, prove it, that I said they preached nothing but a covenant of works. . . .

Dep. Gov. If they do not preach a covenant of grace, clearly, then, they preach a covenant of works.

Mrs. H. No, sir, one may preach a covenant of grace more clearly than another, so I said.

Dudley was faring worse than Winthrop, and the divines, who had been bursting with impatience, could hold no longer. The Rev. Hugh Peters broke in : " That which concerns us to speak unto, as yet we are sparing in, unless the court command us to speak, then we shall answer to Mrs. Hutchinson, notwith-standing our brethren are very unwilling to answer." And without further urging, that meek servant of Christ went on to tell how he and others had heard that the prisoner said they taught a covenant of works, how they had sent for her, and though she was " very tender " at first, yet upon being begged to speak plainly, she had explained that there " was a broad difference between our Brother Mr. Cotton and our-selves. I desired to know the difference. She an-swered ' that he preaches the covenant of grace and you the covenant of works, and that you are not able ministers of the New Testament, and know no more than the apostles did before the resurrection.' " . . .

Mrs. H. If our pastor would shew his writings you should see what I said, and that many things are not so as is reported.

Mr. Wilson. Sister Hutchinson, for the writings you speak of I have them not. . . .

Five more divines followed, who, though they were " loth to speak in that assembly concerning that gentlewoman," yet to ease their consciences in " the relation wherein " they stood " to the Commonwealth and . . . unto God," felt constrained to state that the prisoner had said they were not able ministers of the New Testament, and that the whole of the evidence of Hugh Peters was true, and in so doing they came to an issue of veracity with Cotton.

An adjournment soon followed till next day, and the presiding justice seems to have considered his case against his prisoner as closed.

In the morning Mrs. Hutchinson opened her defence by calling three witnesses, Leverett, Coggeshall, and John Cotton.

Gov. Mr. Coggeshall was not present.

Mr. C. Yes, but I was, only I desired to be silent till I should be called.

Gov. Will you . . . say that she did not say so ?

Mr. C. Yes, I dare say that she did not say all that which they lay against her.

Mr. Peters. How dare you look into the court to say such a word ?

Mr. C. Mr. Peters takes upon him to forbid me. I shall be silent. . . .

Gov. Well, Mr. Leverett, what were the words ? I pray speak.

Mr. L. To my best remembrance . . . Mr. Peters did with much vehemency and entreaty urge her to tell what difference there was between Mr. Cotton and them, and upon his urging of her she said : " The fear of man is a snare, but they that trust upon the Lord shall be safe." And . . . that they did not preach a covenant of grace so clearly as Mr. Cotton did, and she gave this reason of it, because that as the apostles were for a time without the Spirit so until they had received the witness of the Spirit they could not preach a covenant of grace so clearly.

The Rev. John Cotton was then called. He was much embarrassed in giving his evidence, but, if he is to be believed, his brethren, in their anxiety to make out a case, had colored material facts. He closed his account of the interview in these words : " I must say that I did not find her saying they were under a covenant of works, nor that she said they did preach a covenant of works."

Gov. You say you do not remember, but can you say she did not speak so ?

Mr. C. I do remember that she looked at them as the apostles before the ascension. . . .

Dep. Gov. They affirm that Mrs. Hutchinson did say they were not able ministers of the New Testament.

Mr. C. I do not remember it.

Mrs. Hutchinson had shattered the case of the government in a style worthy of a leader of the bar, but
she now ventured on a step for which she has been
generally condemned. She herself approached the
subject of her revelations. To criticise the introduction of evidence is always simpler than to conduct a
cause, but an analysis of her position tends to show
not only that her course was the result of mature
reflection, but that her judgment was in this instance
correct. She probably assumed that when the more
easily proved charges had broken down she would be
attacked here; and in this assumption she was undoubtedly right. The alternative presented to her,
therefore, was to go on herself, or wait for Winthrop
to move. If she waited she knew she should give the
government the advantage of choosing the ground,
and she would thus be subjected to the danger of having fatal charges proved against her by hearsay or
distorted evidence. If she took the bolder course, she
could explain her revelations as monitions coming to
her through texts in Scripture, and here she was certain of Cotton's support. Before that tribunal she
could hardly have hoped for an acquittal; but if anything could have saved her it would have been the
sanction given to her doctrines by the approval of
John Cotton. At all events, she saw the danger, for
she closed her little speech in these touching words:
"Now if you do condemn me for speaking what in
my conscience I know to be truth, I must commit myself unto the Lord."

Mr. Nowell. How do you know that that was the Spirit?

Mrs. H. How did Abraham know that it was God? . . .

Dep. Gov. By an immediate voice.

Mrs. H. So to me by an immediate revelation.

Then she proceeded to state how, through various texts which she cited, the Lord showed her what He would do; and she particularly dwelt on one from Daniel. So far all was well; she had planted herself on ground upon which orthodox opinion was at least divided; but she now committed the one grave error of her long and able defence. As she went on her excitement gained upon her, and she ended by something like a defiance and denunciation: "You have power over my body, but the Lord Jesus hath power over my body and soul; and assure yourselves thus much, you do as much as in you lies to put the Lord Jesus Christ from you, and if you go on in this course you begin, you will bring a curse upon you and your posterity, and the mouth of the Lord hath spoken it."

Gov. Daniel was delivered by miracle. Do you think to be delivered so too?

Mrs. H. I do here speak it before the court. I look that the Lord should deliver me by his providence. . . .

Dep. Gov. I desire Mr. Cotton to tell us whether you do approve of Mrs. Hutchinson's revelations as she hath laid them down.

Mr. C. I know not whether I do understand her, but this I say, if she doth expect a deliverance in a way of providence, then I cannot deny it.

Gov. . . . I see a marvellous providence of God to bring things to this pass. . . . God by a providence hath answered our desires, and made her to lay open herself and the ground of all these disturbances to be by revelations. . . .

Court. We all consent with you.

Gov. Ey, it is the most desperate enthusiasm in the world. . . .

Mr. Endicott. I speak in reference to Mr. Cotton. . . . Whether do you witness for her or against her.

Mr. C. This is that I said, sir, and my answer is plain, that if she doth look for deliverance from the hand of God by his providence, and the revelation be . . . according to a word [of Scripture] that I cannot deny.

Mr. Endicott. You give me satisfaction.

Dep. Gov. No, no, he gives me none at all. . . .

Mr. C. I pray, sir, give me leave to express myself. In that sense that she speaks I dare not bear witness against it.

Mr. Nowell. I think it is a devilish delusion.

Gov. Of all the revelations that ever I read of I never read the like ground laid as is for this. The enthusiasts and Anabaptists had never the like. . . .

Mr. Peters. I can say the same . . . and I think that is very disputable which our brother Cotton hath spoken. . . .

Gov. I am persuaded that the revelation she brings forth is delusion.

All the court but some two or three ministers cry out, We all believe it, we all believe it. . . .

And then Coddington stood up before that angry meeting like the brave man he was, and said, " I beseech you do not speak so to force things along, for I do not for my own part see any equity in the court in all your proceedings. Here is no law of God that she hath broken, nor any law of the country that she hath broke, and therefore deserves no censure ; and if she say that the elders preach as the apostles did, why they preached a covenant of grace and what wrong is that to them, . . . therefore I pray consider, what you do, for here is no law of God or man broken."

Mr. Peters. I profess I thought Mr. Cotton would never have took her part.

Gov. The court hath already declared themselves satisfied . . . concerning the troublesomeness of her spirit and the danger of her course amongst us which is not to be suffered. Therefore if it be the mind of the court that Mrs. Hutchinson . . . shall be banished out of our liberties and imprisoned till she be sent away let them hold up their hands.

All but three consented.

Those contrary minded hold up yours. Mr. Coddington and Colburn only.

Gov. Mrs. Hutchinson, the sentence of the court you hear is that you are banished from out of our jurisdiction as being a woman not fit for our society, and are to be imprisoned till the court shall send you away.

Mrs. H. I desire to know wherefore I am banished.

Gov. Say no more, the court knows wherefore and is satisfied.[1]

With refined malice she was committed to the custody of Joseph Welde of Roxbury, the brother of the Rev. Thomas Welde who thought her a Jezebel. Here "divers of the elders resorted to her," and under this daily torment rapid progress was made. Probably during that terrible interval her reason was tottering, for her talk came to resemble ravings.[2] When this point was reached the divines saw their object attained, and that "with sad hearts" they could give her up to Satan.[2] Accordingly they "wrote to the church at Boston, offering to make proof of the same," whereupon she was summoned and the lecture appointed to begin at ten o'clock.[3]

"When she was come one of the ruling elders called her forth before the assembly," and read to her the twenty-nine errors of which she was accused, all of which she admitted she had maintained. "Then she asked by what rule such an elder would come to

---

[1] Hutch. *Hist.* vol. ii. App. 2.   [2] *Brief Apologie,* p. 59.
[3] Winthrop, i. 254.

her pretending to desire light and indeede to entrappe her." He answered that he came not to "entrap her but in compassion to her soule. . . ."

"Then presently she grew into passion . . . professing withall that she held none of these things . . . before her imprisonment." [1]

The court sat till eight at night, when "Mr. Cotton pronounced the sentence of admonition . . . with much zeal and detestation of her errors and pride of spirit." [2] An adjournment was then agreed on for a week and she was ordered to return to Roxbury; but this was more than she could bear, and her distress was such that the congregation seem to have felt some touch of compassion, for she was committed to the charge of Cotton till the next lecture day, when the trial was to be resumed. [3] At his house her mind recovered its tone and when she again appeared she not only retracted the wild opinions she had broached while at Joseph Welde's, but admitted "that what she had spoken against the magistrates at the court (by way of revelation) was rash and ungrounded." [4]

But nothing could avail her. She was in the hands of men determined to make her expiation of her crimes a by-word of terror; her fate was sealed. The doctrines she now professed were less objectionable, so she was examined as to former errors, among others "that she had denied inherent righteousness;" she "affirmed that it was never her judgment; and though

---

[1] *Brief Apol.* pp. 59–61.　　[2] Winthrop, i. 256.
[3] *Brief Apol.* p. 62.　　[4] Winthrop, i. 258.

it was proved by many testimonies . . . yet she impudently persisted in her affirmation to the astonishment of all the assembly. So that . . . the church with one consent cast her out. . . . After she was excommunicated her spirit, which seemed before to be somewhat dejected, revived again and she gloried in her sufferings." [1] And all this time she had been alone; her friends were far away.

That no circumstances of horror might be lost, she and one of her most devoted followers, Mary Dyer, were nearing their confinements during this time of misery. Both cases ended in misfortunes over whose sickening details Thomas Welde and his reverend brethren gloated with a savage joy, declaring that " God himselfe was pleased to step in with his casting vote . . . as clearly as if he had pointed with his finger." [2] Let posterity draw a veil over the shocking scene.

Two or three days after her condemnation " the governor sent [her] a warrant . . . to depart . . . she went by water to her farm at the Mount . . . and so to the island in the Narragansett Bay which her husband and the rest of that sect had purchased of the Indians." [3]

This pure and noble but most unhappy woman had sinned against the clergy, past forgiveness here or hereafter. They gibbeted her as Jezebel, and her name became a reproach in Massachusetts through two

[1] Winthrop, i. 258.   [2] *Short Story*, Preface, § 5.
[3] Winthrop, i. 259.

hundred years. But her crimes and the awful ending of her life are best read in the Christian words of the Rev. Thomas Welde, whose gentle spirit so adorned his holy office.

" For the servants of God who came over into New England . . . seeing their ministery was a most precious sweete savour to all the saints before she came hither, it is easie to discerne from what sinke that ill vapour hath risen which hath made so many of her seduced party to loath now the smell of those flowers which they were wont to find sweetnesse in.[1] . . . The Indians set upon them, and slew her and all the family.[2] . . . Some write that the Indians did burne her to death with fire, her house and all the rest named that belonged to her; but I am not able to affirme by what kind of death they slew her, but slaine it seemes she is, according to all reports. I never heard that the Indians in those parts did ever before this, commit the like outrage . . . ; and therefore God's hand is the more apparently seene herein, to pick out this wofull woman, to make her and those belonging to her, an unheard of heavie example of their cruelty above al others." [3]

[1] *Short Story*, p. 40.

[2] Mrs. Hutchinson and her family were killed in a general massacre of the Dutch and English by the Indians on Long Island. Winthrop, ii. 136.

[3] *Short Story*, Preface.

CHAPTER III.

THE CAMBRIDGE PLATFORM.

WITH the ruin of the Antinomians, opposition to the clergy ceased within the church itself, but many causes combined to prevent the bulk of the people from participating in the communion. Of those who were excluded, perhaps even the majority might have found it impossible to have secured their pastor's approbation, but numbers who would have been gladly received were restrained by conscientious scruples; and more shrank from undergoing the ordeal to which they would have been obliged to submit. It was no light matter for a pious but a sincerely honest man to profess his conversion, and how God had been pleased to work " in the inward parts of his soul," when he was not absolutely certain that he had indeed been visited by the Spirit. And it is no exaggeration to say that to sensitive natures the initiation was appalling. The applicant had first to convince the minister of his worthiness, then his name was openly propounded, and those who knew of any objection to his character, either moral or religious, were asked to give notice to the presbytery of elders. If the candidate succeeded in passing this private examination as to his fitness the following scene took place in church : —

" The party appearing in the midst of the assembly
. . . the ruling elder speaketh in this manner: Brethren of this congregation, this man or woman . . . hath
beene heretofore propounded to you, desiring to enter
into church fellowship with us, and we have not since
that heard anything from any of you to the contrary
of the parties admittance but that we may goe on to
receive him: therefore now, if any of you know anything against him, why he may not be admitted, you
may yet speak. . . . Whereupon, sometimes men do
speak to the contrary . . . and so stay the party for
that time also till this new offence be heard before
the elders, so that sometimes there is a space of divers
moneths between a parties first propounding and receiving, and some are so bashfull as that they choose
rather to goe without the communion than undergoe
such publique confessions and tryals, but that is held
their fault." [1]

Those who were thus disfranchised, Lechford, who
knew what he was talking about, goes on to say, soon
began to complain that they were " ruled like slaves ; "
and there can be no doubt that they had to submit to
very substantial grievances. The administration of
justice especially seems to have been defective. " Now
the most of the persons at New England are not admitted of their church, and therefore are not freemen,
and when they come to be tryed there, be it for life or
limb, name or estate, or whatsoever, they must bee tryed
and judged too by those of the church, who are in a

---

[1] Lechford, *Plain Dealing*, pp. 6, 7.

sort their adversaries : how equall that hath been, or may be, some by experience doe know, others may judge." [1]

The government was in fact in the hands of a small oligarchy of saints,[2] who were, in their turn, ruled by their priests, and as the repression of thought inevitable under such a system had roused the Antinomians, who were voters, to demand a larger intellectual freedom, so the denial of ordinary political rights to the majority led to discontent.

Since under the theocracy there was no department of human affairs in which the clergy did not meddle, they undertook as a matter of course to interfere with the militia, and the following curious letter written to the magistrates by the ministers of Rowley shows how far they carried their supervision even so late as 1689.

ROWLEY, *July* 24th, 1689.

May it please your honors,

The occasion of these lines is to inform you that whereas our military company have nominated Abel Platts, for ensign, we conceive that it is our duty to declare that we cannot approve of their choice in that he is corrupt in his judgment with reference to the Lord's Supper, declaring against Christ's words of justification, and hereupon hath withdrawn himself from communion with the church in that holy ordinance some years, besides some other things wherein

[1] *Plain Dealing,* p. 23.

[2] " Three parts of the people of the country remaine out of the church." *Plain Dealing,* p. 73. A. D. 1642.

he hath shown no little vanity in his conversation and hath demeaned himself unbecomingly toward the word and toward the dispensers of it. . . .

SAMUEL PHILLIPS.
EDWARD PAISON.[1]

A somewhat similar difficulty, which happened in Hingham in 1645, produced very serious consequences. A new captain had been chosen for their company; but a dispute having arisen, the magistrates, on the question being submitted to them, set the election aside and directed the old officers to keep their places until the General Court should meet. Notwithstanding this order the commotion continued to increase, and the pastor, Mr. Peter Hubbert, " was very forward to have excommunicated the lieutenant," who was the candidate the magistrates favored.[2] Winthrop happened to be deputy governor that year, and the aggrieved officer applied to him for protection; whereupon, as the defendants seemed inclined to be recalcitrant, several were committed in open court, among whom were three of Mr. Hubbert's brothers.

Forthwith the clergyman in great wrath headed a petition to which he obtained a large number of signatures, in which he prayed the General Court to take cognizance of the cause, since it concerned the public liberty and the liberty of the church.

At its next session, the legislature proceeded to examine the whole case, and Winthrop was brought to

---

[1] *History of Newbury*, p. 80.   [2] Winthrop, ii. 222, 223.

trial for exceeding his jurisdiction as a magistrate. A contest ensued between the deputies and assistants, which was finally decided by the influence of the elders. The result was that Winthrop was acquitted and Mr. Hubbert and the chief petitioners were fined.[1]

In March the constable went to Hingham to collect the money,[2] but he found the minister indisposed to submit in silence. About thirty people had collected, and before them all Mr. Hubbert demanded the warrant; when it was produced he declared it worthless because not in the king's name, and then went on to add that the government " was not more then a corporation in England, and . . . had not power to put men to death . . . that for himself he had neither horn nor hoofe of his own, nor anything wherewith to buy his children cloaths . . . if he must pay the fine he would pay it in books, but that he knew not for what they were fined, unlesse it were for petitioning : and if they were so waspish they might not be petitioned, then he could not tell what to say." [3]

Unluckily for Mr. Hubbert he had taken the popular side in this dispute and had thus been sundered from his brethren, who sustained Winthrop, and in the end carried him through in triumph ; and not only this, but he was suspected of Presbyterian tendencies, and a committee of the elders who had visited Hingham to reconcile some differences in the congregation

[1] Winthrop, ii. 227.   [2] 1645–46, 18 March.
[3] *New Eng. Jonas,* Marvin's ed. p. 5.

had found him in grave fault. The government was not sorry, therefore, to make him a public example, as appeared not only by these proceedings, but by the way he was treated in the General Court the next autumn. He was accordingly indicted for sedition, tried and convicted in June, fined twenty pounds, and bound over to good behavior in forty pounds more.[1] Such a disturbance as this seems to have been all that was needed to bring the latent discontent to a focus.

William Vassal had been an original patentee and was a member of the first Board of Assistants, who were appointed by the king. Being, however, a man of liberal views he had not found Massachusetts congenial; he had returned to England after a stay of only a month, and when he came again to America in 1635, he had settled at Scituate, the town adjoining Hingham, but in the Plymouth jurisdiction. Having both wealth and social position he possessed great influence, and he now determined to lead an agitation for equal rights and liberty of conscience in both colonies at once, by petitioning the legislatures, and in case of failure there, presenting similar petitions to Parliament.

Bradford was this year[2] governor of Plymouth, and Edward Winslow was an assistant. Winslow himself had been governor repeatedly, was a thorough-going churchman, and deep in all the councils of the conservative party. There was, however, no religious qualification for the suffrage in the old

[1] *New Eng. Jonas*, p. 6.   2 June, 1646.   [2] 1645.

colony, and the complexion of its politics was therefore far more liberal than in Massachusetts; so Vassal was able to command a strong support when he
brought forward his proposition. Winslow, writing to
his friend Winthrop at Boston, gives an amusing account of his own and Bradford's consternation, and the
expedients to which they were forced to resort in the
legislature to stave off a vote upon the petition, when
Vassal made his motion in October, 1645.

" After this, the first excepter [Vassal] having been
observed to tender the view of a scroule from man to
man, it came at length to be tendered to myself, and
withall, said he, it may be you will not like this.
Having read it, I told him I utterly abhorred it as
such as would make us odious to all Christian com-
monweales : But at length he told the governor
[Bradford] he had a written proposition to be propounded to the court, which he desired the court to
take into consideration, and according to order, if
thought meet, to be allowed : To this the deputies
were most made beforehand, and the other three assistants, who applauded it as their Diana; and the
sum of it was, to allow and maintaine full and free
tollerance of religion to all men that would preserve
the civill peace and submit unto government; and
there was no limitation or exception against Turke,
Jew, Papist, Arian, Socinian, Nicholaytan, Familist,
or any other, &c. But our governor and divers of us
having expressed the sad consequences would follow,
especially myselfe and Mr. Prence, yet notwithstand-

ing it was required, according to order, to be voted:
But the governor would not suffer it to come to vote,
as being that indeed would eate out the power of God-
lines, &c. . . . You would have admired to have seen
how sweet this carrion relished to the pallate of most
of the deputies! What will be the issue of these
things, our all ordering God onely knows. . . . But if
he have such a judgment for this place, I trust we
shall finde (I speake for many of us that groane under these things) a resting place among you for the
soales of our feet." [1]

As just then nothing more could be done in Plymouth, proceedings were transferred to Massachusetts.
Samuel Maverick is a bright patch of color on the sad
Puritan background. He had a dwelling at Winnisime,
that "in the yeare 1625 I fortified with a pillizado
and fflankers and gunnes both belowe and above in
them which awed the Indians who at that time had a
mind to cutt off the English." [2] When Winthrop
landed, he found him keeping open house, so kindly
and freehanded that even the grim Johnson relaxes
when he speaks of him: "a man of very loving and
curteous behaviour, very ready to entertaine strangers, yet an enemy to the reformation in hand, being
strong for the lordly prelatical power." [3]

This genial English churchman entertained every
one at his home on Noddle's Island, which is now

---

[1] *Hutch. Coll.*, Prince Soc. ed. i. 174.

[2] *Mass. Hist. Soc. Proceedings*, Oct. 1884, p. 236.

[3] *Wonder-Working Providence*, Poole's ed. p. 37.

East Boston : Vane and Lord Ley, and La Tour when he came to Boston ruined, and even Owen when he ran off with another man's wife, and so brought a fine of £100 on his host. Josselyn says with much feeling: " I went a shore upon Noddles Island to Mr. Samuel Maverick, . . . the only hospitable man in the whole countrey." He was charitable also, and Winthrop relates how, when the Indians were dying of the small-pox, he, "his wife and servants, went daily to them, ministered to their necessities, and buried their dead, and took home many of their children." He was generous, too, with his wealth; and when the town had to rebuild the fort on Castle Island much of the money came from him.

But, as Endicott told the Browns, when he shipped them to England, because their practice in adhering to their Episcopal orders tended to " mutiny," " New England was no place for such as they." One by one they had gone, — the Browns first, and afterward William Blackstone, who had found it best to leave Boston because he could not join the church ; and now the pressure on Maverick began to make him restive. Though he had been admitted a freeman in the early days, he was excluded from all offices of importance ; he was taxed to support a church of which he disapproved, yet was forced to attend, though it would not baptize his children ; and he was so suspected that, in March, 1635, he had been ordered to remove to Boston, and was forbidden to lodge strangers for more than one night without leave from a magistrate. Under such circumstances he could not but sympathize with Vassal in his effort to win for all men equal rights before the law. Next after him in consequence was Dr. Robert Childe, who had taken a degree at Padua, and who, though not a freeman, had considerable interests in the country, — a man of property and standing. There were five more signers of the petition: Thomas Burton, John Smith, David Yale, Thomas Fowle, and John Dand, but they do not require particular notice. They prayed that "civil liberty and freedome be forthwith granted to all truly English, equall to the rest of their countrymen, as in all plantations is accustomed to be done, and as all free-borne enjoy in our native country. . . . Further that none of the English nation . . . be banished unless they break the known lawes of England. . . . We therefore humbly intreat you, in whose hands it is to help . . . for the glory of God . . . to give liberty to the members of the churches of England not scandalous in their lives . . . to be taken into your congregations, and to enjoy with you all those liberties and ordinances Christ hath purchased for them, and into whose name they are baptized . . . or otherwise to grant liberty to settle themselves here in a church way according to the best reformations of England and Scotland. If not, we and they shall be necessitated to apply our humble desires to the Honorable Houses of Parliament." [1]

This petition was presented to the court on May

[1] *New Eng. Jonas,* Marvin's ed. pp. 13–15.

19, 1646; but the session was near its close, and it was thought best to take no immediate steps. The elders, however, became satisfied that the moment had come for a thorough organization of the church, and they therefore caused the legislature to issue a general invitation to all the congregations to send representatives to a synod to be held at Cambridge. But notwithstanding the inaction of the authorities, the clergy were perfectly aware of the danger, and they passed the summer in creating the necessary indignation among the voters: they bitterly denounced from their pulpits " the sons of Belial, Judasses, sons of Corah," "with sundry appellations of that nature . . . which seemed not to arise from a gospel spirit." Sometimes they devoted "a whole sermon, and that not very short," to describing the impending ruin and exhorting the magistrates " to lay hold upon " the offenders.[1] Winthrop had been chosen governor in May, and, when the legislature met in October, he was made chairman of a committee to draft an answer to Childe. This document may be found in Hutchinson's Collection. As a state paper devoted to the discussion of questions of constitutional law it has little merit, but it may have been effective as a party manifesto. A short adjournment followed till November, when, on reassembling, the elders were asked for their advice upon this absorbing topic.

" Mr. Hubbard of Hingham came with the rest, but the court being informed that he had an hand in a pe-

[1] *New Eng. Jonas*, Marvin's ed. p. 19.

tition, which Mr. Vassall carried into England against the country in general, the governour propounded, that if any elder present had any such hand, &c., he would withdraw himself." Mr. Hubbert sitting still a good space, one of the deputies stated that he was suspected, whereupon he rose and said he knew nothing of such a petition.

Then Winthrop replied that he "must needs deliver his mind about him," and though he had no proof about the petition, " yet in regard he had so much opposed authority and offered such contempt to it, . . . he thought he would (in discretion) withdraw himself, &c., whereupon he went out." [1]

The ministers who remained then proceeded to define the relations of Massachusetts toward England, and the position they assumed was very simple.

" I. We depend upon the state of England for protection and immunities of Englishmen. . . . II. We conceive . . we have granted by patent such full and ample power . . . of making all laws and rules of our obedience, and of a full and final determination of all cases in the administration of justice, that no appeals or other ways of interrupting our proceedings do lie against us." [2]

In other words, they were to enjoy the privileges and safeguards of British subjects without yielding obedience to British law.

Under popular governments the remedy for discontent is free discussion ; under despotisms it is repres-

[1] Winthrop, ii. 278.   [2] Winthrop, ii. 282.

sion. In Massachusetts energetic steps were promptly taken to punish the ring-leaders in what the court now declared to be a conspiracy. The petitioners were summoned, and on being questioned refused to answer until some charge was made. A hot altercation followed, which ended in the defendants tendering an appeal, which was refused; and they were committed for trial.[1] A species of indictment was then prepared in which they were charged with publishing seditious libels against the Church of Christ and the civil government. The gravamen of the offence was the attempt to persuade the people " that the liberties and privileges in our charter belong to all freeborn Englishmen inhabitants here, whereas they are granted only to such as the governour and company shall think fit to receive into that fellowship." [2] The appeal was held criminal because a denial of the jurisdiction of the government. The trial resembled Wheelwright's. Like him the defendants refused to make submission, but persisted " obstinately and proudly in their evil practice; " that is to say, they maintained the right of petition and the legality of their course. They were therefore fined: Childe £50; Smith £40; Maverick, because he had not yet appealed, £10; and the others £30 each; three magistrates dissented.

Childe at once began hasty preparations to sail. To prevent him Winthrop called the assistants together, without, however, giving the dissenting magistrates notice, and arranged to have him arrested and searched.

[1] Winthrop, ii. 285.   [2] *Idem.*

One striking characteristic of the theocracy was its love for inflicting mental suffering upon its victims. The same malicious vindictiveness which sent Morton to sea in sight of his blazing home, and which imprisoned Anne Hutchinson in the house of her bitterest enemy, now suggested a scheme for making Childe endure the pangs of disappointment, by allowing him to embark, and then seizing him as the ship was setting sail. And though the plan miscarried, and the arrest had to be made the night before, yet even as it was the prisoner took his confinement very "grievously, but he could not help it." [1]

Nothing criminating was found in his possession, but in Dand's study, which was ransacked, copies of two petitions were discovered, with a number of queries relating to certain legal aspects of the charter, and intended to be submitted to the Commissioners for the Plantations at London.

These petitions were substantially those already presented, except that, by way of preamble, the story of the trial was told ; and how the ministers " did revile them, &c., as far as the wit or malice of man could, and that they meddled in civil affaires beyond their calling, and were masters rather than ministers, and ofttimes judges, and that they had stirred up the magistrates against them, and that a day of humiliation was appointed, wherein they were to pray against them." [2]

Such words had never been heard in Massachusetts.

[1] Winthrop, ii. 294.   [2] Winthrop, ii. 293.

The saints were aghast. Winthrop speaks of the offence as "being in nature capital," and Johnson thought the Lord's gracious goodness alone quelled this malice against his people.

Of course no mercy was shown. It is true that the writings were lawful petitions by English subjects to Parliament; that, moreover, they had never been published, but were found in a private room by means of a despotic search. Several of the signers were imprisoned for six months and then were punished in May: —

Doctor Childe, (imprisonment till paid,)				£200
John Smith,	"	"	"	100
John Dand,	"	"	"	200
Tho. Burton,	"	"	"	100

Samuel Maverick, for his offence in being p͞ty to ye conspiracy, (imprisonment till paid,) 100

Samuel Maverick, ffor his offence in breaking his oath and in appealing ag^{nst} ye intent of his oath of a freeman, 50 [1]

The conspirators of the poorer class were treated with scant ceremony. A carpenter named Joy was in Dand's study when the officers entered. He asked if the warrant was in the king's name. "He was laid hold on, and kept in irons about four or five days, and then he humbled himself . . . for meddling in matters belonging not to him, and blessed God for these irons

---

[1] *Mass. Rec.* iii. 113. May 26, 1647. £200 was the equivalent of about $5,000.

upon his legs, hoping they should do him good while he lived." [1]

But though the government could oppress the men, they could not make their principles unpopular, and the next December after Vassal and his friends had left the colony, the orthodox Samuel Symonds of Ipswich wrote mournfully to Winthrop : " I am informed that coppies of the petition are spreading here, and divers (specially young men and women) are taken with it, and are apt to wonder why such men should be troubled that speake as they doe : not being able suddenly to discerne the poyson in the sweet wine, nor the fire wrapped up in the straw." [2] The petitioners, however, never found redress. Edward Winslow had been sent to London as agent, and in 1648 he was able to write that their " hopes and endeavours . . . had been blasted by the special providence of the Lord who still wrought for us." And Winthrop piously adds : " As for those who went over to procure us trouble, God met with them all. Mr. Vassall, finding no entertainment for his petitions, went to Barbadoes," [3] . . . " God had brought " Thomas Fowle " very low, both in his estate and in his rep utation, since he joined in the first petition." And " God had so blasted " Childe's " estate as he was quite broken." [4]

Maverick remained some years in Boston, being probably unable to abandon his property ; during this

[1] Winthrop, ii. 294.   [2] Felt's *Eccl. Hist.* i. 593.
[3] Winthrop, ii. 321.   [4] Winthrop, ii. 322.

interval he made several efforts to have his fine remitted, and he did finally secure an abatement of one half. He then went to England and long afterward came back as a royal commissioner to try his fortune once again in a contest with the theocracy.

Dr. Palfrey has described this movement as a plot to introduce a direct government by England by inducing Parliament to establish Presbyterianism. By other than theological reasoning this inference cannot be deduced from the evidence. All that is certainly known about the leaders is that they were not of any one denomination. Maverick was an Episcopalian; Vassal was probably an Independent like Cromwell or Milton; and though the elders accused Childe of being a Jesuit, there is some ground to suppose that he inclined toward Geneva. So far as the testimony goes, everything tends to prove that the petitioners were perfectly sincere in their effort to gain some small measure of civil and religious liberty for themselves and for the disfranchised majority.

Viewed from the standpoint of history and not of prejudice, the events of these early years present themselves in a striking and unmistakable sequence.

They are the phenomena that regularly attend a certain stage of human development, — the absorption of power by an aristocracy. The clergy's rule was rigid, and met with resistance, which was crushed with an iron hand. Was it defection from their own ranks, the deserters met the fate of Wheelwright, of Williams, of Cotton, or of Hubbert; were politicians contumacious, they were defeated or exiled, like Vane, or Aspinwall, or Coddington; were citizens discontented, they were coerced like Maverick and Childe. The process had been uninterrupted alike in church and state. The congregations, which in theory should have included all the inhabitants of the towns, had shrunk until they contained only a third or a quarter of the people; while the churches themselves, which were supposed to be independent of external interference and to regulate their affairs by the will of the majority, had become little more than the chattels of the priests, and subject to the control of the magistrates who were their representatives. This system has generally prevailed; in like manner the Inquisition made use of the secular arm. The condition of ecclesiastical affairs is thus described by the highest living authority on Congregationalism: —

"Our fathers laid it down — and with perfect truth — that the will of Christ, and not the will of the major or minor part of a church, ought to govern that church. But somebody must interpret that will. And they quietly assumed that Christ would reveal his will to the elders, but would not reveal it to the church-members; so that when there arose a difference of opinion as to what the Master's will might be touching any particular matter, the judgment of the elders, rather than the judgment even of a majority of the membership, must be taken as conclusive. To all intents and purposes, then, this was precisely the aristocracy which they affirmed that it

was not. For the elders were to order business in the
assurance that every truly humble and sincere member would consent thereto. If any did not consent,
and after patient debate remained of another judgment, he was 'partial' and 'factious,' and continu-
ing 'obstinate,' he was 'admonished' and his vote
'nullified;' so that the elders could have their way
in the end by merely adding the insult of the apparent but illusive offer of coöperation to the injury
of their absolute control. As Samuel Stone of Hart-
ford no more tersely than truly put it, this kind of
Congregationalism was simply a 'speaking Aristocracy in the face of a silent Democracy.'"[1]

It is true that Vassal's petition was the event which
made the ministers decide to call a synod[2] by means
of an invitation of the General Court; but it is also
certain that under no circumstances would the meeting of some such council have been long delayed.
For sixteen years the well-known process had been
going on, of the creation of institutions by custom,
having the force of law; the stage of development
had now been reached when it was necessary that
those usages should take the shape of formal enactments. The Cambridge platform therefore marks the
completion of an organization, and as such is the central point in the history of the Puritan Commonwealth. The work was done in August, 1648: the

[1] *Early New England Congregationalism, as seen in its Literature*, p. 429. Dr. Dexter.

[2] Winthrop, ii. 264.

Westminster Confession was promulgated as the creed; the powers of the clergy were minutely defined, and the duty of the laity stated to be " obeying their elders and submitting themselves unto them in the Lord." [1] The magistrate was enjoined to punish " idolatry, blasphemy, heresy," and to coerce any church becoming " schismatical."

In October, 1649, the court commended the platform to the consideration of the congregations; in October, 1651, it was adopted; and when church and state were thus united by statute the theocracy was complete.

The close of the era of construction is also marked by the death of those two remarkable men whose influence has left the deepest imprint upon the institutions they helped to mould : John Winthrop, who died in 1649, and John Cotton in 1652.

Winthrop's letters to his wife show him to have been tender and gentle, and that his disposition was one to inspire love is proved by the affection those bore him who had suffered most at his hands. Williams and Vane and Coddington kept their friendship for him to the end. But these very qualities, so amiable in themselves, made him subject to the influence of men of inflexible will. His dream was to create on earth a commonwealth of saints whose joy would be to walk in the ways of God. But in practice he had to deal with the strongest of human passions. In 1634, though supported by Cotton, he was defeated by Dud-

---

[1] *Cambridge Platform,* ch. x. section 7.

ley, and there can be no doubt that this was caused
by the defection of the body of the clergy. The evidence seems conclusive, for the next year Vane
brought about an interview between the two at which
Haynes was present, and there Haynes upbraided him
with remissness in administering justice.[1] Winthrop
agreed to leave the question to the ministers, who the
next morning gave an emphatic opinion in favor of
strict discipline. Thenceforward he was pliant in
their hands, and with that day opened the dark epoch
of his life. By leading the crusade against the Antinomians he regained the confidence of the elders and
they never again failed him; but in return they ex-
acted obedience to their will; and the rancor with
which he pursued Anne Hutchinson, Gorton, and
Childe cannot be extenuated, and must ever be a
stain upon his fame.

As Hutchinson points out, in early life his tendencies were liberal, but in America he steadily grew
narrow. The reason is obvious. The leader of an
intolerant party has himself to be intolerant. His
claim to eminence as a statesman must rest upon the
purity of his moral character, his calm temper, and
his good judgment; for his mind was not original or
brilliant, nor was his thought in advance of his age.
Herein he differed from his celebrated contemporary,
for among the long list of famous men, who are the
pride of Massachusetts, there are few who in mere
intellectual capacity outrank Cotton. He was not

[1] Winthrop, i. 178.

only a profound scholar, an eloquent preacher, and a famous controversialist, but a great organizer, and a natural politician. He it was who constructed the Congregational hierarchy; his publications were the accepted authority both abroad and at home; and the system which he developed in his books was that which was made law by the Cambridge Platform.

Of medium height, florid complexion, and as he grew old some tendency to be stout, but with snowy hair and much personal dignity, he seems to have had an irresistible charm of manner toward those whom he wished to attract.

Comprehending thoroughly the feelings and prejudices of the clergy, he influenced them even more by his exquisite tact than by his commanding ability; and of easy fortune and hospitable alike from inclination and from interest, he entertained every elder who went to Boston. He understood the art of flattery to perfection; or, as Norton expressed it, "he was a man of ingenuous and pious candor, rejoicing (as opportunity served) to take notice of and testifie unto the gifts of God in his brethren, thereby drawing the hearts of them to him...." [1] No other clergyman has ever been able to reach the position he held with apparent ease, which amounted to a sort of primacy of New England. His dangers lay in the very fecundity of his mind. Though hampered by his education and profession, he was naturally liberal; and his first miscalculation was when, almost immediately on landing, he supported

[1] Norton's *Funeral Sermon,* p. 37.

Winthrop, who was in disgrace for the mildness of his administration, against the austerer Dudley.

The consciousness of his intellectual superiority seems to have given him an almost overweening confidence in his ability to induce his brethren to accept the broader theology he loved to preach; nor did he apparently realize that comprehension was incompatible with a theocratic government, and that his success would have undermined the organization he was laboring to perfect. He thus committed the error of his life in undertaking to preach a religious reformation, without having the resolution to face a martyrdom. But when he saw his mistake, the way in which he retrieved himself showed a consummate knowledge of human nature and of the men with whom he had to deal. Nor did he ever forget the lesson. From that time forward he took care that no one should be able to pick a flaw in his orthodoxy; and whatever he may have thought of much of the policy of his party, he was always ready to defend it without flinching.

Neither he nor Winthrop died too soon, for with the completion of the task of organization the work that suited them was finished, and they were unfit for that which remained to be done. An oligarchy, whose power rests on faith and not on force, can only exist by extirpating all who openly question their pretensions to preëminent sanctity; and neither of these men belonged to the class of natural persecutors, — the one was too gentle, the other too liberal. An example will show better than much argument how little in accord either really was with that spirit which, in the regular course of social development, had thenceforward to dominate over Massachusetts.

Captain Partridge had fought for the Parliament, and reached Boston at the beginning of the winter of 1645. He was arrested and examined as a heretic. The magistrates referred the case to Cotton, who reported that " he found him corrupt in judgment," but " had good hope to reclaim him." [1] An instant recantation was demanded ; it was of course refused, and, in spite of all remonstrance, the family was banished in the snow. Winthrop's sad words were : " But sure, the rule of hospitality to strangers, and of seeking to pluck out of the fire such as there may be hope of, . . . do seem to require more moderation and indulgence of human infirmity where there appears not obstinacy against the clear truth." [2]

But in the savage and bloody struggle that was now at hand there was no place for leaders capable of pity or remorse, and the theocracy found supremely gifted chieftains in John Norton and John Endicott.

Norton approaches the ideal of the sterner orders of the priesthood. A gentleman by birth and breeding, a ripe scholar, with a keen though polished wit, his sombre temper was deeply tinged with fanaticism. Unlike so many of his brethren, temporal concerns were to him of but little moment, for every passion of his gloomy soul was intensely concentrated on the warfare he believed himself waging with the fiend. Doubt

[1] Winthrop, ii. 251.   [2] Winthrop, ii. 251.

or compassion was impossible, for he was commissioned by the Lord. He was Christ's elected minister, and misbelievers were children of the devil whom it was his sacred duty to destroy. He knew by the Word of God that all save the orthodox were lost, and that heretics not only perished, but were the hirelings of Satan, who tempted the innocent to their doom; he therefore hated and feared them more than robbers or murderers. Words seemed to fail him when he tried to express his horror: "The face of death, the King of Terrours, the living man by instinct turneth his face from. An unusual shape, a satanical phantasm, a ghost, or apparition, affrights the disciples. But the face of heresie is of a more horrid aspect than all . . . put together, as arguing some signal inlargement of the power of darkness as being diabolical, prodigeous, portentous." [1] By nature, moreover, he had in their fullest measure the three attributes of a preacher of a persecution, — eloquence, resolution, and a heart callous to human suffering. To this formidable churchman was joined a no less formidable magistrate.

No figure in our early history looms out of the past like Endicott's. The harsh face still looks down from under the black skull-cap, the gray moustache and pointed beard shading the determined mouth, but throwing into relief the lines of the massive jaw. He is almost heroic in his ferocious bigotry and daring, — a perfect champion of the church.

The grim Puritan soldier is almost visible as, stand-

[1] *Heart of New Eng. Rent*, p. 46.

ing at the head of his men, he tears the red cross from the flag, and defies the power of England; or, in that tremendous moment, when the people were hanging breathless on the fate of Christison, when insurrection seemed bursting out beneath his feet, and his judges shrunk aghast before the peril, we yet hear the savage old man furiously strike the table, and, thanking God that he at least dares to do his duty, we see him rise alone before that threatening multitude to condemn the heretic to death.

CHAPTER IV.

THE ANABAPTISTS.

THE Rev. Thomas Shepard, pastor of Charlestown, was such an example, " in word, in conversation, in civility, in spirit, in faith, in purity, that he did let no man despise his youth ; " [1] and yet, preaching an election sermon before the governor and magistrates, he told them that " anabaptisme . . . hath ever been lookt at by the godly leaders of this people as a scab." [2] While the Rev. Samuel Willard, president of Harvard, declared that " such a rough thing as a New England Anabaptist is not to be handled over tenderly." [3]

So early as 1644, therefore, the General Court " Ordered and agreed, y[t] if any pson or psons w[th]in y[e] iurisdiction shall eith[r] openly condemne or oppose y[e] baptiz[g] of infants, or go about secretly to seduce oth[rs] fro[m] y[e] app'bation or use thereof, or shall purposely depart y[e] congregation at y[e] administration of y[e] ordinance, . . . and shall appear to y[e] Co't willfully and obstinately to continue therein after due time and meanes of conviction, every such pson or psons shallbe sentenced to banishm[t]." [4]

The legislation, however, was unpopular, for Win-

[1] *Magnalia*, bk. 4, ch. ix. § 6.   [2] *Eye Salve*, p. 24.
[3] *Ne Sutor*, p. 10.
[4] *Mass. Rec.* ii. 85.   13 November, 1644.

throp relates that in October, 1645, divers merchants
and others petitioned to have the act repealed, because
of the offense taken thereat by the godly in England,
and the court seemed inclined to accede, " but many
of the elders . . . entreated that the law might continue still in force, and the execution of it not suspended, though they disliked not that all lenity and patience should be used for convincing and reclaiming
such erroneous persons. Whereupon the court refused
to make any further order." [1]   And Edward Winslow assured Parliament in 1646, when sent to England to represent the colony, that, some mitigation
being desired, " it was answered in my hearing. 'T is
true we have a severe law, but wee never did or will
execute the rigor of it upon any. . . . But the reason wherefore wee are loath either to repeale or alter
the law is, because wee would have it . . . to beare witnesse against their judgment, . . . which we conceive
. . . to bee erroneous." [2]

Unquestionably, at that time no one had been banished; but in 1644 " one Painter, for refusing to let
his child be baptized, . . . was brought before the
court, where he declared their baptism to be anti-
Christian. He was sentenced to be whipped, which
he bore without flinching, and boasted that God had
assisted him." [3] Nor was his a solitary instance of
severity. Yet, notwithstanding the scorn and hatred
which the orthodox divines felt for these sectaries,

[1] Winthrop, ii. 251.   [2] *Hypocrisie Unmasked*, 101.
[3] Hutch. *Hist.* i. 208, note.

many very eminent Puritans fell into the errors of that persuasion. Roger Williams was a Baptist, and Henry Dunster, for the same heresy, was removed from the presidency of Harvard, and found it prudent to end his days within the Plymouth jurisdiction. Even that great champion of infant baptism, Jonathan Mitchell, when thrown into intimate relations with Dunster, had doubts.

"That day . . . after I came from him I had a strange experience; I found hurrying and pressing suggestions against Pædobaptism, and injected scruples and thoughts whether the other way might not be right, and infant baptism an invention of men; and whether I might with good conscience baptize children and the like. And these thoughts were darted in with some impression, and left a strange confusion and sickliness upon my spirit. Yet, methought, it was not hard to discern that they were from the *Evil One;* . . . And it made me fearful to go needlessly to Mr. D.; for methought I found a venom and poison in his insinuations and discourses against Pædobaptism."[1]

Henry Dunster was an uncommon man. Famed for piety in an age of fanaticism, learned, modest, and brave, by the unremitting toil of thirteen years he raised Harvard from a school to the position which it has since held; and though very poor, and starving on a wretched and ill-paid pittance, he gave his beloved college one hundred acres of land at the mo-

[1] *Magnalia*, bk. 4, ch. iv. § 10.

ment of its sorest need.[1] Yet he was a criminal, for he would not baptize infants, and he met with the "lenity and patience" which the elders were not unwilling should be used toward the erring.

He was indicted and convicted of disturbing church ordinances, and deprived of his office in October, 1654. He asked for leave to stay in the house he had built for a few months, and his petition in November ought to be read to understand how heretics were made to suffer : —

"1st. The time of the year is unseasonable, being now very near the shortest day, and the depth of winter.

"2d. The place unto which I go is unknown to me and my family, and the ways and means of subsistance. . . .

"3d. The place from which I go hath fire, fuel, and all provisions for man and beast, laid in for the winter. . . . The house I have builded upon very damageful conditions to myself, out of love for the college, taking country pay in lieu of bills of exchange on England, or the house would not have been built. . . .

"4th. The persons, all beside myself, are women and children, on whom little help, now their minds lie under the actual stroke of affliction and grief. My wife is sick, and my youngest child extremely so, and hath been for months, so that we dare not carry him out of doors, yet much worse now than before. . . . Myself will willingly bow my neck to any yoke of per-

[1] Quincy's *History of Harvard*, i. 15.

sonal denial, for I know for what and for whom, by grace I suffer." [1]

He had before asked Winthrop to cause the government to pay him what it owed, and he ended his prayer in these words : " Considering the poverty of the country, I am willing to descend to the lowest step; and if nothing can comfortably be allowed, I sit still appeased; desiring nothing more than to supply me and mine with food and raiment." [2]   He received that mercy which the church has ever shown to those who wander from her fold; he was given till March, and then, with dues unpaid, was driven forth a broken man, to die in poverty and neglect.

But Jonathan Mitchell, pondering deeply upon the wages he saw paid at his very hearthstone, to the sin of his miserable old friend, snatched his own soul from Satan's jaws.   And thenceforward his path lay in pleasant places, and he prospered exceedingly in the world, so that " of extream lean he grew extream fat; and at last, in an extream hot season, a fever arrested him, just after he had been preaching. . . . Wonderful were the lamentations which this deplorable death fill'd the churches of New England withal. . . . Yea . . . all New England shook when that pillar fell to the ground." [3]

Notwithstanding, therefore, clerical promises of gentleness, Massachusetts was not a comfortable place of residence for Baptists, who, for the most part, went to

[1] *History of Harvard,* i. 18.   [2] *Idem,* i. 20.
[3] *Magnalia,* bk. 4, ch. iv. § 16.

Rhode Island; and John Clark [1] became the pastor of
the church which they formed at Newport about 1644.
He had been born about 1610, and had been educated
in London as a physician.   In 1637 he landed at Boston, where he seems to have become embroiled in the
Antinomian controversy; at all events, he fared so ill
that, with several others, he left Massachusetts 'resolving, through the help of Christ, to get clear of all
[chartered companies] and be of ourselves.'   In the
course of their wanderings they fell in with Williams,
and settled near him.

Clark was perhaps the most prominent man in the
Plantations, filled many public offices, and was the
commissioner who afterward secured for the colony
the famous charter that served as the State Constitution till 1842.

Obediah Holmes, who succeeded him as Baptist
minister of Newport, is less well known. He was educated at Oxford, and when he emigrated he settled
at Salem; from thence he went to Seaconk, where he
joined the church under Mr. Newman.   Here he soon
fell into trouble for resisting what he maintained was
an "unrighteous act" of his pastor's; in consequence
he and several more renounced the communion, and
began to worship by themselves; they were baptized
and thereafter they were excommunicated; the inevitable indictment followed, and they, too, took refuge
in Rhode Island.[2]

[1] For sketch of Clark's life see Allen's *Biographical Dictionary.*
[2] Holmes's Narrative, Backus, i. 213.

William Witter[1] of Lynn was an aged Baptist, who had already been prosecuted, but, in 1651, being blind and infirm, he asked the Newport church to send some of the brethren to him, to administer the communion, for he found himself alone in Massachusetts.[2] Accordingly Clark undertook the mission, with Obediah Holmes and John Crandall.

They reached Lynn on Saturday, July 19, 1651, and on Sunday stayed within doors in order not to disturb the congregation. A few friends were present, and Clark was in the midst of a sermon, when the house was entered by two constables with a warrant signed by Robert Bridges, commanding them to arrest certain " erroneous persons being strangers." The travellers were at once seized and carried to the tavern, and after dinner they were told that they must go to church.

Gorton, like many another, had to go through this ordeal, and he speaks of his Sundays with much feeling : " Only some part of those dayes they brought us forth into their congregations, to hear their sermons . . . which was meat to be digested, but only by the heart or stomacke of an ostrich." [3]

The unfortunate Baptists remonstrated, saying that were they forced into the meeting-house, they should be obliged to dissent from the service, but this, the constable said, was nothing to him, and so he carried

---

[1] For the following events, see " *Ill Newes from New England,*" *Mass. Hist. Coll.* fourth series, vol. ii.

[2] Backus, i. 215.

[3] *Simplicitie's Defence*, p. 57.

them away. On entering, during the prayer, the prisoners took off their hats, but presently put them on again and began reading in their seats. Whereupon Bridges ordered the officers to uncover their heads, which was done, and the service was then quietly finished. When all was over, Clark asked leave to speak, which, after some hesitation, was granted, on condition he would not discuss what he had heard. He began to explain how he had put on his hat because he could not judge that they were gathered according to the visible order of the Lord ; but here he was silenced, and the three were committed to custody for the night. On Tuesday they were taken to Boston, and on the 31st were brought before Governor Endicott. Their trial was of the kind reserved by priests for heretics. No jury was impanelled, no indictment was read, no evidence was heard, but the prisoners were reviled by the bench as Anabaptists, and when they repudiated the name were asked if they did not deny infant baptism. The theological argument which followed was cut short by a recommitment to await sentence.

That afternoon John Cotton exhorted the judges from the pulpit. He expounded the law, and commanded them to do their duty ; he told them that the rejection of infant baptism would overthrow the church ; that this was a capital crime, and therefore the captives were " foul murtherers." [1] Thus inspired, the court came in toward evening.

[1] *Ill Newes,* p. 56.

The record recites a number of misdemeanors, such as wearing the hat in church, administering the communion to the excommunicated, and the like, but no attempt was made to prove a single charge.[1] The reason is obvious: the only penalty provided by statute for the offence of being a Baptist was banishment, hence the only legal course would have been to dismiss the accused. Endicott condemned them to fines of twenty, thirty, and five pounds, respectively, or to be whipped. Clark understood his position perfectly, and from the first had demanded to be shown the law under which he was being tried. He now, after sentence, renewed the request. Endicott well knew that in acting as the mouthpiece of the clergy he was violating alike justice, his oath of office, and his honor as a judge; and, being goaded to fury, he broke out: You have deserved death; I will not have such trash brought into our jurisdiction.[2] Holmes tells the rest: "As I went from the bar, I exprest myself in these words, — I blesse God I am counted worthy to suffer for the name of Jesus ; whereupon John Wilson (their pastor, as they call him) strook me before the judgement seat, and cursed me, saying, The curse of God . . . goe with thee ; so we were carried to the prison."[3]

All the convicts maintained that their liberty as English subjects had been violated, and they refused to pay their fines. Clark's friends, however, alarmed for his safety, settled his for him, and he was discharged.

[1] *Ill Newes*, pp. 31–44.　　[2] *Idem*, p. 33.　　[3] *Idem*, p. 47.

Crandall was admitted to bail, but being misinformed as to the time of surrender, he did not appear, his bond was forfeited, and on his return to Boston he found himself free.

Thus Holmes was left to face his punishment alone. Actuated apparently by a deep sense of duty toward himself and his God, he refused the help of friends, and steadfastly awaited his fate. As he lay in prison he suffered keenly as he thought of his birth and breeding, his name, his worldly credit, and the humiliation which must come to his wife and children from his public shame; then, too, he began to fear lest he might not be able to bear the lash, might flinch or shed tears, and bring contempt on himself and his religion. Yet when the morning came he was calm and resolute; refusing food and drink, that he might not be said to be sustained by liquor, he betook himself to prayer, and when his keeper called him, with his Bible in his hand, he walked cheerfully to the post. He would have spoken a few words, but the magistrate ordered the executioner to do his office quickly, for this fellow would delude the people; then he was seized and stripped, and as he cried, " Lord, lay not this sin unto their charge," he received the first blow.[1]

They gave him thirty lashes with a three-thonged whip, of such horrible severity that it was many days before he could endure to have his lacerated body touch the bed, and he rested propped upon his hands and knees.[2] Yet, in spite of his torture, he stood firm

[1] *Ill Newes*, pp. 48, 56.

[2] Backus, i. 237, note.   MS. of Gov. Jos. Jencks.

and calm, showing neither pain nor fear, breaking out at intervals into praise to God; and his dignity and courage so impressed the people that, in spite of the danger, numbers flocked about him when he was set free, in sympathy and admiration. John Spur, being inwardly affected by what he saw and heard, took him by the hand, and, with a joyful countenance, said: " Praised be the Lord," and so went back with him. That same day Spur was arrested, charged with the crime of succoring a heretic. Then said the undaunted Spur: "Obediah Holmes I do look upon as a godly man: and do affirm that he carried himself as did become a Christian, under so sad an affliction." " We will deal with you as we have dealt with him," said Endicott. " I am in the hands of God," answered Spur; and then his keeper took him to his prison.[1]

Perhaps no persecutor ever lived who was actuated by a single motive: Saint Dominic probably had some trace of worldliness; Henry VIII. some touch of bigotry; and this was preëminently true of the Massachusetts elders. Doubtless there were among them men like Norton, whose fanaticism was so fierce that they would have destroyed the heretic like the wild beast, as a child of the devil, and an abomination to God. But with the majority worldly motives predominated: they were always protesting that they did not constrain men's consciences, but only enforced orderly living. Increase Mather declared: in " the same church there have been Presbyterians, Independents, Epis-

[1] *Ill Newes*, p. 57.

copalians, and Antipædobaptists, all welcome to the
same table of the Lord when they have manifested to
the judgment of Christian charity a work of regener-
ation in their souls." [1] And Winslow solemnly assured
Parliament, " Nay, some in our churches " are " of
that judgment, and as long as they [Baptists] carry
themselves peaceably as hitherto they doe, wee will
leave them to God." [2]

Such statements, although intended to convey a
false impression, contained this much truth : provided
a man conformed to all the regulations of the church,
paid his taxes, and held his tongue, he would not, in
ordinary circumstances, have been molested under the
Puritan Commonwealth. But the moment he refused
implicit obedience, or, above all, if he withdrew from
his congregation, he was shown no mercy, because
such acts tended to shake the temporal power. John
Wilson, pastor of Boston, was a good example of the
average of his order. On his death-bed he was asked
to declare what he thought to be the worst sins of the
country. " 'I have long feared several sins, whereof
one,' he said, 'was Corahism : that is, when people
rise up as Corah against their ministers, as if they took
too much upon them, when indeed they do but rule
for Christ, and according to Christ.' " [3] Permeated
with this love of power, and possessed of a superb
organization, the clergy never failed to act on public

---

[1] *Vindication of New Eng.* p. 19.
[2] *Hypocrisie Unmasked*, p. 101. A. D. 1646.
[3] *Magnalia*, bk. 3, ch. iii. § 17.

opinion with decisive effect whenever they saw their worldly interests endangered. Childe has described the attack which overwhelmed him, and Gorton gives a striking account of their process of inciting a crusade : —

" These things concluded to be heresies and blasphemies. . . . The ministers did zealously preach unto the people the great danger of such things, and the guilt such lay under that held them, stirring the people up to labour to find such persons out and to execute death upon them, making persons so execrable in the eyes of the people, whom they intimated should hold such things, yea some of them naming some of us in their pulpits, that the people that had not seen us thought us to be worse by far in any respect then those barbarous Indians are in the country. . . . Whereupon we heard a rumor that the Massachusets was sending out an army of men to cut us off." [1]

The persecution of the Baptists lays bare this selfish clerical policy. The theory of the suppression of heresy as a sacred duty breaks down when it is conceded that the heretic may be admitted to the orthodox communion without sin ; therefore the motives for cruelty were sordid. The ministers felt instinctively that an open toleration would impair their power ; not only because the congregations would divide, but because these sectaries listened to " John Russell the shoemaker." [2] Obviously, were cobblers to usurp the sacerdotal functions, the superstitious reverence of the

---

[1] *Simplicitie's Defence,* p. 32.   [2] *Ne Sutor,* p. 26.

people for the priestly office would not long endure:
and it was his crime in upholding this sacrilegious
practice which made the Rev. Thomas Cobbett cry
out in his pulpit " against Gorton, that arch-heretick,
who would have al men to be preachers." [1]

Therefore, though Winslow solemnly protested before the Commissioners at London that Baptists who
lived peaceably would be left unmolested, yet such of
them as listened to "foul-murtherers" [2] were denounced by the divines as dangerous fanatics who
threatened to overthrow the government, and were
hunted through the country like wolves.

Thomas Gould was an esteemed citizen of Charlestown, but, unfortunately for himself, he had long felt
doubt concerning infant baptism; so when, in 1655,
a child was born to him, he "durst not" have it
christened.   " The elder pressed the church to lay me
under admonition, which the church was backward
to do.   Afterward I went out at the sprinkling of
children, which was a great trouble to some honest
hearts, and they told me of it.   But I told them I
could not stay, for I lookt upon it as no ordinance of
Christ.   They told me that now I had made known
my judgment I might stay. . . . So I stayed and sat
down in my seat when they were at prayer and ad-
ministring the service to infants.   Then they dealt
with me for my unreverent carriage." [3]   That is to

---

[1] *Simplicitie's Defence*, p. 32.   See *Ne Sutor*, p. 26.

[2] " *Ill Newes*," *Mass. Hist. Coll.* fourth series, vol. ii. p. 56.

[3] Gould's Narrative, Backus, i. 364–366.

say, his pastor, Mr. Symmes, caused him to be admonished and excluded from the communion. In October, 1656, he was presented to the county court for " denying baptism to his child," convicted, admonished, and given till the next term to consider of his error; and gradually his position at Charlestown became so unpleasant that he went to church at Cambridge, which was a cause of fresh offence to Mr. Symmes.[1]

From this time forward for several years, though no actual punishment seems to have been inflicted, Gould was subjected to perpetual annoyance, and was repeatedly summoned and admonished, both by the courts and the church, until at length he brought matters to a crisis by withdrawing, and with eight others forming a church, on May 28, 1665.

He thus tells his story: " We sought the Lord to direct us, and taking counsel of other friends who dwelt among us, who were able and godly, they gave us counsel to congregate ourselves together; and so we did, . . . to walk in the order of the gospel according to the rule of Christ, yet knowing it was a breach of the law of this country. . . . After we had been called into one or two courts, the church understanding that we were gathered into church order, they sent three messengers from the church to me, telling me the church required me to come before them the next Lord's day." [2] That Sunday he could not go.

[1] *History of Charlestown*, Frothingham, p. 164.
[2] Gould's Narrative, Backus, i. 369.

but he promised to attend on the one following ;[1] and his wife relates what was then done : "The word was carried to the elder, that if they were alive and well they would come the next day, yet they were so hot upon it that they could not stay, but master Sims, when he was laying out the sins of these men, before he had propounded it to the church, to know their mind, the church having no liberty to speak, he wound it up in his discourse, and delivered them up to Satan, to the amazement of the people, that ever such an ordinance of Christ should be so abused, that many of the people went out; and these were the excommunicated persons."[2] The sequence is complete: so long as Gould confined his heresy to pure speculation upon dogma he was little heeded; when he withheld his child from baptism and went out during the ceremony he was admonished, denied the sacrament, and treated as a social outcast; but when he separated, he was excommunicated and given to the magistrate to be crushed.

Passing from one tribunal to another the sectaries came before the General Court in October, 1665 : such as were freemen were disfranchised, and all were sentenced, upon conviction before a single magistrate of continued schism, to be imprisoned until further order.[3] The following April they were fined four pounds and put in confinement, where they lay till

---

[1] Gould's Narrative, Backus, i. 371.

[2] Mrs. Gould's Answer, Backus, i. 384.

[3] *Mass. Rec.* vol. iv. pt. 2, p. 291.

the 11th of September, when the legislature, after a hearing, ordered them to be discharged upon payment of fines and costs.[1]

How many Baptists were prosecuted, and what they suffered, is not known, as only an imperfect record remains of the fortunes of even the leaders of the movement; this much, however, is certain, they not only continued contumacious, but persecution added to their numbers. So at length the clergy decided to try what effect a public refutation of these heretics would have on popular opinion. Accordingly the governor and council, actuated by " Christian candor," ordered the Baptists to appear at the meeting-house, at nine o'clock in the morning, on the 14th of April, 1668; and six ministers were deputed to conduct the disputation.[2]

During the immolation of Dunster the Rev. Mr. Mitchell had made up his mind that he " would have an argument able to remove a mountain " before he would swerve from his orthodoxy; he had since confirmed his faith by preaching " more than half a score ungainsayable sermons " " in defence of this comfortable truth," and he was now prepared to maintain it against all comers. Accordingly this " worthy man was he who did most service in this disputation; whereof the effect was, that although the erring brethren, as is usual in such cases, made this their last answer to the arguments which had cast them into much confusion : ' Say what you will we will hold our

---

[1] *Mass. Rec.* vol. iv. pt. 2, p. 316.   [2] Backus, i. 375.

mind.' Yet others were happily established in the right ways of the Lord." [1]

Such is the account of Cotton Mather : but the story of the Baptists presents a somewhat different view of the proceedings. " It is true there were seven elders appointed to discourse with them . . . and when they were met, there was a long speech made by one of them of what vile persons they were, and how they acted against the churches and government here, and stood condemned by the court. The others desiring liberty to speak, they would not suffer them, but told them they stood there as delinquents and ought not to have liberty to speak. . . . Two days were spent to little purpose; in the close, master Jonathan Mitchel pronounced that dreadful sentence against them in Deut. xvii. 8, to the end of the 12th, and this was the way they took to convince them, and you may see what a good effect it had." [2]

The sentence pronounced by Mitchell was this : " And the man that will do presumptuously, and will not hearken unto the priest that standeth to minister there before the Lord thy God, or unto the judge, even that man shall die : and thou shalt put away the evil from Israel." [3]

On the 27th of May, 1668, Gould, Turner, and Farnum, " obstinate & turbulent Annabaptists," were banished under pain of perpetual imprisonment.[4]   They

[1] *Magnalia*, bk. 4, ch. iv. § 10.
[2] Mrs. Gould's Answer, Backus, i. 384, 385.
[3] *Deut.* xvii. 12.   [4] *Mass. Rec.* vol. iv. pt. ii, pp. 373–375.

determined to stay and face their fate: afterward they wrote to the magistrates : —

HONOURED SIRS: . . . After the tenders of our service according to Christ, his command to your selves and the country, wee thought it our duty and concernment to present your honours with these few lines to put you in remembrance of our bonds: and this being the twelfth week of our imprisonment, wee should be glad if it might be thought to stand with the honour and safety of the country, and the present government thereof, to be now at liberty. For wee doe hereby seriously profess, that as farre as wee are sensible or know anything of our own hearts, wee do prefer their peace and safety above our own, however wee have been resented otherwise : and wherein wee differ in point of judgment wee humbly beeseech you, let there be a bearing with us, till god shal reveale otherwise to us; for there is a spirit in man and the inspiration of the Almighty giveth them understanding, therefore if wee are in the dark, wee dare not say that wee doe see or understand, till the Lord shall cleare things up to us. And to him wee can appeale to cleare up our innocency as touching the government, both in your civil and church affaires. That it never was in our hearts to thinke of doing the least wrong to either : but have and wee hope, by your assistance, shal alwaies indeavour to keepe a conscience void of offence towards god and men. And if it shal be thought meete to afforde us our liberty, that wee

may take that care, as becomes us, for our families,
wee shal engage ourselves to be alwayes in a readi-
nes to resigne up our persons to your pleasure.   Hoping your honours will be pleased seriously to consider
our condition, wee shall commend both you and it to
the wise disposing and blessing of the Almighty, and
remaine your honours faithful servants in what we
may.

THO: GOLD
WILL: TURNER
JOHN FARNUM.[1]

Such were the men whom the clergy daily warned
their congregations "would certainly undermine the
churches, ruine order, destroy piety, and introduce pro-
phaneness." [2]   And when they appealed to their spotless lives and their patience under affliction, they were
told "that the vilest hereticks and grossest blasphemers have resolutely and cheerfully (at least sullenly
and boastingly) suffered as well as the people of
God." [3]

The feeling of indignation and of sympathy was,
notwithstanding, strong ; and in spite of the danger of
succoring heretics, sixty-six inhabitants, among whom
were some of the most respected citizens of Charlestown, petitioned the legislature for mercy : "They being aged and weakly men ; . . . the sense of this their
. . . most deplorable and afflicted condition hath

---

[1] *Mass. Archives,* x. 220.   [2] *Ne Sutor,* p. 11.

[3] *Ne Sutor,* p. 9.

sadly affected the hearts of many . . . Christians, and such as neither approve of their judgment or practice; especially considering that the men are reputed godly, and of a blameless conversation. . . . We therefore most humbly beseech this honored court, in their Christian mercy and bowels of compassion, to pity and relieve these poor prisoners."[1] On November 7, 1668, the petition was voted " scandalous & reproachful," the two chief promoters were censured, admonished, and fined ten and five pounds respectively; the others were made, under their own hands, to express their sorrow, " for giving the court such just ground of offence."[2]

The shock was felt even in England. In March, 1669, thirteen of the most influential dissenting ministers wrote from London earnestly begging for moderation lest they should be made to suffer from retaliation; but their remonstrance was disregarded.[3] What followed is not exactly known; the convicts would seem to have lain in jail about a year, and they are next mentioned in a letter to Clark written in November, 1670, in which he was told that Turner had been again arrested, but that Gould had eluded the officers, who were waiting for him in Boston; and was on Noddle's Island. Subsequently all were taken and treated with the extremest rigor; for in June, 1672, Russell was so reduced that it was supposed he could not live, and he was reported to have died in prison.

---

[1] Backus, i. 380, 381. [2] *Mass. Rec.* vol. iv. pt. 2, p. 413.
[3] Backus, i. 395.

Six months before Gould and Turner had been thought past hope; their sufferings had brought them all to the brink of the grave.[1] But relief was at hand; the victory for freedom had been won by the blood of heretics, as devoted, as fearless, but even unhappier than they; and the election of Leverett, in 1673, who was opposed to persecution, marks the moment when the hierarchy admitted their defeat. During his administration the sectaries usually met in private undisturbed; and soon every energy of the theocracy became concentrated on the effort to repulse the ever contracting circle of enemies who encompassed it.

During the next few years events moved fast. In 1678 the ecclesiastical power was so shattered that the Baptists felt strong enough to build a church; but the old despotic spirit lived even in the throes of death, and the legislature passed an act forbidding the erection of unlicensed meeting-houses under penalty of confiscation. Nevertheless it was finished, but on the Sunday on which it was to have been opened the marshal nailed the doors fast and posted notices forbidding all persons to enter, by order of the court. After a time the doors were broken open, and services were held; a number of the congregation were summoned before the court, admonished, and forbidden to meet in any public place;[2] but the handwriting was now glowing on the wall, priestly threats had lost their terror; the order was disregarded; and now for al-

[1] Backus, i. 398–404, 405.
[2] June 11, 1680. *Mass. Rec.* v. 271.

most two hundred years Massachusetts has been foremost in defending the equal rights of men before the law.

The old world was passing away, a new era was opening, and a few words are due to that singular aristocracy which so long ruled New England. For two centuries Increase Mather has been extolled as an eminent example of the abilities and virtues which then adorned his order. In 1681, when all was over, he published a solemn statement of the attitude the clergy had held toward the Baptists, and from his words posterity may judge of their standard of morality and of truth.

" The Annabaptists in New England have in their narrative lately published, endeavoured to . . . make themselves the innocent persons and the Lord's servants here no better than persecutors. . . . I have been a poor labourer in the Lord's Vineyard in this place upward of twenty years; and it is more than I know, if in all that time, any of those that scruple infant baptism, have met with molestation from the magistrate merely on account of their opinion." [1]

[1] Preface to *Ne Sutor.*

CHAPTER V.

THE QUAKERS.

THE lower the organism, the less would seem to be the capacity for physical adaptation to changed conditions of life; the jelly-fish dies in the aquarium, the dog has wandered throughout the world with his master. The same principle apparently holds true in the evolution of the intellect; for while the oyster lacks consciousness, the bee modifies the structure of its comb, and the swallow of her nest, to suit unforeseen contingencies, while the dog, the horse, and the elephant are capable of a high degree of education.[1]

Applying this law to man, it will be found to be a fact that, whereas the barbarian is most tenacious of custom, the European can adopt new fashions with comparative ease. The obvious inference is, that in proportion as the brain is feeble it is incapable of the effort of origination; therefore, savages are the slaves of routine. Probably a stronger nervous system, or a peculiarity of environment, or both combined, served to excite impatience with their surroundings among the more favored races, from whence came a desire for innovation. And the mental flexibility thus slowly developed has passed by inheritance, and has been

[1] *Mental Evolution in Animals*, Romanes, Am. ed. pp. 203–210.

strengthened by use, until the tendency to vary, or think independently, has become an irrepressible instinct among some modern nations. Conservatism is the converse of variation, and as it springs from mental inertia it is always a progressively salient characteristic of each group in the descending scale. The Spaniard is less mutable than the Englishman, the Hindoo than the Spaniard, the Hottentot than the Hindoo, and the ape than the Hottentot. Therefore, a power whose existence depends upon the fixity of custom must be inimical to progress, but the authority of a sacred caste is altogether based upon an unreasoning reverence for tradition, — in short, on superstition ; and as free inquiry is fatal to a belief in those fables which awed the childhood of the race, it has followed that established priesthoods have been almost uniformly the most conservative of social forces, and that clergymen have seldom failed to slay their variable brethren when opportunity has offered. History teems with such slaughters, some of the most instructive of which are related in the Old Testament, whose code of morals is purely theological.

Though there may be some question as to the strict veracity of the author of the Book of Kings, yet, as he was evidently a thorough churchman, there can be no doubt that he has faithfully preserved the traditions of the hierarchy ; his chronicle therefore presents, as it were, a perfect mirror, wherein are reflected the workings of the ecclesiastical mind through many generations. According to his account, the theocracy only triumphed after a long and doubtful struggle. Samuel must have been an exceptionally able man, for, though he failed to control Saul, it was through his intrigues that David was enthroned, who was profoundly orthodox ; yet Solomon lapsed again into heresy, and Jeroboam added to schism the even blacker crime of making "priests of the lowest of the people, which were not of the sons of Levi," [1] and in consequence he has come down to posterity as the man who made Israel to sin. Ahab married Jezebel, who introduced the worship of Baal, and gave the support of government to a rival church. She therefore roused a hate which has made her immortal; but it was not until the reign of her son Jehoram that Elisha apparently felt strong enough to execute a plot he had made with one of the generals to precipitate a revolution, in which the whole of the house of Ahab should be murdered and the heretics exterminated. The awful story is told with wonderful power in the Bible.

" And Elisha the prophet called one of the children of the prophets, and said unto him, Gird up thy loins, and take this box of oil in thine hand, and go to Ramoth-gilead: and when thou comest thither, look out there Jehu, . . . and make him arise up . . . and carry him to an inner chamber ; then take the box of oil, and pour it on his head, and say, Thus saith the Lord, I have anointed thee king over Israel. . . .

" So the young man . . . went to Ramoth-gilead.

[1] 1 *Kings* xii. 31.

. . . And he said, I have an errand to thee, O cap, tain. . . .

" And he arose, and went into the house; and he poured the oil on his head, and said unto him, Thus saith the Lord God of Israel, I have anointed thee king over the people of the Lord, even over Israel.

" And thou shalt smite the house of Ahab thy mas· ter, that I may avenge the blood of my servants the prophets. . . .

" For the whole house of Ahab shall perish: . . . and I will make the house of Ahab like the house of Jeroboam the son of Nebat, . . . and the dogs shall eat Jezebel. . . .

" Then Jehu came forth to the servants of his lord : . . . And he said, Thus spake he to me, saying, Thus saith the Lord, I have anointed thee king over Israel.

" Then they hasted, . . . and blew with trumpets, saying, Jehu is king. So Jehu . . . conspired against Joram. . . .

" But king Joram was returned to be healed in Jez- reel of the wounds which the Syrians had given him, when he fought with Hazael king of Syria. . . .

" So Jehu rode in a chariot, and went to Jezreel ; for Joram lay there. . . .

" And Joram . . . went out . . . in his chariot, . . . against Jehu. . . . And it came to pass, when Joram saw Jehu, that he said, Is it peace, Jehu ? And he answered, What peace, so long as the whoredoms of thy mother Jezebel and her witchcrafts are so many ?

" And Joram turned his hands, and fled, and said to Ahaziah, There is treachery, O Ahaziah.

" And Jehu drew a bow with his full strength, and smote Jehoram between his arms, and the arrow went out at his heart, and he sunk down in his chariot. . . .

" But when Ahaziah the king of Judah saw this, he fled by the way of the garden house. And Jehu followed after him, and said, Smite him also in the chariot. And they did so. . . .

" And when Jehu was come to Jezreel, Jezebel heard of it; and she painted her face, and tired her head, and looked out at a window.

" And as Jehu entered in at the gate, she said, Had Zimri peace, who slew his master? . . .

" And he said, Throw her down. So they threw her down : and some of her blood was sprinkled on the wall, and on the horses : and he trod her under foot. . . .

" And Ahab had seventy sons in Samaria. And Jehu wrote letters, . . . to the elders, and to them that brought up Ahab's children, saying, . . . If ye be mine, . . . take ye the heads of . . . your master's sons, and come to me to Jezreel by to-morrow this time. . . . And it came to pass, when the letter came to them, that they took the king's sons, and slew seventy persons, and put their heads in baskets, and sent him them to Jezreel. . . .

" And he said, Lay ye them in two heaps at the entering in of the gate until the morning. . . .

" So Jehu slew all that remained of the house of

Ahab in Jezreel, and all his great men, and his kins-folks, and his priests, until he left him none remaining.

"And he arose and departed, and came to Samaria. And as he was at the shearing house in the way, Jehu met with the brethren of Ahaziah king of Judah. . . .

"And he said, Take them alive. And they took them alive, and slew them at the pit of the shearing house, even two and forty men; neither left he any of them. . . .

"And when he came to Samaria, he slew all that re-mained unto Ahab in Samaria, till he had destroyed him, according to the saying of the Lord, which he spake to Elijah.

"And Jehu gathered all the people together, and said unto them, Ahab served Baal a little; but Jehu shall serve him much. Now therefore call unto me all the prophets of Baal, all his servants, and all his priests; let none be wanting: for I have a great sac-rifice to do to Baal; whosoever shall be wanting, he shall not live. But Jehu did it in subtilty, to the intent that he might destroy the worshippers of Baal. . . .

"And Jehu sent through all Israel: and all the wor-shippers of Baal came, so that there was not a man left that came not. And they came into the house of Baal; and the house of Baal was full from one end to another. . . .

"And it came to pass, as soon as he had made an end of offering the burnt offering, that Jehu said to the guard and to the captains, Go in, and slay them;

let none come forth. And they smote them with the edge of the sword; and the guard and the captains cast them out. . . .

" Thus Jehu destroyed Baal out of Israel." [1]

Viewed from the standpoint of comparative history, the policy of theocratic Massachusetts toward the Quakers was the necessary consequence of antecedent causes, and is exactly parallel with the massacre of the house of Ahab by Elisha and Jehu. The power of a dominant priesthood depended on conformity, and the Quakers absolutely refused to conform; nor was this the blackest of their crimes: they believed that the Deity communicated directly with men, and that these revelations were the highest rule of conduct. Manifestly such a doctrine was revolutionary. The influence of all ecclesiastics must ultimately rest upon the popular belief that they are endowed with attributes which are denied to common men. The syllogism of the New England elders was this: all revelation is contained in the Bible; we alone, from our peculiar education, are capable of interpreting the meaning of the Scriptures: therefore we only can declare the will of God. But it was evident that, were the dogma of " the inner light " once accepted, this reasoning must fall to the ground, and the authority of the ministry be overthrown. Necessarily those who held so subversive a doctrine would be pursued with greater hate than less harmful heretics, and thus contemplating the situation there is no difficulty in understanding why the Rev. John Wilson, pastor of

[1] 2 *Kings* ix., x.

Boston, should have vociferated in his pulpit, that " he would carry fire in one hand and faggots in the other, to burn all the Quakers in the world ; "[1] why the Rev. John Higginson should have denounced the "inner light" as "a stinking vapour from hell;"[2] why the astute Norton should have taught that "the justice of God was the devil's armour;"[3] and why Endicott sternly warned the first comers, "Take heed you break not our ecclesiastical laws, for then ye are sure to stretch by a halter."[4]

Nevertheless, this view has not commended itself to those learned clergymen who have been the chief historians of the Puritan commonwealth. They have, on the contrary, steadily maintained that the sectaries were the persecutors, since the company had exclusive ownership of the soil, and acted in self-defence.

The case of Roger Williams is thus summed up by Dr. Dexter : " In all strictness and honesty he persecuted them — not they him ; just as the modern ' Come-outer,' who persistently intrudes his bad manners and pestering presence upon some private company, making himself, upon pretence of conscience, a nuisance there ; is — if sane — the persecutor, rather than the man who forcibly assists, as well as courteously requires, his desired departure."[5]

---

[1] *New England Judged,* ed. 1703, p. 124.
[2] *Truth and Innocency Defended,* ed. 1703, p. 80.
[3] *New England Judged,* ed. 1703, p. 9.
[4] *Idem,* p. 9.
[5] *As to Roger Williams,* p. 90.

Dr. Ellis makes a similar argument regarding the Quakers: "It might appear as if good manners, and generosity and magnanimity of spirit, would have kept the Quakers away. Certainly, by every rule of right and reason, they ought to have kept away. They had no rights or business here. . . . Most clearly they courted persecution, suffering, and death; and, as the magistrates affirmed, 'they rushed upon the sword.' Those magistrates never intended them harm, . . . except as they believed that all their successive measures and sharper penalties were positively necessary to secure their jurisdiction from the wildest lawlessness and absolute anarchy." [1] His conclusion is: "It is to be as frankly and positively affirmed that their Quaker tormentors were the aggressive party ; that they wantonly initiated the strife, and with a dogged pertinacity persisted in outrages which drove the authorities almost to frenzy. . . ." [2]

The proposition that the Congregationalists owned the territory granted by the charter of Charles I. as though it were a private estate, has been considered in an earlier chapter; and if the legal views there advanced are sound, it is incontrovertible, that all peaceful British subjects had a right to dwell in Massachusetts, provided they did not infringe the monopoly in trade. The only remaining question, therefore, is whether the Quakers were peaceful. Dr. Ellis, Dr. Palfrey, and Dr. Dexter have carefully collected a certain number of cases of misconduct, with the view

[1] *Mass. and its Early History,* p. 110.
[2] *Idem,* p. 104.

of proving that the Friends were turbulent, and the government had reasonable grounds for apprehending such another outbreak as one which occurred a century before in Germany and is known as the Peasants' War. Before, however, it is possible to enter upon a consideration of the evidence intelligently, it is necessary to fix the chronological order of the leading events of the persecution.

The twenty-one years over which it extended may be conveniently divided into three periods, of which the first began in July, 1656, when Mary Fisher and Anne Austin came to Boston, and lasted till December, 1661, when Charles II. interfered by commanding Endicott to send those under arrest to England for trial. Hitherto John Norton had been preëminent, but in that same December he was appointed on a mission to London, and as he died soon after his return, his direct influence on affairs then probably ceased. He had been chiefly responsible for the hangings of 1659 and 1660, but under no circumstances could they have been continued, for after four heretics had perished, it was found impossible to execute Wenlock Christison, who had been condemned, because of popular indignation.

Nevertheless, the respite was brief. In June, 1662, the king, in a letter confirming the charter, excluded the Quakers from the general toleration which he demanded for other sects, and the old legislation was forthwith revived; only as it was found impossible to kill the schismatics openly, the inference, from what occurred subsequently, is unavoidable, that the elders sought to attain their purpose by what their reverend historians call "a humaner policy," [1] or, in plain English, by murdering them by flogging and starvation. Nor was the device new, for the same stratagem had already been resorted to by the East India Company, in Hindostan, before they were granted full criminal jurisdiction.[2]

The Vagabond Act was too well contrived for compassing such an end, to have been an accident, and portions of it strongly suggest the hand of Norton. It was passed in May, 1661, when it was becoming evident that hanging must be abandoned, and its provisions can only be explained on the supposition that it was the intention to make the infliction of death discretionary with each magistrate. It provided that any foreign Quaker, or any native upon a second conviction, might be ordered to receive an unlimited number of stripes. It is important also to observe that the whip was a two-handed implement, armed with lashes made of twisted and knotted cord or catgut.[3] There can be no doubt, moreover, that sundry of the judgments afterward pronounced would have resulted fatally had the people permitted their execution. During the autumn following its enactment this statute was suspended, but it was revived in about ten months.

[1] *As to Roger Williams*, p. 134.
[2] Mill's *British India*, i. 48, note.
[3] *New England Judged*, ed. 1703, p. 357, note.

Endicott's death in 1665 marks the close of the second epoch, and ten comparatively tranquil years followed. Bellingham's moderation may have been in part due to the interference of the royal commissioners, but a more potent reason was the popular disgust, which had become so strong that the penal laws could not be enforced.

A last effort was made to rekindle the dying flame in 1675, by fining constables who failed in their duty to break up Quaker meetings, and offering one third of the penalty to the informer. Magistrates were required to sentence those apprehended to the House of Correction, where they were to be kept three days on bread and water, and whipped.[1] Several suffered during this revival, the last of whom was Margaret Brewster. At the end of twenty-one years the policy of cruelty had become thoroughly discredited and a general toleration could no longer be postponed ; but this great liberal triumph was only won by heroic courage and by the endurance of excruciating torments. Marmaduke Stevenson, William Robinson, Mary Dyer, and William Leddra were hanged, several were mutilated or branded, two at least are known to have died from starvation and whipping, and it is probable that others were killed whose fate cannot be traced. The number tortured under the Vagabond Act is unknown, nor can any estimate be made of the misery inflicted upon children by the ruin and exile of parents.

[1] *Mass. Rec.* v. 60.

The early Quakers were enthusiasts, and therefore occasionally spoke and acted extravagantly ; they also adopted some offensive customs, the most objectionable of which was wearing the hat; all this is immaterial. The question at issue is not their social attractiveness, but the cause whose consequence was a virulent persecution.   This can only be determined by an analysis of the evidence.   If, upon an impartial review of the cases of outrage which have been collected, it shall appear probable that the conduct of the Friends was sufficiently violent to make it credible that the legislature spoke the truth, when it declared that "the prudence of this court was exercised onely in making provission to secure the peace & order heere established against theire attempts, whose designe (wee were well assured by our oune experjence, as well as by the example of theire predecessors in Munster) was to vndermine & ruine the same;"[1] then the reverend historians of the theocracy must be considered to have established their proposition.   But if, on the other hand, it shall seem apparent that the intense vindictiveness of this onslaught was due to the bigotry and greed of power of a despotic priesthood, who saw in the spread of independent thought a menace to the ascendency of their order, then it must be held to be demonstrated that the clergy of New England acted in obedience to those natural laws, which have always regulated the conduct of mankind.

[1] *Mass. Rec.* vol. iv. pt. 1, p. 385.

CHRONOLOGY.

1656, July.   First Quakers came to Boston.

1656, 14 Oct.   First act against Quakers passed. Providing that ship-masters bringing Quakers should be fined £100.   Quakers to be whipped and imprisoned till expelled.   Importers of Quaker books to be fined.   Any defending Quaker opinions to be fined, first offence, 40s. ; second, £4 ; third, banishment.

1657, 14 Oct.   By a supplementary act ; Quakers returning after one conviction for first offence, for men, loss of one ear; imprisonment till exile.   Second offence, loss other ear, like imprisonment.   For females ; first offence, whipping, imprisonment.   Second offence, idem.   Third offence, men and women alike ; tongue to be bored with a hot iron, imprisonment, exile.[1]

1658.   In this year Rev. John Norton actively exerted himself to secure more stringent legislation ; procured petition to that effect to be presented to court.

1658, 19 Oct.   Enacted that undomiciled Quakers returning from banishment should be hanged.   Domiciled Quakers upon conviction, refusing to apostatize, to be banished, under pain of death on return.[2]

Under this act the following persons were hanged :

1659, 27 Oct.   Robinson and Stevenson hanged.

1660, 1 June.   Mary Dyer hanged.   (Previously condemned, reprieved, and executed for returning.)

1660–1661, 14 Mar.   William Leddra hanged.

[1] *Mass. Rec.* vol. iv. pt. 1, p. 309.   [2] *Idem,* p. 346.

1661, June. Wenlock Christison condemned to death ; released.

1661, 22 May. Vagabond Act. Any person convicted before a county magistrate of being an undomiciled or vagabond Quaker to be stripped naked to the middle, tied to the cart's tail, and flogged from town to town to the border. Domiciled Quakers to be proceeded against under Act of 1658 to banishment, and then treated as vagabond Quakers. The death penalty was still preserved but not enforced.[1]

1661, 9 Sept. King Charles II. wrote to Governor Endicott directing the cessation of corporal punishment in regard to Quakers, and ordering the accused to be sent to England for trial.

1661, 27 Nov. Vagabond Act suspended.

1662, 28 June. The company's agents, Bradstreet and Norton, received from the king his letter of pardon, etc., wherein, however, Quakers are excepted from the demand made for religious toleration.

1662, 8 Oct. Encouraged by the above letter the Vagabond law revived.

1664–5, 15 March. Death of John Endicott. Bellingham governor. Commissioners interfere on behalf of Quakers in May. The persecution subsides.

1672, 3 Nov. Persecution revived by passage of law punishing persons found at Quaker meeting by fine or imprisonment and flogging. Also fining constables for neglect in making arrests and giving one third the fine to informers.[2]

[1] *Mass. Rec.* vol. iv. pt. 2, p. 3.   [2] *Mass. Rec.* v. 60.

1677, Aug. 9. Margaret Brewster whipped for entering the Old South in sackcloth.

TURBULENT QUAKERS.

1656, Mary Prince.	1662, Deborah Wilson.
1658, Sarah Gibbons.	1663, Thomas Newhouse.
" Dorothy Waugh.	" Edward Wharton.
1660, John Smith.	1664, Hannah Wright.[1]
1661, Katherine Chatham.	" Mary Tomkins.
" George Wilson.	1665, Lydia Wardwell.
1662, Elizabeth Hooton.	1677, Margaret Brewster.

" It was in the month called July, of this present year [1656] when Mary Fisher and Ann Austin arrived in the road before Boston, before ever a law was made there against the Quakers; and yet they were very ill treated; for before they came ashore, the deputy governor, Richard Bellingham (the governor himself being out of town) sent officers aboard, who searched their trunks and chests, and took away the books they found there, which were about one hundred, and carried them ashore, after having commanded the said women to be kept prisoners aboard; and the said books were, by an order of the council, burnt in the market-place by the hangman. . . . And then they were shut up close prisoners, and command was given that none should come to them without leave; a fine of five pounds being laid on any that should otherwise come at, or speak with them, tho' but at the window. Their pens, ink, and paper were

---

[1] Uncertain.

taken from them, and they not suffered to have any candle-light in the night season; nay, what is more, they were stript naked, under pretence to know whether they were witches [a true touch of sacerdotal malignity] tho' in searching no token was found upon them but of innocence. And in this search they were so barbarously misused that modesty forbids to mention it: And that none might have communication with them a board was nailed up before the window of the jail. And seeing they were not provided with victuals, Nicholas Upshal, one who had lived long in Boston, and was a member of the church there, was so concerned about it, (liberty being denied to send them provision) that he purchas'd it of the jailor at the rate of five shillings a week, lest they should have starved. And after having been about five weeks prisoners, William Chichester, master of a vessel, was bound in one hundred pound bond to carry them back, and not suffer any to speak with them, after they were put on board; and the jailor kept their beds . . . and their Bible, for his fees." [1]

Endicott was much dissatisfied with the forbearance of Bellingham, and declared that had he " been there . . . he would have had them well whipp'd." [2] No exertion was spared, nevertheless, to get some hold upon them, the elders examining them as to matters of faith, with a view to ensnare them as heretics. In this, however, they were foiled.

[1] Sewel, p. 160.
[2] *New England Judged*, ed. 1703, p. 10.

On the authority of Hutchinson, Dr. Dexter [1] and Dr. Palfrey complain [2] that Mary Prince reviled two of the ministers, who " with much moderation and tenderness endeavored to convince her of her errors." [3] A visitation of the clergy was a form of torment from which even the boldest recoiled ; Vane, Gorton, Childe, and Anne Hutchinson quailed under it, and though the Quakers abundantly proved that they could bear stripes with patience, they could not endure this. She called them " Baal's priests, the seed of the serpent." Dr. Ellis also speaks of "stinging objurgations screamed out . . . from between the bars of their prisons." [4] He cites no cases, but he probably refers to the same woman who called to Endicott one Sunday on his way from church : " Woe unto thee, thou art an oppressor." [5] If she said so she spoke the truth, for she was illegally imprisoned, was deprived of her property, and subjected to great hardship.

In October, 1656, the first of the repressive acts was passed, by which the " cursed " and " blasphemous " intruders were condemned to be " comĩtted to the house of correction, and at theire entrance to be seuerely whipt and by the master thereof to be kept constantly to worke, and none suffered to converse or speak wth them ; " [6] and any captain knowingly bringing them within the jurisdiction to be fined one hundred pounds, with imprisonment till payment.

---

[1] *As to Roger Williams*, p. 127.   [2] Palfrey, ii. 464.

[3] Hutch. *Hist.* i. 181.   [4] *Mem. Hist. of Boston*, i. 182.

[5] Hutch. *Hist.* i. 181.   [6] *Mass. Rec.* vol. iv. pt. 1, p. 278.

" When this law was published at the door of the aforenamed Nicholas Upshall, the good old man, grieved in spirit, publickly testified against it; for which he was the next morning sent for to the General Court, where he told them that: ' The execution of that law would be a forerunner of a judgment upon their country, and therefore in love and tenderness which he bare to the people and place, desired them to take heed, lest they were found fighters against God.' For this, he, though one of their church-members, and of a blameless conversation, was fined £20 and £3 more for not coming to church, whence the sense of their wickedness had induced him to absent himself. They also banished him out of their jurisdiction, allowing him but one month for his departure, though in the winter season, and he a weakly ancient man: Endicott the governor, when applied to on his behalf for a mitigation of his fine, churlishly answered, ' I will not bate him a groat.' " [1]

Although, after the autumn of 1656, whippings, fines, and banishments became frequent, no case of misconduct is alleged until the 13th of the second month, 1658, when Sarah Gibbons and Dorothy Waugh broke two bottles in Mr. Norton's church, after lecture, to testify to his emptiness;[2] both had previously been imprisoned and banished, but the ferocity with which Norton at that moment was forcing on the persecution was the probable incentive to the trespass. " They were sent to the house of correction, where, after being kept three days without

---

[1] Besse, ii. 181.   [2] This charge is unproved.

any food, they were cruelly whipt, and kept three days longer without victuals, though they had offered to buy some, but were not suffered." [1]

In 1661 Katharine Chatham walked through Boston, in sackcloth. This was during the trial of Christison for his life, when the terror culminated, and hardly needs comment.

George Wilson is charged with having " rushed through the streets of Boston, shouting: 'The Lord is coming with fire and sword!'" [2] The facts appear to be these : in 1661, just before Christison's trial, he was arrested, without any apparent reason, and, as he was led to prison, he cried, that the Lord was coming with fire and sword to plead with Boston. [3] At the general jail delivery [4] in anticipation of the king's order, he was liberated, but soon rearrested, " sentenced to be tied to the cart's tail," and flogged with so severe a whip that the Quakers wanted to buy it " to send to England for the novelty of the cruelty, but that was not permitted." [5]

Elizabeth Hooton coming from England in 1661, with Joan Brooksup, " they were soon clapt up in prison, and, upon their discharge thence, being driven with the rest two days' journey into the vast, howling wilderness, and there left . . . without necessary provisions." [6] They escaped to Barbadoes. "Upon

---

[1] Besse, ii. 184.   [2] *As to Roger Williams*, p. 133.

[3] *New England Judged*, ed. 1703, p. 351.

[4] *Mass. Rec.* vol. iv. pt. 2, p. 19.   Order passed 28 May, 1661.

[5] Besse, ii. 224.   [6] Besse, ii. 228, 229.

their coming again to Boston, they were presently apprehended by a constable, an ignorant and furious
zealot, who declared, ' It was his delight, and he could
rejoice in following the Quakers to their execution
as much as ever.' " Wishing to return once more,
she obtained a license from the king to buy a house in
any plantation. Though about sixty, she was seized
at Dover, where the Rev. Mr. Rayner was settled, put
into the stocks, and imprisoned four days in the dead
of winter, where she nearly perished from cold.[1] Afterward, at Cambridge, she exhorted the people to
repentance in the streets,[2] and for this crime, which
is cited as an outrage to Puritan decorum,[3] she was
once more apprehended and " imprisoned in a close,
stinking dungeon, where there was nothing either to
lie down or sit on, where she was kept two days and
two nights without bread or water," and then sentenced to be whipped through three towns. " At
Cambridge she was tied to the whipping-post, and
lashed with ten stripes with a three-stringed whip,
with three knots at the end : At Watertown she was
laid on with ten stripes more with rods of willow : At
Dedham, in a cold frosty morning, they tortured her
aged body with ten stripes more at a cart's tail."
The peculiar atrocity of flogging from town to town
lay in this : that the victim's wounds became cold

[1] Besse, ii. 229.

[2] " Repentance ! Repentance ! A day of howling and sad
lamentation is coming upon you all from the Lord."

[3] *As to Roger Williams,* p. 133.

between the times of punishment, and in winter sometimes frozen, which made the torture intolerably
agonizing. Then, as hanging was impossible, other
means were tried to make an end of her: "Thus
miserably torn and beaten, they carried her a weary
journey on horseback many miles into the wilderness, and toward night left her there among wolves,
bears, and other wild beasts, who, though they did
sometimes seize on living persons, were yet to her less
cruel than the savage - professors of that country.
When those who conveyed her thither left her, they
said, 'They thought they should never see her
more.'"[1]

The intent to kill is obvious, and yet Elizabeth
Hooton suffered less than many of those convicted
and sentenced after public indignation had forced the
theocracy to adopt what their reverend successors are
pleased to call the "humaner policy" of the Vagabond Act.[2]

Any want of deference to a clergyman is sure to be
given a prominent place in the annals of Massachusetts; and, accordingly, the breaking of bottles in
church, which happened twice in twenty-one years, is
never omitted.

In 1663 "John Liddal, and Thomas Newhouse,
having been at meeting" (at Salem), "were apprehended and . . . sentenced to be whipt through three
towns as vagabonds," which was accordingly done.

[1] Besse, ii. 229. See *New England Judged*, p. 413.
[2] *As to Roger Williams*, p. 134.

" Not long after this, the aforesaid Thomas New-house was again whipt through the jurisdiction of Boston for testifying against the persecutors in their meeting-house there; at which time he, in a prophetick manner, having two glass bottles in his hands, threw them down, saying, ' so shall you be dashed in pieces.' " [1]

The next turbulent Quaker is mentioned in this way by Dr. Dexter : " Edward Wharton was 'pressed in spirit' to repair to Dover and proclaim ' Wo, ven-geance, and the indignation of the Lord ' upon the court in session there." [2] This happened in the sum-mer of 1663, and long ere then he had seen and suffered the oppression that makes men mad. He was a peaceable and industrious inhabitant of Salem ; in 1659 he had seen Robinson and Stevenson done to death, and, being deeply moved, he said, "the guilt of [their] blood was so great that he could not bear it ; " [3] he was taken from his home, given twenty lashes and fined twenty pounds; the next year, just at the time of Christison's trial, he was again seized, led through the country like a notorious offender, and thrown into prison, "where he was kept close, night and day, with William Leddra, sometimes in a very little room, little bigger than a saw-pit, having no lib-erty granted them."

" Being brought before their court, he again asked, ' What is the cause, and wherefore have I been

---

[1] Besse, ii. 232.   [2] *As to Roger Williams*, p. 133.
[3] Besse, ii. 205.

fetcht from my habitation, where I was following my
honest calling, and here laid up as an evil-doer?'
They told him, that 'his hair was too long, and that
he had disobeyed that commandment which saith,
Honour thy father and mother.' He asked, 'Wherein?' 'In that you will not,' said they, 'put off your
hat to magistrates.' Edward replied, 'I love and
own all magistrates and rulers, who are for the punishment of evil doers, and for the praise of them that
do well.' " [1]

Then Rawson pronounced the sentence: " You are
upon pain of death to depart this jurisdiction, it being
the 11th of this instant March, by the one and twentieth of the same, on the pain of death. . . . 'Nay
[said Wharton], I shall not go away; therefore be
careful what you do.' " [2]

And he did not go, but was with Leddra when he
died upon the tree. On the day Leddra suffered,
Christison was brought before Endicott, and commanded to renounce his religion; but he answered:
" Nay, I shall not change my religion, nor seek to
save my life; . . . but if I lose my life for Christ's
sake and the preaching of the gospel, I shall save
it." They then sent him back to prison to await his
doom. At the next court he was brought to the bar,
where he demanded an appeal to England; but in the
midst a letter was brought in from Wharton, signify-
ing, " That whereas they had banished him on pain of
death, yet he was at home in his own house at Salem,

[1] Besse, ii. 220. [2] Besse, ii. 221.

and therefore proposing, ' That they would take off their wicked sentence from him, that he might go about his occasions out of their jurisdiction.' " [1]

Endicott was exasperated to frenzy, for he felt the ground crumbling beneath him; he put the fate of Christison to the vote, and failed to carry a condemnation. " The governor seeing this division, said, ' I could find it in my heart to go home; ' being in such a rage, that he flung something furiously on the table. . . . Then the governor put the court to vote again; but this was done confusedly, which so incensed the governor that he stood up and said, ' You that will not consent record it: I thank God I am not afraid to give judgment. . . . Wenlock Christison, hearken to your sentence: You must return unto the place from whence you came, and from thence to the place of execution, and there you must be hang'd until you are dead, dead, dead.' " [2] Thereafter Wharton invoked the wrath of God against the theocracy.

To none of the enormities committed during these years are the divines more keenly alive than to the crime of disturbing what they call " public Sabbath worship; " [3] and since their language conveys the impression that such acts were not only very common, but also unprovoked, whereas the truth is that they were rare, it cannot fail to be instructive to relate the causes which led to the interruption of the ordination

---

[1] Besse, ii. 222, 223.
[2] Sewel, p. 279.
[3] *As to Roger Williams*, p. 139.

of that Mr. Higginson, who called the " inner light "
" a stinking vapour from hell." [1]

John and Margaret Smith were members of the Salem church, and John was a freeman. In 1658, Margaret became a Quaker, and though in feeble health, she
was cast into prison, and endured the extremities of
privation; her sufferings and her patience so wrought
upon her husband that he too became a convert, and
a few weeks before the ceremony wrote to Endicott:

" O governour, governour, do not think that my love
to my wife is at all abated, because I sit still silent,
and do not seek her . . . freedom, which if I did would
not avail. . . . Upon examination of her, there being
nothing justly laid to her charge, yet to fulfil your
wills, it was determined, that she must have ten stripes
in the open market place, it being very cold, the snow
lying by the walls, and the wind blowing cold. . . .
My love is much more increased to her, because I see
your cruelty so much enlarged to her." [2]

Yet, though laboring under such intense excitement, the only act of insubordination wherewith this
man is charged was saying in a loud voice during the
service, " What you are going about to set up, our
God is pulling down." [3]

Dr. Dexter also speaks with pathos of the youth of
some of the criminals.

" Hannah Wright, a mere girl of less than fifteen
summers, toiled . . . from Oyster Bay . . . to Boston,

[1] Ordained July 8, 1660. *Annals of Salem.*
[2] Besse, ii. 208, 209.   [3] Hutch. *Hist.* i. 187.

that she might pipe in the ears of the court ' a warning in the name of the Lord.' " [1] This appears to have happened in 1664,[2] yet the name of Hannah Wright is recorded among those who were released in the general jail delivery in 1661,[3] when she was only twelve; and her sister had been banished.[4]

But of all the scandals which have been dwelt on for two centuries with such unction, none have been made more notorious than certain extravagances committed by three women; and regarding them, the reasoning of Dr. Dexter should be read in full.

"The Quaker of the seventeenth century . . . was essentially a coarse, blustering, conceited, disagreeable, impudent fanatic; whose religion gained subjective comfort in exact proportion to the objective comfort of which it was able to deprive others; and which broke out into its choicest exhibitions in acts which were not only at that time in the nature of a public scandal and nuisance, but which even in the brightest light of this nineteenth century . . . would subject those who should be guilty of them to the immediate and stringent attention of the police court. The disturbance of public Sabbath worship, and the indecent exposure of the person — whether conscience be pleaded for them or not — are punished, and rightly punished, as crimes by every civilized government." [5]

[1] As to Roger Williams, p. 133.
[2] Besse, ii. 234. New England Judged, ed. 1703, p. 461.
[3] Besse, ii. 224.   [4] New England Judged, ed. 1703, p. 461.
[5] As to Roger Williams, pp. 138, 139.

This paragraph undoubtedly refers to Mary Tomkins, who "on the First Day of the week at Oyster
River, broke up the service of God's house . . . the
scene ending in deplorable confusion; "[1] and to Lydia
Wardwell and Deborah Wilson, who appeared in
public naked.

Mary Tomkins and Alice Ambrose came to Massachusetts in 1662; landing at Dover, they began preaching at the inn, to which a number of people resorted.
Mr. Rayner, hearing the news, hurried to the spot,
and in much irritation asked them what they were
doing there? This led to an argument about the
Trinity, and the authority of ministers, and at last
the clergyman "in a rage flung away, calling to his
people, at the window, to go from amongst them."[2]
Nothing was done at the moment, but toward winter
the two came back from Maine, whither they had
gone, and then Mr. Rayner saw his opportunity. He
caused Richard Walden to prosecute them, and as the
magistrate was ignorant of the technicalities of the
law, the elder acted as clerk, and drew up for him
the following warrant: —

To the Constables of Dover, Hampton, Salisbury,
Newbury, Rowley, Ipswich, Wenham, Linn, Bos-
ton, Roxbury, Dedham, and until these vagabond
Quakers are carried out of this jurisdiction.
You and every of you are required, in the King's

[1] *As to Roger Williams*, p. 133.
[2] *New England Judged*, ed. 1703, p. 362.

Majesty's name, to take these vagabond Quakers, Anne Coleman, Mary Tomkins and Alice Ambrose, and make them fast to the cart's tail, and driving the cart through your several towns, to whip them on their backs, not exceeding ten stripes apiece on each of them in each town, and so to convey them from constable to constable, till they come out of this jurisdiction, as you will answer it at your peril: and this shall be your warrant.

Per me   RICHARD WALDEN.

At Dover, dated December the 22d, 1662.[1]

The Rev. John Rayner pronounced judgment of death by flogging, for the weather was bitter, the distance to be walked was eighty miles, and the lashes were given with a whip, whose three twisted, knotted thongs cut to the bone.

" So, in a very cold day, your deputy, Walden, caused these women to be stripp'd naked from the middle upward, and tyed to a cart, and after a while cruelly whipp'd them, whilst the priest stood and looked, and laughed at it. . . . They went with the executioner to Hampton, and through dirt and snow at Salisbury, half way the leg deep, the constable forced them after the cart's tayl at which he whipp'd them." [2]

Had the Reverend John Rayner but followed the cart, to see that his three hundred and thirty lashes were all given with the same ferocity which warmed his heart to mirth at Dover, before his journey's end

[1] Besse, ii. 227.   [2] *New England Judged*, pp. 366, 367.

he would certainly have joyed in giving thanks to
God over the women's gory corpses, freezing amid the
snow. His negligence saved their lives, for when the
ghastly pilgrims passed through Salisbury, the people
to their eternal honor set the captives free.

Soon after, on Sunday, — "Whilst Alice Ambrose
was at prayer, two constables . . . came . . . and
taking her . . . dragged her out of doors, and then
with her face toward the snow, which was knee deep,
over stumps and old trees near a mile; when they had
wearied themselves they . . . left the prisoner in an
house . . . and fetched Mary Tomkins, whom in like
manner they dragged with her face toward the snow.
. . . On the next morning, which was excessive cold,
they got a canoe . . . and so carried them to the har-
bour's mouth, threatning, that 'They would now so do
with them, as that they would be troubled with them no
more.' The women being unwilling to go, they forced
them down a very steep place in the snow, dragging
Mary Tomkins over the stumps of trees to the water
side, so that she was much bruised, and fainted under
their hands : They plucked Alice Ambrose into the
water, and kept her swimming by the canoe in great
danger of drowning, or being frozen to death. They
would in all probability have proceeded in their wicked
purpose to the murthering of those three women, had
they not been prevented by a sudden storm, which
drove them back to the house again. They kept the
women there till near midnight, and then cruelly
turned them out of doors in the frost and snow, Alice

Ambrose's clothes being frozen hard as boards. . . .
It was observable that those constables, though wicked
enough of themselves, were animated by a ruling elder
of their church, whose name corresponded not with his
actions, for he was called Hate-evil Nutter, he put
those men forward, and by his presence encouraged
them." [1]

Subsequently, Mary Tomkins committed the breach
of the peace complained of, which was an interruption
of a sermon against Quaker preaching.[2]

Deborah Wilson, one of the women who went
abroad naked, was insane, the fact appearing of record subsequently as the judgment of the court.[3] She
was flogged.

Lydia Wardwell was the daughter of Isaac Per-
kins, a freeman. She married Eliakim Wardwell,
son of Thomas Wardwell, who was also a citizen.
They became Quakers ; and the story begins when
the poor young woman had been a wife just three
years. "At Hampton, Priest Seaborn Cotton, understanding that one Eliakim Wardel had entertained
Wenlock Christison, went with some of his herd to
Eliakim's house, having like a sturdy herdsman put
himself at the head of his followers, with a truncheon
in his hand." [4]   Eliakim was fined for harboring
Christison, and "a pretty beast for the saddle, worth
about fourteen pound, was taken . . . the overplus of

---

[1] Besse, ii. 228.

[2] *New England Judged*, ed. 1703, p. 386.

[3] *Quaker Invasion*, p. 104.   [4] Sewel, p. 340.

which to make up to him, your officers plundred old
William Marston of a vessel of green ginger, which
for some fine was taken from him, and forc'd it into
Eliakim's house, where he let it lie and touched it
not ; . . . and notwithstanding he came not to your
invented worship, but was fined ten shillings a day's
absence, for him and his wife, yet was he often rated
for priest's hire ; and the priest (Seaborn Cotton, old
John Cotton's son) to obtain his end and to cover
himself, sold his rate to a man almost as bad as himself, . . . who coming in pretence of borrowing a little
corn for himself, which the harmless honest man
willingly lent him ; and he finding thereby that he
had corn, which was his design, Judas-like, he went
. . . and measured it away as he pleased."

" Another time, the said Eliakim being rated to the
said priest, Seaborn Cotton, the said Seaborn having
a mind to a pied heifer Eliakim had, as Ahab had to
Naboth's vineyard, sent his servant nigh two miles to
fetch her ; who having robb'd Eliakim of her, brought
her to his master." . . .

" Again the said Eliakim was had to your court,
and being by them fined, they took almost all his
marsh and meadow-ground from him to satisfie it,
which was for the keeping his cattle alive in winter
. . . and [so] seized and took his estate, that they
plucked from him most of that he had." [1]

Lydia Wardwell, thus reduced to penury, and
shaken by the daily scenes of unutterable horror

[1] *New England Judged,* ed. 1703, pp. 374–376.

through which she had to pass, was totally unequal to endure the strain under which the masculine intellect of Anne Hutchinson had reeled. She was pursued by her pastor, who repeatedly commanded her to come to church and explain her absence from communion.[1] The miserable creature, brooding over her blighted life and the torments of her friends, became possessed with the delusion that it was her duty to testify against the barbarity of flogging naked women; so she herself went in among them naked for a sign. There could be no clearer proof of insanity, for it is admitted that in every other respect her conduct was exemplary.

Her judges at Ipswich had her bound to a rough post of the tavern, in which they sat, and then, while the splinters tore her bare breasts, they had her flesh cut from her back with the lash.[2]

"Thus they served the wife, and the husband escaped not free; . . . he taxing Simon Broadstreet, . . . for upbraiding his wife . . . and telling Simon of his malitious reproaching of his wife who was an honest woman . . . and of that report that went abroad of the known dishonesty of Simon's daughter, Seaborn Cotton's wife; Simon in a fierce rage, told the court, 'That if such fellows should be suffered to speak so in the court, he would sit there no more:' So to please Simon, Eliakim was sentenc'd to be stripp'd from his waste upward, and to be bound to an oak-

[1] Besse, ii. 235.

[2] *New England Judged*, ed. 1703, p. 377.

tree that stood by their worship-house, and to be whipped fifteen lashes; . . . as they were having him out . . . he called to Seaborn Cotton . . . to come and see the work done (so far was he from being daunted by their cruelty), who hastned out and followed him thither, and so did old Wiggins, one of the magistrates, who when Eliakim was tyed to the tree and stripp'd, said . . . to the whipper . . . ' Whip him a good ;' which the executioner cruelly performed with cords near as big as a man's little finger ; . . . Priest Cotton standing near him . . . Eliakim . . . when he was loosed from the tree, said to him, amongst the people, 'Seaborn, hath my py'd heifer calv'd yet ? ' Which Seaborn, the priest, hearing stole away like a thief." [1]

As Margaret Brewster was the last who is known to have been whipped, so is she one of the most famous, for she has been immortalized by Samuel Sewall, an honest, though a dull man.

"July 8, 1677. New Meeting House Mane : In sermon time there came in a female Quaker, in a canvas frock, her hair disshevelled and loose like a Periwigg, her face as black as ink, led by two other Quakers, and two other followed. It occasioned the greatest and most amazing uproar that I ever saw. Isaiah 1. 12, 14." [2]

In 1675 the persecution had been revived, and the stories the woman heard of the cruelties that were perpetrated on those of her own faith inspired her

---

[1] *New England Judged*, ed. 1703, pp. 377–379.
[2] *Mass. Hist. Coll.* fifth series, v. 43.

with the craving to go to New England to protest against the wrong; so she journeyed thither, and entered the Old South one Sunday morning clothed in sackcloth, with ashes on her head.

At her trial she asked for leave to speak: "Governour, I desire thee to hear me a little, for I have something to say in behalf of my friends in this place : . . . Oh governour! I cannot but press thee again and again, to put an end to these cruel laws that you have made to fetch my friends from their peaceable meetings, and keep them three days in the house of correction, and then whip them for worshipping the true and living God: Governour! Let me entreat thee to put an end to these laws, for the desire of my soul is, that you may act for God, and then would you prosper, but if you act against the Lord and his blessed truth, you will assuredly come to nothing, the mouth of the Lord hath spoken it." . . .

"Margaret Brewster, You are to have your clothes stript off to the middle, and to be tied to a cart's tail at the South Meeting House, and to be drawn through the town, and to receive twenty stripes upon your naked body."

"The will of the Lord be done: I am contented." . . .

Governour. "Take her away." [1]

So ends the sacerdotal list of Quaker outrages, for, after Margaret Brewster had expiated her crime of protesting against the repression of free thought, there

[1] Besse, ii. 263, 264.

came a toleration, and with toleration a deep tranquillity, so that the very name of Quaker has become synonymous with quietude. The issue between them and the Congregationalists must be left to be decided upon the legal question of their right as English subjects to inhabit Massachusetts; and secondarily upon the opinion which shall be formed of their conduct as citizens, upon the testimony of those witnesses whom the church herself has called. But regarding the great fundamental struggle for liberty of individual opinion, no presentation of the evidence could be historically correct which did not include at least one example of the fate that awaited peaceful families, under this ecclesiastical government, who roused the ire of the priests.

Lawrence and Cassandra Southwick were an aged couple, members of the Salem church, and Lawrence was a freeman. Josiah, their eldest son, was a man; but they had beside a younger boy and girl named Daniel and Provided.

The father and mother were first arrested in 1657 for harboring two Quakers; Lawrence was soon released, but a Quaker tract was found upon Cassandra.[1] Although no attempt seems to have been made to prove heresy to bring the case within the letter of the law, the paper was treated as a heretical writing, and she was imprisoned for seven weeks and fined forty shillings.

Persecution made converts fast, and in Salem par-

[1] Besse, ii. 183.

ticularly a number withdrew from the church and began to worship by themselves. All were soon arrested, and the three Southwicks were again sent to Boston, this time to serve as an example. They arrived on the 3d of February, 1657; without form of trial they were whipped in the extreme cold weather and imprisoned eleven days. Their cattle were also seized and sold to pay a fine of £4 13s. for six weeks' absence from worship on the Lord's day.

The next summer, Leddra, who was afterwards hanged, and William Brend went to Salem, and several persons were seized for meeting with them, among whom were the Southwicks. A room was prepared for the criminals in the Boston prison by boarding up the windows and stopping ventilation.[1] They were refused food unless they worked to pay for it; but to work when wrongfully confined was against the Quaker's conscience, so they did not eat for five days. On the second day of fasting they were flogged, and then, with wounds undressed, the men and women together were once more locked in the dark, close room, to lie upon the bare boards, in the stifling July heat; for they were not given beds. On the fourth day they were told they might go if they would pay the jail fees and the constables; but they refused, and so were kept in prison. On the morrow the jailer, thinking to bring them to terms, put Brend in irons, neck and heels, and he lay without food for sixteen hours upon his back lacerated with flogging.

[1] *New England Judged*, ed. 1703, p. 64.

The next day the miserable man was ordered to work, but he lacked the strength, had he been willing, for he was weak from starvation and pain, and stiffened by the irons. And now the climax came. The jailer seized a tarred rope and beat him till it broke; then, foaming with fury, he dragged the old man down stairs, and, with a new rope, gave him ninety-seven blows, when his strength failed; and Brend, his flesh black and beaten to jelly, and his bruised skin hanging in bags full of clotted blood, was thrust into his cell. There, upon the floor of that dark and fetid den, the victim fainted. But help was at hand; an outcry was raised, the people could bear no more, the doors were opened, and he was rescued.[1]

The indignation was deep, and the government was afraid. Endicott sent his own doctor, but the surgeon said that Brend's flesh would " rot from off his bones," and he must die. And now the mob grew fierce and demanded justice on the ruffian who had done this deed, and the magistrates nailed a paper on the church door promising to bring him to trial.

Then it was that the true spirit of his order blazed forth in Norton, for the jailer was fashioned in his own image, and he threw over him the mantle of the holy church. He made the magistrates take the paper down, rebuking them for their faintness of heart, saying to them: —

William " Brend endeavoured to beat our gospel ordinances black and blue, if he then be beaten black

[1] *New England Judged,* ed. 1703, p. 66.

and blue, it is but just upon him, and I will appear in his behalf that did so." [1]   And the man was justified, and commanded to whip " the Quakers in prison . . . twice a week, if they refused to work, and the first time to add five stripes to the former ten, and each time to add three to them. . . . Which order ye sent to the jaylor, to strengthen his hands to do yet more cruelly; being somewhat weakened by the fright of his former doings." [2]

After this the Southwicks, being still unable to obtain their freedom, sent the following letter to the magistrates, which is a good example of the writings of these " coarse, blustering, . . . impudent fanatics : " [3] —

This to the Magistrates at Court in Salem.

FRIENDS,

Whereas it was your pleasures to commit us, whose names are under-written, to the house of correction in Boston, altho' the Lord, the righteous Judge of heaven and earth, is our witness, that we had done nothing worthy of stripes or of bonds; and we being committed by your court, to be dealt withal as the law provides for foreign Quakers, as ye please to term us; and having some of us, suffered your law and pleasures, now that which we do expect, is, that whereas we have suffered your law, so now to be set free by

[1] Besse, ii. 186.
[2] *New England Judged*, ed. 1703, p. 67.
[3] *As to Roger Williams*, p. 138.

the same law, as your manner is with strangers, and
not to put us in upon the account of one law, and
execute another law upon us, of which, according to
your own manner, we were never convicted as the law
expresses. If you had sent us upon the account of
your new law, we should have expected the jaylor's
order to have been on that account, which that it was
not, appears by the warrant which we have, and the
punishment which we bare, as four of us were whipp'd,
among whom was one that had formerly been whipp'd,
so now also according to your former law. Friends,
let it not be a small thing in your eyes, the exposing
as much as in you lies, our families to ruine. It's
not unknown to you the season, and the time of the
year, for those that live of husbandry, and what their
cattle and families may be exposed unto; and also
such as live on trade; we know if the spirit of Christ
did dwell and rule in you, these things would take
impression on your spirits. What our lives and
conversations have been in that place, is well known;
and what we now suffer for, is much for false reports,
and ungrounded jealousies of heresie and sedition.
These thing lie upon us to lay before you. As for our
parts, we have true peace and rest in the Lord in all
our sufferings, and are made willing in the power and
strength of God, freely to offer up our lives in this
cause of God, for which we suffer; Yea and we do
find (through grace) the enlargements of God in our
imprisoned state, to whom alone we commit ourselves
and families, for the disposing of us according to his

infinite wisdom and pleasure, in whose love is our rest and life.

From the House of Bondage in Boston wherein we are made captives by the wills of men, although made free by the Son, John 8, 36. In which we quietly rest, this 16th of the 5th month, 1658.

LAWRENCE ⎫
CASSANDRA ⎬ SOUTHWICK
JOSIAH ⎭
SAMUEL SHATTOCK
JOSHUA BUFFUM.[1]

What the prisoners apprehended was being kept in prison and punished under an *ex post facto* law, and this was precisely what was done. When brought into court they demanded to be told the crime wherewith they were charged. They were answered: " It was ' Entertaining the Quakers who were their enemies; not coming to their meetings; and meeting by themselves.' They adjoyned, ' That as to those things they had already fastned their law upon them.' . . . So ye had nothing left but the hat, for which (then) ye had no law. They answered — that they intended no offence to ye in coming thither . . . for it was not their manner to have to do with courts. And as for withdrawing from their meetings, or keeping on their hats, or doing anything in contempt of them, or their laws,

[1] *New England Judged*, ed. 1703, p. 74.

they said, the Lord was their witness . . . that they did it not. So ye rose up, and bid the jaylor take them away." [1]

An acquittal seemed certain; yet it was intolerable to the clergy that these accursed blasphemers should elude them when they held them in their grasp; wherefore, the next day, the Rev. Charles Chauncy, preaching at Thursday lecture, thus taught Christ's love for men: "Suppose ye should catch six wolves in a trap . . . [there were six Salem Quakers] and ye cannot prove that they killed either sheep or lambs; and now ye have them they will neither bark nor bite: yet they have the plain marks of wolves. Now I leave it to your consideration whether ye will let them go alive, yea or nay." [2]

Then the divines had a consultation, "and your priests were put to it, how to prove them as your law had said: and ye had them before you again, and your priests were with you, every one by his side (so came ye to your court) and John Norton must ask them questions, on purpose to ensnare them, that by your standing law for hereticks, ye might condemn them (as your priests before consulted) and when this would not do (for the Lord was with them, and made them wiser than your teachers) ye made a law to banish them, upon pain of death. . . ." [3]

After a violent struggle, the ministers, under Norton's lead, succeeded, on the 19th of October, 1658,

[1] *New England Judged*, ed. 1703, p. 85.
[2] *Idem*, pp. 85, 86.　　　　　　[3] *Idem*, p. 87.

in forcing the capital act through the legislature, which contained a clause making the denial of reverence to superiors, or in other words, the wearing the hat, evidence of Quakerism.[1]

On that very day the bench ordered the prisoners at Ipswich to be brought to the bar, and the Southwicks were bidden to depart before the spring elections.[2] They did not go, and in May were once more in the felon's dock. They asked what wrong they had done. The judges told them they were rebellious for not going as they had been commanded. The old man and woman piteously pleaded " that they had no otherwhere to go," nor had they done anything to deserve banishment or death, though £100 (all they had in the world) had been taken from them for meeting together.[3]

" Major-General Dennison replied, that ' they stood against the authority of the country, in not submitting to their laws : that he should not go about to speak much concerning the error of their judgments : but,' added he, ' you and we are not able well to live together, and at present the power is in our hand, and therefore the stronger must send off.' " [4]

The father, mother, and son were banished under pain of death. The aged couple were sent to Shelter Island, but their misery was well-nigh done; they

---

[1] *New England Judged*, ed. 1703, pp. 100, 101 ; *Mass. Rec.* vol. iv. pt. 1, p. 346.

[2] *Mass. Rec.* vol. iv. pt. 1, p. 349.

[3] *New England Judged*, ed. 1703, p. 106.   [4] Besse, ii. 198.

perished within a few days of each other, tortured to death by flogging and starvation.

Josiah was shipped to England, but afterward returned, was seized, and in the " seventh month, 1661, you had him before you, and at which according to your former law, he should have been tried for his life."

" But the great occasion you took against him, was his hat, which you commanded him to pull off : ' He told your governour he could not.' You said, ' He would not.' He told you, ' It was a cross to his will to keep it on ; . . . and that he could not do it for conscience sake.' . . . But your governour told him, ' That he was to have been tryed for his life, but that you had made your late law to save his life, which, you said, was mercy to him.' Then he asked you, ' Whether you were not as good to take his life now, as to whip him after your manner, twelve or fourteen times at the cart's tail, through your towns, and then put him to death afterward ? ' " He was condemned to be flogged through Boston, Roxbury, and Dedham ; but he, when he heard the judgment, " with arms stretched out, and hands spread before you, said, ' Here is my body, if you want a further testimony of the truth I profess, take it and tear it in pieces . . . it is freely given up, and as for your sentence I matter it not.' " [1]

This coarse, blustering, impudent fanatic had, indeed, " with a dogged pertinacity persisted in out-

[1] *New England Judged*, ed. 1703, pp. 354–356.

rages which" had driven "the authorities almost to frenzy;" therefore they tied him to a cart and lashed him for fifteen miles, and while he "sang to the praise of God," his tormentor swung with all his might a tremendous two-handed whip, whose knotted thongs were made of twisted cat-gut; [1] "thence he was carried fifteen miles from any town into the wilderness." [2]

An end had been made of the grown members of the family, but the two children were still left. To reach them, the device was conceived of enforcing the penalty for not attending church, since "it was well known they had no estate, their parents being already brought to poverty by their rapacious persecutors." [3]

Accordingly, they were summoned and asked to account for their absence from worship. Daniel answered "that if they had not so persecuted his father and mother perhaps he might have come." [4] They were fined; and on the day on which they lost their parents forever, the sale as slaves of this helpless boy and girl was authorized to satisfy the debt.[5]

Edmund Batter, treasurer of Salem, brought the children to the town, and went to a shipmaster who was about to sail, to engage a passage to Barbadoes.

[1] *New England Judged*, ed. 1703, p. 357, note.
[2] Besse, ii. 225.
[3] Sewel, p. 223.
[4] *New England Judged*, ed. 1703, p. 381.
[5] *Mass. Rec.* vol. iv. pt. 1, p. 366.

The captain made the excuse that they would corrupt his ship's company. "Oh, no," said Batter, "you need not fear that, for they are poor harmless creatures, and will not hurt any body." . . . "Will they not so?" broke out the sailor, "and will ye offer to make slaves of so harmless creatures?" [1]

Thus were free-born English subjects and citizens of Massachusetts dealt with by the priesthood that ruled the Puritan Commonwealth.

None but ecclesiastical partisans can doubt the bearing of such evidence. It was the mortal struggle between conservatism and liberality, between repression and free thought. The elders felt it in the marrow of their bones, and so declared it in their laws, denouncing banishment under pain of death against those "adhering to or approoving of any knoune Quaker, or the tenetts & practices of the Quakers, . . . manifesting thereby theire compljance wth those whose designe it is to ouerthrow the order established in church and comonwealth." [2]

Dennison spoke with an unerring instinct when he said they could not live together, for the faith of the Friends was subversive of a theocracy. Their belief that God revealed himself directly to man led with logical certainty to the substitution of individual judgment for the rules of conduct dictated by a sacred class, whether they claimed to derive their authority from their skill in interpreting the Scriptures, or from

[1] *New England Judged*, ed. 1703, p. 112.
[2] *Mass. Rec.* vol. iv. pt. 1, p. 346.

traditions preserved by Apostolic Succession. Each man, therefore, became, as it were, a priest unto himself, and they repudiated an ordained ministry. Hence, their crime resembled that of Jeroboam, the son of Nebat, who "made priests of the lowest of the people, which were not of the sons of Levi;" [1] and it was for this reason that John Norton and John Endicott resolved upon their extermination, even as Elisha and Jehu conspired to exterminate the house of Ahab.

That they failed was due to no mercy for their victims, nor remorse for the blood they made to flow, but to their inability to control the people. Nothing is plainer upon the evidence, than that popular sympathy was never with the ecclesiastics in their ferocious policy; and nowhere does the contrast of feeling shine out more clearly than in the story of the hanging of Robinson and Stevenson.

The figure of Norton towers above his contemporaries. He held the administration in the hollow of his hand, for Endicott was his mouthpiece; yet even he, backed by the whole power of the clergy, barely succeeded in forcing through the Chamber of Deputies the statute inflicting death.

" The priests and rulers were all for blood, and they pursued it. . . . This the deputies withstood, and it could not pass, and the opposition grew strong, for the thing came near. Deacon Wozel was a man much affected therewith; and being not well at that time that

---

[1] Jeroboam's sin is discussed in *Ne Sutor*, p. 25 ; *Divine Right of Infant Baptism*, p. 26.

he supposed the vote might pass, he earnestly desired the speaker . . . to send for him when it was to be, lest by his absence it might miscarry. The deputies that were against the . . . law, thinking themselves strong enough to cast it out, forbore to send for him. The vote was put and carried in the affirmative, — the speaker and eleven being in the negative and thirteen in the affirmative: so one vote carried it; which troubled Wozel so . . . that he got to the court, . . . and wept for grief, . . . and said ' If he had not been able to go, he would have crept upon his hands and knees, rather than it should have been.' " [1]

After the accused had been condemned, the people, being strongly moved, flocked about the prison, so that the magistrates feared a rescue, and a guard was set.

As the day approached the murmurs grew, and on the morning of the execution the troops were under arms and the streets patrolled. Stevenson and Robinson were loosed from their fetters, and Mary Dyer, who also was to die, walked between them; and so they went bravely hand in hand to the scaffold. The prisoners were put behind the drums, and their voices drowned when they tried to speak; for a great multitude was about them, and at a word, in their deep excitement, would have risen.[2]

As the solemn procession moved along, they came to where the Reverend John Wilson, the Boston pastor,

[1] *New England Judged*, ed. 1703, pp. 101, 102.
[2] *Idem*, pp. 122, 123.

stood with others of the clergy. Then Wilson "fell a taunting at Robinson, and, shaking his hand in a light, scoffing manner, said, ' Shall such Jacks as you come in before authority with your hats on?' with many other taunting words." Then Robinson replied, "Mind you, mind you, it is for the not putting off the hat we are put to death." [1]

When they reached the gallows, Robinson calmly climbed the ladder and spoke a few words. He told the people they did not suffer as evil-doers, but as those who manifested the truth. He besought them to mind the light of Christ within them, of which he tes-tified and was to seal with his blood.

He had said so much when Wilson broke in upon him: " Hold thy tongue, be silent; thou art going to dye with a lye in thy mouth." [2] Then they seized him and bound him, and so he died; and his body was "cast into a hole of the earth," where it lay uncovered.

Even the voters, the picked retainers of the church, were almost equally divided, and beyond that narrow circle the tide of sympathy ran strong.

The Rev. John Rayner stood laughing with joy to see Mary Tomkins and Alice Ambrose flogged through Dover, on that bitter winter day; but the men of Salisbury cut those naked, bleeding women from the cart, and saved them from their awful death.

The Rev. John Norton sneered at the tortures of Brend, and brazenly defended his tormentor; but the

[1] *New England Judged,* ed. 1703, p. 124.
[2] *Idem,* p. 125.

Boston mob succored the victim as he lay fainting on the boards of his dark cell.

The Rev. Charles Chauncy, preaching the word of God, told his hearers to kill the Southwicks like wolves, since he could not have their blood by law; but the honest sailor broke out in wrath when asked to traffic in the flesh of our New England children.

The Rev. John Wilson jeered at Robinson on his way to meet his death, and reviled him as he stood beneath the gibbet, over the hole that was his grave; but even the savage Endicott knew well that all the trainbands of the colony could not have guarded Christison to the gallows from the dungeon where he lay condemned.

Yet awful as is this Massachusetts tragedy, it is but a little fragment of the sternest struggle of the modern world. The power of the priesthood lies in submission to a creed. In their onslaughts on rebellion they have exhausted human torments; nor, in their lust for earthly dominion, have they felt remorse, but rather joy, when slaying Christ's enemies and their own. The horrors of the Inquisition, the Massacre of St. Bartholomew, the atrocities of Laud, the abominations of the Scotch Kirk, the persecution of the Quakers, had one object, — the enslavement of the mind.

Freedom of thought is the greatest triumph over tyranny that brave men have ever won; for this they fought the wars of the Reformation; for this they have left their bones to whiten upon unnumbered fields of battle; for this they have gone by thousands to the dungeon, the scaffold, and the stake. We owe to their heroic devotion the most priceless of our treasures, our perfect liberty of thought and speech; and all who love our country's freedom may well reverence the memory of those martyred Quakers by whose death and agony the battle in New England has been won.

CHAPTER VI.

THE SCIRE FACIAS.

HAD the Puritan Commonwealth been in reality the thing which its historians have described; had it been a society guided by men devoted to civil liberty, and as liberal in religion as was consistent with the temper of their age, the early relations of Massachusetts toward Great Britain might now be a pleasanter study for her children. Cordiality toward Charles I. would indeed have been impossible, for the Puritans well knew the fate in store for them should the court triumph. Gorges was the representative of the despotic policy toward America, and so early as 1634, probably at his instigation, Laud became the head of a commission, with absolute control over the plantations, while the next year a writ of *quo warranto* was brought against the patent.[1] With Naseby, however, these dangers vanished, and thenceforward there would have been nothing to mar an affectionate confidence in both Parliament and the Protector.

In fact, however, Massachusetts was a petty state, too feeble for independence, yet ruled by an autocratic priesthood whose power rested upon legislation antagonistic to English law; therefore the ecclesiastics

[1] See introduction to *New Canaan*, Prince Soc. ed.

were jealous of Parliament, and had little love for Cromwell, whom they found wanting in "a thorough testimony against the blasphemers of our days." [1]

The result was that the elders clung obstinately to every privilege which served their ends, and repudiated every obligation which conflicted with their ambition. Clerical political morality seldom fails to be instructive, and the following example is typical of that peculiar mode of reasoning. The terms of admission to ordinary corporations were fixed by each organization for itself, but in case of injustice the courts could give relief by setting aside unreasonable ordinances, and sometimes Parliament itself would interfere, as it did upon the petition against the exactions of the Merchant Adventurers. Now there was nothing upon which the theocracy more strongly insisted than that "our charter doeth expresly give vs an absolute & free choyce of our oune members;" [2] because by means of a religious test the ministers could pack the constituencies with their tools; but on the other hand they as strenuously argued "that no appeals or other ways of interrupting our proceedings do lie against us," [3] because they well knew that any bench of judges before whom such questions might come would annul the most vital of their statutes as repugnant to the British Constitution.

Unfortunately for these churchmen, their objects,

[1] Diary of Hull, Palfrey, ii. 400, 401, and note.
[2] *Mass. Rec.* v. 287.
[3] Winthrop, ii. 283.

as ecclesiastical politicians, could seldom be reconciled with their duty as English subjects. At the outset, though made a corporation within the realm, they felt constrained to organize in America to escape judicial supervision. They were then obliged to incorporate towns and counties, to form a representative assembly, and to levy general taxes and duties, none of which things they had power to do. Still, such irregularities as these, had they been all, most English statesmen would have overlooked as unavoidable. But when it came to adopting a criminal code based on the Pentateuch, and, in support of a dissenting form of worship, fining and imprisoning, whipping, mutilating, and hanging English subjects without the sanction of English law; when, finally, the Episcopal Church itself was suppressed, and peaceful subjects were excluded from the corporation for no reason but because they partook of her communion, and were forbidden to seek redress by appealing to the courts of their king, it seems impossible that any self-respecting government could have long been passive.

At the Restoration Massachusetts had grown arrogant from long impunity. She thought the time of reckoning would never come, and even in trivial matters seemed to take a pride in slighting Great Britain and in vaunting her independence. Laws were enacted in the name of the Commonwealth, the king's name was not in the writs, nor were the royal arms upon the public buildings; even the oath of allegiance was rejected, though it was unobjectionable in form.

She had grown to believe that were offence taken she had only to invent pretexts for delay, to have her fault forgotten in some new revolution. General Denison, at the Quaker trials, put the popular belief in a nut-shell: " This year ye will go to complain to the Parliament, and the next year they will send to see how it is ; and the third year the government is changed." [1]

But, beside these irritating domestic questions, the corporation was bitterly embroiled with its neighbors. Samuel Gorton and his friends were inhabitants of Rhode Island, and were, no doubt, troublesome to deal with; but their particular offence was ecclesiastical. An armed force was sent over the border and they were seized. They were brought to Boston and tried on the charge of being " blasphemous enemies of the true religion of our Lord Jesus Christ, and of all his holy ordinances, and likewise of all civil government among his people, and particularly within this juris-diction." [2] All the magistrates but three thought that Gorton ought to die, but he was finally sentenced to an imprisonment of barbarous cruelty. The invasion of Rhode Island was a violation of an independent jurisdiction, the arrest was illegal, the sentence an arbitrary outrage.[3]

Massachusetts was also at feud in the north, and none of her quarrels brought more serious results than

---

[1] Sewel, p. 280.   [2] Winthrop, ii. 146.

[3] See paper of Mr. Charles Deane, *New Eng. Historical and Genealogical Register*, vol. iv.

this with the proprietors of New Hampshire and
Maine. The grant in the charter was of all lands
between the Charles and Merrimack, and also all
lands within the space of three miles to the northward
of the said Merrimack, or to the northward of any
part thereof, and all lands lying within the limits
aforesaid from the Atlantic to the South Sea.

Clearly the intention was to give a margin of three
miles beyond a river which was then supposed to flow
from west to east, and accordingly the territory to the
north, being unoccupied, was granted to Mason and
Gorges. Nor was this construction questioned before
1639 — the General Court having at an early day
measured off the three miles and marked the boundary by what was called the Bound House.

Gradually, however, as it became known that the
Merrimack rose to the north, larger claims were made.
In 1641 the four New Hampshire towns were absorbed with the consent of their inhabitants, who thus
gained a regular government; another happy consequence was the settlement of sundry eminent divines, by whose ministrations the people " were very
much civilized and reformed." [1]

In 1652 a survey was made of the whole river, and
43° 40' 12" was fixed as the latitude of its source. A
line extended east from three miles north of this point
came out near Portland, and the intervening space
was forthwith annexed. The result of such a policy
was that Charles had hardly been crowned before

[1] Neal's *New England*, i. 210.

complaints poured in from every side. Quakers, Baptists, Episcopalians, all who had suffered persecution, flocked to the foot of the throne; and beside these came those who had been injured in their estates, foremost of whom were the heirs of Mason and Gorges. The pressure was so great and the outcry so loud that, in September, 1660, it was thought in London a governor-general would be sent to Boston; [1] and, in point of fact, almost the first communication between the king and his colony was his order to spare the Quakers.

The outlook was gloomy, and there was hesitation as to the course to pursue. At length it was decided to send Norton and Bradstreet to England to present an address and protect the public interests. The mission was not agreeable; Norton especially was reluctant, and with reason, for he had been foremost in the Quaker persecutions, and was probably aware that in the eye of English law the executions were homicide.

However, after long vacillation, " the Lord so encouraged and strengthened " his heart that he ventured to sail.[2] So far as the crown was concerned apprehension was needless, for Lord Clarendon was prime minister, whose policy toward New England was throughout wise and moderate, and the agents were well received. Still they were restless in London, and Sewel tells an anecdote which may partly account for their impatience to be gone.

[1] Leverett to Endicott. *Hutch. Coll.,* Prince Soc. ed. ii. 40.
[2] Feb. 11, 1661–2. Palfrey, ii. 524.

"Now the deputies of New England came to London, and endeavored to clear themselves as much as possible, but especially priest Norton, who bowed no less reverently before the archbishop, than before the king. . . .

"They would fain have altogether excused themselves; and priest Norton thought it sufficient to say that he did not assist in the bloody trial, nor had advised to it. But John Copeland, whose ear was cut off at Boston, charged the contrary upon him: and G. Fox, the elder, got occasion to speak with them in the presence of some of his friends, and asked Simon Broadstreet, one of the New England magistrates, 'whether he had not a hand in putting to death those they nicknamed Quakers?' He not being able to deny this confessed he had. Then G. Fox asked him and his associates that were present, 'whether they would acknowledge themselves to be subjects to the laws of England? and if they did by what law they had put his friends to death?' They answered, 'They were subjects to the laws of England; and they had put his friends to death by the same law, as the Jesuits were put to death in England.' Hereupon G. Fox asked, 'whether they did believe that those his friends, whom they had put to death, were Jesuits, or jesuitically affected?' They said 'Nay.' 'Then,' replied G. Fox, 'ye have murdered them; for since ye put them to death by the law that Jesuits are put to death here in England, it plainly appears, you have put them to death arbitrarily, without any law.' Thus

Broadstreet, finding himself and his company ensnar'd by their own words, ask'd, 'Are you come to catch us?' But he told them 'They had catch'd themselves, and they might justly be questioned for their lives; and if the father of William Robinson (one of those that were put to death) were in town, it was probable he would question them, and bring their lives into jeopardy. For he not being of the Quakers persuasion, would perhaps not have so much regard to the point of forbearance, as they had.' Broadstreet seeing himself thus in danger began to flinch and to sculk; for some of the old royalists were earnest with the Quakers to prosecute the New England persecutors. But G. Fox and his friends said, ' They left them to the Lord, to whom vengeance belonged, and he would repay it.' Broadstreet however, not thinking it safe to stay in England, left the city, and with his companions went back again to New England." [1]

The following June the agents were given the king's answer [2] to their address and then sailed for home. It is certainly a most creditable state paper. The people of Massachusetts were thanked for their good will, they were promised oblivion for the past, and were assured that they should have their charter confirmed to them and be safe in all their privileges and liberties, provided they would make certain reforms in their government. They were required to repeal such statutes as were contrary to the laws of England, to

[1] Sewel, p. 288.

[2] 1662, June 28.

take the oath of allegiance, and to administer justice in the king's name. And then followed two propositions that were crucial: " And since the principle and foundation of that charter was and is the freedom of liberty of conscience, wee do hereby charge and require you that that freedom and liberty be duely admitted," especially in favor of those " that desire to use the Book of Common Prayer." And secondly, " that all the freeholders of competent estates, not vicious in conversations, orthodox in religion (though of different perswasions concerning church government) may have their vote in the election of all officers civill or millitary." [1]

However judicious these reforms may have been, or howsoever strictly they conformed with the spirit of English law, was immaterial. They struck at the root of the secular power of the clergy, and they roused deep indignation. The agents had braved no little danger, and had shown no little skill in behalf of the commonwealth; and the fate of John Norton enables us to realize the rancor of theological feeling. The successor of Cotton, by general consent the leading minister, in some respects the most eminent man in Massachusetts, he had undertaken a difficult mission against his will, in which he had acquitted himself well; yet on his return he was so treated by his brethren and friends that he died in the spring of a broken heart.[2]

[1] *Hutch. Coll.*, Prince Soc. ed. ii. 101–103.
[2] April 5, 1663.

The General Court took no notice of the king's demands except to order the writs to run in the royal name.[1] And it is a sign of the boldness, or else of the indiscretion, of those in power, that this crisis was chosen for striking a new coin,[2] — an act confessedly illegal and certain to give offence in England, both as an assumption of sovereignty and an interference with the currency.

From the first Lord Clarendon paid some attention to colonial affairs, and he appears to have been much dissatisfied with the condition in which he found them. At length, in 1664, he decided to send a commission to New England to act upon the spot.

Great pressure must have been brought by some who had suffered, for Samuel Maverick, the Episcopalian, who had been fined and imprisoned in 1646 for petitioning with Childe, was made a member. Colonel Richard Nichols, the head of the board, was a man of ability and judgment; the choice of Sir Robert Carr and Colonel George Cartwright was less judicious.

The commissioners were given a public and private set of instructions,[3] and both were admirable. They were to examine the condition of the country and its laws, and, if possible, to make some arrangement by which the crown might have a negative at least upon the choice of the governor; they were to urge the re-

---

[1] Oct. 8, 1662. *Mass. Rec.* vol. iv. pt. 2, p. 58.

[2] 1662, May 7.

[3] Public Instructions, Hutch. *Hist.* i. 459.

forms already demanded by the king, especially a
larger toleration, for "they doe in truth deny that
liberty of conscience to each other, which is equally
provided for and granted to every one of them by
their charter." [1] They were directed to be concilia-
tory toward the people, and under no circumstances
to meddle with public worship, nor were they to press
for any sudden enforcement of the revenue acts. On
one point alone they were to insist: they were instructed to sit to hear appeals in causes in which
the parties alleged they had been wronged by colonial decisions.

Unquestionably the chancellor was right in principle. The only way whereby such powerful corporations as the trade-guilds or the East India Company
could be kept from acts of oppression was through the
appellate jurisdiction, by which means their enactments could be brought before the courts, and those
annulled which in the opinion of the judges tran-
scended the charters. The Company of Massachusetts Bay was a corporation having jurisdiction over
many thousand English subjects, only a minority of
whom were freemen and voters. So long, therefore,
as she remained within the empire, the crown was
bound to see that the privileges of the English Constitution were not denied within her territory. Yet,
though this is true, it is equally certain that the erection of a commission of appeal without an act of Parliament was irregular. The stretch of prerogative,

[1] Private Instructions, *O'Callaghan Documents,* iii. 58.

nevertheless, cannot be considered oppressive when it is remembered that Massachusetts was a corporation which had escaped from the realm to avoid judicial process, and which refused to appear and plead; hence Lord Clarendon had but this alternative: he could send judges to sit upon the spot, or he could proceed against the charter in London. The course he chose may have been illegal, but it was the milder of the two.

The commissioners landed on July 23, 1664, but they did not stay in Boston. Their first business was to subdue the Dutch at New York, and they soon left to make the attack. The General Court now recurred, for the first time, to the dispatch which their agents had brought home, and proceeded to amend the law relating to the franchise. They extended the qualification by enacting that Englishmen who presented a certificate under the hands of the minister of the town that they were orthodox in religion and not vicious in life, and who paid, beside, 10s. at a single rate, might become freemen, as well as those who were church-members.[1] The effect of such a change could hardly have been toward liberality, rather, probably, toward concentration of power in the church. However slight, there was some popular control over the rejection of an applicant to join a congregation; but giving a certificate was an act that must have depended on the pastor's will alone.

The court then drew up an address to the king: " If your poore subjects, . . . doe . . . prostrate

[1] *Mass. Rec.* vol. iv. pt. 2, p. 117.

themselues at your royal feet₃, & begg yor favor, wee
hope it will be graciously accepted by your majestje,
and that as the high place you sustejne on earth
doeth number you here among the gods, [priests can
cringe as well as torture] so you will jmitate the
God of heaven, in being ready . . . to receive their
crjes. . . ." [1] And he was implored to reflect on the
affliction of heart it was to them, that their sins had
provoked God to permit their adversaries to procure
a commission, under the great seal, to four persons to
hear appeals. When this address reached London it
caused surprise. The chancellor was annoyed. He
wrote to America, pointing out that His Majesty would
hardly think himself well used at complaints before
a beginning had been made, and a demand that his
commission should be revoked before his commissioners had been able to deliver their instructions. " I
know," he said, " they are expressly inhibited from
intermedling with, or instructing the administration
of justice, according to the formes observed there ; but
if in truth, in any extraordinary case, the proceedings
there have been irregular, and against the rules of
justice, as some particular cases, particularly recommended to them by His Majesty, seeme to be, it cannot be presumed that His Majesty hath or will leave
his subjects of New England, without hope of re-
dresse by an appeale to him, which his subjects of all
his other kingdomes have free liberty to make." [2]

The campaign against New York was short and

[1] *Mass. Rec.* vol. iv. pt. 2, p. 129.   [2] Hutch. *Hist.* i. 465.

successful, and the commissioners were soon at leisure. As they had reason to believe that Massachusetts would prove stubborn, they judged it wiser to
begin with the more tractable colonies first. They
therefore went to Plymouth,[1] and, on their arrival, according to their instructions, submitted the four following propositions : —

First. That all householders should take the oath
of allegiance, and that justice should be administered
in the king's name.

Second. That all men of competent estates and civil
conversation, though of different judgments, might be
admitted to be freemen, and have liberty to choose
and be chosen officers, both civil and military.

Third. That all men and women of orthodox opinions, competent knowledge, and civil lives not scandalous, should be admitted to the Lord's Supper [and
have baptism for their children, either in existing
churches or their own].

Fourth. That all laws . . . derogatory to his majesty should be repealed.[2]

Substantially the same proposals were made subsequently in Rhode Island and Connecticut. They
were accepted without a murmur. A few appeal
cases were heard, and the work was done.

The commissioners reported their entire satisfaction
to the government, the colonies sent loyal addresses,
and Charles returned affectionate answers.

Massachusetts alone remained to be dealt with, but

[1] Feb. 1664–5.   [2] Palfrey, ii. 601.

her temper was in striking contrast to that of the rest
of New England. The reason is obvious. Nowhere
else was there a fusion of church and state. The
people had, therefore, no oppressive statutes to up-
hold, nor anything to conceal. Provided the liberty
of English subjects was secured to them they were
content to obey the English Constitution. On the
other hand, Massachusetts was a theocracy, the power
of whose priesthood rested on enactments contrary to
British institutions, and which, therefore, would have
been annulled upon appeal. Hence the clerical party
were wild with fear and rage, and nerved themselves
to desperate resistance.

" But alasse, sir, the commission impowering those
commisioners to heare and determine all cases whatever, . . . should it take place, what would become
of our civill government which hath binn, under God,
the heade of that libertie for our consciences for which
the first adventurers . . . bore all . . . discourage-
ments that encountered them . . . in this wildernes."
Rather than submit, they protested they had " sooner
leave our place and all our pleasant outward injoy-
ments." [1]

Under such conditions a direct issue was soon
reached. The General Court, in answer to the commissioners' proposals, maintained that the observance
of their charter was inconsistent with appeals; that
they had already provided an oath of allegiance; that
they had conformed to his majesty's requirements in

---

[1] Court to Boyle. *Hutch. Coll.*, Prince Soc. ed. ii. 113.

regard to the franchise; and lastly, in relation to toleration, there was no equivocation.   " Concerning the
vse of the Comõn Prayer Booke " . . . we had not
become " voluntary exiles from our deare native country, . . . could wee haue seene the word of God,
warranting us to performe our devotions in that way,
& to haue the same set vp here; wee conceive it is
apparent that it will disturbe our peace in our present
enjoyments." [1]

Argument was useless.   The so-called oath of allegiance was not that required by Parliament; the alteration in the franchise was a sham; while the two
most important points, appeals to England and toleration in religion, were rejected.   The commissioners,
therefore, asked for a direct answer to this question :
" Whither doe yow acknowledge his majestjes comis-
sion . . . to be of full force ? " [2]   They were met by
evasion.   On the 23d of May they gave notice that
they should sit the next morning to hear the case of
Thos. Deane et al. *vs.* The Gov. & Co. of Mass. Bay,
a revenue appeal.   Forthwith the General Court proclaimed by trumpet that the hearing would not b̤
permitted.

Coercion was impossible, as no troops were at
hand.   The commissioners accordingly withdrew and
went to Maine, which they proceeded to sever from
Massachusetts.[3]   In this they followed the king's instructions, who himself acted upon the advice of the

---

[1] 1665.   *Mass. Rec.* vol. iv. pt. 2, p. 200.
[2] *Mass. Rec.* vol. iv. pt. 2, p. 204.   [3] June, 1665.

law officers of the crown, who had given an opinion sustaining the claim of Gorges.[1]

The triumph was complete. All that the English government was then able to do was to recall the commissioners, direct that agents should be sent to London at once, and forbid interference with Maine. No notice was taken of the order to send agents; and in 1668 possession was again taken of the province, and the courts of the company once more sat in the county of York.[2]

This was the culmination of the Puritan Commonwealth. The clergy were exultant, and the Rev. Mr. Davenport of New Haven wrote in delight to Leverett: —

" Their claiming power to sit authoritatively as a court for appeales, and that to be managed in an arbitrary way, was a manifest laying of a groundworke to undermine your whole government established by your charter. If you had consented thereunto, you had plucked downe with your owne hands that house which wisdom had built for you and your posterity. . . . As for the solemnity of publishing it, in three places, by sounding a trumpet, I believe you did it upon good advice, . . . for declaring the courage and resolution of the whole countrey to defend their charter liberties and priviledges, and not to yeeld up theire right voluntarily, so long as they can hold it,

---

[1] Charles II.'s letter to Inhabitants of Maine. *Hutch. Coll.*, Prince Soc. ed. ii. 110 ; Palf. ii. 622.

[2] July, 1668. Report of Com. *Mass. Rec.* vol. iv. pt. 2, p. 401.

in dependence upon God in Christ, whose interest is
in it, for his protection and blessing, who will be with
you while you are with him." [1]

Although the colonists were alarmed at their own
success, there was nothing to fear. At no time before
or since could England have been so safely defied.
In 1664 war was begun against Holland; 1665 was
the year of the plague; 1666 of the fire. In June,
1667, the Dutch, having dispersed the British fleets,
sailed up the Medway, and their guns were heard in
London. Peace became necessary, and in August
Clarendon was dismissed from office. The discord
between the crown and Parliament paralyzed the nation, and the wastefulness of Charles kept him always
poor. By the treaty of Dover in 1670 he became a
pensioner of Louis XIV. The Cabal followed, probably the worst ministry England ever saw; and in
1672, at Clifford's suggestion, the exchequer was
closed and the debt repudiated to provide funds for
the second Dutch war. In March fighting began, and
the tremendous battles with De Ruyter kept the navy
in the Channel. At length, in 1673, the Cabal fell,
and Danby became prime minister.

Although during these years of disaster and disgrace Massachusetts was not molested by Great Britain,
they were not all years during which the theocracy
could tranquilly enjoy its victory.

So early as 1671 the movements of the Indians
began to give anxiety; and in 1675 Philip's War

[1] Davenport to Leverett. *Hutch. Coll.*, Prince Soc. ed. ii. 119.

broke out, which brought the colony to the brink of
ruin, and in which the clergy saw the judgment of
God against the Commonwealth, for tenderness toward
the Quakers.[1]

With the rise of Danby a more regular administration opened, and, as usual, the attention of the government was fixed upon Massachusetts by the clamors
of those who demanded redress for injuries alleged to
have been received at her hands.   In 1674 the heirs
of Mason and Gorges, in despair at the reoccupation
of Maine, proposed to surrender their claim to the
king, reserving one third of the product of the customs for themselves.   The London merchants also
had become restive under the systematic violation of
the Navigation Acts.   The breach in the revenue
laws had, indeed, been long a subject of complaint,
and the commissioners had received instructions relating thereto ; but it was not till this year that these
questions became serious.

The first statute had been passed by the Long Parliament, but the one that most concerned the colonies was not enacted till 1663.   The object was not
only to protect English shipping, but to give her the
entire trade of her dependencies.   To that end it was
made illegal to import European produce into any
plantation except through England; and, conversely,
colonial goods could only be exported by being landed
in England.

The theory upon which this legislation was based is

[1] *Reforming Synod, Magnalia,* bk. 5, pt. 4.

exploded; enforced, it would have crippled commerce; but it was then, and always had been, a dead letter at Boston. New England was fast getting its share of the carrying trade. London merchants already began to feel the competition of its cheap and untaxed ships, and manufacturers to complain that they were undersold in the American market, by goods brought direct from the Continental ports. A petition, therefore, was presented to the king, to carry the law into effect. No colonial office then existed; the affairs of the dependencies were assigned to a committee of the Privy Council, called the Lords of Committee of Trade and Plantations; and on these questions being referred by them to the proper officers, the commissioners of customs sustained the merchants; the attorney-general, the heirs of Mason and Gorges.[1] The famous Edward Randolph now appears. The government was still too deeply embarrassed to act with energy. A temporizing policy was therefore adopted; and as the experiment of a commission had failed, Randolph was chosen as a messenger to carry the petitions and opinions to Massachusetts; together with a letter from the king, directing that agents should be sent in answer thereto. After delivering them, he was ordered to devote himself to preparing a report upon the country. He reached Boston June 10, 1676. Although it was a time of terrible suffering from the ravages of the Indian war, the temper of the magistrates was harsher than ever.

[1] Palfrey, iii. 281; Chalmers's *Political Annals of the United Colonies,* p. 262.

The repulse of the commissioners had convinced them that Charles was not only lazy and ignorant, but too poor to use force; and they also believed him to be so embroiled with Parliament as to make his overthrow probable. Filled with such feelings, their reception of Randolph was almost brutal. John Leverett was governor, who seems to have taken pains to mark his contempt in every way in his power. Randolph was an able, but an unscrupulous man, and probably it would not have been difficult to have secured his good-will. Far however from bribing, or even flattering him, they so treated him as to make him the bitterest enemy the Puritan Commonwealth ever knew.

Being admitted into the council chamber, he delivered the letter.[1] The governor opened it, glanced at the signature, and, pretending never to have heard of Henry Coventry, asked who he might be. He was told he was his majesty's principal secretary of state. He then read it aloud to the magistrates. Even the fierce Endicott, when he received the famous " missive " from the Quaker Shattock, "laid off his hat . . . [when] he look'd upon the papers," [2] as a mark of respect to his king; but Leverett and his council remained covered. Then the governor said " that the matters therein contained were very inconsiderable things and easily answered, and it did no way concern that government to take any notice thereof; " and so

[1] Randolph's Narrative. *Hutch. Coll.,* Prince Soc. ed. ii. 240.
[2] Sewel, p. 282.

Randolph was dismissed. Five days after he was again sent for, and asked whether he "intended for London by that ship that was ready to saile?" If so, he could have a duplicate of the answer to the king, as the original was to go by other hands. He replied that he had other business in charge, and inquired whether they had well considered the petitions, and fixed upon their agents so soon. Leverett did not deign to answer, but told him "he looked upon me as Mr. Mason's agent, and that I might withdraw." The next day he saw the governor at his own house, who took occasion, when Randolph referred to the Navigation Acts, to expound the legal views of the theocracy. "He freely declared to me that the lawes made by your majestie and your Parliament obligeth them in nothing but what consists with the interest of that colony, that the legislative power is and abides in them solely . . . and that all matters in difference are to be concluded by their finall determination, without any appeal to your majestie, and that your majestie ought not to retrench their liberties, but may enlarge them." [1] One last interview took place when Randolph went for dispatches for England, after his return from New Hampshire; then he "was entertained by" Leverett "with a sharp reproof for publishing the substance of my errand into those parts, contained in your majestie's letters, . . . telling me that I designed to make a mutiny. . . . I told him, if I had done anything amisse, upon com-

[1] Randolph's Narrative. *Hutch. Coll.*, Prince Soc. ed. ii. 243.

plaint made to your majestie he would certainly have justice done him." . . .

"At my departure . . . he . . . intreated me to give a favourable report of the country and the magistrates thereof, adding that those that blessed them God would blesse, and those that cursed them God would curse." And that "they were a people truely fearing the Lord and very obedient to your majestie." [1] And so the royal messenger was dismissed in wrath, to tell his story to the king.

The legislature met in August, 1676, and a decision had to be made concerning agents. On the whole, the clergy concluded it would be wiser to obey the crown, "provided they be, with vtmost care & caution, qualified as to their instructions." [2] Accordingly, after a short adjournment, the General Court chose William Stoughton and Peter Bulkely; and having strictly limited their power to a settlement of the territorial controversy, they sent them on their mission.[3]

Almost invariably public affairs were seen by the envoys of the Company in a different light from that in which they were viewed by the clerical party at home, and these particularly had not been long in London before they became profoundly alarmed. There was, indeed, reason for grave apprehension. The selfish and cruel policy of the theocracy had borne its natural fruit: without an ally in the world,

[1] *Hutch. Coll.*, Prince Soc. ed. ii. 248.
[2] *Mass. Rec.* v. 99.   [3] *Mass. Rec.* v. 114.

372 *THE SCIRE FACIAS.*

Massachusetts was beset by enemies. Quakers, Baptists, and Episcopalians whom she had persecuted and exiled; the heirs of Mason and Gorges, whom she had wronged; Andros, whom she had maligned;[1] and Randolph, whom she had insulted, wrought against her with a government whose sovereign she had offended and whose laws she had defied. Even her English friends had been much alienated.[2]

The controversy concerning the boundary was referred to the two chief justices, who promptly decided against the Company;[3] and the easy acquiescence of the General Court must raise a doubt as to their faith in the soundness of their claims. And now again the fatality which seemed to pursue the theocracy in all its dealings with England led it to give fresh provocation to the king by secretly buying the title of Gorges for twelve hundred and fifty pounds.[4]

Charles had intended to settle Maine on the Duke of Monmouth. It was a worthless possession, whose revenue never paid for its defence; yet so stubborn was the colony that it made haste to anticipate the crown and thus become "Lord Proprietary" of a burdensome province at the cost of a slight which was never forgiven. Almost immediately the Privy

---

[1] He had been accused of countenancing aid to Philip when governor of New York. *O'Callaghan Documents,* iii. 258.

[2] Palfrey, iii. 278, 279.

[3] See Opinion; Chalmers's *Annals,* p. 504.

[4] May, 1677. Chalmers's *Annals,* pp. 396, 397. See notes, Palfrey, iii. 312.

Council had begun to open other matters, such as coining and illicit trade; and the attorney-general drew up a list of statutes which, in his opinion, were contrary to the laws of England. The agents protested that they were limited by their instructions, but were sharply told that his majesty did not think of treating with his own subjects as with foreigners, and it would be well to intimate the same to their principals.[1] In December, 1677, Stoughton wrote in great alarm that something must be done concerning the Navigation Acts or a breach would be inevitable.[2] And the General Court saw reason in this emergency to increase the tension by reviving the obnoxious oath of fidelity to the country,[3] — the substitute for the oath of allegiance, — and thus gave Randolph a new and potent weapon. In the spring[4] the law officers gave an opinion that the misdemeanors alleged against Massachusetts were sufficient to avoid her patent; and the Privy Council, in view of the encroachments and injuries which she had continually practised on her neighbors, and her contempt of his majesty's commands, advised that a *quo warranto* should be brought against the charter. Randolph was appointed collector at Boston.[5]

Even Leverett now saw that some concessions must be made, and the General Court ordered the oath of

---

[1] Palfrey, iii. 309.   [2] Hutch. *Hist.* i. 288.

[3] *Mass. Rec.* v. 154.

[4] Palfrey, iii. 316, 317 ; Chalmers's *Annals*, p. 439.

[5] 1678, May 31.

allegiance to be taken ; nothing but perversity seems
to have caused the long delay.[1] The royal arms were
also carved in the court-house ; and this was all, for
the clergy were determined upon those matters touching their authority. The agents were told, "that
which is farr more considerable then all these is the
interest of the Lord Jesus & of his churches . . .
wch ought to be farr dearer to us than our liues; and
. . . wee would not that by any concessions of ours,
or of yo^{rs} . . . the least stone should be put out of
the wall."[2]

Both agents and magistrates were, nevertheless,
thoroughly frightened, and being determined not to
yield, in fact, they resorted to a policy of misrepre-
sentation, with the hope of deceiving the English
government.[3] Stoughton and Bulkely had already
assured the Lords of Committee that the "rest of
the inhabitants were very inconsiderable as to number, compared with those that were acknowledged
church-members."[4] They were in fact probably as
five to one. The General Court had been censured
for using the word Commonwealth in official documents, as intimating independence. They hastened to
assure the crown that it had not of late been used,
and should not be thereafter;[5] yet in November, 1675,

[1] Oct. 2, 1678. *Mass. Rec.* v. 193. See Palfrey, iii. 320,
note 2.   [2] *Mass. Rec.* v. 202.

[3] See Answers of Agents, Chalmers's *Annals*, p. 450.

[4] Palfrey, iii. 318.

[5] *Mass. Rec.* v. 198. And see, in general, the official correspondence, pp. 197–203.

commissions were thus issued.[1] But the breaking out of the Popish plot began to absorb the whole attention of the government at London; and the agents, after receiving a last rebuke for the presumption of the colony in buying Maine, were at length allowed to depart.[2]

Nearly half a century had elapsed since the emigration, and with the growth of wealth and population changes had come. In March, John Leverett, who had long been the head of the high-church party, died, and the election of Simon Bradstreet as his successor was a triumph for the opposition. Great as the clerical influence still was, it had lost much of its old despotic power, and the congregations were no longer united in support of the policy of their pastors. This policy was singularly desperate. Casting aside all but ecclesiastical considerations, the clergy consistently rejected any compromise with the crown which threatened to touch the church. Almost from the first they had recognized that substantial independence was necessary in order to maintain the theocracy. Had the colony been strong, they would doubtless have renounced their allegiance; but its weakness was such that, without the protection of England, it would have been seized by France. Hence they resorted to expedients which could only end in disaster, for it was impossible for Massachusetts, while part of the British Empire, to refuse obedience at her pleasure to laws which other colonies cheerfully obeyed.

[1] Palfrey, iii. 322.　　　　[2] Nov. 1679.

Without an ally, no resistance could be made to England, when at length her sovereignty should be asserted; and an armed occupation and military government were inevitable upon a breach.

Though such considerations are little apt to induce
a priesthood to surrender their temporal power, they
usually control commercial communities. Accordingly, Boston and the larger towns favored concession, while the country was the ministers' stronghold.
The result of this divergence of opinion was that the
moderate party, to which Bradstreet and Dudley belonged, predominated in the Board of Assistants, while
the deputies remained immovable. The branches of
the legislature thus became opposed; no course of action could be agreed on, and the theocracy drifted to
its destruction.

The duplicity characteristic of theological politics
grew daily more marked. In May, 1679, a law had
been passed forbidding the building of churches without leave from the freemen of the town or the General Court.[1] On the 11th of June, 1680, three persons representing the society of Baptists were summoned before the legislature, charged with the crime
of erecting a meeting-house. They were admonished and forbidden to meet for worship except with
the established congregations; and their church was
closed.[2] That very day an address was voted to the
king, one passage of which is as follows: "Concern-

[1] *Mass. Rec.* v. 213.
[2] *Mass. Rec.* v. 271.

ing liberty of conscience, . . . that after all, a multitude of notorious errors . . . be openly broached, . . . amongst us, as by the Quakers, &c., wee presume his majesty doeth not intend; and as for other Prottestant dissenters, that carry it peaceably & soberly, wee trust there shallbe no cause of just complaint against us on their behalfe." [1]

Meanwhile Randolph had renewed his attack. He declared that in spite of promises and excuses the revenue laws were not enforced; that his men were beaten, and that he hourly expected to be thrown into prison; whereas in other colonies, he asserted, he was treated with great respect.[2] There can be no doubt ingenuity was used to devise means of annoyance, and certainly the life he was made to lead was hard. In March [3] he sailed for home, and while in London he made a series of reports to the government which seem to have produced the conviction that the moment for action had come. In December he returned, commissioned as deputy - surveyor and auditor - general for all New England, except New Hampshire. When Stoughton and Bulkely were dismissed, the colony had been commanded to send new agents within six months. In September, 1680, another royal letter had been written, in which the king dwelt upon the misconduct of his subjects, "when . . . we signified unto you our gracious inclination to have all past deeds forgotten . . . wee then little thought that

---

[1] *Mass. Rec.* v. 287.

[2] June, 1680. Palfrey, iii. 340.   [3] March 15, 1680–1.

those markes of our grace and favour should have found no better acceptance amoung you. . . . We doe therefore by these our letters, strictly command and require you, as you tender your allegiance unto us, and will deserve the effects of our grace and favour (which wee are enclyned to afford you) seriously to reflect upon our commands ; . . . and particularly wee doe hereby command you to send over, within three months after the receipt hereof, such . . . persons as you shall think fitt to choose, and that you give them sufficient instructions to attend the regulation and settlement of that our government." [1]

The General Court had not thought fit to regard these communications, and now Randolph came charged with a long and stern dispatch, in which agents were demanded forthwith, " in default whereof, we are fully resolved, in Trinity Term next ensuing, to direct our attorney-general to bring a quo warranto in our court of kings-bench, whereby our charter granted unto you, with all the powers thereof, may be legally evicted and made void ; and so we bid you fare-wel." [2]

Hitherto the clerical party had procrastinated, buoyed up by the hope that in the fierce struggle with the commons Charles might be overthrown ; but this dream ended with the dissolution of the Oxford Par, liament, and further inaction became impossible. Jo seph Dudley and John Richards were chosen agents,

---

[1] Sept. 30. *Hutch. Coll.*, Prince Soc. ed. ii. 261.
[2] Chalmers's *Annals*, p. 449.

and provided with instructions bearing the peculiar
tinge of ecclesiastical statesmanship.

They were directed to represent that appeals would
be intolerable; and, for their private guidance, the
legislature used these words: " We therefore doe not
vnderstand by the regulation of the gouernment, that
any alteration of the patent is intended; yow shall
therefore neither doe nor consent to any thing that
may violate or infringe the libertjes & priuiledges
granted to us by his maj^ties royall charter, or the gouernment established thereby; but if any thing be propounded that may tend therevnto, yow shall say, yow
haue received no instruction in that matter." [1] With
reference to the complaints made against the colony,
they were to inform the king " that wee haue no law
prohibbiting any such as are of the perswasion of the
church of England, nor haue any euer desired to worship God accordingly that haue been denied." [2]

Such a statement cannot be reconciled with the
answer made the commissioners; and the laws com-
pelled Episcopalians to attend the Congregational
worship, and denied them the right to build churches
of their own.

" As for the Annabaptists, they are now subject to
no other pœnal statutes then those of the Congregational way." This sophistry is typical. The law
under which the Baptist church was closed applied
in terms to all inhabitants, it is true ; but it was contrived to suppress schism, it was used to coerce here-

[1] *Mass. Rec.* v. 349. [2] *Mass. Rec.* v. 347. March 23.

tics, and it was unrepealed. Moreover, it would seem as though the statute inflicting banishment must then have still been in force.

The assurances given in regard to the reform of the suffrage were precisely parallel : —

" For admission of ffreemen, wee humbly conceive it is our liberty, by charter, to chuse whom wee will admitt into our oune company, wch yet hath not binn restrayned to Congregational men, but others haue been admitted, who were also provided for according to his maj^ties direction." [1]

Such insincerity gave weight to Randolph's words when he wrote : "My lord, I have but one thing to reminde your lordship, that nothing their agents can say or doe in England can be any ground for his majestie to depend upon." [2]

With these documents and one thousand pounds for bribery, soon after increased to three,[3] Dudley and Richards sailed. Their powers were at once rejected at London as insufficient, and the decisive moment came.[4] The churchmen of Massachusetts had to determine whether to accept the secularization of their government or abandon every guaranty of popular liberty. The clergy did not hesitate before the momentous alternative : they exerted themselves to the utmost, and turned the scale for the last time.[5] In

[1] 1681–2, March 23.

[2] Randolph to Clarendon. *Hutch. Coll.*, Prince Soc. ed. ii. 277

[3] Chalmers's *Annals*, p. 461.

[4] *Idem*, p. 413.   [5] Hutch. *Hist.* i. 303, note.

fresh instructions the agents were urged to do what was possible to avert, or at least delay, the stroke; but they were forbidden to consent to appeals, or to alterations in the qualifications required for the admission of freemen.[1] They had previously been directed to pacify the king by a present of two thousand pounds; and this ill-judged attempt at bribery had covered them with ridicule.[2]

Further negotiation would have been futile. Proceedings were begun at once, and Randolph was sent to Boston to serve the writ of *quo warranto;*[3] he was also charged with a royal declaration promising that, even then, were submission made, the charter should be restored with only such changes as the public welfare demanded.[4] Dudley, who was a man of much political sagacity, had returned and strongly urged moderation. The magistrates were not without the instincts of statesmanship: they saw that a breach with England must destroy all safeguards of the common freedom, and they voted an address to the crown accepting the proffered terms.[5] But the clergy strove against them: the privileges of their order were at stake; they felt that the loss of their importance would be " destructive to the interest of religion and of Christ's kingdom in the colony,"[6] and they roused their congregations to resist. The deputies did

---

[1] 1683, March 30. *Mass. Rec.* v. 390.

[2] Hutch. *Hist.* i. 303, note.   [3] 1683, July 20.

[4] *Mass. Rec.* v. 422, 423.

[5] 1683, 15 Nov. Hutch. *Hist.* i. 304.   [6] Palfrey, iii. 381.

not represent the people, but the church. They were men who had been trained from infancy by the priests, who had been admitted to the communion and the franchise on account of their religious fervor, and who had been brought into public life because the ecclesiastics found them pliable in their hands. The influence which had moulded their minds and guided their actions controlled them still, and they rejected the address.[1] Increase Mather took the lead. He stood up at a great meeting in the Old South, and exhorted the people, "telling them how their forefathers did purchase it [the charter], and would they deliver it up, even as Ahab required Naboth's vineyard, Oh! their children would be bound to curse them." [2]

All that could be resolved on was to retain Robert Humphrys of the Middle Temple to interpose such delays as the law permitted; but no attempt was made at defence upon the merits of their cause, probably because all knew well that no such defence was possible.

Meanwhile, for technical reasons, the *quo warranto* had been abandoned, and a writ of *scire facias* had been issued out of chancery. On June 18, 1684, the lord keeper ordered the defendant to appear and plead on the first day of the next Michaelmas Term. The time allowed was too short for an answer from America, and judgment was entered by default.[3] The

[1] Nov. 30. Palfrey, iii. 385.   [2] Palfrey, iii. 388, note 1.
[3] Decree entered June 21, 1684; confirmed, Oct. 23. Palfrey, iii. 393, note.

decree was arbitrary, but no effort was made to obtain relief. The story, however, is best told by Humphrys himself : —

" It is matter of astonishment to me, to think of the returnes I haue had from you in the affaire of yor charter; that a prudent people should think soe little, in a thing of the greatest moment to them.

" Which charge I humbly justify in the foll^g particulars, and yet at the same time confess that all you could haue done would but haue gained more time, and spent more money, since the breaches assigned ag^t you, were as obvious as vnanswerable, soe as all the service yor councill and friends could haue done you here, would haue onely served to deplore, not prevent the inevitable loss.

" When I sent you the lord keeper's order of the 18th of June 1684 requireing yor appeareing peromptorily the first day of Michas Tearme then next, and pleading to yssue . . . you may remember I sent with it such drafts of lres of attorney, to pass vnder your comon seale as were essentially necessary to empower and justify such appearance, and pleading for you here, which you could not imagine but that you must haue had due time to returne them in, noe law compelling impossibilities.

" When the first day of that Michas Tearme came, and yor lres of attorney neither were, nor indeed could be return'd . . . I applyd by councill to the Court of Chancery to enlarge that time urgeing the impossibility of hauing a returne from you in the time allotted.

. . . But it is true my lord keeper cutt the ground
from under us which wee stood upon, by telling us the
order of the 18th of June was a surprize upon his
lo^p and that he ought not to haue granted it, for
that every corporacon ought to haue an attorney in
every court to appeare to his ma^{ts} suite, and that
London had such. . . . However certainely you ought
when my łres were come to you, nunc pro tunc, to
haue past the łres of attorney I sent you under your
comon seale and sent them me, and not to haue stopt
them upon any private surmises from other hands
then his you had entrusted in that matter; and the
rather for that the judgm^{ts} of law, espetially those
taken by defaults for non appearances, are not like
the laws of the Medes and Persians irrevocable, but
are often on just grounds sett aside by the court
here, and the defendants admitted to plead as if noe
such judgm^{ts} had been entred vp, and the very order
it selfe of the 18th of June guies you a home instance
of it.

" And indeed I did therefore forbeare giueing you
an acco^t of a further time being denyd, and the entry
of judgm^t ag^t you, expecting you would before such
łre could haue reacht you haue sent me the łres of
attorney vnder your corporacon seale that the court
might haue been moved to admitt yor appearance
and plea and waiued the judgm^t.

" But instead of those łres of attorney under your
seale you sent me an address to his late ma^{ty}, I confess judiciously drawne. But it is my wonder in which

of yor capacityes you could imagine it should be presented to his ma^{ty}, for if as a corporacon, a body poli-
tique, it should have been putt under your corporacon
seale if as a private comunity it should haue been
signed by your order. But the paper has neither
private hand nor publique seale to it and soe must
be lost. . . .

" In this condicon what could a man doe for you,
nothing publiquely for he had noe warrant from you
to justify the accon." [1]

So perished the Puritan Commonwealth. The
child of the Reformation, its life sprang from the
assertion of the freedom of the mind; but this great
and noble principle is fatal to the temporal power of
a priesthood, and during the supremacy of the clergy
the government was doomed to be both persecuting
and repressive. Under no circumstance could the
theocracy have endured: it must have fallen by revolt
from within if not by attack from without. That
Charles II. did in fact cause its overthrow gives him
a claim to our common gratitude, for he then struck a
decisive blow for the emancipation of Massachusetts;
and thus his successor was enabled to open before her
that splendid career of democratic constitutional liberty which was destined to become the basis of the
jurisprudence of the American Union.

[1] *Mass. Archives,* cvi. 343.

CHAPTER VII.

THE WITCHCRAFT.

THE history of the years between the dissolution of the Company of Massachusetts Bay and the reorganization of the country by William III. in 1692 has little bearing upon the development of the people; for the presidency of Dudley and the administration of Andros were followed by a revolution that paralyzed all movement. During the latter portion of this interval the colony was represented at London by three agents, of whom Increase Mather was the most influential, who used every effort to obtain the reëstablishment of the old government; they met, however, with insuperable obstacles. Quietly to resume was impossible; for the obstinacy of the clergy, in refusing all compromise with Charles II., had caused the patent to be cancelled; and thus a new grant had become necessary. Nor was this all, for the attorney and solicitor general, with whom the two chief justices concurred,[1] gave it as their opinion that, supposing no decree had been rendered, and the same powers were exercised as before, a writ of *scire facias* would certainly be issued, upon which a similar judgment would inevitably be entered. These considerations, however,

[1] *Parentator*, p. 139.

became immaterial, as the king was a statesman, and
had already decided upon his policy. His views had
little in common with those held by the Massachusetts
ecclesiastics, and when the Rev. Mr. Mather first read
the instrument in which they had been embodied, he
declared he " would sooner part with his life than consent unto such minutes." [1] He grew calmer, however,
when told that his "consent was not expected nor desired ; " and with that energy and decision for which
he was remarkable, at once secured the patronage.

The constitutional aspect of the Provincial Charter
is profoundly interesting, and it will be considered in
its legal bearings hereafter. Its political tendencies,
however, first demand attention, for it wrought a complete social revolution, since it overthrew the temporal
power of the church. Massachusetts, Maine, and
Plymouth were consolidated, and within them toleration was established, except in regard to Papists;
the religious qualification was swept away, and in
its stead freeholders of forty shillings per annum, or
owners of personal property to the value of forty
pounds sterling, were admitted to the franchise; the
towns continued to elect the house of representatives,
and the whole Assembly chose the council, subject to
the approval of the executive.[2] The governor, lieutenant-governor, and secretary were appointed by the
crown; the governor had a veto, and the king reserved the right to disallow legislation within three
years of the date of its enactment. Thus the theoc-

[1] *Parentator*, p. 134.   [2] Hutch. *Hist*. ii. 15, 16.

racy fell at a single blow ; and it is worthy of remark that thenceforward prosecutions for sedition became unknown among the people of the Province of Massachusetts Bay. Yet, though the clerical oligarchy was no longer absolute, the ministers still exerted a prodigious influence upon opinion. Not only did they speak with all the authority inherited with the traditions of the past; not only had they or their predecessors trained the vast majority of the people from their cradles to reverence them more than anything on earth, but their compact organization was as yet unimpaired, and at its head stood the two Mathers, the pastors of the Old North Church. Thus venerated and thus led, the elders were still able to appeal to the popular superstition and fanaticism with terrible effect.

Widely differing judgments have been formed of these two celebrated divines; the ecclesiastical view is perhaps well summed up by the Rev. John Eliot, who thus describes the President of Harvard: " He was the father of the New England clergy, and his name and character were held in veneration, not only by those, who knew him, but by succeeding generations." [1] All must admit his ability and learning, while in sanctimoniousness of deportment he was unrivalled. His son Cotton says he had such a " gravity as made all sorts of persons, wherever he came, to be struck with a sensible awe of his presence, . . . yea, if he laughed on them, they believed it not." " His very counte-

[1] *Biographical Dictionary*, p. 312.

nance carried the force of a sermon with it." [1] He
kept a strict account of his mental condition, and always was pleased when able to enter in his diary at
the end of the day, "heart serious." He was unctuous
in his preaching, and wept much in the pulpit; he
often mentions being "quickened at the Lord's table
[during which] tears gushed from me before the
Lord," [2] but of his self-sacrifice, his mercy, and his
truth, his own acts and words are the best evidence
that remain.

When the new government was about to be put in
operation, an extraordinary amount of patronage lay
at the disposal of the crown; for, beside the regular
executive officers, the entire council had to be named,
since they could not be elected until a legislature had
been organized to choose them. Increase Mather,
Elisha Cooke, and Thomas Oakes were acting as
agents, and all had been bitterly opposed to the new
charter; but of the three, the English ministers
thought Mather the most important to secure. And
now an odd coincidence happened in the life of this
singular man. He suddenly one day announced himself convinced that the king's project was not so intolerable as to be unworthy of support; and then it
very shortly transpired that he had been given all the
spoil before the patent had passed the seals. [3] The
proximity of these events is interesting as bearing on
the methods of ecclesiastical statesmen, and it is also

[1] *Parentator*, p. 40. [2] *Parentator*, p. 48.
[3] Palfrey, iv. 85.

instructive to observe how thorough a master of the situation this eminent divine proved himself to be. He not only appointed all his favorite henchmen to office, but he rigidly excluded his colleagues at London, who had continued their opposition, and every one else who had any disposition to be independent. His creature, Sir William Phips, was made governor; William Stoughton, who was bred for the church, and whose savage bigotry endeared him to the clergy, was lieutenant-governor; and the council was so packed that his excellent son broke into a shout of triumph when he heard the news : —

"The time has come! the set time has come! I am now to receive an answer of so many prayers. All the councellors of the province are of my own father's nomination ; and my father-in-law, with several related unto me, and several brethren of my own church are among them. The governor of the province is not my enemy, but one whom I baptized ; namely, Sir William Phips, one of my own flock, and one of my dearest friends." [1] Such was the government the theocracy left the country as its legacy when its own power had passed away, and dearly did Massachusetts rue that fatal gift in her paroxysms of agony and blood.

At the close of the seventeenth century the belief in witchcraft was widespread, and among the more ignorant well-nigh universal. The superstition was, moreover, fostered by the clergy, who, in adopting this

[1] Cotton Mather's *Diary ;* Quincy's *History of Harvard,* i. 60.

policy, were undoubtedly actuated by mixed motives. Their credulity probably made them for the most part sincere in the unbounded confidence they professed in the possibility of compacts between the devil and mankind ; but, nevertheless, there is abundant evidence in their writings of their having been keenly alive to the fact that men horror-stricken at the sight of the destruction of their wives and children by magic would grovel in the submission of abject terror at the feet of the priest who promised to deliver them.

The elders began the agitation by sending out a paper of proposals for collecting stories of apparitions and witchcrafts, and in obedience to their wish Increase Mather published his " Illustrious Providences " in 1683-4. Two chapters of this book were devoted to sorceries, and the reverend author took occasion to intimate his opinion that those who might doubt the truth of his relations were probably themselves either heretics or wizards. This movement of the clergy seems to have highly inflamed the popular imagination,[1] yet no immediate disaster followed; and the nervous exaltation did not become deadly until 1688. In the autumn of that year four children of a Boston mason named Goodwin began to mimic the symptoms they had so often heard described; the father, who was a pious man, called in the ministers of Boston and Charlestown, who fasted and prayed, and succeeded in delivering the youngest, who was five. Meanwhile, one of the daughters had " cried out

[1] Hutch. *Hist.* ii. 24.

upon " an unfortunate Irish washerwoman, with whom she had quarrelled. Cotton Mather was now in his element. He took the eldest girl home with him and tried a great number of interesting experiments as to the relative power of Satan and the Lord; among others he gravely relates how when the sufferer was tormented elsewhere he would carry her struggling to his own study, into which entering, she stood immediately upon her feet, and cried out, "They are gone! They are gone! They say they cannot —— God won't let 'em come here." [1]

It is not credible that an educated and a sane man could ever have honestly believed in the absurd stuff which he produced as evidence of the supernatural; his description of the impudence of the children is amazing.

" They were divers times very near burning or drowning of themselves, but . . . by their own pittiful and seasonable cries for help still procured their deliverance: which made me consider, whether the little ones had not their angels, in the plain sense of our Saviour's intimation. . . . And sometimes, tho' but seldome, they were kept from eating their meals, by having their teeth sett when they carried any thing to their mouthes." [2]

And it was upon such evidence that the washerwoman was hanged. There is an instant in the battle as the ranks are wavering, when the calmness of

[1] *Memorable Providences*, pp. 27, 28.
[2] *Idem*, pp. 15–17.

the officers will avert the rout; and as to have held their soldiers then is deemed their highest honor, so to have been found wanting is their indelible disgrace; the people stood poised upon the panic's brink, their pastors lashed them in.

Cotton Mather forthwith published a terrific account of the ghostly crisis, mixed with denunciations of the Sadducee or Atheist who disbelieved; and to the book was added a preface, written by the four other clergymen who had assisted with their prayers, the character of which may be judged by a single extract. "The following account will afford to him that shall read with observation, a further clear confirmation, that, there is both a God, and a devil, and witchcraft: that there is no outward affliction, but what God may, (and sometimes doth) permit Satan to trouble his people withal." [1] Not content with this, Mather goaded his congregation into frenzy from the pulpit. "Consider also, the misery of them whom witchcraft may be let loose upon. What is it to fall into the hands of devils? ... O what a direful thing is it, to be prickt with pins, and stab'd with knives all over, and to be fill'd all over with broken bones? 'T is impossible to reckon up the varieties of miseries which those monsters inflict where they can have a blow. No less than death, and that a languishing and a terrible death will satisfie the rage of those formidable dragons." [2] The pest was sure to spread in a credulous

[1] *Memorable Providences*, Preface.
[2] *Discourse on Witchcraft*, p. 19.

community, fed by their natural leaders with this morbid poison, and it next broke out in Salem village in February, 1691–2. A number of girls had become intensely excited by the stories they had heard, and two of them, who belonged to the family of the clergyman, were seized with the usual symptoms. Of Mr. Parris it is enough to say that he began the investigation with a frightful relish. Other ministers were called in, and prayer-meetings lasting all day were held, with the result of throwing the patients into convulsions.[1] Then the name of the witch was asked, and the girls were importuned to make her known. They refused at first, but soon the pressure became too strong, and the accusations began. Among the earliest to be arrested and examined was Goodwife Cory. Mr. Noyes, teacher of Salem, began with prayer, and when she was brought in the sufferers "did vehemently accuse her of afflicting them, by biting, pinching, strangling, &c., and they said, they did in their fits see her likeness coming to them, and bringing a book for them to sign."[2] By April the number of informers and of the suspected had greatly increased and the prisons began to fill. Mr. Parris behaved like a madman; not only did he preach inflammatory sermons, but he conducted the examinations, and his questions were such that the evidence was in truth nothing but what he put in the mouths of the witnesses; yet he seems to have been guilty of

[1] Calef's *More Wonders*, p. 90 *et seq.*

[2] *Idem*, p. 92.

a darker crime, for there is reason to suppose he gar-
bled the testimony it was his sacred duty to truly
record.[1] And in all this he appears to have had the
approval and the aid of Mr. Noyes. Such was the
crisis when Sir William Phips landed on the 14th
of May, 1692; he was the Mathers' tool, and the result could have been foretold. Uneducated and credulous, he was as clay in the hands of his creators;
and his first executive act was to cause the miserable prisoners to be fettered. Jonathan Cary has
described what befell his wife: "Next morning the
jaylor put irons on her legs (having received such a
command) the weight of them was about eight pounds;
these irons and her other afflictions, soon brought her
into convulsion fits, so that I thought she would have
died that night."[2]

At the beginning of June the governor, by an arbitrary act, created a court to try the witches, and at
its head put William Stoughton. Even now it is impossible to read the proceedings of this sanguinary
tribunal without a shudder, and it has left a stain
upon the judiciary of Massachusetts that can never be
effaced.

Two weeks later the opinion of the elders was
asked, as it had been of old, and they recommended
the " speedy and vigorous prosecutions of such as
have rendered themselves obnoxious," [3] nor did their

[1] *Grounds of Complaint against Parris,* § 6 ; *More Wonders,*
p. 96 (*i. e.* 56).

[2] *More Wonders,* p. 97.   [3] Hutch. *Hist.* ii. 53.

advice fall upon unwilling ears. Stoughton was already at work, and certain death awaited all who were dragged before that cruel and bloodthirsty bigot; even when the jury acquitted, the court refused to receive the verdict. The accounts given of the legal proceedings seem monstrous. The preliminary examinations were conducted amid such " hideous clamours and screechings," that frequently the voice of the defendant was drowned, and if a defence was attempted at a trial, the victim was browbeaten and mocked by the bench.[1]

The ghastly climax was reached in the case of George Burroughs, who had been the clergyman at Wells. At his trial the evidence could hardly be heard by reason of the fits of the sufferers. " The chief judge asked the prisoner, who he thought hindered these witnesses from giving their testimonies? and he answered, he supposed it was the devil. That honourable person then replied, How comes the devil so loath to have any testimony born against you? Which cast him into very great confusion." Presently the informers saw the ghosts of his two dead wives, whom they charged him with having murdered, stand before him " crying for vengeance; " yet though much appalled, he steadily denied that they were there. He also roused his judges' ire by asserting that " there neither are, nor ever were, witches." [2]

He and those to die with him were carried through

---

[1] *More Wonders*, p. 102.
[2] *Idem.* pp. 115–119.

the streets of Salem in a cart. As he climbed the
ladder he called God to witness he was innocent, and
his words were so pathetic that the people sobbed
aloud, and it seemed as though he might be rescued
even as he stood beneath the tree. Then when at last
he swung above them, Cotton Mather rode among the
throng and told them of his guilt, and how the fiend
could come to them as an angel of light, and so the
work went on. They cut him down and dragged him
by his halter to a shallow hole among the rocks, and
threw him in, and there they lay together with the
rigid hand of the wizard Burroughs still pointing upward through his thin shroud of earth.[1]

By October it seemed as though the bonds of society
were dissolving; nineteen persons had been hanged,
one had been pressed to death, and eight lay condemned; a number had fled, but their property had
been seized and they were beggars; the prisons were
choked, while more than two hundred were accused
and in momentary fear of arrest;[2] even two dogs had
been killed. The plague propagated itself; for the
only hope for those cried out upon was to confess their
guilt and turn informers. Thus no one was safe.
Mr. Willard, pastor of the Old South, who began to
falter, was threatened; the wife of Mr. Hale, pastor
of Beverly, who had been one of the great leaders of
the prosecutions, was denounced; Lady Phips herself was named. But the race who peopled New Eng-

[1] *More Wonders*, pp. 103, 104.
[2] *Idem*, p. 110.

land had a mental vigor which even the theocracy could not subdue, and Massachusetts had among her sons liberal and enlightened men, whose voice was heard, even in the madness of the terror. Of these, the two Brattles, Robert Calef, and John Leverett were the foremost; and they served their mother well, though the debt of gratitude and honor which she owes them she has never yet repaid.

On the 8th, four days before the meeting of the legislature, and probably at the first moment it could be done with safety, Thomas Brattle wrote an admirable letter,[1] in which he exposed the folly and wickedness of the delusion with all the energy the temper of the time would bear; had he miscalculated, his error of judgment would probably have cost him his life. At the meeting of the General Court the illegal and blood-stained commission came to an end, and as the reaction slowly and surely set in, Phips began to feel alarm lest he should he called to account in England; accordingly, he tried to throw the blame on Stoughton: "When I returned, I found people much dissatisfied at the proceedings of the court; . . . The deputy - governor, [Stoughton] notwithstanding, persisted vigorously in the same method. . . . When I put an end to the court, there was at least fifty persons in prison, in great misery by reason of the extreme cold and their poverty. . . . I permitted a special superior court to be held at Salem, . . . on the third day of January, the lieutenant-governor being

1 *Mass. Hist. Coll.* first series, v. 61.

chief judge. . . . All . . . were cleared, saving three.
. . . The deputy-governor signed a warrant for their
speedy execution, and also of five others who were
condemned at the former court. . . . But . . . I sent
a reprieve; . . . the lieutenant-governor upon this
occasion was enraged and filled with passionate anger,
and refused to sit upon the bench at a superior court,
at that time held at Charlestown; and, indeed, hath
from the beginning hurried on these matters with
great precipitancy, and by his warrant hath caused
the estates, goods, and chattels of the executed to be
seized and disposed of without my knowledge or consent." [1] Some months earlier, also, just before the
meeting of the legislature, he had called on Cotton
Mather to defend him against the condemnation he
had even then begun to feel, and the elder had responded with a volume which remains as a memorial of him and his compeers.[2] He gave thanks for
the blood that had already flowed, and prayed to God
for more. "They were some of the gracious words,
inserted in the advice, which many of the neighbouring
ministers, did this summer humbly lay before our honourable judges: 'We cannot but with all thankfulness, acknowledge the success which the merciful God
has given unto the sedulous and assiduous endeavours of our honourable rulers, to detect the abom-
inable witchcrafts which have been committed in the

[1] Phips to the Earl of Nottingham, Feb. 21, 1693. Palfrey,
iv. 112, note 2.

[2] *Wonders of the Invisible World.*

country; humbly praying that the discovery of those
mysterious and mischievous wickednesses, may be per-
fected.' If in the midst of the many dissatisfactions
among us, the publication of these trials, may promote
such a pious thankfulness unto God, for justice being
so far, executed among us, I shall rejoyce that God is
glorified; and pray that no wrong steps of ours may
ever sully any of his glorious works." [1]

"These witches . . . have met in hellish randez-
vouszes. . . . In these hellish meetings, these monsters have associated themselves to do no less a thing
than to destroy the kingdom of our Lord Jesus Christ,
in these parts of the world. . . . We are truly come
into a day, which by being well managed might be
very glorious, for the exterminating of those, accursed
things, . . . But if we make this day quarrelsome, . . .
Alas, O Lord, my flesh trembles for fear of thee, and
I am afraid of thy judgments." [2]

While reading such words the streets of Salem rise
before the eyes, with the cart dragging Martha Cory
to the gallows while she protests her innocence, and
there, at her journey's end, at the gibbet's foot, stands
the Rev. Nicholas Noyes, pointing to the dangling
corpses, and saying: "What a sad thing it is to see
eight firebrands of hell hanging there." [3]

The sequence of cause and effect is sufficiently obvious. Although at a moment when the panic had

[1] *Wonders of the Invisible World*, pp. 82, 83.
[2] *Idem*, pp. 49–60.
[3] *More Wonders*, p. 108.

got beyond control, even the most ultra of the clergy
had been forced by their own danger to counsel moderation, the conservatives were by no means ready to
abandon their potent allies from the lower world;
the power they gave was too alluring. " 'Tis a strange
passage recorded by Mr. Clark, in the life of his father, That the people of his parish refusing to be re-
claimed from their Sabbath breaking, by all the zealous testimonies which that good man bore against it;
at last [one night] . . . there was heard a great noise,
with rattling of chains, up and down the town, and an
horrid scent of brimstone. . . . Upon which the guilty
consciences of the wretches, told them, the devil was
come to fetch them away; and it so terrify'd them,
that an eminent reformation follow'd the sermons
which that man of God preached thereupon." [1] They
therefore saw the constant acquittals, the abandonment of prosecutions, and the growth of incredulity with regret. The next year Cotton Mather laid
bare the workings of their minds with cynical frank-
ness. " The devils have with most horrendous opera-
tions broke in upon our neighbourhood, and God has
at such a rate overruled all the fury and malice of
those devils, that . . . the souls of many, especially
of the rising generation, have been thereby waken'd
unto some acquaintance with religion; our young people who belonged unto the praying meetings, of both
sexes, apart would ordinarily spend whole nights by
the whole weeks together in prayers and psalms upon

---

[1] *Wonders of the Invisible World*, p. 65.

these occasions; . . . and some scores of other young people, who were strangers to real piety, were now struck with the lively demonstrations of hell . . . before their eyes. . . . In the whole — the devil got just nothing, but God got praises, Christ got subjects, the Holy Spirit got temples, the church got addition, and the souls of men got everlasting benefits." [1]

Mather prided himself on what he had done. " I am not so vain as to say that any wisdom or virtue of mine did contribute unto this good order of things; but I am so just as to say, I did not hinder this good." [2] Men with such beliefs, and lured onward by such temptations, were incapable of letting the tremendous power superstition gave them slip from their grasp without an effort on their own behalf; and accordingly it was not long before the Mathers were once more at work. On the 10th of September, 1693, or about nine months after the last spasms at Salem, and when the belief in enchantments was fast falling into disrepute, a girl named Margaret Rule was taken with the accustomed symptoms in Boston. Forthwith these two godly divines repaired to her bedside, and this is what took place : —

Then Mr. M—— father and son came up, and others with them, in the whole were about thirty or forty persons, they being sat, the father on a stool, and the son upon the bedside by her, the son began to question her :

[1] *More Wonders*, p. 12.   [2] *Idem*, p. 12.

Margaret Rule, how do you do? Then a pause without any answer.

Question. What. Do there a great many witches sit upon you? *Answer.* Yes.

Question. Do you not know that there is a hard master?

Then she was in a fit. He laid his hand upon her face and nose, but, as he said, without perceiving breath; then he brush'd her on the face with his glove, and rubb'd her stomach (her breast not being covered with the bed clothes) and bid others do so too, and said it eased her, then she revived.

Q. Don't you know there is a hard master? *A.* Yes.

Reply. Don't serve that hard master, you know who.

Q. Do you believe? Then again she was in a fit, and he again rub'd her breast &c. . . . He wrought his fingers before her eyes and asked her if she saw the witches? *A.* No. . . .

Q. Who is it that afflicts you? *A.* I know not, there is a great many of them. . . .

Q. You have seen the black man, hant you? *A.* No.

Reply. I hope you never shall.

Q. You have had a book offered you, hant you? *A.* No.

Q. The brushing of you gives you ease, don't it? *A.* Yes. She turn'd herselfe, and a little groan'd.

Q. Now the witches scratch you, and pinch you,

and bite you, don't they ?   A. Yes.   Then he put his
hand upon her breast and belly, viz. on the clothes
over her, and felt a living thing, as he said; which
moved the father also to feel, and some others.

Q. Don't you feel the live thing in the bed?
A. No. . . .

Q. Shall we go to pray . . . spelling the word.
A. Yes.   The father went to prayer for perhaps half
an hour, chiefly against the power of the devil and
witchcraft, and that God would bring out the afflict-
ers. . . . After prayer he [the son] proceeded.

Q. You did not hear when we were at prayer did
you?   *A.* Yes.

Q. You don't hear always? you don't hear sometimes past a word or two, do you?   *A.* No.   Then
turning him about said, this is just another Mercy
Short. . . .

Q. What does she eat or drink?   *A.* Not eat at
all ; but drink rum.[1]

To sanctify to the godly the ravings of this drunken
and abandoned wench was a solemn joy to the heart
of this servant of Christ, who gave his life to " un-
wearied cares and pains, to rescue the miserable from
the lions and bears of hell," [2] therefore he prepared
another tract.   But his hour was well-nigh come.
Though it was impossible that retribution should be
meted out to him for his crimes, at least he did not

---

[1] *More Wonders,* pp. 13, 14.
[2] *Idem,* p. 10.

escape unscathed, for Calef and the Brattles, who had
long been on his father's track and his, now seized
him by the throat. He knew well they had been
with him in the chamber of Margaret Rule, that they
had gathered all the evidence; and so when Calef
sent him a challenge to stand forth and defend himself, he shuffled and equivocated.

At length a rumor spread abroad that a volume was
to be published exposing the whole black history, and
then the priest began to cower. His Diary is full of
his prayers and lamentations. " The book is printed,
and the impression is this week arrived here. . . . I
set myself to humble myself before the Lord under
these humbling and wondrous dispensations, and obtain the pardon of my sins, that have rendered me
worthy of such dispensations. . . .

" 28d. 10m. Saturday. — The Lord has permitted
Satan to raise an extraordinary storm upon my father
and myself. All the rage of Satan against the holy
churches of the Lord falls upon us. First Calf's book,
and then Coleman's, do set the people in a mighty
ferment. All the adversaries of the churches lay their
heads together, as if, by blasting of us, they hoped
utterly to blow up all. The Lord fills my soul with
consolations, inexpressible consolations, when I think
on my conformity to my Lord Jesus Christ in the
injuries and reproaches that are cast upon me. . . .

" 5d. 2m. Saturday [1701]. — I find the enemies of
the churches are set with an implacable enmity against
myself; and one vile fool, namely, R. Calf, is employed

by them to go on with more of his filthy scribbles to hurt my precious opportunities of glorifying my Lord Jesus Christ. I had need be much in prayer unto my glorious Lord that he would preserve his poor servant from the malice of this evil generation, and of that vile man particularly." [1]

" More Wonders of the Invisible World " appeared in 1700, and such was the terror the clergy still inspired it is said it had to be sent to London to be printed, and when it was published no bookseller in Boston dared to offer it in his shop.[2] Yet though it was burnt in the college yard by the order of Increase Mather, it was widely read, and dealt the death-blow to the witchcraft superstition of New England. It did more than this: it may be said to mark an era in the intellectual development of Massachusetts, for it shook to its centre that moral despotism which the pastors still kept almost unimpaired over the minds of their congregations, by demonstrating to the people the necessity of thinking for themselves. But what the fate of its authors would have been had the priests still ruled may be guessed by the onslaught made on them by those who sat at the Mathers' feet. " Spit on, Calf; thou shalt be but like the viper on Pauls hand, easily shaken off, and without any damage to the servant of the Lord." [3]

[1] *Mass. Hist. Soc. Proc.* 1855–58, pp. 290–293.
[2] *Some Few Remarks*, p. 9.
[3] *Idem*, p. 22.

CHAPTER VIII.

BRATTLE CHURCH.

If the working of the human mind is mechanical, the quality of its action must largely depend upon the training it receives. Viewed as civilizing agents, therefore, systems of education might be tested by their tendency to accelerate or retard the intellectual development of the race. The proposition is capable of being presented with almost mathematical precision; the receptive faculty begins to fail at a comparatively early age; thereafter new opinions are assimilated with increasing difficulty until the power is lost. This progressive period of life, which is at best brief, may, however, be indefinitely shortened by the interposition of artificial obstacles, which have to be overcome by a waste of time and energy, before the reason can act with freedom; and when these obstacles are sufficiently formidable, the whole time is consumed and men are stationary. The most effectual impediments are those prejudices which are so easily implanted in youth, and which acquire tremendous power when based on superstitious terrors. Herein, then, lies the radical divergence between theological and scientific training: the one, by inculcating that tradition is sacred, that accurate investigation is sacrilege, certain to be visited with terrific punishment, and that the highest moral virtue is submission to authority, seeks to paralyze exact thought, and to produce a condition in which dogmatic statements of fact, and despotic rules of conduct, will be received with abject resignation; the other, by stimulating the curiosity, endeavors to provoke inquiry, and, by encouraging a scrutiny of what is obscure, tries to put the mind in an impartial and questioning attitude toward all the phenomena of the universe.

The two methods are irreconcilable, and spring from the great primary instincts which are called conservatism and liberality. Necessarily the movement of any community must correspond exactly with the preponderance of liberalism. Where the theological incubus is unresisted it takes the form of a sacred caste, as among the Hindoos; appreciable advance then ceases, except from some external pressure, such as conquest. The same tendencies in a mitigated form are seen in Spain, whereas Germany is scientific.

Such being the ceaseless conflict between these natural forces, the vantage-points for which the opposing parties have always struggled in western Europe are the pulpits and the universities. Through women the church can reach children at their most impressionable age, while at the universities the teachers are taught. Obviously, if a priesthood can control both positions their influence must be immense. At the beginning of any movement the conservatives are almost necessarily in possession, and their worst reverses

have come from defection from within; for unless
their organization is so perfect as not only to be animated by a single purpose, but capable of being controlled by a single will, liberals will penetrate within
the fold, and if they can maintain their footing and
preach with the authority of the ancient tradition it
leads to revolution. It was thus the Reformation was
accomplished.

The clergy of Massachusetts, with the true priestly
instinct, took in the bearings of their situation from
the instant they recognized that their political supremacy was passing away, and in order to keep their
organization in full vigor they addressed themselves
with unabated energy to enforcing the discipline which
had been established; at the same time they set the
ablest of their number on guard at Harvard. But
the task was beyond their strength; they might as
well have tried to dam the rising tide with sand.

There is a limit to the capacity of even the most
gifted man, and Increase Mather committed a fatal
error when he tried to be professor, clergyman, and
statesman at once. He was, it is true, made president in 1685, but the next year John Leverett and
William Brattle were chosen tutors and fellows, who
soon developed into ardent liberals; so it happened
that when the reverend rector went abroad in 1688,
in his character of politician, he left the college in
the complete control of his adversaries. He was absent four years, and during this interval the man
was educated who was destined to overthrow the Cam-

bridge Platform, the corner-stone of the conservative power.

Benjamin Colman was one of Leverett's favorite pupils and the intimate friend of Pemberton. As he was to be a minister, he stayed at Cambridge until he took his master's degree in 1695; he then sailed at once for England in the Swan. When she had been some weeks at sea she was attacked by a French privateer, who took her after a sharp action. During the fight Colman attracted attention by his coolness; but he declared that though he fired like the rest, " he was sensible of no courage but of a great deal of fear; and when they had received two or three broadsides he wondered when his courage would come, as he had heard others talk." [1]

After the capture the Frenchmen stripped him and put him in the hold, and had it not been for a Madame Allaire, who kept his money for him, he might very possibly have perished from the exposure of an imprisonment in France, for his lungs were delicate. Moreover, at this time of his life he was always a pauper, for he was not only naturally generous, but so innocent and confiding as to fall a victim to any clumsy sharper. Of course he reached London penniless and in great depression of spirits; but he soon became known among the dissenting clergy, and at length settled at Bath, where he preached two years. He seems to have formed singularly strong friendships while in England, one of which was with Mr.

[1] *Life of B. Colman,* p. 6.

Walter Singer, at whose house he passed much time, and who wrote him at parting, " Methinks there is one place vacant in my affections, which nobody can fill beside you.   But this blessing was too great for me, and God has reserved it for those that more deserved it. — I cannot but hope sometimes that Providence has yet in store so much happiness for me, that I shall yet see you." [1]

Meanwhile opinion was maturing fast at home ; the passions of the witchcraft convulsion had gone deep, and in 1697 a movement began under the guidance of Leverett and the Brattles to form a liberal Congregational church.   The close on which the meeting-house was to stand was conveyed by Thomas Brattle to trustees on January 10, 1698, and from the outset there seems to have been no doubt as to whom the pastor should be.   On the 10th of May, 1699, a formal invitation was dispatched to Colman by a committee, of which Thomas Brattle was chairman, and it was accompanied by letters from many prominent liberals.   Leverett wrote, " I shall exceedingly rejoice at your return to your country.   We want persons of your character.   The affair offered to your consideration is of the greatest moment."   William Brattle was even more emphatic, while Pemberton assured him that " the gentlemen who solicit your return are mostly known to you — men of repute and figure, from whom you may expect generous treatment ; . . . I believe your return will be pleasing **to**

[1] *Life of B. Colman,* p. 48.

all that know you, I am sure it will be inexpressibly so to your unfeigned friend and servant." [1]   It
was, however, thought prudent to have him ordained
in London, since there was no probability that the
clergy of Massachusetts would perform the rite.
When he landed in November, after an absence of
four years, he was in the flush of early manhood,
highly trained for theological warfare, having seen
the world, and by no means in awe of his old pastor,
the reverend president of Harvard.

The first step after his arrival was to declare the
liberal policy, and this was done in a manifesto which
was published almost at once.[2]   The efficiency of the
Congregational organization depended upon the perfection of the guard which the ministers and the congregations mutually kept over each other.   On the
one hand no dangerous element could creep in among
the people through the laxness of the elder, since all
candidates for the communion had to pass through
the ordeal of a public examination ; on the other the
orthodoxy of the ministers was provided for, not only
by restricting the elective body to the communicants,
but by the power of the ordained clergy to " except
against any election of a pastor who . . . may be
. . . unfit for the common service of the gospel." [3]

The declaration of the Brattle Street "undertakers"

---

[1] *Life of B. Colman*, pp. 43, 44.

[2] *History of Brattle St. Church*, p. 20.

[3] Propositions determined by the Assembly of Ministers. *Magnalia*, bk. 5, Hist. Remarks, § 8.

cut this system at the root, for they announced their intention to dispense with the relation of experiences, thus practically throwing their communion open to all respectable persons who would confess the Westminster Creed; and more fatal still, they absolutely destroyed the homogeneousness of the ecclesiastical constituency: "We cannot confine the right of chusing a minister to the male communicants alone, but we think that every baptized adult person who contributes to the maintenance, should have a vote in electing." [1]

They also proposed several innovations of minor importance, such as relaxing the baptismal regulations, and somewhat changing the established service by having the Bible read without comment.

Their temporal power was gone, toleration was the law of the land they had once possessed, and now an onslaught was to be made upon the intellectual ascendency which the clergy felt certain of maintaining over their people, if only they could enforce obedience in their own ranks. The danger, too, was the more alarming because so insidious; for, though their propositions seemed reasonable, it was perfectly obvious that should the liberals succeed in forcing their church within the pale of the orthodox communion, discipline must end, and the pulpits might at any time be filled with men capable of teaching the most subversive doctrines. Although such might be the inexorable destiny of the Massachusetts hierarchy, it was not in

---

[1] *History of Brattle St. Church*, p. 25, Prop. 16.

ecclesiastical human nature to accept the dispensation
with meekness, and the utterances of the conservative
divines seem hardly to breathe the spirit of that gospel they preached at such interminable length.

Yet it was very difficult to devise a scheme of resistance. They were powerless to coerce ; for, although Increase Mather had taken care, when at the
summit of his power, to have a statute passed which
had the effect of reënacting the Cambridge Platform,
it had been disapproved by the king ; therefore, moral
intimidation was the only weapon which could be employed. Now, aside from the fact that men like
Thomas Brattle and Leverett were not timorous, their
position was at this moment very strong from the
stand they had taken in the witchcraft troubles, and
worst of all, they were openly supported by William
Brattle, who was already a minister, and by Pemberton, who was a fellow of Harvard, and soon to be
ordained.

The attack was, however, begun by Mr. Higginson,
and Mr. Noyes, of witchcraft memory, in a long rebuke, whose temper may be imagined from such a
sentence as this : " We cannot but think you might
have entered upon your declaration with more reverence and humility than so solemnly to appeal to
God, your judge, that you do it with all the sincerity
and seriousness the nature of your engagement commands from you ; seeing you were most of you much
unstudied in the controversial points of church order
and discipline, and yet did not advise with the neigh-

boring churches . . . but with a great deal of confidence and freedom, set up by yourselves." The
letter then goes on to adjure them to revoke the manifesto, and adjust matters with the "neighbouring
elders," "that so the right hand of fellowship may
be given to your pastor by other pastors, . . . and
that you may not be the beginning of a schism that
will dishonour God, . . . and be a matter of triumph
to the bad." [1]

Cotton Mather's Diary, however, gives the most
pleasing view of the high churchmen : —

" 1699. 7th, 10th m. (Dec.) I see another day of
temptation begun upon the town and land. A company of headstrong men in the town, the chief of
whom are full of malignity to the holy ways of our
churches, have built in the town another meeting-
house. To delude many better meaning men in their
own company, and the churches in the neighbourhood,
they passed a vote in the foundation of the proceedings that they would not vary from the practice of
these churches, except in one little particular.

" But a young man born and bred here, and hence
gone for England, is now returned hither at their invitation, equipped with an ordination to qualify him
for all that is intended on his returning and arriving
here ; these fallacious people desert their vote, and
without the advice or knowledge of the ministers in
the vicinity, they have published, under the title of a
manifesto, certain articles that utterly subvert our

[1] *History of Brattle St. Church*, pp. 29–37.

churches, and invite an ill party, through all the country, to throw all into confusion on the first opportunities.   This drives the ministers that would be faithful unto the Lord Jesus Christ, and his interests in the churches, unto a necessity of appearing for their defence.   No little part of these actions must unavoidably fall to my share.   I have already written a large monitory letter to these innovators, which, though most lovingly penned, yet enrages their violent and imperious lusts to carry on the apostacy."

"1699. 5th d. 11th m. (Saturday.) I see Satan beginning a terrible shake in the churches of New England, and the innovators that had set up a new church in Boston (a new one indeed!) have made a day of temptation among us. The men are ignorant, arrogant, obstinate, and full of malice and slander, and they fill the land with lies, in the misrepresentations whereof I am a very singular sufferer. Wherefore I set apart this day again for prayer in my study, to cry mightily unto God." [1]

" 21st d. 11th m. The people of the new church in Boston, who, by their late manifesto, went on in an ill way, and in a worse frame, and the town was filled with sin, and especially with slanders, wherein especially my father and myself were sufferers. We two, with many prayers and studies, and with humble resignation of our names unto the Lord, prepared a faithful antidote for our churches against the infection of the example, which we feared this company

[1] *History of Harvard,* Quincy, i. 486, 487, App. x.

had given them, and we put it into the press. But when the first sheet was near composed at the press, I stopped it, with a desire to make one attempt more for the bringing of this people to reason. I drew up a proposal, and, with another minister, carried it unto them, who at first rejected it, but afterward so far embraced it, as to promise that they will the next week publicly recognize their covenant with God and one another, and therewithall declare their adherence to the Heads of Agreement of the United Brethren in England, and request the communion of our churches in that foundation." [1]

This last statement is marked by the exuberance of imagination for which the Mathers are so famed. In truth, Dr. Mather had nothing to do with the settlement. The facts were these : after Brattle Street Church was organized, the congregation voted that Mr. Colman should ask the ministers of the town to keep a day of prayer with them. On the 28th of December, 1699, they received the following suggestive answer : —

Mr. Colman :

Whereas you have signified to us that your society have desired us to join with them in a public fast, in order to your intended communion, our answer is, that as we have formerly once and again insinuated unto you, that if you would in due manner lay aside what you call your manifesto, and resolve and

[1] *History of Harvard,* i. 487, App. x.

declare that you will keep to the heads of agreement on which the United Brethren in London have made their union, and then publicly proceed with the presence, countenance, and concurrence of the New England churches, we should be free to give you our fellowship and our best assistance, which things you have altogether declined and neglected to do ; thus we must now answer, that, if you will give us the satisfaction which the law of Christ requires for your disorderly proceedings, we shall be happy to gratify your desires ; otherwise, we may not do it, lest . . . we become partakers of the guilt of those irregularities by which you have given just cause of offence. . . .

INCREASE MATHER.

JAMES ALLEN.[1]

Under the theocracy a subservient legislature would have voted the association " a seditious conspiracy," and the country would have been cleared of Leverett, Colman, the Brattles, and their abettors ; but in 1700 the priests no longer manipulated the constituencies, and there was actual danger to the conservative cause from their violence ; therefore Stoughton exerted himself to muzzle the Mathers, and he did succeed in quieting them for the moment, though Sewall seems to intimate that they submitted with no very good grace : [$\frac{1699}{1700}$.] "Jany 24th. The Lt Govr [Stoughton] calls me with him to Mr. Willards, where out of two papers Mr. Wm Brattle drew up a third for an accomo-

---

[1] *History of Brattle St. Church*, p. 55.

dation to bring on an agreement between the new-church and our ministers; Mr. Colman got his brethren to subscribe it. . . . Jany 25th. Mr. I. Mather, Mr. C. Mather, Mr. Willard, Mr. Wadsworth, and S. S. wait on the Lt Govr at Mr. Coopers : to confer about the writing drawn up the evening before. Was some heat; but grew calmer, and after lecture agreed to be present at the fast which is to be observed Jany 31." [1]

Humility has sometimes been extolled as the crowning grace of Christian clergymen, but Cotton Mather's Diary shows the intolerable arrogance of the early Congregational divines.

" A wonderful joy filled the hearts of our good people far and near, that we had obtained thus much from them. Our strife seemed now at an end; there was much relenting in some of their spirits, when they saw our condescension, our charity, our compassion. We overlooked all past offences. We kept the public fast with them . . . and my father preached with them on following peace with holiness, and I concluded with prayer." [2]

Yet, although there had been this ostensible reconciliation, those who have appreciated the sensitiveness to sin, of him whom Dr. Eliot calls the patriarch and his son, must already feel certain they were incapable of letting Colman's impiety pass unrebuked; indeed, the Diary says the " faithful antidote " was at that moment in the press, and it was not long before it was

---

[1] *Mass. Hist. Coll.* fifth series, vi. 2.
[2] *History of Harvard*, i. 487, App. x.

published, sanctified by their prayers. The patriarch
began by telling how he was defending the "cause
of Christ and of his churches in New England,"
and "if we espouse such principles . . . we then give
away the whole Congregational cause at once." [1] He
assured his hearers that a "wandering Levite" like
Colman was no more a pastor than he who "has no
children is a father," [2] he was shocked at the abandonment of the relation of experiences, and was so
scandalized at reading the Bible without comment he
could only describe it as "dumb." In a word, there
was nothing the new congregation had done which
was not displeasing to the Lord; but if they had offended in one particular more than another it was in
establishing a man in "the pastoral office without the
approbation of neighbouring churches or elders." [3] To
this solemn admonition Colman and William Brattle
had the irreverence to prepare a reply smacking of
levity; nevertheless, they began with a grave and noble definition of their principles. "The liberties and
privileges which our Lord Jesus Christ has given to
his church . . . consist . . . in . . . that our consciences be not imposed on by men or their traditions." "We are reflected on as casting dishonour
on our parents, & their pious design in the first settlement of this land. . . . Some have made this the great
design, to be freed from the impositions of men in

[1] *Order of the Gospel*, pp. 8, 9.

[2] *Idem*, p. 102.

[3] *Idem*, p. 8.

the worship of God. . . . In this we are risen up to
make good their grounds." [1]

They then went on to expose the abuse of public
relations of experiences: " But this is the misery, the
more meek and fearful are hereby kept out of God's
house, while the more conceited and presumptuous
never boggle at this, or anything else. But it seems
there is a gross corruption of this laudable practice
which the author does well to censure ; and that is,
when some, who have no good intention of their own,
get others to devise a relation for them." [2] They even
dared to intimate that it did not savor of modesty for
the patriarch " to think any one of his sermons, or
short comments, can edifie more than the reading of
twenty chapters." [3] And then they added some sentences, which were afterward declared by the venerable victim to be as scurrilous as other portions of the
pamphlet were profane.

" We are assured, the author is esteemed more a
Presbyterian than a Congregational man, by scores
of his friends in London. He is lov'd and reverenced
for a moderate spirit, a peaceable disposition, and a
temper so widely different from his late brothers in
London. . . . Did our reverend author appear the
same here, we should be his easie proselites too. But
we are loath to say how he forfeits that venerable
character, which might have consecrated his name to

---

[1] *Gospel Order Revived*, Epistle Dedicatory.
[2] *Idem*, p. 9.
[3] *Idem*, p. 15.

posterity, more than his learning, or other honorary titles can." [1]

No printer in Boston dared to be responsible for this ribaldry, and when it came home from New York and was actually cast before the people, words fail to convey the condition into which the patriarch was thrown. At last his emotions found a vent in a tract which he prepared jointly with his son.

"A moral heathen would not have done as he has done.[2] . . . There is no one thing, which does more threaten or disgrace New-England, than want of due respect unto superiors.[3] . . . It is a disgrace to the name of Presbyterian, that such as he is should pretend unto it [4] . . . and if our children should learn from them, . . . we may tremble to think, what a flood of profaneness and atheism would break in upon us, and ripen us for the dreadfullest judgments of God.[5] . . . They assault him [the aged president] with a volley of rude jeers and taunts, as if they were so many children of Bethel." [6] Among these taunts some struck deep, for they are quoted at length. "'Abundance of people have long obstinately believed, that the contest on his part, is more for lordship and dominion, than for truth.' But there are many more such passages, which laid altogether, would make a considerable dunghil." [7] They dwelt with pathos upon those sacred rites

[1] *Gospel Order Revived*, pp. 34, 35.
[2] *Collection of Some of the More Offensive Matters*, Preface.
[3] *Idem*, p. 10.   [4] *Idem*, p. 12.   [5] *Idem*, p. 7.
[6] *Idem*, p. 8.   [7] *Idem*, p. 9.

desecrated by these " unsanctified" " young men " in
their " miserable pamphlet." " The Lord is exceedingly glorified, and his people are edified, by the accounts, which the candidates, of the communion in our
churches give of that self-examination which is by plain
institution . . . a qualification, of the communicants.
Now these think it not enough to charge the churches,
which require & expect such accounts, with exceedingly provoking the Lord. But of the tears dropt
by holy souls on those occasions, they say with a scoff,
' whether they be for joy or grief, we are left in the
dark.' " [1] But the suffering divines found peace in
knowing that Christ himself would inflict the punishment upon these abandoned men which the priests
would have meted out with holy joy had they still
possessed the power.

" Considering that the things contained in their
pamphlet, are a deep apostasy, in conjunction with
such open impiety, and profane scurrility against the
holy wayes in which our fathers walked, in case it become the sin of the land, (as it will do if not duely
testified against) we may fear that some heavy judgment will come upon the whole land. And will not
the holy Lord Jesus Christ, who walks in the midst
of his golden candlesticks, make all the churches to
know . . . that these men have provoked the Lord! " [2]

Yet, notwithstanding the Mathers' piteous prayers,
God heeded them not, and the rising tide that was

[1] *Collection of Some of the More Offensive Matters,* p. 6.
[2] *Idem,* pp. 18, 19.

sweeping over them soon drowned their cries. Brattle Street congregation became an honored member of the orthodox communion, the principles which animated its founders spread apace, and the name of Benjamin Colman waxed great in the land. The liberals had penetrated the stronghold of the church.

CHAPTER IX.

FOR more than two centuries one ceaseless anthem of adulation has been chanted in Massachusetts in honor of the ecclesiastics who founded Harvard University, and this act has not infrequently been cited as incontrovertible proof that they were both liberal and progressive at heart. The laudation of ancestors is a task as easy as it is popular; but history deals with the sequence of cause and effect, and an examination of facts, apart from sentiment, tends to show that in building a college the clergy were actuated by no loftier motive than intelligent self-interest, if, indeed, they were not constrained thereto by the inexorable exigencies of their position.

The truth of this proposition becomes apparent if the soundness of the following analysis be conceded.

There would seem to be a point in the pathway of civilization where every race passes more or less completely under the dominion of a sacred caste; when and how the more robust have emerged into freedom is uncertain, but enough is known to make it possible to trace the process by which this insidious power is acquired, and the means by which it is perpetuated. A flood of light has, moreover, been shed on this class of subjects by the recent remarkable investigations among the Zuñis.[1]

Most American Indians are in the matriarchal period of development, which precedes the patriarchal; and it is then, should they become sedentary, that caste appears to be born.   Some valuable secret, such as a cure for the bite of the rattlesnake, is discovered, and this gives the finder, and chosen members of his clan with whom he shares it, a peculiar sanctity in the eyes of the rest of the tribe.   Like facts, however, become known to other clans, and then coalitions are made which take the form of esoteric societies, and from these the stronger savages gradually exclude the weaker and their descendants.   Meanwhile an elaborate ritual is developed, and so an hereditary priesthood comes into life, which always claims to have received its knowledge by revelation, and which teaches that resistance to its will is sacrilege.   Nevertheless the sacerdotal power is seldom firmly established without a struggle, the memory whereof is carefully preserved as a warning of the danger of incurring the divine wrath.   A good example of such a myth is the fable of the rebellious Zuñi fire-priest, who at the prayer of his orthodox brethren was destroyed with all his clan by a boiling torrent poured from the burning mountain, sacred to their order, by the avenging gods.   Compare this with the story of Korah; and it is interesting to observe how the priestly chron-

[1] Made by Mr. F. H. Cushing, of the Bureau of Ethnology, Smithsonian Institution.

*i*cler, in order to throw the profounder awe about his class, has made the great national prophet the author of the exclusion of the body of the Levites from the caste, in favor of his own brother. " And they gathered themselves together against Moses and against Aaron, and said unto them, Ye take too much upon you, seeing all the congregation are holy, . . . wherefore then lift ye up yourselves above the congregation of the Lord ?

" And when Moses heard it, he fell upon his face." Then he told Korah and his followers, who were descendants of Levi and legally entitled to act as priests by existing customs, to take censers and burn incense, and it would appear whether the Lord would respect their offering. So every man took his censer, and Korah and two hundred and fifty more stood in the door of the tabernacle.

Then Moses said, if " the earth open her mouth, and swallow them up, with all that appertain unto them, and they go down quick into the pit; then ye shall understand that these men have provoked the Lord. . . .

" And the earth opened her mouth, and swallowed them up, and their houses, and all the men that appertained unto Korah, and all their goods.

" They, and all that appertained to them, went down alive into the pit, and the earth closed upon them: . . . And all Israel that were round about them fled at the cry of them : for they said, Lest the earth swallow us up also." [1]

[1] *Numbers* xvi.

Traces of a similar conflict are found in Hindoo sacred literature, and probably the process has been well-nigh universal. The caste, therefore, originates in knowledge, real and pretended, kept by secret tradition in certain families, and its power is maintained by systematized terrorism. But to learn the mysteries and ritual requires a special education, hence those destined for the priesthood have careful provision made for their instruction. The youthful Zuñi is taught at the sacred college at the shrine of his order; the pious Hindoo lives for years with some famous Brahmin; as soon as the down came on the cheek, the descendants of Aaron were taken into the Temple at Jerusalem, and all have read how Hannah carried the infant Samuel to the house of the Lord at Shiloh, and how the child did minister unto the Lord before Eli the priest.

These facts seem to lead to well-defined conclusions when applied to New England history. In their passionate zeal the colonists conceived the idea of reproducing, as far as they could, the society of the Pentateuch, or, in other words, of reverting to the archaic stage of caste; and in point of fact they did succeed in creating a theocratic despotism which lasted in full force for more than forty years. Of course, in the seventeenth century such a phase of feeling was ephemeral; but the phenomena which attended it are exceptionally interesting, and possibly they are somewhat similar to those which accompany the liberation of a primitive people.

The knowledge which divided the Massachusetts clergy from other men was their supposed proficiency in the interpretation of the ancient writings containing the revelations of God. For the perpetuation of this lore a seminary was as essential to them as an association of priests for the instruction of neophytes is to the Zuñi now, or as the training at the Temple was to the Jews. In no other way could the popular faith in their special sanctity be sustained. It is also true that few priesthoods have made more systematic use of terror. The slaughter of Anne Hutchinson and her family was exultingly declared to be the judgment of God for defaming the elders. Increase Mather denounced the disobedient Colman in the words of Moses to Korah; Cotton Mather revelled in picturing the torments of the bewitched; and, even in the last century Jonathan Edwards frightened people into convulsions by his preaching. On the other hand, it is obvious that the reproduction of the Mosaic law could not in the nature of things have been complete; and the two weak points in the otherwise strong position of the clergy were that the spirit of their age did not permit them to make their order hereditary, nor, although their college was a true theological school, did they perceive the danger of allowing any lay admixture. The tendency to weaken the force of the discipline is obvious, yet they were led to abandon the safe Biblical precedent, not only by their own early associations, but by their hatred of anything savoring of Catholicism.

Men to be great leaders must exalt their cause above themselves; and if so godly a man as the Rev. Increase Mather can be said to have had a human failing it was an inordinate love of money and of flattery. The first of these peculiarities showed itself early in life when, as his son says, he was reluctant to settle at the North Church, because of "views he had of greater service elsewhere."[1] In other words, the parish was not liberal; for it seems "the deacons . . . were not spirited like some that have succeeded them; and the leaders of the more honest people also, were men of a low, mean, sordid spirit. . . . For one of his education, and erudition, and gentlemanly spirit, and conversation, to be so creepled and kept in such a depressing poverty! — In these distresses, it was to little purpose for him to make his complaint unto man! If he had, it would have been basely improved unto his disadvantage."[2] His diary teemed with repinings. "Oh! that the Lord Jesus, who hears my complaints before him, would either give an heart to my people to look after my comfortable subsistance among them, or . . . remove me to another people, who will take care of me, that so I may be in a capacity to attend his work, and glorify his name in my generation."[3] However, matters mended with him, for we are assured that "the Glorious One who knew the works, and the service and the patience of this tempted man, ordered it, that several gentlemen of good estate, and of better spirit, were become the

[1] *Parentator*, p. 25.   [2] *Idem*, p. 30.   [3] *Idem*, p. 33.

members of his church ; " and from them he had " such filial usages . . . as took away from him all room of repenting, that he had not under his temptations prosecuted a removal from them." [1]

The presidency of Harvard, though nominally the highest place a clergyman could hold in Massachusetts, had always been one of poverty and self-denial ; for the salary was paid by the legislature, which, as the unfortunate Dunster had found, was not disposed to be generous. Therefore, although Mr. Mather was chosen president in 1685, and was afterward confirmed as rector by Andros, he was far too pious to be led again into those temptations from which he had been delivered by the interposition of the Glorious One ; and the last thing he proposed was to go into residence and give up his congregation. Besides, he was engrossed in politics and went to England in 1688, where he stayed four years. Meanwhile the real control of education was left in the hands of Leverett, who was appointed tutor in 1686, and of William Brattle, who was in full sympathy with his policy. Among the many powers usurped by the old trading company was that of erecting corporations ; hence the effect of the judgment vacating the patent had been to annul the college charter which had been granted by the General Court ; [2] and although the institution had gone on much as usual after the Revolution, its position was felt to be precarious. Such being the situation when

[1] *Parentator*, pp. 34, 35.   [2] 23 May, 1650.   *Mass. Rec.* iii. 195.

the patriarch came home in 1692 in the plenitude of
power, he conceived the idea of making himself the
untrammelled master of the university, and he forthwith caused a bill to be introduced into the legislature
which would certainly have produced that result.[1]
Nor did he meet with any serious opposition in Massachusetts, where his power was, for the moment, well-
nigh supreme. His difficulty lay with the king, since
the fixed policy of Great Britain was to foster Episcopalianism, and of course to obtain some recognition
for that sect at Cambridge. And so it came to pass
that all the advantage he reaped by the enactment of
this singular law was a degree of Doctor of Divinity [2]
which he gave himself between the approval of the
bill by Phips and its rejection at London. The com-
pliment was the more flattering, however, as it was the
first ever granted in New England. But the clouds
were fast gathering over the head of this good man.
Like many another benefactor of his race, he was
doomed to experience the pangs inflicted by ingratitude, and indeed his pain was so acute he seldom lost
an opportunity of giving it public expression; to use
his own words of some years later, " these are the last
lecture sermons . . . to be preached by me. . . . The
ill treatment which I have had from those from whom
I had reason to have expected better, have discouraged me from being any more concerned on such occasions." [3]

[1] *Province Laws,* 1692–93, c. 10.

[2] Sept. 5, 1692. Quincy's *History of Harvard,* i. 71.

[3] Address to Sermon, *The Righteous Man a Blessing,* 1702.

Certainly he was in a false position; he was necessarily unappreciated by the liberals, and he had not
only alienated many staunch conservatives by his acceptance of the charter, but he had embittered them
by rigorously excluding all except his particular faction from Phips's council.   To his deep chagrin, the
elections of 1693 went in favor of many of these
thankless men, and his discontent soon took the form
of an intense longing to go abroad in some official
position which would give him importance.   The only
possible opening seemed to be to get himself made
agent to negotiate a charter for Harvard; and therefore he soon had "angelical" suggestions that God
needed him in England to glorify his name.

"1693.   September 3d.   As I was riding to preach
at Cambridge, I prayed to God, — begged that my
labors might be blessed to the souls of the students;
at the which I was much melted.   Also saying to the
Lord, that some workings of his Providence seemed
to intimate, that I must be returned to England
again; . . . I was inexpressibly melted, and that for
a considerable time, and a stirring suggestion, that to
England I must go.   In this there was something extraordinary, either divine or angelical."

" December 30th.   Meltings before the Lord this
day when praying, desiring being returned to England
again, there to do service to his name, and persuasions
that the Lord will appear therein."

"1694.   January 27th.   Prayers and supplications
that tidings may come from England, that may be

some direction to me, as to my returning thither or otherwise, as shall be most for his glory."

" March 13th. This morning with prayers and tears I begged of God that I might hear from my friends and acquaintance in England something that should encourage and comfort me. Such tidings are coming, but I know not what it is. God has heard me." [1]

His craving to escape from the country was increased by the nagging of the legislature; for so early as December, 1693, the representatives passed the first of a long series of resolves, " that the president of Harvard College for the time being shall reside there, as hath been accustomed in time past." [2] Now this was precisely what the Reverend Doctor was determined he would not do ; nor could he resign without losing all hope of his agency ; so it is not surprising that as time went on he wrestled with the Deity.

1698. " September 25th. This day as I was wrestling with the Lord, he gave me glorious and heart-melting persuasions, that he has work for me to do in England, for the glory of his name. My soul rejoiceth in the Lord." [3]

Doubtless his trials were severe, but the effect upon his temper was unfortunate. He brought forward scheme after scheme, and the corporation was made

[1] *History of Harvard*, i. 475, 476, App. ix.
[2] *Court Rec.* vi. 316.
[3] *History of Harvard*, i. 480, App. ix.

to address the legislature, and then the legislature was pestered to accede to the prayer of the corporation, until everybody was wrought to a pitch of nervous irritation ; he himself was always jotting in his Diary what he had on foot, mixed with his hopes and prayers.

" 1696. December 11th. I was with the representatives in the General Court, and did acquaint them with my purpose of undertaking a voyage for England in the spring (if the Lord will), in order to the attainment of a good settlement for the college."

" December 28th. The General Court have done nothing for the poor college. . . . The corporation are desirous that I should go to England on the college's account."

1696. " April 19th (Sabbath.) In the morning, as I was praying in my closet, my heart was marvellously melted with the persuasion, that I should glorify Christ in England."

" 1697. June 7th. Discourse with ministers about the college, and the corporation unanimously desired me to take a voyage for England on the college's account." [1]

But of what the senior tutor was doing with the rising generation he took no note at all. His attention was probably first attracted by rumors of the Brattle Church revolt, for not till 1697 was he able to divert his thoughts from himself long enough to observe that all was not as it should be at Cambridge. Then, at

[1] *History of Harvard*, i. 476, App. ix.

length, he made an effort to get rid of Leverett by striking his name from the list of fellows when a bill for incorporation was brought into the legislature; but this crafty politician had already become too strong in the house of representatives, of which he was soon after made speaker.

Two years later, however, the conservative clergy made a determined effort and prepared a bill containing a religious test, which they supported with a petition praying " that, in the charter for the college, our holy religion may be secured to us and unto our posterity, by a provision, that no person shall be chosen president, or fellow, of the college, but such as declare their adherence unto the principles of reformation, which were espoused and intended by those who first settled the country . . . and have hitherto been the general profession of New England." [2] This time they narrowly missed success, for the bill passed the houses, but was vetoed by Lord Bellomont.

Hitherto Cotton Mather had shown an unfilial lack of interest in his father's ambition to serve the public; but this summer he also began to have assurances from God. One cause for his fervor may have been the death of the Rev. Mr. Morton, who was conceded to stand next in succession to the presidency, and he therefore supposed himself to be sure of the office should a vacancy occur.[3]

---

[1] *History of Harvard,* i. 87.

[2] *Idem,* i. 99.

[3] *Idem,* i. 102.

" 1699. 7th d. 4th m. (June.) The General Court has, divers times of late years, had under consideration the matter of the settlement of the college, which was like still to issue in a voyage of my father to England, and the matter is now again considered. I have made much prayer about it many and many a time. Nevertheless, I never could have my mind raised unto any particular faith about it, one way or another. But this day, as I was (may I not say) in the spirit, it was in a powerful manner assured me from heaven, that my father should one day be carried into England, and that he shall there glorify the Lord Jesus Christ ; . . . And thou, O Mather the younger, shalt live to see this accomplished ! " [1]

" 16th d. 5th m. (July.) Being full of distress in my spirit, as I was at prayer in my study at noon, it was told me from heaven, that my father shall be carried from me unto England, and that my opportunities to glorify the Lord Jesus Christ will, on that occasion, *be gloriously accommodated.*"

" 18th d. 5th m. . . . And now behold a most unintelligible dispensation ! At this very time, even about noon, instead of having the bill for the college enacted, as was expected, the governor plainly rejected it, because of a provision therein, made for the religion of the country."

After the veto the patriarch seems to have got the upper hand for a season, and to have made some arrangement by which he evicted his adversary, as ap-

---

[1] *History of Harvard*, i. 482, 483, App. x.

pears by a very dissatisfied letter written by Leverett in August, 1699 : " As soon as I got home I was informed, that Rev. President (I. M.), held a corporation at the college the 7th inst., and the said corporation, after the publication of the *new settlement*, made choice of Mr. Flynt to be one of the tutors at college. . . . I have not the late act for incorporating the college at hand, nor have I seen the new temporary settlement; but I perceive, that all the members of the late corporation were not notified to be at the meeting. I can't say how legal these late proceedings are; but it is wonderful, that an establishment for so short a time as till October next, should be made use of so soon to introduce an unnecessary addition to that society." [1]

A long weary year passed, during which Dr. Mather must have suffered keenly from the public ingratitude; still, at its end he was happy, since he felt certain of being rewarded by the Lord ; for, just as the earl's administration was closing, he had succeeded by unremitting toil in so adjusting the legislature as to think the spoil his own ; when, alas, suddenly, without warning, in the most distressing manner, the prize slipped into Bellomont's pocket. How severely his faith was tried appears from his son's Diary.

"1700. 16th d. 4th mo. (Lord's Day.) I am going to relate one of the most astonishing things that ever befell in all the time of my pilgrimage.

---

[1] *History of Harvard,* i. 500, App. xvi.

"A particular faith had been unaccountably produced in my father's heart, and in my own, that God will carry him unto England, and there give him a short but great opportunity to glorify the Lord Jesus Christ, before his entrance into the heavenly kingdom. There appears no probability of my father's going thither but in an agency to obtain a charter for the college. This matter having been for several years upon the very point of being carried in the General Assembly, hath strangely miscarried when it hath come to the birth. It is now again before the Assembly, in circumstances wherein if it succeed not, it is never like to be revived and resumed any more. . . .

"But the matter in the Assembly being likely now to come unto nothing, I was in this day in extreme distress of spirit concerning it. . . . After I had finished all the other duties of this day, I did in my distress cast myself prostrate on my study floor before the Lord. . . . I spread before him the consequences of things, and the present posture and aspect of them, and, having told the Lord, that I had always taken a particular faith to be a work of heaven on the minds of the faithful, but if it should prove a deceit in that remarkable instance which was now the cause of my agony, I should be cast into a most wonderful confusion ; I then begged of the Lord, that, if my particular faith about my father's voyage to England were not a delusion, he would be pleased to renew it upon me. All this while my heart had the coldness of a stone upon it, and the straitness that is to be expected from

the lone exercise of reason. But now all on the sudden I felt an inexpressible force to fall on my mind,
an afflatus, which cannot be described in words; *none
knows it but he that has it.* . . . It was told me, that
the Lord Jesus Christ loved my father, and loved me,
and that he took delight in us, as in two of his faithful servants, and that he had not permitted us to be
deceived in our particular faith, but that my father
should be carried into England, and there glorify the
Lord Jesus Christ before his passing into glory. . . .

"Having left a flood of tears from me, by these
rages from the invisible world, on my study floor, I
rose and went into my chair. There I took up my
Bible, and the first place that I opened was at Acts
xxvii. 23–25, 'There stood by me an angel of God,
whose I am, and whom I serve, saying, Fear not, thou
must be brought before Cæsar.' . . . A new flood of
tears gushed from my flowing eyes, and I broke out
into these expressions. 'What! shall my father yet
appear before Cæsar! Has an angel from heaven told
me so! And must I believe what has been told me!
Well then, it shall be so! It shall be so!'"

"And now what shall I say! When the affair of
my father's agency after this came to a turning point
in the court, it strangely miscarried! All came to
nothing! Some of the Tories had so wrought upon
the governor, that, though he had first moved this
matter, and had given us both directions and promises about it, yet he now (not without base unhand-
someness) deferred it. The lieutenant-governor, who

had formerly been for it, now (not without great ebullition of unaccountable prejudice and ingratitude) appeared, with all the little tricks imaginable, to confound it. It had for all this been carried, had not some of the council been inconveniently called off and absent. But now the whole affair of the college was left unto the management of the Earl of Bellamont, so that all expectation of a voyage for my father unto England, on any such occasion, is utterly at an end." [1]

During all these years the legislature had been steadily passing resolutions requiring the president to go into residence; and in 1698 they went so far as to vote him the liberal salary, for that age, of two hundred pounds, and appointed a committee to wait upon him. Judge Sewall describes the interview: —

"Mr. President expostulated with Mr. Speaker . . . about the votes being alter'd from 250 [£. ?]." . . . "We urg'd his going all we could; I told him of his birth and education here; that he look'd at work rather than wages, all met in desiring him. . . . Objected want of a house, bill for corporation not pass'd . . . must needs preach once every week, which he preferred before the gold and silver of the West-Indies. I told him would preach twice aday to the students. He said that [exposition] was nothing like preaching." [2] And in this the patriarch spoke the truth; for if there was anything he loved more than

[1] *History of Harvard*, i. 484–486, App. x.
[2] Sewall's *Diary. Mass. Hist. Coll.* fifth series, v. 487.

money it was the incense of adulation which steamed
up to his nostrils from a great congregation. Of
course he declined; and yet this importunity pained
the good man, not because there was any conflict in
his mind between his duty to a cause he held sacred
and his own interest, but because it was "a thing contrary to the faith marvellously wrought into my soul,
that God will give me an opportunity to serve and
glorify Christ in England, I set the day apart to cry
to heaven about it." [1]

There were limits, however, even to the patience of
the Massachusetts Assembly with an orthodox divine;
and no sooner was the question of the agency decided
by the appointment of Bellomont, than it addressed
itself resolutely to the seemingly hopeless task of forcing Dr. Mather to settle in Cambridge or resign his
office. On the 10th of July, 1700, they voted him
two hundred and twenty pounds a year, and they
appointed a committee to obtain from him a categori-
cal answer. This time he thought it prudent to feign
compliance; and after a "suitable place . . . for the
reception and entertainment of the president" had
been prepared at the public expense, he moved out of
town and stayed till the 17th of October, when he
went back to Boston, and wrote to tell Stoughton his
health was suffering. His disingenuousness seems to
have given Leverett the opportunity for which he had
been waiting; and his acting as chairman of a committee appointed by the representatives suggests his

[1] *History of Harvard*, vi. 481, App. ix.

having forced the issue; it was resolved that, should
Mr. Mather be absent from the college, his duties
should devolve upon Samuel Willard, the vice-president;[1] and in March the committee apparently reported the president's house to be in good condition.
Stimulated by this hint, the doctor went back to Cambridge and stayed a little more than three months,
when he wrote a characteristic note to Stoughton, who
was acting governor. " I promised the last General
Court to take care of the college until the Commencement. Accordingly I have been residing in Cambridge these three months. I am determined (if the
Lord will) to return to Boston the next week, and no
more return to reside in Cambridge; for it is not reasonable to desire me to be (as, out of respect to the
public interest, I have been six months within this
twelve) any longer absent from my family. . . . I
do therefore earnestly desire, that the General Court
would . . . think of another president. . . . It would
be fatal to the interest of religion, if a person disaf-
fected to the order of the Gospel, professed and practised in these churches, should preside over this society. I know the General Assembly, out of their
regard to the interest of Christ, will take care to prevent it." [2] Yet though he himself begged the legislature to select his successor, in his inordinate vanity
he did not dream of being taken at his word; so
when he was invited to meet both houses in the coun-

[1] *History of Harvard,* i. 111 ; *Court Rec.* vii. 172, 175.
[2] *History of Harvard,* i. 501, App. xvii.

cil chamber he explained with perfect cheerfulness how "he was now removed from Cambridge to Boston, and . . . did not think fitt to continue his residence there, . . . but, if the court thought fit to desire he should continue his care of the colledge as formerly, he would do so." [1]

Increase Mather delighted to blazon himself as Christ's foremost champion in the land. He predicted, and with reason, that should those who had been already designated succeed him at Harvard, it would be fatal to that cause to which his life was vowed. The alternative was presented of serving himself or God, and to him it seemed unreasonable of his friends to expect of him a choice. And yet when, as was his wont, he would describe himself from the pulpit, as a refulgent beacon blazing before New England, he would use such words as these: " Every . . . one of a publick spirit . . . will deny himself as to his worldly interests, provided he may thereby promove the welfare of his people. . . . He will not only deny himself, but if called thereto, will encounter the greatest difficulties and dangers for the publicks sake." [2]

The man had presumed too far; the world was wearying of him. On September 6, 1701, the government was transferred to Samuel Willard, the vice-president, and Harvard was lost forever.[3]

[1] *Court Records,* vii. 229.

[2] Sermon, *The Publick Spirited Man,* pp. 7, 9.

[3] *History of Harvard,* i. 116.

No education is so baleful as the ecclesiastical, because it breeds the belief in men that resistance to their will is not only a wrong to their country and themselves, but a sacrilege toward God. The Mathers were now to give an illustration of the degree to which the theocratic training debauched the mind; and it is only necessary to observe that Samuel Sewall, who tells the story, was educated for the ministry, and was perhaps as staunch a conservative as there was in the province.

1701, " Oct.ʳ 20. Mr. Cotton Mather came to Mr. Wilkins's shop, and there talked very sharply against me as if I had used his father worse than a neger; spake so loud that people in the street might hear him. . . . I had read in the morn Mr. Dod's saying; Sanctified afflictions are good promotions. I found it now a cordial."

" Oct.ʳ 9. I sent Mr. Increase Mather a hanch of very good venison; I hope in that I did not treat him as a negro."

" Octob.ʳ 22. 1701. I, with Major Walley and Capt. Sam¹ Checkly, speak with Mr. Cotton Mather at Mr. Wilkins's. . . . I told him of his book of the Law of Kindness for the Tongue, whether this were correspondent with that. Whether correspondent with Christ's rule:

" He said, having spoken to me before there was no need to speak to me again; and so justified his reviling me behind my back. Charg'd the council with lying, hypocrisy, tricks, and I know not what all. I ask'd him if it were done with that meekness as it should; Answer'd, Yes. Charg'd the council in general, and then shew'd my share, which was my speech in council; viz. If Mr. Mather should goe to Cambridge again to reside there with a resolution not to read the Scriptures, and expound in the Hall: I fear the example of it will do more hurt than his going thither will doe good. This speech I owned. . . . I ask'd him if I should suppose he had done somthing amiss in his church as an officer; whether it would be well for me to exclaim against him in the street for it."

" Thursday Oct.ᴿ 23. Mr. Increase Mather said at Mr. Wilkins's, If I am a servant of Jesus Christ, some great judgment will fall on Capt. Sewall, or his family."[1]

Had the patriarch been capable of a disinterested action, for the sake of those principles he professed to love, he would have stopped Willard's presidency, no matter at what personal cost, for he knew him to be no better than a liberal in disguise, and he had already quarrelled bitterly with him in 1697 when he was trying to eject Leverett. Sewall noted on " Nov.ᴿ 20. . . . Mr. Willard told me of the falling out between the president and him about chusing fellows last Monday. Mr. Mather has sent him word, he will never come to his house more till he give him satisfaction."[2] But they had in reality separated years be-

[1] Sewall's *Diary. Mass. Hist. Coll.* fifth series, vi. 43–45.
[2] *Mass. Hist. Coll.* fifth series, v. 464.

fore ; for when, in the witchcraft terror, Willard was
cried out upon, and had to look a shameful death in
the face, he learned to feel that the men who were
willing to risk their lives to save him were by no
means public enemies. And so, as the vice-president
lived in Boston, the administration of the college was
left very much to Leverett and the Brattles, who were
presently reinstated.

Joseph Dudley was the son of that old governor
who wrote the verses about the cockatrice to be
hatched by toleration, yet he inherited very little of
his father's disposition. He was bred for the ministry, and as the career did not attract him, he turned to
politics, in which he made a brilliant opening. At first
he was the hope of the high churchmen, but they afterward learned to hate him with a rancor exceptional
even toward their enemies. And he gave them only
too good a handle against him, for he was guilty of
the error of selling himself without reserve to the Andros government. At the Revolution he suffered a
long imprisonment, and afterward went to England,
where he passed most of William's reign. There his
ability soon brought him forward, he was made lieutenant-governor of the Isle of Wight, was returned to
Parliament, and at last appointed governor by Queen
Anne. Though Massachusetts owes a deeper debt to
few of her chief magistrates, there are few who have
found scantier praise at the hands of her historians.
He was, it is true, an unscrupulous politician and
courtier, but his mind was broad and vigorous, his

policy wise and liberal, and at the moment of his power his influence was of inestimable value.

Among his other gifts, he was endowed with infinite tact, and when working for his office he managed not only to conciliate the Mathers, but even to induce the son to write a letter in his favor ; and so when he arrived in 1702 they were both sedulous in their attentions in the expectation of controlling him. A month had not passed, however, before this ominous entry was made in the younger's diary : —

"June 16, 1702. I received a visit from Governour Dudley. . . . I said to him . . . I should be content, I would approve it, . . . if any one should say to your excellency, 'By no means let any people have cause to say, that you take all your measures from the two Mr. Mathers.' By the same rule I may say without offence, 'By no means let any people say, that you go by no measures in your conduct, but Mr. Byfield's and Mr. Leverett's.' . . . The WRETCH went unto those men and told them, that I had advised him to be no ways advised by them; and inflamed them into an implacable rage against me." [1]

Leverett, on the contrary, now reached his zenith ; from the house he passed into the council and became one of Dudley's most trusted advisers. The Mathers were no match for these two men, and few routs have been more disastrous than theirs. Lord Bellomont's sudden death had put an end to all hope of obtaining a charter by compromise with England, and no fur-

[1] *Mass. Hist. Coll.* first series, iii. 137.

ther action had been taken, when, on September 12, 1707, Willard died. On the 28th of October the fellows met and chose John Leverett president of Harvard College; and then came a demonstration which proved not only Increase Mather's prescience, when he foretold how a liberal university would kill a disciplined church, but which shows the mighty influence a devoted teacher can have upon his age. Thirty-nine ministers addressed Governor Dudley thus: —

"We have lately, with great joy, understood the great and early care that our brethren, who have the present care and oversight of the college at Cambridge, have taken, . . . by their unanimous choice of Mr. John Leverett, . . . to be the president . . . Your Excellency personally knows Mr. Leverett so well, that we shall say the less of him. However, we cannot but give this testimony of our great affection to and esteem for him; that we are abundantly satisfied . . . of his religion, learning, and other excellent accomplishments for that eminent service, a long experience of which we had while he was senior fellow of that house; for that, under the wise and faithful government of him, and the Rev. Mr. Brattle, of Cambridge, the greatest part of the now rising ministry in New England were happily educated; and we hope and promise ourselves, through the blessing of the God of our fathers, to see religion and learning thrive and flourish in that society, under Mr. Leverett's wise conduct and influence, as much as ever yet it hath done." [1]

[1] *History of Harvard,* i. 504, App. xx.

His salary was only one hundred and fifty pounds a year; but the man worked for love of a great cause, and did not stop to haggle. Nor were he and Dudley of the temper to leave a task half done. Undoubtedly at the governor's instigation, a resolve was introduced into the Assembly reviving the Act of 1650 by which the university had been incorporated, and it is by the sanction of this lawless and masterly feat of statesmanship that Harvard has been administered for almost two hundred years.

Sewall tells how Dudley went out in state to inaugurate his friend. " The gov^r prepar'd a Latin speech for instalment of the president. Then took the president by the hand and led him down into the hall; . . . The gov^r sat with his back against a noble fire. . . . Then the gov^r read his speech . . . and mov'd the books in token of their delivery. Then president made a short Latin speech, importing the difficulties discouraging, and yet that he did accept: . . . Clos'd with the hymn to the Trinity. Had a very good diñer upon 3 or 4 tables. . . . Got home very well. *Laus Deo.*" [1]

Nor did Dudley fail to provide the new executive with fit support. By the old law he had revived the corporation was reduced to seven; of this board Leverett himself was one, and on the day he took his office both the Brattles and Pemberton were also appointed. And more than this, when, a few years later, Pemberton died, the arch-rebel, Benjamin Colman, was

[1] *Mass. Hist. Coll.* fifth series, vi. 209.

chosen in his place. The liberal triumph was complete, and in looking back through the vista of the past, there are few pages of our history more strongly stamped with the native energy of the New England mind than this brilliant capture of Harvard, by which the ancient cradle of bigotry and superstition was made the home of American liberal thought. As for the Mathers, when they found themselves beaten in fair fight, they conceived a revenge so dastardly that Pemberton declared with much emotion he would humble them, were he governor, though it cost him his head. Being unable longer to withstand Dudley by honorable means, they tried to blast him by charging him with felony. Their letters are too long to be reproduced in full; but their purport may be guessed by the extracts given, and to this day they remain choice gems of theocratic morality.

Sir, That I have had a singular respect for you, the Lord knows; but that since your arrival to the government, my charitable expectations have been greatly disappointed, I may not deny. . . .

1st. I am afraid you cannot clear yourself from the guilt of bribery and unrighteousness. . . .

2d. I am afraid that you have not been true to the interest of your country, as God (considering his marvellous dispensations towards you) and his people have expected from you. . . .

3d. I am afraid that you cannot clear yourself from the guilt of much hypocrisy and falseness in the affair of the college. . . .

4th. I am afraid that the guilt of innocent blood is still crying in the ears of the Lord against you. I mean the blood of Leister and Milburn. My Lord Bellamont said to me, that he was one of the committee of Parliament who examined the matter; and that those men were not only murdered, but barbarously murdered. . . .

5th. I am afraid that the Lord is offended with you, in that you ordinarily forsake the worship of God in the holy church to which you are related, in the afternoon on the Lord's day, and after the publick exercise, spend the whole time with some persons reputed very ungodly men. I am sure your father did not so. . . . Would you choose to be with them or such as they are in another world, unto which you are hastening? . . . I am under pressures of conscience to bear a publick testimony without respect of persons. . . . I trust in Christ that when I am gone, I shall obtain a good report of my having been faithful before him. To his mercy I commend you, and remain in him,

Yours to serve,

I. MATHER.[1]

BOSTON, *January* 20, 1707–8.
  To the Governour.

BOSTON, *Jan.* 20, 1707–8.

SIR, There have appeared such things in your conduct, that a just concern for the welfare of your excellency seems to render it necessary, that you should be *faithfully* advised of them. . . . You will

[1] *Mass. Hist. Coll.* first series, iii. 126.

give me leave to write nothing, but in a style, whereof
an ignorant mob, to whom (as well as the General
Assembly) you think fit to communicate what *fragments* you please of my letters, must be *competent
judges*. I must proceed accordingly. . . . I weakly
believed that the wicked and horrid things done before the righteous Revolution, had been heartily repented of; and that the rueful business at New York,
which many illustrious persons . . . called a barbarous
murder, . . . had been considered with such a repentance, as might save you and your family from any further storms of heaven for the revenging of it. . . . Sir,
your *snare* has been that thing, the *hatred* whereof is
most expressly required of the ruler, namely COVET-
OUSNESS. When a governour shall make his government more an engine to enrich himself, than to *be-
friend his country*, and shall by the unhallowed hunger of riches be prevailed withal to do many wrong,
base, dishonourable things; it is a covetousness which
will shut out from the kingdom of heaven; and sometimes the *loss of a government on earth* also is the
punishment of it. . . . The main channel of that covetousness has been the reign of bribery, which you,
sir, have set up in the land, where it was hardly
known, till you brought it in fashion. . . . And there
lie affidavits before the queen and council, which affirm
that you have been guilty of it in very many instances.
I do also know that you have. . . .

Sir, you are sensible that there is a judgment to
come, wherein the glorious Lord will demand, how far

you aimed at serving him in your government; . . . how far you did in your government encourage those that had most of his image upon them, or place your eyes on the wicked of the land. Your *age* and *health*, as well as other circumstances, greatly invite you, sir, to entertain *awful thoughts* of this matter, and solicit the divine mercy through the only sacrifice. . . . Yet if the troubles you brought on yourself should procure your abdication and recess unto a more private condition, and your present *parasites* forsake you, as you *may be sure they will*, I should think it my duty to do you all the good offices imaginable.

Finally, I can forgive and forget injuries; and I hope I am somewhat ready for *sunset ;* the more for having discharged the duty of this letter. . . .

Your humble and faithful servant,

COTTON MATHER.[1]

But these venomous priests had tried their fangs upon a resolute and an able man. Dudley shook them off like vermin.

GENTLEMEN, Yours of the 20th instant I received ; and the contents, both as to the matter and manner, astonish me to the last degree. I must think you have extremely forgot your own station, as well as my character; otherwise it had been impossible to have made such an open breach upon all the laws of decency, honour, justice, and Christianity, as you have

---

[1] *Mass. Hist. Coll.* first series, iii. 128.

done in treating me with an air of superiority and contempt, which would have been greatly culpable towards a Christian of the lowest order, and is insufferably rude toward one whom divine Providence has honoured with the character of your governour. . . .

Why, gentlemen, have you been so long silent? and suffered sin to lie upon me years after years? You cannot pretend any new information as to the main of your charge; for you have privately given your tongues a loose upon these heads, I am well assured, when you thought you could serve yourselves by exposing me. Surely murder, robberies, and other such flaming immoralities were as reprovable then as now. . . .

Really, gentlemen, conscience and religion are things too solemn, venerable, or sacred, to be played with, or made a covering for actions so disagreeable to the gospel, as these your endeavours to expose me and my most faithful services to contempt; nay, to unhinge the government. . . .

I desire you will keep your station, and let fifty or sixty good ministers, your equals in the province, have a share in the government of the college, and advise thereabouts as well as yourselves, and I hope all will be well. . . .

I am your humble servant,

J. DUDLEY.

To the Reverend Doctors Mathers.[1]

[1] *Mass. Hist. Coll.* first series, iii. 135.

CHAPTER X.

THE LAWYERS.

In the age of sacred caste the priest is likewise the law-maker and the judge, and as succeeding generations of ecclesiastics slowly spin the intricate web of their ceremonial code, they fail not to teach the people that their holy ordinances were received of yore from divine lips by some great prophet. This process is beautifully exemplified in the Old Testament: though the complicated ritualism of Leviticus was always reverently attributed to Moses, it was evidently the work of a much later period; for the present purpose, however, its date is immaterial, it suffices to follow the account the scribes thought fit to give in Kings.

Long after the time of Solomon, Josiah one day sent to inquire about some repairs then being made at the Temple, when suddenly, "Hilkiah the high priest said unto Shaphan the scribe, I have found the book of the law in the house of the Lord." And he gave the book to Shaphan.

"And it came to pass, when the king had heard the words of the book . . . he rent his clothes." And he was greatly alarmed for fear of the wrath of the Lord, because their fathers had not hearkened unto the words of this book; as indeed it was impossible they should, since they knew nothing about it. So, to find out what was best to be done, he sent Hilkiah and others to Huldah the prophetess, who told them that the wrath of the Lord was indeed kindled, and he would bring evil unto the land; but, because Josiah's heart had been tender, and he had humbled himself, and rent his clothes, and wept when he had heard what was spoken, he should be gathered into his grave in peace, and his eyes should not see the evil.[1]

Such is an example of the process whereby a compilation of canonical statutes is brought into practical operation by adroitly working upon the superstitious fears of the civil magistrate; at an earlier period the priests administer justice in person.

Eli judged Israel forty years, and Samuel went on circuit all the days of his life; "and he went from year to year in circuit to Bethel, and Gilgal, and Mizpeh, and judged Israel in all those places." [2] But, sooner or later, the time must come when a soldier is absolutely necessary, both to fight foreign enemies and to enforce obedience at home; and then some chief is set up whom the clergy think they can control: thus Samuel anointed Saul to be captain over the Lord's inheritance.[3] So long as the king is submissive to authority all goes well, but any insubordination is promptly punished; and this was the fate of Saul. On one occasion, when he was in difficulty and Samuel happened to be away, he was so rash as to

[1] 2 *Kings* xxii.   [2] 1 *Samuel* iv., vii.   [3] 1 *Samuel* x.

sacrifice a burnt offering himself; his presumption offended the prophet, who forthwith declared that his kingdom should not continue.[1] After this the relations between them went from bad to worse, and it was not long before the priest began to intrigue with David, whom he presently anointed.[2] The end of it was that Saul was defeated in battle, as Samuel's ghost foretold, for not obeying " the voice of the Lord; " and after a struggle between the houses of Saul and David, all the elders of Israel went to Hebron, where David made a league with them, and in return they anointed him king.[3]

Thenceforward, or from the moment when a layman assumed control of the temporal power, the Jewish chronicles teem with the sins and the disasters of those rulers who did not walk in the way of their fathers, or who, in other words, were restive under ecclesiastical dictation.

So long as this period lasts, during which the sovereign is forced to obey the behests of the priesthood, an arbitrary despotism is inevitable; nor can the foundation of equal justice and civil liberty be laid until first the military, and then the legal profession, has become distinct and emancipated from clerical control, and jurisprudence has grown into the recognized calling of a special class.

These phenomena tend to explain the peculiar and original direction taken by legal thought in Massachusetts, for they throw light upon the influences un-

[1] 1 *Samuel* xiii. [2] *Idem,* xvi. [3] 2 *Samuel* v.

der which her first generation of lawyers grew up, whose destiny it was to impress upon her institutions the form they have ever since retained.

The traditions inherited from the theocracy were vicious in the extreme. For ten years after the settlement the clergy and their aristocratic allies stubbornly refused either to recognize the common law or to enact a code; and when at length further resistance to the demands of the freemen was impossible, the Rev. Nathaniel Ward drew up "The Body of Liberties," which, though it perhaps sufficiently defined civil obligations, contained this extraordinary provision concerning crimes : —

"No mans life shall be taken away, no mans honour or good name shall be stayned, no mans person shall be arested, restrayned, banished, dismembred, nor any wayes punished, . . . unlesse it be by virtue or equitie of some expresse law of the country waranting the same, . . . or in case of the defect of a law in any parteculer case by the word of God. And in capitall cases, or in cases concerning dismembring or banishment according to that word to be judged by the Generall Court." [1]

The whole of the subtle policy, whereof this legislation forms a part, well repays attentive study. The relation of the church to the state was not unlike that of Samuel toward Saul, for no public man could withstand its attack, as was demonstrated by the fate of Vane. Much of the story has been told already in

---

[1] *Mass. Hist. Coll.* third series, viii. 216.

describing the process whereby the clergy acquired a substantial ascendency over the executive and legislature, through their command of the constituencies, which it was the labor of their lives to fill with loyal retainers. Nothing therefore remains to be done but to trace the means they employed to invest their order with judicial attributes.

From the outset lawyers were excluded from practice, so the magistrates were nothing but common politicians who were nominated by the priests; thus the bench was not only filled with trusty partisans without professional training or instincts, but also, as they were elected annually, they were practically removable at pleasure should they by any chance rebel. Upon these points there is abundant evidence: " The government was first by way of charter, which was chiefly managed by the preachers, who by their power with the people made all the magistrates & kept them so intirely under obedience, that they durst not act without them. Soe that whensoever anything strange or unusuall was brought before them, they would not determine the matter without consulting the preachers, for should any bee soe sturdy as to presume to act of himself without takeing advice & directions, he might bee sure of it, his magistracy ended with the year. He could bee noe magistrate for them, that was not approved and recommended from the pulpit, & he could expect little recommendation who was not the preacher's most humble servant. Soe they who treated, caressed & presented the preachers most, were the rulers & magistrates among the people." [1]

From the decisions of such a judiciary the only appeal lay to a popular assembly, which could always be manipulated. Obviously, ecclesiastical supervision over the ordinary course of litigation was amply provided for. The adjudication of the more important controversies was reserved; for it was expressly enacted that doubtful questions and the higher crimes should be judged according to the Word of God. This master-stroke resembled Hilkiah's when he imposed his book on Josiah; for on no point of discipline were the ministers so emphatic as on the sacred and absolute nature of their prerogative to interpret the Scriptures; nor did they fail to impress upon the people that it was a sin akin to sacrilege for the laity to dispute their exposition of the Bible.

The deduction to be drawn from these premises is plain. The assembled elders, acting in their advisory capacity, constituted a supreme tribunal of last resort, wholly superior to carnal precedent, and capable of evolving whatsoever decrees they deemed expedient from the depths of their consciousness.[2] The result exemplifies the precision with which a cause operating upon the human mind is followed by its consequence; and the action of this resistless force is painfully apparent in every state prosecution under the Puri-

[1] An Account of the Colonies, etc., Lambeth MSS. Perry's *Historical Collections*, iii. 48.

[2] See Gorton's case, Winthrop, ii. 146.

tan Commonwealth, from Wheelwright's to Margaret Brewster's. The absorption of sacerdotal, political, and juridical functions by a single class produces an arbitrary despotism; and before judges greedy of earthly dominion, flushed by the sense of power, unrestrained by rules of law or evidence, and unopposed by a resolute and courageous bar, trials must become little more than conventional forms, precursors of predetermined punishments.

After a period of about half a century these social conditions underwent radical change, but traditions remained that deeply affected the subsequent development of the people, and produced a marked bent of thought in the lawyers who afterward wrote the Constitution.

At the accession of William III. great progress had been made in the science of colonial government; charters had been granted to Connecticut and Rhode Island in 1662 and 1663, which, except in the survival of the ancient and meaningless jargon of incorporation, had a decidedly modern form. By these regular local representative governments were established with full power of legislation, save in so far as limited by clauses requiring conformity with the law of England; and they served their purpose well, for both were kept in force many years after the Revolution, Rhode Island's not having been superseded until 1843.

The stubborn selfishness of the theocracy led to the adoption of a less liberal policy toward Massachusetts. The nomination of the executive officers was retained

by the crown, and the governor was given very substantial means of maintaining his authority; he could
reject the councillors elected by the Assembly; he appointed the judges and sheriffs with the advice of this
body, whose composition he could thus in a measure
control; he had a veto, and was commander-in-chief.
Appeals to the king in council were also provided
for in personal actions where the matter in difference
exceeded three hundred pounds.

On the other hand, the legislature made all appro-
priations, including those for the salaries of the governor and judges, and was only limited in its capacity
to enact statutes by the clause invariably inserted in
these patents.

This, therefore, is the precise moment when the
modern theory of constitutional limitations first appears defined; distinct from the ancient corporate
precedents. By a combination of circumstances also,
a sufficient sanction for the written law happened to
be provided, thus making the conception complete,
for the tribunal of last resort was an English court
sustained by ample physical force; nevertheless the
great principle of coördinate departments of government was not yet understood, and substantial relief
against legislative usurpation had to be sought in a
foreign jurisdiction. To lawyers of our own time it
is self-evident that the restrictions of an organic code
must be futile unless they are upheld by a judiciary
not only secure in tenure and pay, but removed as far
as may be from partisan passions. This truth, how-

ever, remained to be discovered amid the abuses of the eighteenth century, for the position of the provincial bench was unsatisfactory in the last degree. The justices held their commissions at the king's pleasure, but their salaries were at the mercy of the deputies; they were therefore subject to the caprice of antagonistic masters. Nor was this the worst, for the charter did not isolate the judicial office. Under the theocracy the policy of the clergy had been to suppress the study of law in order to concentrate their own power; hence no training was thought necessary for the magistrate, no politician was considered incompetent to fill the judgment-seat because of ignorance of his duty, and the office-hunter, having got his place by influence, was deemed at liberty to use it as a point of vantage, from whence to prosecute his chosen career. For example, the first chief justice was Stoughton, who was appointed by Phips, probably at the instigation of Increase Mather. As he was bred for the church, he could have had no knowledge to recommend him, and his peculiar qualifications were doubtless family connections and a narrow and bigoted mind; he was also lieutenant - governor, a member of the council, and part of the time commander-in-chief.

Thomas Danforth was the senior associate, who is described by Sewall as "a very good husbandman, and a very good Christian, and a good councillor;" but his reputation as a jurist rested upon a spotless record, he having been the most uncompromising of the high church managers.

Wait Winthrop was a soldier, and was not only in the council, but so active in public life that years afterward, while on the bench, he was set up as a candidate for governor in opposition to Dudley.

John Richards was a merchant, who had been sent to England as agent in 1681, just when the troubles came to a crisis; but the labors by which he won the ermine seem plain enough, for he was bail for Increase Mather when sued by Randolph, and was appointed by Phips. Samuel Sewall was brought up to preach, took to politics on the conservative side, and was regularly chosen to the council.

This motley crew, who formed the first superior court, had but one trait in common: they belonged to the clique who controlled the patronage; and as it began so it continued to the end, for Hutchinson, the last chief justice but one, was a merchant; yet he was also probate judge, lieutenant-governor, councillor, and leader of the Tories. In so intelligent a community such prostitution of the judicial office would have been impossible but for the pernicious tradition that the civil magistrate needed no special training to perform his duty, and was to take his law from those who expounded the Word of God.

And there was another inheritance, if possible, more baleful still. The legislature, under the Puritan Commonwealth, had been the court of last resort, and it was by no means forward to abandon its prerogative. It was consequently always ready to listen to the complaints of suitors who thought themselves

aggrieved by the decisions of the regular tribunals,
and it was fond of altering the course of justice
to make it conform to what the members were
pleased to call equity. This abuse finally took such
proportions that Hutchinson remonstrated vigorously
in a speech to the houses in 1772.

" Much time is usually spent . . . in considering
petitions for new trials at law, for leave to sell the
real estates of persons deceased, by their executors,
or administrators, and the real estates of minors, by
their guardians. All such private business is properly cognizable by the established judicatories. . . .
A legislative body . . . is extremely improper for
such decisions. The polity of the English government seldom admits of the exercise of this executive
and judiciary power by the legislature, and I know of
nothing special in the government of this province, to
give countenance to it." [1]

The disposition to interfere in what did not concern them was probably aggravated by the presence
of judicial politicians in the popular assemblies, who
seem to have been unable to resist the temptation of
intriguing to procure legislation to affect the litigation
before them. But the simplest way to illustrate the
working of the system in all its bearings will be to
give a history of a celebrated case finally taken on appeal to the Privy Council. The cause arose in Connecticut, it is true, but the social condition of the two
colonies was so similar as to make this circumstance
immaterial.

[1] *Mass. State Papers*, 1765–1775, p. 314.

Wait Winthrop,[1] grandson of the first John Winthrop, died intestate in 1717, leaving two children, John, of New London, and Anne, wife of Thomas Lechmere, of Boston. The father intended his son should take the land according to the family tradition, and in pursuance of this purpose he put him in actual possession of the Connecticut property in 1711; but he neglected to make a will.

By the common law of England real estate descended to the eldest son of him who was last seised; but in 1699 the Assembly had passed a statute of distribution, copied from a Massachusetts act, which directed the probate court, after payment of debts, to make a " distribution of . . . all the residue . . . of the real and personal estate by equal portions to and among the children . . . except the eldest son . . . who shall have two shares."

Here, then, at the threshold, the constitutional question had to be met, as to whether the colonial enactment was not in conflict with the restriction in the charter, and therefore void. Winthrop took out letters of administration, and Lechmere became one of the sureties on his bond. There was no disagreement about the personalty, but the son's claim to the land was disputed, though suit was not brought against him till 1723.

The litigation began in Boston, but was soon transferred to New London, where, in July, 1724, Lech-

---

[1] This report of Winthrop *v.* Lechmere is taken from a MS. brief in the possession of Hon. R. C. Winthrop.

mere petitioned for an account. Winthrop forthwith exhibited an inventory of the chattels, and moved that it should be accepted as final; but the judge of probate declined so to rule. Then Lechmere prayed for leave to sue on the bond in the name of the judge. His prayer was granted, and he presently began no less than six actions in different forms.

Much time was consumed in disposing of technicalities, but at length two test cases were brought before the superior court. One, being in substance an action on the bond, was tried on the general issue, and the verdict was for the defendant. The other was a writ of partition, wherein Anne was described as coheir with her brother. It was argued on demurrer to the declaration, and the defendant again prevailed.

Thus, so far as judicial decision could determine private rights to property, Winthrop had established his title; but he represented the unpopular side in the controversy, and his troubles were just beginning. Christopher Christophers was the judge of probate, he was also a justice of the superior court, and a member of the Assembly, of which body the plaintiff's counsel was speaker. In April, 1725, when Lechmere had finally exhausted his legal remedies, he addressed a petition to the legislature, where he had this strong support, and which was not to meet till May, stating the impossibility of obtaining relief by ordinary means, and asking to have one of the judgments set aside and a new trial ordered, in such form as to enable him to maintain his writ of partition, notwithstanding the solemn decision against him by the court of last resort. The defendant in vain protested that no error was alleged, no new evidence produced, nor any matter of equity advanced which might justify interference: the Assembly had determined to sustain the statute of distributions, and it accordingly resolved that in cases of this description relief ought to be given in probate by means of a new grant of administration, to be executed according to the terms of the act.

Winthrop was much alarmed, and with reason, for he saw at once the intention of the legislature was to induce the judges to assume an unprecedented jurisdiction; he therefore again offered his account, which Christophers rejected, and he appealed from the decision. Lechmere also applied for administration on behalf of his wife; and upon his prayer being denied, pending a final disposition of Winthrop's cause, he too went up. In March, 1725–6, final judgment was rendered, the judges holding that both real and personal property should be inventoried. Winthrop thereupon entered his appeal to the Privy Council, whose jurisdiction was peremptorily denied.

From what afterward took place, the inference is that Christophers shrank from assuming alone so great a responsibility as now devolved upon him, and persuaded his brethren to share it with him; for the superior court proceeded to issue letters of administration to Lechmere, and took his bond, drawn to themselves personally, for the faithful performance of his trust. This was a most high-handed usurpation, for

the function of the higher tribunal in these matters
was altogether appellate, it having nothing to do with
such executive business as taking bonds, which was
the province of the judge of probate.

However this may have been, progress was thenceforward rapid.   In April Lechmere produced a sched-
ule of debts, which have at this day a somewhat suspicious look, and when they were allowed, he petitioned the legislature for leave to sell land to pay
them.   Winthrop appeared and presented a remonstrance, which " the Assembly, observing the common
course of justice, and the law of the colony being by
application to the said Assembly, when the judgments
of the superior courts are grievous to any person . . .
dismissed," and immediately passed an act authorizing
the sale, and making the administrators' deed good to
convey a title.

Then Winthrop was so incautious as to make a final
effort: he filed a protest and caution against any illegal
interference with his property pending his appeal, declaring the action already taken to be contrary to the
common and statute law of England, and to the tenor
of the charter.

The Assembly being of the opinion that this protest
" had in it a great show of contempt," caused Winthrop to be arrested and brought to the bar; there he
not only defended his representations as reasonable,
but avowed his determination to lay all these proceedings before the king in council.   " This was treated as
an insolent contemptuous and disorderly behaviour "

in the prisoner, " as declaring himself *coram non ju-
dice*, and putting himself on a par with them, and im-
peaching their authoritys and the charter; and his said
protest was declared to be full of reflections, and to
terrifie so far as in him lay all the authorities established by the charter." So they imprisoned him three
days and fined him twenty pounds for his contemptuous words.

This leading case was afterward elaborately argued
in London, and judgment was entered for Winthrop,
upon the ground that the statute of distribution was
in conflict with the charter and therefore void; but
as Connecticut resolutely refused to abandon its own
policy, the utmost confusion prevailed for seventeen
years regarding the settlement of estates. During all
this time the local government made unremitting efforts to obtain relief, and seems to have used pecuniary as well as legal arguments to effect its purpose; at
all events, it finally secured a majority in the Privy
Council, who reversed Winthrop *v.* Lechmere, in Clark
v. Tousey. The same question was raised in Massachusetts in 1737, in Phillips *v.* Savage, but enough influence was brought to bear to prevent an adverse decision.[1] A possible distinction between the two cases
also lay in the fact that the Massachusetts act had received the royal assent.

The history of this litigation is interesting, not only
as illustrating the defects in provincial justice, but as

[1] *Conn. Coll. Rec.* vii. 191, note ; *Proc. Mass. Hist. Soc.*
1860–62, pp. 64–80, 165–171.

showing the process by which the conception of constitutional limitations became rooted in the minds of
the first generation of lawyers; and in point of fact,
they were so thoroughly impregnated with the theory
as to incline to carry it to unwarrantable lengths.
For example, so justly eminent a counsel as James
Otis, in his great argument on the Writs of Assistance in 1761, solemnly maintained the utterly untenable proposition that an act of Parliament " against
the Constitution is void: an act against natural equity
is void: and if an act of Parliament should be made,
in the very words of this petition, it would be void." [1]
While so sound a man, otherwise, as John Adams wrote,
in 1776, to Mr. Justice Cushing: "You have my
hearty concurrence in telling the jury the nullity of
acts of Parliament. . . . I am determined to die of
that opinion, let the *jus gladii* say what it will." [2]

On looking back at Massachusetts as she was in the
year 1700, permeated with the evil theocratic traditions, without judges, teachers, or books, the mind
can hardly fail to be impressed with the unconquer-
able energy which produced great jurists from such a
soil; and yet in 1725 Jeremiah Gridley graduated from
Harvard, who may fairly be said to have been th
progenitor of a famous race; for long before the Revolution, men like Prat, Otis, and John Adams could
well have held their own before any court of Common
Law that ever sat. Such powerful counsel naturally

[1] Quincy's *Reports*, p. 474.
[2] *Works of J. Adams*, ix. 390.

felt a contempt for the ignorant politicians who for
the most part presided over them, which they took
little pains to hide. Ruggles one day had an aged
female witness who could find no chair and complained to him of exhaustion. He told her to go and
sit on the bench. His honor, in some irritation, calling him to account, he replied: "I really thought
that place was made for old women." Hutchinson
says of himself: "It was an eyesore to some of the
bar to have a person at the head of the law who had
not been bred to it." But he explains with perfect
simplicity how his occupation as chief justice "engaged his attention, and he applied his intervals to
reading the law." [1]

The British supremacy closed with the evacuation
of Boston, and the colony then became an independent state; yet in that singularly homogeneous community, which had always been taught to regard their
royal patents as the bulwark of their liberties, no one
seems to have seriously thought it possible to dispense
with a written instrument to serve as the basis of the
social organization. Accordingly, in 1779, the legislature called a convention to draft a Constitution; and it
was the good fortune of the lawyers, who were chosen
as delegates, to have an opportunity, not only to correct those abuses from which the administration of
justice had so long suffered, but to carry into practical
operation their favorite theory, of the limitation of
legislative power by the intervention of the courts.

[1] *Diary and Letters of Thomas Hutchinson,* p. 66.

The course pursued was precisely what might have
been predicted of the representatives of a progressive
yet sagacious people. Taking the old charter as the
foundation whereon to build, they made only such alterations as their past experience had shown them to
be necessary; they adopted no fanciful schemes, nor
did they lightly depart from a system with which they
were acquainted; and their almost servile fidelity to
their precedent,wherever it could be followed, is shown
by the following extracts relating to the legislative
and executive departments.

And we doe further for vs our heires and successors
give and grant to the said governor and the Great and
Generall Court or Assembly of our said province or
territory for the time being full power and authority
from time to time to make ordaine and establish all
manner of wholsome and reasonable orders laws statutes and ordinances directions and instructions either
with penalties or without (soe as the same be not repugnant or contrary to the lawes of this our realme of
England) as they shall judge to be for the good and
welfare of our said province or territory and for the
gouernment and ordering thereof and of the people
inhabiting or who shall inhabit the same and for the
necessary support and defence of the government
thereof.

CONSTITUTION.

And further, full power and authority are hereby given and granted to the said General Court, from time to time, to make, ordain, and establish, all manner of wholesome and reasonable orders, laws, statutes, and ordinances, directions and instructions, either with penalties or without; so as the same be not repugnant or contrary to this constitution, as they shall judge to be for the good and welfare of this commonwealth, and for the government and ordering thereof, and of the subjects of the same, and for the necessary support and defence of the government thereof.

CHARTER.

The governour of our said province for the time being shall have authority from time to time at his discretion to assemble and call together the councillors or assistants of our said province for the time being and that the said governour with the said assistants or councillors or seaven of them at the least shall and may from time to time hold and keep a councill for the ordering and directing the affaires of our said province.

CONSTITUTION.

The governour shall have authority, from time to time at his discretion, to assemble and call together the councillors of this commonwealth for the time being; and the governour, with the said councillors, or five of them at least, shall, and may, from time to time, hold and keep a council, for the ordering and directing the affairs of the commonwealth, agreeably to the constitution and the laws of the land.

The clause concerning the council is curious as an instance of the survival of an antiquated form. In the province the body had a use, for it was a regular upper chamber; but when, in 1779, a senate was added, it became an anomalous and meaningless third house; yet it is still regularly elected, though its inutility is obvious. So long ago as 1814 John Adams had become very tired of it; he then wrote: " This constitution, which existed in my handwriting, made the governor annually elective, gave him the executive power, shackled with a council, that I now wish was annihilated." [1]

On the other hand, the changes made are even more . interesting, as an example of the evolution of institutions. The antique document was simplified by an orderly arrangement and division into sections; the obsolete jargon of incorporation was eliminated, which had come down from the mediæval guilds; in the dispute with England the want of a bill of rights had been severely felt, so one was prefixed; and then the convention, probably out of regard to symmetry, blotted their otherwise admirable work by creating an unnecessary senate. But viewed as a whole, the grand original conception contained in this instrument, making it loom up a landmark in history, is the

[1] *Works of J. Adams*, vi. 465.

theory of the three coördinate departments in the administration of a democratic commonwealth, which has ever since been received as the corner-stone of American constitutional jurisprudence.

Though this assertion may at first sight seem too sweeping, it is borne out by the facts. During the first sessions of the Continental Congress no question was more pressing than the reorganization of the colonies should they renounce their allegiance to the crown, nor was there one in regard to which the majority of the delegates were more at sea. From their peculiar education the New Englanders were exceptions to the general rule, and John Adams in particular had thought out the problem in all its details. His conversation so impressed some of his colleagues that he was asked to put his views in a popular form. His first attempt was a short letter to Richard Henry Lee, in November, 1775, in which he starts with this proposition as fundamental : "A legislative, an executive, and a judicial power comprehend the whole of what is meant and understood by government. It is by balancing each of these powers against the other two, that the efforts in human nature towards tyranny can alone be checked and restrained, and any degree of freedom preserved in the constitution." [1]

His next tract, written in 1776 at the request of Wythe of Virginia, was printed and widely circulated, and similar communications were sent in reply to applications from New Jersey, North Carolina, and pos-

[1] *Works of J. Adams,* iv. 186.

sibly other States. The effect of this discussion is apparent in all of the ten constitutions afterward drawn, with the exception of Pennsylvania's, which was a failure; but none of them passed beyond the tentative or embryonic stage. It therefore remained for Massachusetts to present the model, which in its main features has not yet been superseded.

A first attempt was deservedly rejected by the people, and the work was not done until 1779; but the men who then met in convention at Cambridge knew precisely what they meant to do. Though the executive and the legislature were a direct inheritance, needing but little change, a deep line was drawn between the three departments, and the theory of the coördinate judiciary was first brought to its maturity within the jurisdiction where it had been born. To attain this cherished object was the chief labor of the delegates, for to the supreme court was to be intrusted the dangerous task of grappling with the representative chambers and enforcing the popular charter. Therefore they made the tenure of the judges permanent; they secured their pay; to obtain impartiality they excluded them from political office; while on the other hand they confined the legislature within its proper sphere, to the end that the government they created might be one of laws and not of men.

The experiment has proved one of those memorable triumphs which mark an era. Not only has the great conception of New England been accepted as the fundamental principle of the Federal Union, but it has been adopted by every separate State; and more than this, during the one hundred and six years since the people of our Commonwealth wrote their Constitution, they have had as large a measure of liberty and safety under the law as men have ever known on earth. There is no jurisdiction in the world where justice has been purer or more impartial; nor, probably, has there ever been a community, of equal numbers, which has produced more numerous or more splendid specimens of juridical and forensic talent.

When freed from the incubus of the ecclesiastical oligarchy the range of intellectual activity expanded, and in 1780 Massachusetts may be said, without exaggeration, to have led the liberal movement of the world; for not only had she won almost in perfection the three chief prizes of modern civilization, liberty of speech, toleration, and equality before the law; but she had succeeded in formulating those constitutional doctrines by which, during the nineteenth century, popular self-government has reached the highest efficiency it has ever yet attained.

A single example, however, must suffice to show what the rise of the class of lawyers had done for individual security and liberty in that comparatively short interval of ninety years.

Theocratic justice has been described; the trials of Wheelwright, and of Anne Hutchinson, of Childe, of Holmes, and of Christison have been related; and also the horrors perpetrated before that ghastly tribunal of untrained bigots, which condemned the miserable witches undefended and unheard.[1] For the honor of our Commonwealth let the tale be told of a state prosecution after her bar was formed.

In 1768 the British Ministry saw fit to occupy Boston with a couple of regiments, a force large enough to irritate, but too small to overawe, the town. From the outset bad feeling prevailed between the citizens and the soldiers, but as the time went on the exasperation increased, and early in 1770 that intense passion began to glow which precedes the outbreak of civil war. Yet though there were daily brawls, no blood was shed until the night of the 5th of March, when a rabble gathered about the sentry at the custom-house in State Street. He became frightened and called for help, Captain Preston turned out the guard, the mob pelted them, and they fired on the people without warning. A terrific outbreak was averted by a species of miracle, but the troops had to be withdrawn, and Preston and his men were surrendered and indicted for murder.

John Adams, who was a liberal, heart and soul, had just come into leading practice. His young friend

[1] In England, throughout the eighteenth century, counsel were allowed to speak in criminal trials, in cases of treason and misdemeanor only. . Nor is the conduct of Massachusetts in regard to witches peculiar. Parallel atrocities might probably be adduced from the history of every European nation, even though the procedure of the courts were more regular than was that of the Commission of Phips. The relation of the priest to the sorcerer is a most interesting phenomenon of social development; but it would require a treatise by itself.

Josiah Quincy was even more deeply pledged to the popular cause. On the morning after the massacre, Preston, doubtless at Hutchinson's suggestion, sent Adams a guinea as a retaining fee, which, though it seemed his utter ruin to accept, he did not dream of refusing. What Quincy went through may be guessed from his correspondence with his father.

BRAINTREE, *March* 22, 1770.

MY DEAR SON, I am under great affliction at hearing the bitterest reproaches uttered against you, for having become an advocate for those criminals who are charged with the murder of their fellow-citizens. Good God! Is it possible? I will not believe it.

Just before I returned home from Boston, I knew, indeed, that on the day those criminals were committed to prison, a sergeant had inquired for you at your brother's house; but I had no apprehension that it was possible an application would be made to you to undertake their defence. Since then I have been told that you have actually engaged for Captain Preston; and I have heard the severest reflections made upon the occasion, by men who had just before manifested the highest esteem for you, as one destined to be a saviour of your country. I must own to you, it has filled the bosom of your aged and infirm parent with anxiety and distress, lest it should not only prove true, but destructive of your reputation and interest;

and I repeat, I will not believe it, unless it be confirmed by your own mouth, or under your own hand.

> Your anxious and distressed parent,
>
> JOSIAH QUINCY.

BOSTON, *March* 26, 1770.

HONOURED SIR, I have little leisure, and less inclination, either to know or to take notice of those
ignorant slanderers who have dared to utter their
"bitter reproaches" in your hearing against me, for
having become an advocate for criminals charged with
murder. . . . Before pouring their reproaches into
the ear of the aged and infirm, if they had been
friends, they would have surely spared a little reflection on the nature of an attorney's oath and duty. . . .

Let such be told, sir, that these criminals, charged
with murder, are not yet legally proved guilty, and
therefore, however criminal, are entitled, by the laws
of God and man, to all legal counsel and aid; that
my duty as a man obliged me to undertake; that my
duty as a lawyer strengthened the obligation. . . .
This and much more might be told with great truth;
and I dare affirm that you and this whole people will
one day rejoice that I became an advocate for the
aforesaid "criminals," charged with the murder of
our fellow-citizens.

I never harboured the expectation, nor any great desire, that all men should speak well of me. To enquire
my duty, and to do it, is my aim. . . . When a plan
of conduct is formed with an honest deliberation,

neither murmuring, slander, nor reproaches move. . . . There are honest men in all sects, — I wish their approbation; — there are wicked bigots in all parties, — I abhor them.

I am, truly and affectionately, your son,

JOSIAH QUINCY, JR.[1]

Many of the most respected citizens asserted and believed that the soldiers had fired with premeditated malice, for the purpose of revenge; and popular indignation was so deep and strong that even the judges were inclined to shrink. As Hutchinson was acting governor at the time, the chief responsibility fell on Benjamin Lynde, the senior associate, who was by good fortune tolerably competent. He was the son of the elder Lynde, who, with the exception of Paul Dudley, was the only provincial chief justice worthy to be called a lawyer.

The juries were of course drawn from among those men who afterward fought at Lexington and Bunker Hill, and, like the presiding judge and the counsel, they sympathized with the Revolutionary cause. Yet the prisoners were patiently tried according to the law and the evidence; all that skill, learning, and courage could do for them was done, the court charged impartially, and the verdicts were, Not guilty.

[1] *Memoir of Josiah Quincy, Jr.* pp. 26, 27.

CHAPTER XI.

THE REVOLUTION.

STATUS appears to be that stage of civilization whence advancing communities emerge into the era of individual liberty. In its most perfect development it takes the form of caste, and the presumption is the movement toward caste begins upon the abandonment of a wandering life, and varies in intensity with the environment and temperament of each race, the feebler sinking into a state of equilibrium, when change by spontaneous growth ceases to be perceptible. So long as the brain remains too feeble for sustained original thought, and man therefore lacks the energy to rebel against routine, this condition of existence must continue, and its inevitable tendency is toward rigid distinctions of rank, and as a necessary consequence toward the limitation of the range of ambition, by the conventional lines dividing the occupations of the classes. Such at least in a general way was the progression of the Jews, and in a less marked degree of the barbarians who overran the Roman Empire. Yet even these, when they acquired permanent abodes, gravitated strongly enough toward caste to produce a social system based on monopoly and privilege which lasted through many centuries. On the other hand, the democratic formula of "equality before the law" best defines the modern conception of human relations, and this maxim indicates a tone of thought directly the converse of that which begot status; for whereas the one strove to raise impassable barriers against free competition in the struggle for existence, the ideal of the other is to offer the fullest scope for the expansion of the faculties.

As in Western Europe church and state alike rested upon the customs of the Middle Ages, a change so fundamental must have wrought the overthrow, not only of the vastest vested interests, but of the profoundest religious prejudices, consequently, it could not have been accomplished peaceably; and in point of fact the conservatives were routed in two terrific outbreaks, whereof the second was the sequence of the first, though following it after a considerable interval of time. By the wars of the Reformation freedom of thought was gained; by the revolutions of the eighteenth century, which swept away the incubus of feudalism, liberty of action was won; and as Massachusetts had been colonized by the radicals of the first insurrection, it was not unnatural that their children should have led the second. So much may be readily conceded, and yet the inherited tendency toward liberalism alone would have been insufficient to have inspired the peculiar unanimity of sentiment which animated her people in their resistance to Great Britain, and which perhaps was stronger among her clergy, whose instincts regarding domestic affairs were intensely conservative, than among any other portion of her population. The reasons for this phenomenon are worthy of investigation, for they are not only interesting in themselves, but they furnish an admirable illustration of the irresistible action of antecedent and external causes on the human mind.

Under the Puritan Commonwealth the church gave distinction and power, and therefore monopolized the ability which sought professional life; but under the provincial government new careers were opened, and intellectual activity began to flow in broader channels. John Adams illustrates the effect produced by the changed environment; when only twenty he made this suggestive entry in his Diary: "The following questions may be answered some time or other, namely, — Where do we find a precept in the Gospel requiring Ecclesiastical Synods? Convocations? Councils? Decrees? Creeds? Confessions? Oaths? Subscriptions? and whole cart-loads of other trumpery that we find religion encumbered with in these days?" [1]

Such men became lawyers, doctors, or merchants; theology ceased to occupy their minds; and gradually the secular thought of New England grew to be coincident with that of the other colonies.

Throughout America the institutions favored individuality. No privileged class existed among the whites. Under the careless rule of Great Britain habits of personal liberty had taken root, which

---

[1] *Works of J. Adams,* ii. 5.

showed themselves in the tenacity wherewith the people clung to their customs of self-government; and so long as these usages were respected, under which they had always lived, and which they believed to be as well established as Magna Charta, there were not in all the king's broad dominions more loyal subjects than men like Washington, Jefferson, and Jay.

The generation now living can read the history of the Revolution dispassionately, and to them it is growing clear that our ancestors were technically in the wrong. For centuries Parliament has been theoretically absolute; therefore it might constitutionally tax the colonies, or do whatsoever else with them it pleased. Practically, however, it is self-evident that the most perfect despotism must be limited by the extent to which subjects will obey, and this is a matter of habit; rebellions, therefore, are usually caused by the conservative instinct, represented by the will of the sovereign, attempting to enforce obedience to customs which a people have outgrown.

In 1776, though the Middle Ages had passed, their traditions still prevailed in Europe, and probably the antagonism between this survival of a dead civilization and the modern democracy of America was too deep for any arbitrament save trial by battle. Identically the same dispute had arisen in England the century before, when the commons rebelled against the prerogatives of the crown, and Cromwell fought like Washington, in the cause of individual emancipation; but the movement in Great Britain was too radical for the age, and was followed by a reaction whose force was not spent when George III. came to the throne.

Precedent is only inflexible among stationary races, and advancing nations glory in their capacity for change; hence it is precisely those who have led revolt successfully who have won the brightest fame. If, therefore, it be admitted that they should rank among mankind's noblest benefactors, who have risked their lives to win the freedom we enjoy, and which seems destined to endure, there are few to whom posterity owes a deeper debt than to our early statesmen; nor, judging their handiwork by the test of time, have many lived who in genius have surpassed them. In the fourth article of their Declaration of Rights, the Continental Congress resolved that the colonists " are entitled to a free and exclusive power of legislation in their several provincial legislatures, . . . in all cases of taxation and internal polity, subject only to the negative of their sovereign, in such manner as has been heretofore used and accustomed. But, . . . we cheerfully consent to the operation of such acts of Parliament as are, *bonâ fide*, restrained to the regulation of our external commerce."

In 1778 a statute was passed, of which an English jurist wrote in 1885: "One act, indeed, of the British Parliament might, looked at in the light of history, claim a peculiar sanctity. It is certainly an enactment of which the terms, we may safely predict, will never be repealed and the spirit never be violated. . . . It pro-

vides that Parliament ' will not impose any duty, tax
or assessment whatever, payable in any of his majesty's colonies . . . except only such duties as it may
be expedient to impose for the regulation of commerce.' " [1]

Thus is the memory of their grievance held sacred
by the descendants of their adversaries after the lapse
of a century, and the local self-government for which
they pleaded has become the immutable policy of the
empire. The principles they laid down have been
equally enduring, for they proclaimed the equality of
men before the law, the corner-stone of modern civilization, and the Constitution they wrote still remains
the fundamental charter of the liberties of the republic of the United States.

Nevertheless it remains true that secular liberalism
alone could never have produced the peculiarly acrimonious hostility to Great Britain wherein Massachusetts stood preëminent, whose causes, if traced, will be
found imbedded at the very foundation of her social
organization, and to have been steadily in action ever
since the settlement. Too little study is given to ecclesiastical history, for probably nothing throws so
much light on certain phases of development; and
particularly in the case of this Commonwealth the im-
pulses which moulded her destiny cannot be understood unless the events that stimulated the passions
of her clergy are steadily kept in view.

The early aggrandizement of her priests has been

[1] *The Law of the Constitution*, Dicey, p. 62.

described; the inevitable conflict with the law into which their ambition plunged them, and the overthrow of the theocracy which resulted therefrom, have been related; but the causes that kept alive the old exasperation with England throughout the eighteenth century have not yet been told.

The influence of men like Leverett and Colman tended to broaden the church, but necessarily the process was slow; and there is no lack of evidence that the majority of the ministers had little relish for the toleration forced upon them by the second charter. It is not surprising, therefore, to find the sectaries soon again driven to invoke the protection of the king.

Though doubtless some monastic orders have been vowed to poverty, it will probably be generally conceded that a life of privation has not found favor with divines as a class; and one of the earliest acts of the provincial legislature bid each town choose an able and orthodox minister to dispense the Word of God, who should be "suitably encouraged" by an assessment on all inhabitants without distinction. This was for many years a bitter grievance to the dissenting minority; but there was worse to come; for sometimes the majority were heterodox, when pastors were elected who gave great scandal to their evangelical brethren. Therefore, for the prevention of "atheism, irreligion and prophaness," [1] it was enacted in 1775 that the justices of the county should report any town

[1] *Province Laws,* 1715, c. 17.

without an orthodox minister, and thereupon the General Court should settle a candidate recommended to them by the ordained elders, and levy a special tax for his support. Nor could men animated by the fervent piety which raised the Mathers to eminence in their profession be expected to sit by tamely while blasphemers not only worshipped openly, but refused to contribute to their incomes.

" We expect no other but Satan will show his rage against us for our endeavors to lessen his kingdom of darkness. He hath grievously afflicted me (by God's permission) by infatuating or bewitching three or four who live in a corner of my parish with Quaker notions, [who] now hold a separate meeting by themselves." [1]

The heretics, on their side, were filled with the same stubborn spirit which had caused them " obstinately and proudly " to " persecute " Norton and Endicott in earlier days. In 1722 godly preachers were settled at Dartmouth and Tiverton, under the act, the majority of whose people were Quakers and Baptists ; and the Friends tell their own story in a petition they presented to the crown in 1724 : "That the said Joseph Anthony and John Siffon were appointed assessors of the taxes for the said town of Tiverton, and the said John Akin and said Philip Tabor for the town of Dartmouth, but some of the said assessors being of the people called Quakers, and others of them also

[1] Rev. S. Danforth, 1720. *Mass. Hist. Coll.* fourth series, i. 258.

dissenting from the Presbyterians and Independents, and greatest part of the inhabitants of the said towns being also Quakers or Anabaptists . . . the said assessors duly assessed the other taxes . . . relating to the support of government . . . yet they could not in conscience assess any of the inhabitants of the said towns anything for or towards the maintenance of any ministers.

" That the said Joseph Anthony, John Siffon, John Akin and Philip Tabor, (on pretence of their non-compliance with the said law) were on the 25th of the month called May, 1723, committed to the jail aforesaid, where they still continue prisoners under great sufferings and hardships both to themselves and families, and where they must remain and die, if not relieved by the king's royal clemancy and favour." [1]

A hearing was had upon this petition before the Privy Council, and in June, 1724, an order was made directing the remission of the special taxes and the release of the prisoners, who were accordingly liberated in obedience thereto, after they had been incarcerated for thirteen months.

The blow was felt to be so severe that the convention of ministers the next May decided to convene a synod, and Dr. Cotton Mather was appointed to draw up a petition to the legislature.

" Considering the great and visible decay of piety in the country, and the growth of many miscarriages, which we fear may have provoked the glorious Lord

[1] Gough's *Quakers,* iv. 222, 223.

in a series of various judgments wonderfully to distress us. . . . It is humbly desired that . . . the . . . churches . . . meet by their pastors . . . in a synod, and from thence offer their advice upon. . . . What are the miscarriages whereof we have reason to think the judgments of heaven, upon us, call us to be more generally sensible, and what may be the most evangelical and effectual expedients to put a stop unto those or the like miscarriages." [1]

The " evangelical expedient " was of course to revive the Cambridge Platform; nor was such a scheme manifestly impossible, for the council voted " that the synod . . . will be agreeable to this board, and the reverend ministers are desired to take their own time, for the said assembly; and it is earnestly wished the issue thereof may be a happy reformation." [2] In the house of representatives this resolution was read and referred to the next session.

Meanwhile the Episcopalian clergymen of Boston, in much alarm, presented a memorial to the General Court, remonstrating against the proposed measure; but the council resolved " it contained an indecent reflection on the proceedings of that board," [3] and dismissed it. Nothing discouraged, the remonstrants applied for protection to the Bishop of London, who brought the matter to the attention of the law officers of the crown. In their opinion to call a synod would be " a contempt of his majesty's prerogative," and if

[1] Hutch. *Hist.* 3d ed. ii. 292, note.
[2] Chalmers's *Opinions*, i. 8.   [3] *Idem*, p. 9.

" notwithstanding, . . . they shall continue to hold their assembly, . . . the principal actors therein [should] be prosecuted . . . for a misdemeanour." [1]

Steadily and surely the coil was tightening which was destined to strangle the established church of Massachusetts; but the resistance of the ministers was desperate, and lent a tinge of theological hate to the outbreak of the Revolution. They believed it would be impossible for them to remain a dominant priesthood if Episcopalianism, supported by the patronage of the crown, should be allowed to take root in the land; yet the Episcopalians represented conservatism, therefore they were forced to become radicals, and the liberalism they taught was fated to destroy their power.

Meanwhile their sacred vineyard lay open to attack upon every side. At Boston the royal governors went to King's Chapel and encouraged the use of the liturgy, while an inroad was made into Connecticut from New York. Early in the century a certain Colonel Heathcote organized a regular system of invasion. He was a man eminently fitted for the task, being filled with zeal for the conversion of dissenters. "I have the charity to believe that, after having heard one of our ministers preach, they will not look upon our church to be such a monster as she is represented; and being convinced of some of the cheats, many of them may duly consider of the sin of schism." [2]

" They have abundance of odd kind of laws, to pre-

[1] Chalmers's *Opinions*, p. 13.
[2] *Conn. Church Documents*, i. 12.

vent any dissenting . . . and endeavour to keep the people in as much blindness and unacquaintedness with any other religion as possible, but in a more particular manner the church, looking upon her as the most dangerous enemy they have to grapple withal, and abundance of pains is taken to make the ignorant think as bad as possible of her; and I really believe that more than half the people in that government think our church to be little better than the Papist, and they fail not to improve every little thing against us." [1]

He had little liking for the elders, whom he described as being " as absolute in their respective parishes as the Pope of Rome;" but he felt kindly toward "the passive, obedient people, who dare not do otherwise than obey." [2] He explained the details of his plan in his letters, and though he was aware of the difficulties, he did not despair, his chief anxiety being to get a suitable missionary. He finally chose the Rev. Mr. Muirson, and in 1706 began a series of proselytizing tours. Nevertheless, the clergyman was wroth at the treatment he received.

HONOR'D SIR, I entreat your acceptance of my most humble and hearty thanks for the kind and Christian advice you were pleased to tender me in relation to Connecticut. . . . I know that meekness and moderation is most agreeable to the mind of our blessed Saviour, Christ, who himself was meek and lowly, and would have all his followers to learn that

---

[1] *Conn. Church Documents*, i. 9.   [2] *Idem*, i. 10.

lesson of him. . . . I have duly considered all these things, and have carried myself civilly and kindly to the Independent party, but they have ungratefully resented my love; yet I will further consider the obligations that my holy religion lays upon me, to forgive injuries and wrongs, and to return good for their evil. . . . I desired only a liberty of conscience might be allowed to the members of the National Church of England; which, notwithstanding, they seemed unwilling to grant, and left no means untried, both foul and fair, to prevent the settling the church among them; for one of their justices came to my lodging and forewarned me, at my peril, from preaching, telling me that I did an illegal thing in bringing in new ways among them; the people were likewise threatened with prison, and a forfeiture of £5 for coming to hear me. It will require more time than you will willingly bestow on these lines to express how rigidly and severely they treat our people, by taking their estates by distress, when they do not willingly pay to support their ministers. . . . They tell our people that they will not suffer the house of God to be defiled with idolatrous worship and superstitious ceremonies. . . . They say the sign of the cross is the mark of the beast and the sign of the devil, and that those who receive it are given to the devil. . . .

Honored sir, your most assured friend, . . .

GEO. MUIRSON.

RYE, *9th January,* 1707–8.[1]

---

[1] *Conn. Church Documents,* i. 29.

However, in spite of his difficulties, he was able to boast that " I have . . . in one town, . . . baptized about 32, young and old, and administered the Holy Sacrament to 18, who never received it before. Each time I had a numerous congregation." [1]

The foregoing correspondence was with the secretary of the Society for the Propagation of the Gospel, which had been incorporated in 1701, and had presently afterward appointed Colonel Heathcote as their agent. They could have chosen no more energetic representative, nor was it long before his exertions began to bear fruit. In 1707 nineteen inhabitants of Stratford sent a memorial to the Bishop of London, the forerunner of many to come. " Because by reason of the said laws we are not able to support a minister, we further pray your lordship may be pleased to send one over with a missionary allowance from the honourable corporation, invested with full power, so as that he may preach and we hear the blessed Gospel of Jesus Christ, without molestation and terror." [2]

The Anglican prelates conceived it to be their duty to meddle with the religious concerns of New England; therefore, by means of the organization of the venerable society, they proceeded to plant a number of missions throughout the country, whose missionaries were paid from the corporate funds. Whatever opinion may be formed of the wisdom of a policy certain to exasperate deeply so powerful and so

[1] *Conn. Church Documents,* i. 23.
[2] *Idem,* i. 34.

revengeful a class as the Congregational elders, there can be no doubt the Episcopalians achieved a measure of success, in the last degree alarming, not only among the laity, but among the clergy themselves. Mr. Reed, pastor of Stratford, was the first to go over, and was of course deprived of his parish; his defection was followed in 1722 by that of the rector of Yale and six other ministers; and the Rev. Joseph Webb, who thought the end was near, wrote in deep affliction to break the news to his friends in Boston.

FAIRFIELD, *Oct.* 2, 1722.

REVEREND AND HONOURED SIR, The occasion of my now giving you the trouble of these few lines is to me, and I presume to many others, melancholy enough. You have perhaps heard before now, or will hear before these come to hand, (I suppose) of the revolt of several persons of figure among us unto the Church of England. There's the Rev. Mr. Cutler, rector of our college, and Mr. Daniel Brown, the tutor thereof. There are also of ordained ministers, pastors of several churches among us, the Rev. Messieurs following, viz. John Hart of East Guilford, Samuel Whittlesey of Wallingford, Jared Eliot of Kennelworth, . . . Samuel Johnson of West-Haven, and James Wetmore of North-Haven. They are the most of them reputed men of considerable learning, and all of them of a virtuous and blameless conversation. I apprehend the axe is hereby laid to the root of our civil and sacred enjoyments; and a doleful gap opened for trouble and confusion in our churches. . . . It is a very dark day with us; and we need pity, prayers and counsel.[1]

From the tone in which these tidings were received it is plain that the charity and humility of the golden age of Massachusetts were not yet altogether extinct among her ecclesiastics. The ministers published their "sentiments" in a document beginning as follows: —

"These new Episcopalians have declared their desire to introduce an usurpation and a superstition into the church of God, clearly condemned in the sacred Scriptures, which our loyalty and chastity to our Saviour, obliges us to keep close unto; and a tyranny, from which the whole church, which desires to be reformed, has groaned that it may be delivered. . . . The scandalous conjunction of these unhappy men with the Papists is, perhaps, more than what they have themselves duly considered." [2]   In "A Faithful Relation" of what had happened it was observed: "It has caused some indignation in them," (the people) "to see the vile indignity cast by these cudweeds upon those excellent servants of God, who were the leaders of the flock that followed our Saviour into this wilderness: and upon the ministry of them, and their suc-

[1] Rev. Joseph Webb to Dr. C. Mather. *Mass. Hist. Coll.* second series, ii. 131.

[2] The Sentiments of the Several Ministers in Boston. *Mass. Hist. Coll.* second series, ii. 133.

cessours, in which there has been seen for more than forescore years together, the power and blessing of God for the salvation of many thousands in the successive generations; with a success beyond what any of them which set such an high value on the Episcopal ordination could ever boast of! . . . It is a sensible addition, unto their horrour, to see the horrid character of more than one or two, who have got themselves qualified with Episcopal ordination, . . . and come over as missionaries, perhaps to serve scarce twenty families of such people, in a town of several hundred families of Christians, better instructed than the very missionaries: to think, that they must have no other ministers, but such as are ordained, and ordered by them, who have sent over such tippling sots unto them: instead of those pious and painful and faithful instructors which they are now blessed withal!"[1]

Only three of the converts had the fortitude to withstand the pressure to which they were exposed: Cutler, Johnson, and Brown went to England for ordination; there Brown died of small-pox, but Cutler returned to Boston as a missionary, and as he, too, possessed a certain clerical aptitude for forcible expression, it is fitting he should relate his own experiences: —

"I find that, in spite of malice and the basest arts our godly enemies can easily stoop to, that the interest

[1] "A Faithful Relation of a Late Occurrence." *Mass. Hist. Coll.* second series, ii. 138, 139.

of the church grows and penetrates into the very heart of this country. . . . This great town swarms with them " (churchmen), " and we are so confident of our power and interest that, out of four Parliament-men which this town sends to our General Assembly, the church intends to put up for two, though I am not very sanguine about our success in it. . . . My church grows faster than I expected, and, while it doth so, I will not be mortified by all the lies and affronts they pelt me with. My greatest difficulty ariseth from another quarter, and is owing to the covetous and malicious spirit of a clergyman in this town, who, in lying and villany, is a perfect overmatch for any dissenter that I know ; and, after all the odium that he contracted heretofore among them, is fully reconciled and endeared to them by his falsehood to the church." [1]

Time did not tend to pacify the feud. There was no bishop in America, and candidates had to be sent to England for ordination ; nor without such an official was it found possible to enforce due discipline ; hence the anxiety of Dr. Johnson, and, indeed, of all the Episcopalian clergy, to have one appointed for the colonies was not unreasonable. Nevertheless, the opposition they met with was acrimonious in the extreme, so much so as to make them hostile to the charters themselves, which they thought sheltered their adversaries.

[1] Dr. Timothy Cutler to Dr. Zachary Grey, April 2, 1725. Perry's *Collection*, iii. 663.

" The king, by his instructions to our governor, demands a salary; and if he punishes our obstinacy by vacating our charter, I shall think it an eminent blessing of his illustrious reign." [1]   " As I said, infidelity prevails also among us.   Chubb's and Dr. Clarke's works, etc., do much mischief among us.   One Kent, a dissenting teacher, is now suspended by a council for Arianism and Arminianism, though the latter is grown so venial that it would have been hushed had it not been for the former." [2]

Whitefield came in 1740, and the tumult of the great revival roused fresh animosities.

" When Mr. Whitefield first arrived here the whole town was alarmed. . . . The conventicles were crowded; but he chose rather our Common, where multitudes might see him in all his awful postures; besides that, in one crowded conventicle, before he came in, six were killed in a fright.   The fellow treated the most venerable with an air of superiority.   But he forever lashed and anathematized the Church of England; and that was enough.

" After him came one Tennent, a monster! impudent and noisy, and told them all they were damn'd, damn'd, damn'd!   This charmed them, and in the most dreadful winter that I ever saw, people wallowed in the snow night and day for the benefit of his

[1] Dr. Cutler to Dr. Grey, April 20, 1731. Perry's *Coll.* iii. 672.

[2] Dr. Cutler to Dr. Grey, June 5, 1735. Perry's *Coll.* iii. 674

beastly brayings ; and many ended their days under these fatigues. Both of them carried more money out of these parts than the poor could be thankful for." [1]

The excitement was followed by its natural reaction conversions became numerous, and the unevangelical temper this bred between the rival clergymen is painfully apparent in a correspondence wherein Dr. Johnson became involved. Mr. Gold, the Congregationalist minister of Stratford, whom he called a dissenter, had said of him "that he was a thief, and robber of churches, and had no business in the place ; that his church doors stood open to all mischief and wickedness, and other words of like import." He therefore wrote to defend himself : "As to my having no business here, I will only say that to me it appears most evident that I have as much business here at least as you have, — being appointed by a society in England incorporated by royal charter to provide ministers for the church people in America ; nor does his majesty allow of any establishment here, exclusive of the church, much less of anything that should preclude the society he has incorporated from providing and sending ministers to the church people in these countries." [2] To which Mr. Gold replied : —

As for the pleas which you make for Col. Lewis, and others that have broke away disorderly from our church,

[1] Dr. Cutler to Dr. Grey. Sept. 24, 1743. Perry's *Coll.* iii. 676.

[2] *Life of Dr. Samuel Johnson,* p. 108.

I think there's neither weight nor truth in them; nor do I believe such poor shifts will stand them nor you in any stead in the awful day of account; and as for your saying that as bad as you are yet you lie open to conviction, — for my part I find no reason to think you do, seeing you are so free and full in denying plain matters of fact. . . . I don't think it worth my while to say anything further in the affair, and as you began the controversy against rule or justice, so I hope modesty will induce you to desist; and do assure you that if you see cause to make any more replies, my purpose is, without reading of them, to put them under the pot among my other thorns and there let one flame quench the matter. . . .   Hez. Gold.

Stratford, *July* 21, 1741.[1]

And so by an obvious sequence of cause and effect it came to pass that the clergy were early ripe for rebellion, and only awaited their opportunity. Nor could it have been otherwise. An autocratic priesthood had seen their order stripped of its privileges one by one, until nothing remained but their moral empire over their parishioners, and then at last not only did an association of rival ecclesiastics send over emissaries to steal away their people, but they proposed to establish a bishop in the land. The thought was wormwood. He would be rich, he would live in a palace, he would be supported by the patronage and pomp of the royal governors; the imposing ceremo-

[1] *Life of Dr. Samuel Johnson*, p. 111.

nial would become fashionable; and in imagination they already saw themselves reduced to the humble position of dissenters in their own kingdom. Jonathan Mayhew was called a heretic by his more conservative brethren, but he was one of the ablest and the most acrid of the Boston ministers. He took little pains to disguise his feelings, and so early as 1750 he preached a sermon, which was once famous, wherein he told his hearers that it was their duty to oppose the encroachment of the British prelates, if necessary, by force.

" Suppose, then, it was allowed, in general, that the clergy were a useful order of men; that they ought to be esteemed very highly in love for their work's sake, and to be decently supported by those they serve, ' the laborer being worthy of his reward.' Suppose, further, that a number of reverend and right reverend drones, who worked not; who preached, perhaps, but once a year, and then not the gospel of Jesus Christ, but the divine right of tithes, the dignity of their office as ambassadors of Christ, . . . suppose such men as these, spending their lives in effeminacy, luxury, and idleness; . . . suppose this should be the case, . . . would not everybody be astonished at such insolence, injustice, and impiety ? " [1]   " Civil tyranny is usually small in its beginning, like ' the drop of a bucket,' till at length, like a mighty torrent . . . it bears down all before it. . . . Thus it is as to eccle-

[1] " Discourse concerning Unlimited Submission," Jonathan Mayhew. Thornton's *American Pulpit*, pp. 71, 72.

siastical tyranny also — the most cruel, intolerable,
and impious of any. From small beginnings, ' it ex-
alts itself above all that is called God and that is
worshipped.' People have no security against being
unmercifully priest-ridden but by keeping all imperious bishops, and other clergymen who love to ' lord
it over God's heritage,' from getting their foot into
the stirrup at all. . . . For which reason it becomes
every friend to truth and human kind, every lover of
God and the Christian religion, to bear a part in opposing this hateful monster." [1]

Between these envenomed priests peace was impossible; each year brought with it some new aggression
which added fuel to the flame. In 1763, Mr. Apthorp,
missionary at Cambridge, published a pamphlet, in
answer, as he explained, to " some anonymous libels
which appeared in our newspapers . . . grossly re-
flecting on the society & their missionaries, & in particular on the mission at Cambridge." [2]

By this time the passions of the Congregationalist
divines had reached a point when words seemed hardly
adequate to give them expression. The Rev. Ezra
Stiles wrote to Dr. Mayhew in these terms: —

" Shall we be hushed into silence, by those whose
tender mercies are cruelty ; and who, notwithstanding
their pretence of moderation, wish the subversion of

[1] Preface to " A Discourse concerning Unlimited Submission," Jonathan Mayhew. Thornton's *Amer. Pulpit*, pp. 50, 51.
[2] East Apthorp to the Secretary, June 25, 1763. Perry's
Coll. iii. 500.

our churches, and are combined, in united, steady and vigorous effort, by all the arts of subtlety and intreague, for our ruin ? " [1]

Mr. Stiles need have felt no anxiety, for, according to Mr. Apthorp, "this occasion was greedily seized, . . . by a dissenting minister of Boston, a man of a singular character, of good abilities, but of a turbulent & contentious disposition, at variance, not only with the Church of England, but in the essential doctrines of religion, with most of his own party." [2] He alluded to a tract written by Dr. Mayhew in answer to his pamphlet, in which he reproduced the charge made by Mr. Stiles: "The society have long had a formal design to dissolve and root out all our New-England churches; or, in other words, to reduce them all to the Episcopal form." [3] And withal he clothed his thoughts in language which angered Mr. Caner: —

"A few days after, M.ʳ Apthorpe published the enclosed pamphlet, in vindication of the institution and conduct of the society, which occasioned the ungenteel reflections which your grace will find in D.ʳ Mayhew's pamphlet, in which, not content with the personal abuse of M.ʳ Apthorpe, he has insulted the missions in general, the society, the Church of England, in short, the whole rational establishment, in so dirty a manner, that it seems to be below the character of a gentleman to enter into controversy with him. In

[1] Dr. Ezra Stiles to Dr. Mayhew, 1763. *Life of Mayhew*, p. 246.
[2] East Apthorp to the Secretary. Perry's *Coll.* iii. 500.
[3] *Observations on the Charter, etc. of the Society*, p. 107.

most of his sermons, of which he published a great number, he introduces some malicious invectives against the society or the Church of England, and if at any time the most candid and gentle remarks are made upon such abuse, he breaks forth into such bitter and scurrilous personal reflections, that in truth no one cares to have anything to do with him. His doctrinal principles, which seem chiefly copied from Ld Shaftsbury, Bolingbroke, &c., are so offensive to the generalty of the dissenting ministers, that they refuse to admit him a member of their association, yet they appear to be pleased with his abusing the Church of England." [1]

The Archbishop of Canterbury himself now interfered, and tried to calm the tumult by a candid and dignified reply to Dr. Mayhew, in which he labored to show the harmlessness of the proposed bishopric.

" Therefore it is desired, that two or more bishops may be appointed for them, to reside where his majesty shall think most convenient [not in New England, but in one of the Episcopalian colonies] ; that they may have no concern in the least with any person who do not profess themselves to be of the Church of England, but may ordain ministers for such as do ; . . . and take such oversight of the Episcopal clergy, as the Bishop of London's commissaries in those parts have been empowered to take, and have taken, without offence. But it is not desired in the least that they

[1] Rev. Mr. Caner to the Archbishop of Canterbury, June 8, 1763. Perry's *Coll.* iii. 497, 498.

should hold courts . . . or be vested with any authority, now exercised either by provincial governors or subordinate magistrates, or infringe or diminish any privileges and liberties enjoyed by any of the laity, even of our own communion." [1]

But the archbishop should have known that the passions of rival ecclesiastics are not to be allayed. The Episcopalians had become so exasperated as to want nothing less than the overthrow of popular government. Dr. Johnson wrote in 1763: "Is there then nothing more that can be done either for obtaining bishops or demolishing these pernicious charter governments, and reducing them all to one form in immediate dependence on the king? I cannot help calling them pernicious, for they are indeed so as well for the best good of the people themselves as for the interests of true religion." [2]

The Congregationalists, on the other hand, inflamed with jealousy, were ripe for rebellion. On March 22, 1765, the Stamp Act became law, and the clergy threw themselves into the combat with characteristic violence. Oliver had been appointed distributor, but his house was attacked and he was forced to resign. The next evening but one the rabble visited Hutchinson, who was lieutenant-governor, and broke his windows; and there was general fear of further rioting. In the midst of this crisis on the 25th of Au-

[1] *An Answer to Dr. Mayhew's Observations*, etc. Dr. Secker, p. 51.

[2] *Life of Samuel Johnson*, p. 279.

gust, Dr. Mayhew preached a sermon in the West Meeting-house from the text, "I would they were even cut off which trouble you."[1] That this discourse was in fact an incendiary harangue is demonstrated by what followed. At nightfall on the 26th a fierce mob forced the cellars of the comptroller of the customs, and got drunk on the spirits stored within; then they went on to Hutchinson's dwelling: "The doors were immediately split to pieces with broad axes, and a way made there, and at the windows, for the entry of the mob; which poured in, and filled, in an instant, every room. . . . They continued their possession until daylight; destroyed . . . everything . . . except the walls, . . . and had begun to break away the brick-work."[2] His irreplaceable collection of original papers was thrown into the street; and when a bystander interfered in the hope of saving some of them, "answer was made, that it had been resolved to destroy everything in the house; and such resolve should be carried to effect."[3] Malice so bitter bears the peculiar ecclesiastical tinge, and is explained by the confession of one of the ring-leaders, who, when subsequently arrested, said he had been excited by the sermon, "and that he thought he was doing God service."[4]

The outbreak met with general condemnation, and Dr. Mayhew, who saw he had gone too far, tried to excuse himself : —

[1] *Galatians* v. 12.
[2] Hutch. *Hist.* iii. 124.
[3] *Idem*, p. 125, note.
[4] *Idem*, p. 123.

" SIR, — I take the freedom to write you a few lines, by way of condolence, on account of the almost unparalleled outrages committed at your house last evening; and the great damage which I understand you have suffered thereby. God is my witness, that, from the bottom of my heart, I detest these proceedings; that I am most sincerely grieved at them, and have a deep sympathy with you and your distressed family on this occasion." [1]

Nevertheless, the repeal of the Stamp Act, which pacified the laity, left the clergy as hot as ever; and so early as 1768, when no one outside of the inmost ecclesiastical circle yet dreamed of independence, but when the Rev. Andrew Eliot thought the erection of the bishopric was near, he frankly told Hollis he anticipated war.

" You will see by this pamphlet, how we are cajoled. A colony bishop is to be a more innocent creature than ever a bishop was, since diocesan bishops were introduced to lord it over God's heritage. . . . Can the A-b-p, and his tools, think to impose on the colonists by these artful representations. . . . The people of New England are greatly alarmed; the arrival of a bishop would raise them as much as any one thing. . . . Our General Court is now sitting. I have hinted to some of the members, that it will be proper for them to express their fears of the setting up an hierarchy here. I am well assured a motion will be made to this purpose. . . . I may be mistaken,

[1] Mayhew to Hutchinson. *Life of Mayhew*, p. 420.

but I am persuaded the dispute between Great Britain
and her colonies will never be *amicably* settled. . . .
I sent you a few hasty remarks on the A-b-p's sermon.
. . . I am more and more convinced of the meanness,
art — if he was not in so high a station, I should say,
falsehood — of that Arch-Pr-l-te." [1]

An established priesthood is naturally the firmest
support of despotism; but the course of events made
that of Massachusetts revolutionary. This was a social
factor whose importance it is hard to overestimate; for
though the influence of the elders had much declined
during the eighteenth century, their political power
was still immense; and it is impossible to measure
the degree in which the drift of feeling toward independence would have been arrested had they been
thoroughly loyal. At all events, the evidence tends
to show that it is most improbable the first blood
would have been shed in the streets of Boston had it
been the policy of Great Britain to conciliate the
Congregational Church; if, for example, the liberals
had been forced to meet the issue of taxation upon
a statute designed to raise a revenue for the maintenance of the evangelical clergy. How potent an ally
King George lost by incurring their hatred may be
judged by the devotion of the Episcopalian pastors,
many of whom were of the same blood as their Cal-
vinistic brethren, often, like Cutler and Johnson, converts. They all showed the same intensity of feeling;

[1] Thomas Secker. Andrew Eliot to Thomas Hollis, Jan. 5,
1768. *Mass. Hist. Coll.* fourth series, iv. 422.

all were Tories, not one wavered; and they boasted that they were long able to hold their parishioners in check.

In September, 1765, those of Connecticut wrote to the secretary, " although the commotions and disaffection in this country are very great at present, relative to what they call the imposition of stamp duties, yet . . . the people of the Church of England, in general, in this colony, as we hear, . . . and those, in particular, under our respective charges, are of a contrary temper and conduct; esteeming it nothing short of rebellion to speak evil of dignities, and to avow opposition to this last act of Parliament. . . .

" We think it our incumbent duty to warn our hearers, in particular, of the unreasonableness and wickedness of their taking the least part in any tumult or opposition to his majesty's acts, and we have obvious reasons for the fullest persuasion, that they will steadily behave themselves as true and faithful subjects to his majesty's person and government." [1]

Even so late as April, 1775, Mr. Caner, at Boston, felt justified in making a very similar report to the society : " Our clergy have in the midst of these confusions behaved I think with remarkable prudence. None of them have been hindered from exercising the duties of their office since Mr Peters, tho' many of them have been much threat'ned; and as their people have for the most part remained firm and steadfast in their loyalty and attachment to goverment, the clergy

[1] *Conn. Church Doc.* ii. 81.

feel themselves supported by a conscious satisfaction that their labors have not been in vain." [1]

Nor did they shrink because of danger from setting an example of passive obedience to their congregations. The Rev. Dr. Beach graduated at Yale in 1721 and became the Congregational pastor of Newtown. He was afterward converted, and during the war was forbidden to read the prayers for the royal family; but he replied, "that he would do his duty, preach and pray for the king, till the rebels cut out his tongue." [2]

In estimating the energy of a social force, such as ecclesiasticism, the indirect are often more striking than the direct manifestations of power, and this is eminently true of Massachusetts; for, notwithstanding her ministers had always been astute and indefatigable politicians, their greatest triumphs were invariably won by some layman whose mind they had moulded and whom they put forward as their champion. From John Winthrop, who was the first, an almost unbroken line of these redoubtable partisans stretched down to the Revolution, where it ended with him who is perhaps the most celebrated of all.

Samuel Adams has been called the last of the Puritans. He was indeed the incarnation of those qualities which led to eminence under the theocracy. A rigid Calvinist, reticent, cool, and brave, matchless in intrigue, and tireless in purpose, his cause was always holy, and therefore sanctified the means.

[1] Perry's *Coll.* iii. 579.
[2] *O'Callaghan Documents,* iii. 1053, 8vo ed.

Professor Hosmer thus describes him: "It was, however, as a manager of men that Samuel Adams was greatest. Such a master of the methods by which a town-meeting may be swayed, the world has never seen. On the best of terms with the people, the ship-yard men, the distillers, the sailors, as well as the merchants and ministers, he knew precisely what springs to touch. He was the prince of canvassers, the very king of the caucus, of which his father was the inventor. . . . As to his tact, was it ever surpassed?"[1] A bigot in religion, he had the flexibility of a Jesuit; and though he abhorred Episcopalians, he proposed that Mr. Duché should make the opening prayer for Congress, in the hope of soothing the southern members. Strict in all ceremonial observances, he was loose in money matters; yet even here he stood within the pale, for Dr. Cotton Mather was looser,[2] who was the most orthodox of divines.

The clergy instinctively clave to him, and gave him their fullest confidence. When there was any important work to do they went to him, and he never failed them. On January 5, 1768, the Rev. Dr. Eliot told Hollis he had suggested to some of the members of the legislature to remonstrate against the bishops.[3] A week later the celebrated letter of instructions of the house to the agent, De Berdt, was reported, which was written by Adams; and it is interesting to ob-

[1] Hosmer's *Samuel Adams*, p. 363.
[2] See Letter on behalf of Dr. Cotton Mather to Sewall, *Mass. Hist. Coll.* fourth series, ii. 122.
[3] *Mass. Hist. Coll.* fourth series, iv. 422.

serve how, in the midst of a most vigorous protest on the subject, he broke out: " We hope in God such an establishment will never take place in America, and we desire you would strenuously oppose it." [1]

The subtle but unmistakable flavor of ecclesiasticism pervades his whole long agitation. He handled the newspapers with infinite skill, and the way in which he used the toleration granted the Canadian Catholics after the conquest, as a goad wherewith to inflame the dying Puritan fanaticism, was worthy of St. Ignatius. He moved for the committee who reported the resolutions of the town of Boston in 1772; his spirit inspired them, and in these also the grievance of Episcopacy plays a large part. How strong his prejudices were may be gathered from a few words: " We think therefore that every design for establishing . . . a bishop in this province, is a design both against our civil and religious rights." [2]

The liberals, as loyal subjects of Great Britain, grieved over her policy as the direst of misfortunes, which indeed they might be driven to resist, but which they strove to modify.

Washington wrote in 1774: " I am well satisfied, . . . that it is the ardent wish of the warmest advocates for liberty, that peace and tranquillity, upon constitutional grounds, may be restored, and the horrors of civil discord prevented." [3]   Jefferson affirmed:

[1] *Mass. State Papers*, 1765–1775, p. 132.

[2] *Votes and Proceedings of Boston*, Nov. 20, 1772, p. 28.

[3] Washington to Mackenzie. *Washington's Writings*, ii. 402.

" Before the commencement of hostilities . . . I never had heard a whisper of a disposition to separate from Great Britain; and after that, its possibility was contemplated with affliction by all." While John Adams solemnly declared: " For my own part, there was not a moment during the Revolution, when I would not have given everything I possessed for a restoration to the state of things before the contest began, provided we could have had a sufficient security for its continuance." [1]

In such feelings Samuel Adams had no share. In each renewed aggression he saw the error of his natural enemy, which brought ever nearer the realization of the dream of independence he had inherited from the past; for the same fierce passion burned within him that had made Endicott mutilate his flag, and Leverett read his king's letter with his hat on; and the guns of Lexington were music in his ears.

He was not a lawyer, nor a statesman, in the true meaning of the word, but he was a consummate agitator; and if this be remembered, his career becomes clear. When he conceived the idea of the possibility of independence is uncertain; probably soon after the passage of the Stamp Act, but the evidence is strong that so early as 1768 he had deliberately resolved to precipitate some catastrophe which would make reconciliation impossible, and obviously an armed collision would have suited his purpose best.

Troops were then first ordered to Boston, and at

[1] Note of Sparks, *Washington's Writings*, ii. 501.

one moment he was tempted to cause their landing to be resisted.   An old affidavit is still extant, presumably truthful enough, which brings him vividly before the mind as he went about the town lashing up the people.

" Mr. Samuel Adams . . . happened to join the same party . . . trembling and in great agitation. . . . The informant heard the said Samuel Adams then say . . . 'If you are men, behave like men. Let us take up arms immediately, and be free, and seize all the king's officers. We shall have thirty thousand men to join us from the country.' . . . And before the arrival of the troops . . . at the house of the informant . . . the said Samuel Adams said : ' We will not submit to any tax, nor become slaves. . . . The country was first settled by our ancestors, therefore we are free and want no king.' . . . The informant further sayeth, that about a fortnight before the troops arrived, the aforesaid Samuel Adams, being at the house of the informant, the informant asked him what he thought of the times. The said Adams answered, with great alertness, that, on lighting the beacon, we should be joined with thirty thousand men from the country with their knapsacks and bayonets fixed, and added, ' We will destroy every soldier that dare put his foot on shore. His majesty has no right to send troops here to invade the country, and I look upon them as foreign enemies ! ' " [1]

Maturer reflection must have convinced him his

[1] Wells's *Samuel Adams,* i. 210, 211.

design was impracticable, for he certainly abandoned it, and the two regiments disembarked in peace ; but their position was unfortunate. Together they were barely a thousand strong, and were completely at the mercy of the populous and hostile province they had been sent to awe.

The temptation to a bold and unscrupulous revolutionary leader must have been intense. Apparently it needed but a spark to cause an explosion ; the rabble of Boston could be fierce and dangerous when roused, as had been proved by the sack of Hutchinson's house ; and if the soldiers could be goaded into firing on the citizens, the chances were they would be annihilated in the rising which would follow, when a rupture would be inevitable. But even supposing the militia abstained from participating in the outbreak, and the tumult were suppressed, the indignation at the slaughter would be deep enough to sustain him in making demands which the government could not grant.

Hutchinson and the English officers understood the danger, and for many months the discipline was exemplary, but precautions were futile. Though he knew full well how to be all things to all men, the natural affiliations of Samuel Adams were with the clergy and the mob, and in the ship-yards and rope-walks he reigned supreme. Nor was he of a temper to shrink from using to the utmost the opportunity his adversaries had put in his hands, and he forthwith began a series of inflammatory appeals in the newspapers, whereof this is a specimen : " And are the inhabitants

of this town still to be affronted in the night as well
as the day by soldiers arm'd with muskets and fix'd
bayonets? . . . Will the spirits of people, as yet
unsubdued by tyranny, unaw'd by the menaces of
arbitary power, submit to be govern'd by military
force?"[1]

In 1770 it was notorious that "endeavors had been
systematically pursued for many months, by certain
busy characters, to excite quarrels, rencounters, and
combats, single or compound, in the night, between
the inhabitants of the lower class and the soldiers,
and at all risks to enkindle an immortal hatred between them."[2] And it is curious to observe how the
British always quarrelled with the laborers about
the wharves; and how these, the closest friends of
Adams, were all imbued with the theory he maintained, that the military could not use their weapons
without the order of a civil magistrate. Little by
little the animosity increased, until on the 2d of
March there was a very serious fray at Gray's rope-
walk, which was begun by one of the hands, who
knocked down two soldiers who spoke to him in the
street. Although Adams afterward labored to convince the public that the tragedy which happened
three days later was the result of a deliberately matured conspiracy to murder the citizens for revenge,
there is nothing whereon to base such a charge; on
the contrary, the evidence tends to exonerate the

[1] Vindex, *Boston Gazette*, Dec. 5, 1768.
[2] Autobiography of John Adams. *Works of J. Adams*, ii. 229.

troops, and the verdicts show the opinion of the juries. There was exasperation on both sides, but the
rabble were not restrained by discipline, and on the
night of the 5th of March James Crawford swore he
he saw at Calf's corner " about a dozen with sticks, in
Quaker Lane and Green's Lane, met many going toward King Street. Very great sticks, pretty large
cudgells, not common walking canes. . . . At Swing
bridge the people were walking from all quarters with
sticks. I was afraid to go home, . . . the streets in
such commotion as I hardly ever saw in my life. Uncommon sticks such as a man would pull out of an
hedge. . . . Thomas Knight at his own door, 8 or
10 passed with sticks or clubs and one of them said
'D—n their bloods, let us go and attack the main
guard first.'" [1] The crown witnesses testified that
the sentry was surrounded by a crowd of thirty or
forty, who pelted him with pieces of ice "hard and
large enough to hurt any man; as big as one's fist."
And he said " he was afraid, if the boys did not
disperse, there would be " trouble.[2] When the guard
came to his help the mob grew still more violent,
yelling " bloody backs," " lobster scoundrels," " damn
you, fire ! why don't you fire? " striking them with
sticks.

" Did you observe anybody strike Montgomery, or
was a club thrown? The stroke came from a stick
or club that was in somebody's hand, and the blow

---

[1] Kidder's *Massacre*, p. 10.
[2] *Idem*, p. 138.

struck his gun and his arm." "Was he knocked
down? . . . He fell, I am sure. . . . His gun flew
out of hand, and as he stooped to take it up, he fell
himself. . . . Was any number of people standing
near the man that struck his gun? Yes, a whole
crowd, fifty or sixty." [1] When the volley came at last
the rabble fell back, and the 29th was rapidly formed
before the main guard, the front rank kneeling, that
the fire might sweep the street. And now when every
bell was tolling, and the town was called to arms,
and infuriated men came pouring in by thousands,
Hutchinson showed he had inherited the blood of his
great ancestress, who feared little upon earth; but
then, indeed, their adversaries have seldom charged
the Puritans with cowardice in fight. Coming quickly
to the council chamber he passed into the balcony,
which overhung the kneeling regiment and the armed
and maddened crowd, and he spoke with such calmness and courage that even then he was obeyed. He
promised that justice should be done and he commanded the people to disperse. Preston and his men
were at once surrendered to the authorities to await
their trial.

The next day Adams was in his glory. The meeting in the morning was as wax between his fingers,
and his friend, the Rev. Dr. Cooper, opened it with
fervent prayer. A committee was at once appointed
to demand the withdrawal of the troops, but Hutchinson thought he had no power and that Gage alone

[1] Kidder's *Massacre*, pp. 138, 139.

could give the order. Nevertheless, after a conference with Colonel Dalrymple he was induced to propose that the 29th should be sent to the Castle, and the 14th put under strict restraint.[1] To the daring agitator it seemed at last his hour was come, for the whole people were behind him, and Hutchinson himself says "their spirit" was "as high as was the spirit of their ancestors when they imprisoned Andros." As the committee descended the steps of the State House to go to the Old South where they were to report, the dense crowd made way for them, and Samuel Adams as he walked bare-headed through their lines continually bowed to right and left, repeating the catchword, "Both regiments or none." His touch on human passions was unerring, for when the lieutenant-governor's reply was read, the great assembly answered with a mighty shout, "Both regiments or none," and so instructed he returned. Then the nature of the man shone out; the handful of troops were helpless, and he was as inflexible as steel. The thin, strong, determined, gray-eyed Puritan stood before Hutchinson, inwardly exulting as he marked his features change under the torture. "A multitude highly incensed now wait the result of this application. The voice of ten thousand freemen demands that both regiments be forthwith removed. . . . Fail not then at your peril to comply with this requisition!"[2] It was the spirit of Norton and of Endicott

[1] Kidder's *Massacre*, p. 43.
[2] Hosmer's *Samuel Adams*, p. 173.

alive again, and he was flushed with the same stern
triumph at the sight of his victim's pain: "It was
then, if fancy deceived me not, I observed his knees
to tremble. I thought I saw his face grow pale (and
I enjoyed the sight)." [1]

Probably nothing prevented a complete rupture but
the hopeless weakness of the garrison, for Hutchinson,
feeling the decisive moment had come, was full of
fight. He saw that to yield would destroy his authority, and he opposed concession, but he stood alone, the
officers knew their position was untenable, and the
council was unanimous against him. "The L[t] G. endeavoured to convince them of the ill consequence of
this advice, and kept them until late in the evening,
the people remaining assembled; but the council were
resolute. Their advice, therefore, he communicated
to Co[l] Dalrymple, accompanied with a declaration,
that he had no authority to order the removal of the
troops. This part Col. D. was dissatisfied with, and
urged the L[t] G. to withdraw it, but he refused, and
the regiments were removed. He was much distressed, but he brought it all upon himself by his offer
to remove one of the regiments. No censure, however,
was passed upon him." [2]

Had the pacification of his country been the object
near his heart, Samuel Adams, after his victory, would
have abstained from any act however remotely tending to influence the course of justice; for he must

[1] Adams to Warren. Wells's *Samuel Adams,* i. 324.
[2] *Diary and Letters of T. Hutchinson,* p. 80.

have known that it was only by such conduct the colonists could inspire respect for the motives which actuated them in their resistance. A capital sentence would have been doubly unfortunate, for had it been executed it would have roused all England; while had the king pardoned the soldiers, as assuredly he would have done, a deep feeling of wrong would have rankled in America.

A fanatical and revolutionary demagogue, on the other hand, would have longed for a conviction, not only to compass his ends as a politician, but to glut his hate as a zealot.

Samuel Adams was a taciturn, secretive man, whose tortuous course would have been hard to follow a century ago; now the attempt is hopeless. Yet there is one inference it seems permissible to draw: his admirers have always boasted that he was the inspiration of the town meetings, presumably, therefore, the the votes passed at them may be attributed to his manipulation. And starting from this point, with the help of Hutchinson and his own writings, it is still possible to discern the outlines of a policy well worthy of a theocratic statesman.

The March meeting began on the 12th. On the 13th it was resolved : —

" That —— be and they hereby are appointed a committee for and in behalf of the town to find out who those persons are that were the perpetrators of the horred murders and massacres done and committed in King Street on several of the inhabitants in the evening of the 5th instant and take such examinations and depositions as they can procure, and lay the whole thereof before the grand inquest in order that such perpetrators may be indicted and brought to tryal for the same, and upon indictments being found, said committee are desired to prepare matters for the king's attorney, to attend at their tryals in the superior court, subpœna all the witnesses, and do everything necessary for bringing those murtherers to that punishment for such crimes, as the laws of God and man require." [1]

A day or two afterward a number of Adams's friends, among whom were some of the members of this committee, dined together, and Hutchinson tells what he persuaded them to do.

" The time for holding the superior court for the county of Suffolk was the next week after the tragical action in King Street. Although bills were found by the grand jury, yet the court, considering the disordered state of the town, had thought fit to continue the trials over to the next term, when the minds of people would be more free from prejudice." " A considerable number of the most active persons in all publick measures of the town, having dined together, went in a body from table to the superior court then sitting, and Mr. Adams, at their head and in behalf of the town, pressed the bringing on the trial the same term with so much spirit, that the judges did not think it advisable to abide by their own

[1] *Records of Boston*, v. 232.

order, but appointed a day for the trials, and adjourned the court for that purpose." [1]

The justices must afterward have grown ashamed of their cowardice, for Rex *v.* Preston did not come on until the autumn, and altogether very little was accomplished by these attempts to interfere with the due administration of the law. " A committee had been appointed by the town to assist in the prosecution of the soldiers . . . but this was irregular. The courts, according to the practice in the province, required no prosecutors but the officers of the crown ; much less would they have thought it proper for the principal town in the province to have brought all its weight, which was very great, into court against the prisoners." [2]

Nevertheless, Adams had by no means exhausted his resources, for it was possible so to inflame the public mind that dispassionate juries could hardly be obtained.

At the same March meeting another committee was named, who were to obtain a " particular account of all proceedings relative to the massacre in King Street on Monday night last, that a full and just representation may be made thereof ? " [3] The reason assigned for so unwonted a proceeding as the taking of *ex parte* testimony by a popular assembly concerning alleged murders, for which men were to be pres-

[1] Hutch. *Hist.* iii. 285, 286 and note.
[2] *Idem*, iii. 286, note.
[3] Kidder's *Massacre*, p. 23.

ently tried for their lives, was the necessity for con-
troverting the aspersions of the British officials; but
the probable truth of this explanation must be judged
by the course actually pursued. On the 19th the report was made, consisting of "A Short Narrative
of the Horrid Massacre in Boston," together with a
number of depositions; and though perhaps it was
natural, under the circumstances, for such a pamphlet
to have been highly partisan, it was unnatural for its
authors to have assumed the burden of proving that a
deliberately planned conspiracy had existed between
the civilians and the military to murder the citizens;
especially as this tremendous charge rested upon no
better foundation than the fantastic falsehoods of "a
French boy, whose evidence appeared to the justice
so improbable, and whose character was so infamous,
that the justice, who was one of the most zealous in
the cause of liberty, refused to issue a warrant to
apprehend his master, against whom he swore." [1]
"Then I went up to the custom-house door and
knocked, . . . I saw my master and Mr. Munroe come
down-stairs, and go into a room; when four or five
men went up stairs, pulling and hauling me after
them. . . . When I was carried into the chamber, there
was but one light in the room, and that in the corner
of the chamber, when I saw a tall man loading a gun
(then I saw two guns in the room) . . . there was a
number of gentlemen in the room. After the gun was
loaded, the tall man gave it to me, and told me to fire.

[1] Hutch. *Hist.* iii. 279, 280.

and said he would kill me if I did not; I told him I would not. He drawing a sword out of his cane, told me, if I did not fire it, he would run it through my guts. The man putting the gun out of the window, it being a little open, I fired it sideway up the street; the tall man then loaded the gun again. . . . I told him I would not fire again ; he told me again, he would run me through the guts if I did not. Upon which I fired the same way up the street. After I fired the second gun, I saw my master in the room ; he took a gun and pointed it out of the window; I heard the gun go off. Then a tall man came and clapped me on the shoulders above and below stairs, and said, that 's my good boy, I 'll give you some money to-morrow. . . . And I ran home as fast as I could, and sat up all. night in my master's kitchen. And further say, that my master licked me the next night for telling Mrs. Waldron about his firing out of the custom-house. And for fear that I should be licked again, I did deny all that I said before Justice Quincy, which I am very sorry for.[1] . . .

his

" CHARLOTTE + BOURGATE."

mark.

While it is inconceivable that a cool and sagacious politician, whose object was to convince Parliament of the good faith of Massachusetts, should have relied upon such incredible statements to sway the minds of English statesmen and lawyers, it is equally incon-

[5] Kidder's *Massacre*, p. 82. Deposition 58.

ceivable he should not have known they were admirably adapted to still further exasperate an already excited people; and that such was his purpose must be inferred from the immediate publication of the substance of this affidavit in the newspapers.[1]

Without doubt a vote was passed on the 26th of March, a week after the committee had presented their report, desiring them to reserve all the printed copies not sent to Europe, as their distribution might tend to bias the juries; but even had this precaution been observed, it came too late, for the damage was done when the Narrative was read in Faneuil Hall; in fact, however, the order was eluded, for " many copies, notwithstanding, got abroad, and some of a second edition were sent from England, long before the trials of the officer and soldiers came on." [2] And at this cheap rate a reputation for magnanimity was earned.

How thoroughly the clergy sympathized with their champion appears from their clamors for blood. As the time drew near it was rumored Hutchinson would reprieve the prisoners, should they be convicted, till the king's pleasure could be known. Then Dr. Chauncy, the senior minister of Boston, cried out in his pulpit: " Surely he would not counteract the operation of the law, both of God and of man! Surely he would not suffer the town and land to lie under the defilement of blood! Surely he would not make

[1] *Boston Gazette*, March 19, 1770.
[2] Hutch. *Hist.* iii. 279.

himself a partaker in the guilt of murder, by putting a stop to the shedding of their blood, who have murderously spilt the blood of others ! " [1]

Adams attended when the causes were heard and took notes of the evidence; and one of the few occasions in his long life on which his temper seems to have got beyond control was when the accused were acquitted. His writings betray unmistakable chagrin; and nothing is more typical of the man, or of the clerical atmosphere wherein he had been bred, than his comments upon the testimony on which the lives of his enemies hung. His piety caused him to doubt those whose evidence was adverse to his wishes, though they appeared to be trying to speak the truth. " The credibility of a witness perhaps cannot be impeach'd in court, unless he has been convicted of perjury: but an immoral man, for instance one who will commonly prophane the name of his maker, certainly cannot be esteemed of equal credit by a jury, with one who fears to take that sacred name in vain: It is impossible he should in the mind of any man." [2]

And yet this rigid Calvinist, this incarnation of ecclesiasticism, had no scruple in propagating the palpable and infamous lies of Charlotte Bourgate, when by so doing he thought it possible to further his own ends. He was bitterly mortified, for he had been foiled. Yet, though he had failed in precipitating war, he had struck a telling blow, and he had no

---

[1] Hutch. *Hist.* iii. 329, note.

[2] *Boston Gazette*, Jan. 21, 1771.

reason to repine. Probably no single event, before
fighting actually began, left so deep a scar as the Boston massacre; and many years later John Adams
gave it as his deliberate opinion that, on the night of
the 5th of March, 1770, " the foundation of American
independence was laid." Nor was the full realization
of his hopes long delayed. Gage occupied Boston in
1774. During the winter the tireless agitator, from
his place in the Provincial Congress, warned the people to fight any force sent more than ten miles from
the town; and so when Paul Revere galloped through
Middlesex on the night of the 18th of April he found
the farmers ready. Samuel Adams had slept at the
house of the Rev. Jonas Clark. Before sunrise the
detachment sent to seize him was close at hand. While
they advanced, he escaped; and as he walked across
the fields toward Woburn, to the sound of the guns of
Lexington, he exclaimed, in a burst of passionate triumph, " What a glorious morning is this ! "

Massachusetts became the hot-bed of rebellion because of this unwonted alliance between liberality and
sacerdotalism. Liberality was her birthright; for liberalism is the offspring of intellectual variation, which
makes mutual toleration of opinion a necessity; but
that her church should have been radical at this crisis
was due to the action of a long chain of memorable
causes.

The exiles of the Reformation were enthusiasts, for
none would then have dared defy the pains of heresy,
in whom the instinct onward was feebler than the fear

of death; yet when the wanderers reached America the mental growth of the majority had culminated, and they had passed into the age of routine; and exactly in proportion as their youthful inspiration had been fervid was their later formalism intense. But similar causes acting on the human mechanism produce like results; hence bigotry and ambition fed by power led to persecution. Then, as the despotism of the preachers deepened, their victims groaning in their dungeons, or furrowed by their lash, implored the aid of England, who, in defence of freedom and of law, crushed the theocracy at a blow. And the clergy knew and hated their enemy from the earliest days; it was this bitter theological jealousy which flamed within Endicott when he mutilated his flag, and within Leverett when he insulted Randolph; it was a rapacious lust for power and a furious detestation of rival priests which maddened the Mathers in their onslaught upon Dudley, which burned undimmed in Mayhew and Cooper, and in their champion, Samuel Adams, and which at last made the hierarchy cast in its lot with an ally more dangerous far than those prelates whom it deemed its foe. For no church can preach liberality and not be liberalized. Of a truth the momentary spasm may pass which made these conservatives progressive, and they may once more manifest their reactionary nature, but, nevertheless, the impulsion shall have been given to that automatic, yet resistless, machinery which produces innovation; wherefore, in the next generation, the great liberal

secession from the Congregational communion broke
the ecclesiastical power forever. And so, through
toil and suffering, through martyrdoms and war, the
Puritans wrought out the ancient destiny which fated
them to wander as outcasts to the desolate New England shore; there, amidst hardship and apparent failure, they slowly achieved their civil and religious liberty, and conceived that constitutional system which
is the root of our national life; and there in another
century the liberal commonwealth they had builded
led the battle against the spread of human oppression;
and when the war of slavery burst forth her soldiers
rightly were the first to fall; for it is her children's
heritage that, wheresoever on this continent blood
shall flow in defence of personal freedom, there must
the sons of Massachusetts surely be.